Algernon Sidney Crapsey

Algernon Sidney Crapsey:
The Last of the Heretics

By

Stephen T. Neese

Cambridge Scholars Publishing

Algernon Sidney Crapsey: The Last of the Heretics, by Stephen T. Neese

This book first published 2007 by

Cambridge Scholars Publishing

15 Angerton Gardens, Newcastle, NE5 2JA, UK

British Library Cataloguing in Publication Data
A catalogue record for this book is available from the British Library

ISBN (10): 1-84718-395-6, ISBN (13): 9781847183958

TABLE OF CONTENTS

INTRODUCTION

It had not been my intention from the beginning to resurrect the spirit of Algernon Sidney Crapsey. I merely sought to document the details of his life and provide perspective on his famous trial for heresy in 1906. I hoped to deal with how it affected the religious history of the nation, if at all. What I stumbled upon was nearly overwhelming. Studying the life of Crapsey was for me, an incredible, ever- expanding experience. The closer I looked the more I discovered until I had more than I thought I could handle. Had I not found significance in the experiences and expressions of his life I would have gladly let his memory continue on its ever-downward spiral into obscurity. I quickly realized however, that studying Crapsey's life was not only important from a biographical point of view but also as a microcosmic exercise in documenting the social, cultural and intellectual changes of the nation that occurred between the nineteenth and twentieth centuries. There was a definite progressive and independent spirit that rushed forth from the pages of his old books, journal articles, newspaper columns and letters written by and about him. So much so, that the ever-changing voice of Crapsey was able to speak clearly through his writings.

Having been raised in what I considered the conservative city of Rochester, New York, I was amazed that I had never heard of Crapsey or his famous trial until researching American religious history in 1997. I came across a book published in 1966, edited by George H. Shriver about American Religious Heretics. To my surprise one of the articles in the book was about Rochester, New York and a heresy trial that occurred there. Moreover, it was about an Episcopalian, the church of my nativity. My interest was sufficiently stimulated to continue on and to eventually take on the project of writing a biography on Algernon Sidney Crapsey.

Everything written about Crapsey previously concentrated on his trial without going into much detail about his fascinating life. Crapsey also provided an account of the trial in his autobiography published at the age of seventy-five in 1924.[1] His autobiography essentially culminates with the trial. The most scholarly account of the trial has been offered by Hugh M. Jansen Jr. in his narrative entitled, "Algernon S. Crapsey: Heresy at Rochester." Jansen carefully details the trial that took place in Batavia, New York and the subsequent appeal. However, Jansen presents only a

[1] Algernon Sidney Crapsey, *The Last of the Heretics* (New York: Knopf, 1924).

brief synopsis of the events leading up to the trial and very little about what took place afterwards.[2] Since then, Carolyn Swanton has provided a general overview of Crapsey's ministry as a social reformer in Rochester.[3]

The processes involved were intriguing. The more I researched, the more I realized the tremendous changes Crapsey went through to arrive at the point of his disconnection with the Protestant Episcopal Church. The external developments in the secular world and the internal developments in the church influenced Crapsey to deny all that he had been a part of for more than a quarter of a century. The results affected both family and friends regardless of his eventual satisfaction with the appellation of heretic. Nevertheless, the distinction meant something, perhaps much different then than it does today. Most importantly, there were discernable psychological occurrences and a noticeable intellectual progression that culminated in his public utterances and ultimately his conviction for heresy. Crapsey was, in the end, held responsible and judged culpable.

One had to wonder why the Crapsey case stimulated so much public controversy. The attention provoked by the "modern–day heresy trial" held the interest of the nation for nearly two years. Articles that documented the progress of the trial appearing in virtually every major newspaper in America attested to this fact. The *New York Times* was particularly intrigued with the case. Editorial sections in New York, Rochester and elsewhere were jammed with the opinions of people concerned with the ramifications of the trial. But, less than twenty years later another heresy case, this time involving a retired bishop of the same church, caused virtually no public outcry, involvement or excitement at all. What was it about Crapsey that was so demonstrably fascinating to the nation? There were many important questions.

Furthermore, I considered whether heresy was now an outmoded concept, especially in organizations like the Episcopal Church. I wondered to what extent, if any, Crapsey was responsible for the changing conceptions concerning doctrinal orthodoxy that affected the church. I considered whether the Crapsey case could have influenced the later contentions of heresy involving Bishop Pike or the various utterances of

---

[2] Hugh M. Jansen Jr., "Algernon S. Crapsey: Heresy at Rochester," George H. Shriver ed., *American Religious Heretics* (New York, 1966).

[3] Carolyn Swanton, "Dr. Algernon S. Crapsey: Religious Reformer," *Rochester History,* Vol. XLII No. 1 January, 1980. Portions of this paragraph appear in Stephen T. Neese, "Algernon Sidney Crapsey and the Move for Presentment." In *Anglican and Episcopal History* John F. Woolverton ed. Sept. 2001 Vol. LXX No. 3.

Bishop Spong. Certainly Crapsey embodied all of the radical-mindedness of Bishop Pike, as well as the controversial nature of Bishop Spong. Did the historic Crapsey case contribute to their understanding of the changing role of the church? How much, if any responsibility could be laid at the foot of Crapsey's unimposing cemetery plot for any of the subsequent Episcopalian controversies?

Obviously, the Episcopal Church has come a long way since Crapsey's heresy trial in 1906. Documenting the transformation that took place in Crapsey's life provided context and meaning to the historic events that transpired in 1906 and beyond, even if those factors including the concept of heresy has become intellectually outmoded. Perhaps Crapsey was right after all about his legacy, that his trial was the seminal point of intellectual and cultural departure concerning doctrinal orthodoxy in American Christianity.

Crapsey's early life showed little concern with the religious until he stumbled into a Protestant Episcopal Church one cold, snowy evening. He had always been interested in the accumulation of knowledge. Perhaps it was because the nation had not yet loosed itself from its intellectual ties to the religious that Crapsey was truly moved to explore that life further. There has always been a relationship in this country, albeit sometimes tenuous, between the intellectual and the ethical. It has been our national legacy, like it or not, to maintain an association with the academic that pulsates with altruistic, moral undertones. Crapsey realized this fact intuitively, especially considering his family background.

The Protestant Episcopal Church has maintained a sort of younger sibling relationship with the Anglican Church of Great Britain. During the American Revolution the need to disassociate from the Erastian institutional connection and mask the British constitutional relationship resulted in the changing of the name to its present form. The church has always however maintained its commitment to the Anglican liturgy and its traditions. In antebellum years the Protestant Episcopal Church imported both the form and the enthusiasm of the Oxford Movement. Crapsey initially loved the pomp and the ritual associated with the "Catholic sect" of the church. But there was another movement that sprang forth from the great British academic institutions. Broad religiosity encouraged open and rational thinking, Christian socialism, as well as unity in the church. Broad churchmen attempted to break down the walls of separation between the various factions of Anglicanism. In doing so, they targeted dogmatic differences as the culprits of denominational disunity. Their energies would eventually turn to the denominations outside the Anglican

Communion as well, as broad churchmen became leaders in the worldwide, ecumenical movement.

To some extent, they sought to reestablish the dream of James I of reuniting Christendom. However, in the place of sound doctrine, the broad churchmen encouraged a sometimes-superficial morality based upon piety and good works. Anglican Catholicity eventually emphasized ecumenical diversity and a wide appreciation for varied opinions. In the case of some who recognized an incongruity between historic doctrinal perspectives and modernistic thinking there was a compulsion to integrate contemporary scientific theories and modern political, economic and social concepts into the acceptable regimen of the church. For Crapsey and many others, socialism, science and evolution took the lead in the process of displacing the traditional doctrines of the church, expressed by a strict adherence to the creeds. By the beginning of the twentieth century both the old and the new dogmatists, were locked in a definite struggle contending for the hearts and minds of religious America. In the end, "secular humanism" was religion indeed to Crapsey and many others.[4] The Protestant Episcopal Church's factionalism and the Crapsey trial both reflected and accentuated America's struggle with social and intellectual change.

Crapsey started his religious life in the church as a dogmatic Anglo-Catholic. He never had a problem making up his mind or expressing a clear opinion about issues. Much of his "Catholicism" may have been an attraction to what was then considered aberrant and unorthodox behavior by traditionalists in the Protestant denomination. It may have kindled in him a natural rebelliousness that he associated with his maternal grandfather's combativeness over slavery. But when men like Phillips Brooks came on the scene and preached the "gospel of toleration," Crapsey was faced with a weighty decision. All of the social indicators seemed to point to the fact that science and technological development supported the new theories of biological and social evolution. The significant social question that the Crapsey case asked was, would the church adapt to a new dogmatic or persist with the old?

In contrast, social Darwinism presented an interesting challenge to those who sought an increase in democracy to accompany the growth of the academy and changes in the social paradigm. However, after the war had been won to free the black man from physical bondage they were brought immediately back into economic, social and political bondage with the growing cultural acceptance of a social theory that characterized

[4] Crapsey eventually considered himself a secular humanist and this was the term used by him and others to comprehensively describe their experience.

them as lesser beings on the evolutionary scale of development. Social Darwinism would undoubtedly weigh as heavily as the cotton bales slaves were once forced to heave as African-Americans and others now had to deal with scientific racism based upon intellectual misconceptions about mental capacity and inequality. Crapsey however, could effectively detach his newly developed intellectual moorings from his stronger beliefs in American democratic values to make himself, like his grandfather, a friend of the American Negro.

Crapsey's years as an evangelist for Catholic Episcopalianism were spent in intellectual struggle as he grappled over conflicting secular and religious influences and his direction both within and without the church. His concern with bringing all the parties of the church together eventually led him resolutely into broad churchmanship. A complex combination of scientific, religious and personal influences eventually persuaded him to dismiss the significance of doctrinal orthodoxy. Crapsey recognized the conflict between Christian church doctrine and evolutionary science and he worked tirelessly to bring the two into intellectual harmony. Crapsey felt an overriding need first to downplay and then to dismiss dogmatic differences for the cause of homogeneity in the church.

Other influences also affected the way Crapsey responded to the intellectual revolution and the social transformation at the turn of the twentieth century. Lewis Henry Morgan contended that socialism was the next step on the developmental ladder of societal evolution. Crapsey venerated the great anthropologist from Rochester, New York. Morgan's concentration on evolution, science and socialism further influenced Crapsey's turn away from the orthodox, historic Christian faith.

Crapsey felt that broad churchmanship was the way to accomplish unity and introduce a new and multi-faceted dogmatic into the church, while remaining true to his ethical impulses. The Social Gospel further contributed to Crapsey's complex understanding of how the church must progress. It took the focus off individual salvation and placed it squarely onto society as a whole. Furthermore, the rise of Keswickian perfectionism added to the complexity of the religious milieu bringing individual responsibility to bear upon crucial questions about society. All of these influences, coupled with the progressiveness of political reform in the late nineteenth and early twentieth centuries created a dynamic, yet volatile situation for the American church. Inevitably, orthodoxy expressed by an adherence to the creeds was brought into question. Social reform had been one of the traditional occupations of the church. Now however, the church, like society itself, wrestled with its own definition, its place in enacting meaningful reform in light of new social scientific theories and methods, not to mention its significance and continuity in a historical context.

Crapsey was a man given to action personally as well as socially. As such, he was perpetually busy. His intellectual busyness coupled with his love for knowledge caused him first to wonder and then to wander from his religious moorings. He was characteristically prone to seeking truth, as he understood it. He was not a hypocrite. He refused to compromise his thoughts or opinions on matters of the utmost intellectual importance. This led him to be enraptured by the contemporary scholarship then sweeping throughout the Anglican academic institutions and eventually to subscribe to a liberal perspective as a means of bringing the church up to date with the rest of the world. This meant an acceptance of scientifically based, historical research, as well as the employment of "higher criticism" as a means of discovering the "real value" of the biblical texts. For Crapsey, and many others, the scholarly standard had shifted from scriptural infallibility based on faith to the scientific confirmation of theoretic models based on reason as the means for establishing acceptable truth.

Crapsey's respect for the scholarship of men like Brooks, Kingsley, Maurice, Colenso, Morgan, Marx and others persuaded him to make decisions about the accuracy of his faith and to address the hard questions that the new scholarship was bringing to the surface. Crapsey was a man given to great passion and intellectual extremes. He held a high regard for what he considered the truth. But unlike such men as Phillips Brooks who would receive the office of a bishop before his death, Crapsey lacked the discretion necessary to positively challenge and ultimately change the church. He was unable to formulate and articulate concepts that were held by men like Brooks in a religiously acceptable manner. He would eventually question all the cardinal doctrines of the historic Christian faith without regard to the conservative element of the church. In the same way, he completely denied the miraculous and therefore, from a biblically based, literal context, he actually denied the centrality of not just the historic faith, but of faith itself.[5]

Through the prodding of a friend, who went with him on a walking tour of the British Isles, Crapsey hit upon an idea to present a series of lectures about the history of the church. He sought to examine and interpret through his new dogmatic lens the relationship between religion and politics in western society since the times of the Romans. He eventually made some statements about the Virgin Birth that were obviously unorthodox. The press jumped on them. Crapsey would have

---

[5] See Hebrews Chapter 11.

been granted grace by his bishop had he not pushed the issue to the extreme both in his combativeness in the press and in journal articles where he defended his right to think and speak as he felt led. He may have still been granted grace by the diocese but he subsequently chose to publish the lecture series in book form. The publication was representative of Crapsey symbolically thumbing his nose at the religious organization that had employed him for over a quarter of a century. It stated in effect, 'this is in print now and thus it will remain, and so now you must deal with it.' Ultimately the church did.[6]

The bishop of the diocese, William D. Walker, appointed a committee of investigation to inquire into the circumstances at St. Andrew's. While severely criticizing Crapsey's "utterances," the committee finally recommended that Crapsey not be presented for heresy. The popular impression remains that the later presentment was against the prevailing opinion of the diocese. The general consensus in the literature supposes that the continued action against Crapsey was the product of a strong-willed bishop and conservative churchmen who simply overruled the recommendations of the diocesan committee and likewise trumped lay opinion in the diocese. However, a closer examination of the events leading to presentment clearly demonstrates that the bishop did little if anything prior to Crapsey's provocation. When the church refused to act, Crapsey started another series this time denying the veracity and the imminence of the Second Advent. The diocese finally, with the controversy raging in the press, the denomination and the other churches in Rochester, presented him for heresy. Crapsey's incessant public exhibition, including his continuous prodding of the diocese eventually led to his presentment.[7]

Moreover, opinion was clearly divided throughout the diocese, as well as in the country concerning the Crapsey affair. The trial became a sounding board for the opinionates of the day. Diverse perspectives, liberal, moderate and conservative, Catholic and Protestant, relative and absolute, were offered regarding the disposition of the case. Correspondents alternately questioned and supported the traditional concepts and authorities. They offered their opinions on everything, from the intellectual direction that society would take in the twentieth century to the philosophical nature of the truth. It was an enlightening, sometimes

---

[6] Stephen T. Neese, "Algernon Sidney Crapsey and the Move for Presentment." *Anglican and Episcopal History* (Center Sandwich, NH: Sept. 2001). Vol. LXX No.3.

[7] Ibid.

extremely contentious debate that intrigued the nation for the better part of two years. The discussion in the popular press underscored the mood of a society in transition, shaken from its traditional moorings and searching for a sanctuary of intellectual repose.

Crapsey's high profile counsel and his willingness to bait the press made the trial a national spectacle. The defense intended to make the trial a philosophical test case for the truth, as they perceived it. They intended to prove that Crapsey's utterances were not terribly dissimilar to those already being taught in Episcopal institutions all over the nation. But the church advocate, John Lord O'Brian, who would later become the assistant attorney general of the nation, was better prepared. He contended that there remained an undeniable "Catholic" concept concerning doctrine. The church acknowledged it and individual opinions regardless of how prevalent they were would never supercede the time-tested formularies of the great church. He caused the ecclesiastical court to remain focused on the matter at hand, the question of whether or not Crapsey had uttered heretical statements contrary to both the traditional formularies and the current ecclesiastical pronouncements of the church. He was convicted. A subsequent appellate review concurred.[8]

Interestingly, though several church journals demurred, most secular newspapers fully supported the findings of the ecclesiastical court. The drama and the ironies, didn't stop there however, as Crapsey made an impassioned plea to the people of his congregation to remain where they were and to continue to affect the church in the reforms he felt were necessary. Many were heartbroken at the loss of their rector and the Crapsey family members were deeply traumatized through it all.

The sum of the scholarship on Crapsey including his self-aggrandizing account ends there.[9] But Crapsey went on to become a radical, in the strictest sense. He reconstructed the Brotherhood that he had originally established to get the church going and started over again as what he would have described as a secular humanist pastor.[10] His radicalism however got in his way. He eventually became so extreme that those who

---

[8] Crapsey's legal team included a popular upstate New York Congressman, and one of the finest defense lawyers of the day.

[9] This is not solely the opinion of the author but also of Arthur Hunt Crapsey Jr. and other family members. It is the author's opinion that those family members rightly concluded that the autobiography was (perhaps unintentionally) written more as a book justifying his actions and to secure his place in American religious history and less as an exact historical document.

[10] Again, this would have been Crapsey's description.

once supported him, would no longer defend him. They decided he was a detriment rather than the entertaining celebrity he had once been. Many of the same wealthy benefactors who had originally even encouraged his religious heterodoxy, turned their backs on what they considered his social, economic and political aberrations.

He spent his later years writing and walking and working as a parole officer, bringing boys back to the state reform school at Industry outside Rochester, New York. When his age and his conscience could no longer countenance the stress, he retired to write his memoirs. His family and friends took care of him. His wife had become successful as well, by turning a church sewing guild, later a socialist experiment, into a profitable factory. His old friends provided him with an income until his final breath. Only five of Crapsey's children survived him. He buried four others including his marvelously talented daughter who became a well-known poet after her untimely death.

I have attempted to establish through his writings and the historical context in which he lived that studying Algernon Sidney Crapsey is indeed a profitable endeavor. He was significant to both the nation at the turn of the twentieth century and subsequently to those who study cultural and religious history. As his most vocal critics asserted, Crapsey "easily surrendered himself to his intellectual vagaries, and the thing which for the time being appears to be true, he advocates with remarkable eloquence."[11] His "intellectual vagaries" indeeed produced dire consequences for himself, his family, the church and society itself. On the other hand, I trust his eloquence will somehow shine through the pages of this book as well.

Thus, Crapsey's significance includes his role as both a reflection of and a conduit for the flow of ideas from the intellectual sector to the public at a crucial time in American history. His trial, his very life openly displayed the changing ideals of the society he lived in. Conversely, it also reflected the widening intellectual polarization between opposing segments of the American public. It is imperative to note that studying this churchman brings us face to face with the tenor of the times.

Therefore, documenting the life of Crapsey became an exercise in detailing the changing conventions of late nineteenth, early twentieth century society. His early life reflected the impulses and values of the Anglo-Catholic movement in the Episcopal Church during the nineteenth

---

[11]Letter from the Committee of Investigation to Bishop Walker reported in G. Sherman Burrows, *The Diocese of Western New York 1897- 1931* (Buffalo, 1935) pp.124-5.

century. His later life demonstrated the changes that paralleled the transformation of American society through the progressive era of the early twentieth century. America changed warily, yet drastically during this period from a profoundly religious culture to a marginally secular one.

Crapsey was not responsible for instigating those changes. His life, however, influenced, occasioned and expressed them. His educational background was sorely deficient, yet his desire to affect his generation with social and cultural change was compulsive and from this vantagepoint, considerable. In this, he was influenced by an underlying psychological desire to at first, be recognized, and then subsequently attain the goal of religious martyrdom. His biography is a reflection of popular and progressive American culture, as well as religious transformation.

Crapsey was closely coupled to the cultural impulses of his rapidly changing society. His perspective was alternately popular and extreme. Ironically, his limited education and lack of intellectual discipline revealed a special genius about him. He could shake hands with the workingman and speak colloquially about life's deepest mysteries while dining at a table of social elitists. This he did with perfect confidence and ease. He could with candor, correspond with presidential candidates about the important issues of the day, while simultaneously preaching the gospel of socialism to angry mill workers. He was profoundly American. Even his later socially unacceptable radicalism does not alter but rather attests to that fact.

Forever the living irony, Crapsey set out to surmount the religious life including all the precepts and laws of the "straightest sect of his church." But then he ultimately dedicated his life to proving that the old dogma was wrong, by personally demonstrating that one could live morally without the encumbrance of superstitious religiosity. In his religion he was inordinately secular and in his secularity he was profoundly religious. After a life of the most intense and focused religious scrutiny he would subsequently revel in the broadness of a completely open mind. His trial, indeed his life attested to the irony of a changing American ideal, that of the comprehensive character and very nature of cultural truth. His truth was particularistic, relative and rational, in contrast to the absolutist, faith based realities of the past. He was one of the most recognizable men in Rochester during his day, with his characteristic cape and endearing smile. He became a legend that has curiously fallen into obscurity in his adopted home of Rochester, New York. And yet, his life and work continue to reflect both the necessary continuities and the intrinsic differences between the church and society.

Whether he affected the currents of the social history of this nation by influencing people like his fellow Rochesterian, Walter Rauschenbusch, is an interesting question. It is doubtful that Crapsey ever influenced the intellectual direction of Rauschenbusch. But Crapsey's vigor, enthusiasm and earnestness for the liberal cause were unparalleled. Crapsey inspired people. Rauschenbusch could not have lived in Rochester at that time without being affected by the Crapsey debacle. Doubtless, Crapsey inspired Rauschenbusch. Moreover, one must postulate that the religious establishment's reaction to Rauschenbusch's *Christianity and the Social Crisis* might have been quite different, had Crapsey not already taken the brunt of the reactionary criticism about liberal church issues. Nevertheless, Algernon Sidney Crapsey did have his day in the sun, and would be offended, I am sure, with the consideration that his overall significance lay solely in how he affected the writings of someone else to whom history has been more kind.

It is my desire that both popular society and academic historians might look more closely at Crapsey. Both Crapsey's trial and his life accentuated the impulse for change in our culture. Crapsey's presentment through his conviction brought a cacophony of voices out into the public forum. These voices distinguished the polemic that the contemporary society grappled with. But the question remains, what was the character of that change? Ultimately, as Crapsey maintained, questions of how our culture interprets what it considers true is adjudicated in the court of public opinion.[12] Therefore, in light of all that has passed I submit that the Crapsey case is indicative of the way that American society evinced the challenges of the new century. Ironically, the Crapsey case demonstrated how society both embraced the revolutionary ideas forwarded by the recently commissioned academic sector, as well as rejected the perceived radicalism while revealing the depth of intellectual division in America.

In the end, Algernon Sidney Crapsey was defiantly proud to acknowledge his heresy. Something about his rebellious, yet ethical heritage demanded it. One wonders whether the Crapsey case was not illustrative of, or perhaps even instrumental in the cultural process of unfettering the truth from its absolute intellectual base. Eventually, society, like Crapsey himself, moved well beyond modernism to a post-modern philosophical paradigm. However, one must look carefully at the recent swing back toward conservative social, political, religious and intellectual advances in the scholastic and cultural milieu and ask whether the social advances were truly substantive. Based on his humanistic

[12] Letter of resignation from Crapsey to Bishop Walker, Mon. Nov. 26, 1906.

optimism, Crapsey believed he would be exonerated in the court of public opinion. He may have been by the 1960s but at the turn of this new century one wonders if the historic concept of heresy and other definitively collective concepts have not regained socio-cultural validation.

Algernon Sidney Crapsey was more than anything else an American voice. He was indicative of the generation that produced him. Like America itself, he was sometimes an embarrassment, sometimes deeply emotive and inspirational, occasionally profound, at times repulsively egocentric and unusually kind. His life spanned four score years through some of the most turbulently transitional times in our history. Unable to fathom the rapidity of change and development, his generation was both ingenious in their technological achievements, and simultaneously naïve about the progressive development of the soul of mankind. The First World War finally shattered their optimism.

Ultimately, Crapsey's life illustrates the social demarcation between conflicting ideologies in American culture. Our recent experience with political factions arguing about differing philosophical models clearly relates to the depth of this enduring social polemic. The contested presidency of the year 2000 and the ever-widening dispute about the courts' interpretations of the constitution attests to a similar ongoing divergence in the political realm.

I would argue that Crapsey's life and his heresy case represent the depth of division our culture has experienced over the past century. The ongoing dispute in the courts, schools and other social institutions confirm the intensity of this debate. Crapsey's own writings concerning politics and religion illustrate this persistent argument.

Finally, in a comprehensive and popular way, the Crapsey case represents how American society has struggled with our understanding of the truth. Crapsey's case contemplates both how the truth relates to the doctrines, formularies and scriptures of the historic Christian faith, as well as what philosophical, ideological and religious processes society employs to ascertain it. These questions were argued in the editorial sections of the Rochester *Democrat & Chronicle*, the *New York Times* and an entire host of other newspapers interested in the spectacle of the ecclesiastical court at Batavia. The problems that these authors pondered about their contemporary culture and the future of American society were philosophically profound at a time when the discussion was not solely constrained to the ivory halls of academia.[13]

Crapsey stood at the precipice of a paradigmatic shift in American social and religious history. He prescribed an interpretive model in his church and society that struggled with modernistic hermeneutics. He recommended the advancement of science through evolutionary theory and the furtherance of democracy through socialism. The result was expulsion, without dishonor. The religious system he engaged demanded it.

Whether exonerated through time by the church that deposed him, or not, his prophecies underscore his enduring significance. He argued that his generation would be the last to find these doctrinal issues important enough to attend to and reluctantly act upon. He was proven wrong within six months after he published his autobiography. But in retrospect, and given the direction of the Episcopal Church in the twenty-first century, perhaps he was somewhat correct after all. Perhaps Crapsey's rebellion has engendered something in the church and society that refuses to be dismissed after Crapsey, after modernism, after the great World Wars, after communism, after the twentieth century, even now. We struggle in our reluctance to call it heresy still, though we know that it is. To some he is a hero of greater proportion than I have undoubtedly depicted. Conversely, he was perhaps an even more tragic figure than I have portrayed as well. If so I don't apologize, on either account. I recognized something in Crapsey's character, even in his incessant self- assurance, that he would likewise never express any regret for. He was who he was. He paved his own path and carried on with a bounce in his stride. He hoped his work would be his enduring testimony. What that truly means, history has already judged. Therefore, like his daughter that passed on before him, he asserted his own historical legacy, whether one agrees with him or not. And so, according to all that remains relative in American religious history, and by his own obtrusive definition, Algernon Sidney Crapsey remains forever the impenitent, "Last of the Heretics."

---

[13] See Chapter XIX this manuscript concerning letter to the editor from John Williams of Omaha Nebraska. Taken from *The Churchman* Sat. Feb. 3, 1906 Vol. XCIII No. 5, p. 181.

CHAPTER ONE

"That as Ye Have Heard from the Beginning, Ye Should Walk in it"

When Jacob Crapsey first met the diminutive, dark eyed beauty, Rachel Morris, on a stagecoach ride between Cincinnati and the town of Bethel in Clermont County, Ohio, it was love at first sight. Within a year they married. Rachel was an emotional, fiery woman, the daughter of Thomas Morris, former Senator of Ohio. Her son would later write that she was prone to the moodiness that accompanied the passionate Celtic race. He also considered Jacob as deeply poetic in nature, the kind of man given to the philosophic, interested in history and often idle as a result. Together they raised a large family on the western frontier in Ohio.[1]

Algernon Sidney Crapsey was born in Fairmount, Ohio on June 28th, 1847. His eldest brother named him due to his admiration for Algernon Sidney, who fought with Cromwell's parliamentary forces yet, opposed his dictatorial rule. He subsequently published his famous *Discourses Concerning Government* and was later hanged for treason due to his opposition to the restoration of Charles II.[2] One can only postulate what effect Sidney's name had on him as a child. As time progressed, Algernon learned of its significance, living up to his rebellious namesake.[3]

Algernon believed Crapsey was a derivation of the name Kropps. The paternal side of the family was probably German, though possibly Dutch. His immigrant great- grandfather, Jan Ulric or Ulric Jan, was a tenant blacksmith under the patronage of Van Rensellaer, in New York State, during the Revolutionary War. Crapsey assumed that his great grandfather and his brother, originally came to America as mercenaries employed by

---

[1] *Unpublished manuscript* of A.S. Crapsey's autobiography. Arthur Crapsey Jr. Collection. Rare Books Dept. Rush Rhees Library Univ. of Rochester, Rochester, New York. p. 4.

[2] Algernon Sidney *Discourses Concerning Government* London: Printed for A. Millar, 1751.

[3] See Algernon Sidney Crapsey's autobiography, *The Last of the Heretics* (New York: Alfred Knopf: 1924) pp. 1-2.

King George III. After the War, they stayed on, inspired by the vast, untapped potential of the new land.[4]

Algernon's paternal grandfather was a farmer and a Baptist preacher in the town of Parma, New York, then a small farm town in Genesee County, now a suburb of Rochester. His father Jacob Tompkins Crapsey was named after both the biblical patriarch and the governor of New York State. Crapsey mused that due to the circumstances of his birth, his father was a Calvinist and a Democrat.[5]

In his early days, Jacob would find sometimes-drastic ways, like deliberately cutting his foot with his hoe, to get out of work in the fields. He thoroughly despised the hard life of a farmer. Eventually, he was sent to the Baptist Academy in Canandaigua, in the beautiful Finger Lakes Region of New York State. His parents thought the ministry might be his calling. After completing his course work he proceeded to Oberlin College. Algernon noted that educated men could only work in one of two professions at that time, the ministry or law. But unlike his preacher-father, Jacob was not a believer, which severely limited his vocational options. With graduation, his practice of law began. Unfortunately, his mind was more philosophical than practical. He had a tremendous aversion to completing the work that was necessary to prepare oneself for a case. He was a complex man and a dreamer, but polite and kind.[6]

Due to Jacob's aversion to chastisement, "Mrs. Crapsey," as her husband called her, handled the discipline in the large family. She adored little "Algy," but her emotions would sometimes conflict with her love. He remembered well the beatings, especially those that he considered undeserved. Rachel's home was the center of a busy domestic industry steeped in production. In the early days, there was always abundance and the children were never denied an extra helping of food. Rachel was like her father short and diminutive and thoroughly energetic. But she was also moody and could be dancing and singing at one moment and wandering disheartened through the wilderness the next.[7]

Jacob Crapsey for the most part, spent long hours at his law office near Cincinnati, rarely interacting with his children. At one time, he was appointed as the prosecuting attorney of the county. However, the job was totally inappropriate for him. Jacob never considered punishing people. He never raised his hand or voice at home. He treated his children with

---

[4] Ibid., p. 1.
[5] Ibid., p. 2.
[6] Ibid. pp. 1-2.
[7] Ibid., p. 4.

respect and always referred to his young son as Algernon, or sir. Algernon sometimes accompanied him on his Sunday walks when his mother let him skip going to church. Jacob's early attempts at making money were, in general, failures. Algernon considered Jacob, too moral to succeed as a lawyer. Algernon noted that he was too deeply concerned with the meaning of justice and personal integrity to consider the necessary prosecution of a case at any cost. One scheme to create a pleasure park in Cincinnati failed and the family suffered the loss of both income and status. He later recovered some of the family's wealth by becoming the legal counselor to a wealthy entrepreneur in the area.[8]

Algernon loved his father in spite of his failings at the legal profession, farming and business. An educated and resolute heathen, Jacob despaired of the passionate preaching style so familiar in the wake of the Second Great Awakening. While the frontier exhortations rapidly changed the western lands into civilized regions, the democratic, homespun Christianity of the Methodists and Baptists was perhaps too familiar for a complex man like Jacob Crapsey.[9]

Algernon sometimes slipped away with him to walk to the dream park that Jacob envisioned for the people of Cincinnati. They would get "Bavarian beer and black bread and sausages and cheese and sauerkraut and escape to a high place, above that reserved portion of wilderness, to eat and drink and dream." Jacob admired Byron who was then at the peak of his fame. He remembered him "standing on the edge of the ledge of rock, his hat in his hand, his shirt open at the neck, his blond hair blowing in the wind, reciting the opening lines of the Giour:

He who hath bent him oer the dead,
Ere the first day death hath fled,
And marked the mild angelic air,
The rapture of repose that's there.[10]

It was his maternal grandfather however, Thomas Morris that Algernon idolized. Rachel's father migrated from the mountains of Virginia to the Ohio Valley because of his intense hatred for the institution of slavery. He was of Welsh origin and like his daughter, he was given to

[8]A.S. Crapsey, *Manuscript,* p. 31, see also Crapsey, *Heretics*, pp. 20, 24.
[9] For more on the frontier democracy and preaching style of the Second Great Awakening see, Nathan O. Hatch *The Democratization of American Christianity* (New Haven: Yale Univ. Press, 1989).
[10] A.S. Crapsey, *Manuscript,* pp. 25-9.

violent and passionate outbursts. He was also a devoutly religious man.[11] He was a highly moral man driven to challenge the status quo. He started out his career as a lawyer, became a State Supreme Court Justice and eventually a United States Senator from Ohio. He later ran for Vice-President in 1844, with James Birney, on the Liberty Party ballot.[12]

Young Algernon identified deeply with his grandfather. It was his grandfather's wealth that sustained them when his father's commercial plans nearly brought them to the brink of financial ruin. It was his grandfather who had truly made something special out of his life. His grandfather challenged the establishment and paid the price for it. To Algernon, "he was a seer, a prophet, a hero and a martyr." He was a self-made man, self-educated and the only one responsible for his wealth and success. Moreover, he was prophetic in his early anti- slavery stance, a far seeing hero who pushed for the causes he believed in and eventually he was a martyr because of his personal honor and veracity. Algernon was short like his grandfather and filled with the same kinds of passion and energy. He became a political pariah, persecuted for his untarnished integrity."[13]

At a time when the general populace still considered abolitionists as radical troublemakers, Morris stood for his personal convictions. In a fiery answer to a typical Henry Clay speech, seeking compromise between freedom and slavery, Morris was unbending and relentless in his assault upon the immoral institution. He defended,

> the right of petition against it, advocating its abolition in the District of Columbia, calling it a foul thing, cruel to blacks, degrading to whites, a violation of human rights; a contradiction of the fundamental principles of the American Republic, and repugnant to the Word and will of God.

He concluded with the words, "The Negro shall yet be free!" Due to the agitation of the southern senators Morris was soon barred from the

---

[11] Crapsey, *Heretics* p. 3.

[12] James Gillespie Birney wrote a book in 1840 that inflamed religious passions entitled, *The American Churches, The Bulwarks of American Slavery* (Concord, New Hampshire, P. Pillsbury, 1885). Birney moved his law practice from Alabama to Cincinnati, Ohio in the 1830s. He was the editor of one of the first anti- slavery publications in the area, published originally in 1836, *The Philanthropist.*

[13] Morris's relationship with Birney and the anti- church content of many of his writings contributed to his estrangement from the Methodist church. Crapsey, *Heretics,* pp. 2-4.

Democratic Party. He was similarly excommunicated from the Methodist Church. Without the backing of his party he was eventually expelled from the Senate. He was regarded as a social radical, beyond the pale of political and religious orthodoxy.[14]

But Algernon considered him a man beyond his time. He epitomized the explosive character of the growing nation, groping for an identity worthy of its idealistic youth. Morris exemplified all that was just and right about the nation. Algernon realized that time vindicated his grandfather. He was a leader of perhaps the most important movement the American nation would ever know. Yet, for standing up for what he believed he was even deprived of a burial in the Christian church of his choice.[15]

His older brother Marshall's death also made a lasting impression on young Algernon. He truly venerated Marshall, and waited upon him wholeheartedly during the time of his sickness. His death devastated Algernon and the rest of the family. Because they were not members of a church, they called in a stranger to officiate at the funeral. The austere, distinguished man preached the gospel in its entirety including the plan of salvation. He called for those present to profess Christ openly as, only those who were unashamed would inherit the Kingdom. Conversely, he announced that the unbeliever would be constrained to hell. Pointing to Algernon's dead brother lying in the coffin he declared, "As this young man has made no open confession of Christ before men, we cannot expect that he should enter the kingdom of heaven." He then admonished the mourners to make their candid professions unless they wanted the same fate of the lack of God's mercy to happen to them. At this point Mrs. Crapsey became so distressed that she actually fainted over her son's coffin.[16]

In contrast to the fire and brimstone approach of many of the frontier preachers Algernon appreciated the piety and quiet dignity of the Roman Catholic churches in Cincinnati. He pondered about the dignified grace of the inhabitants of the convents and monasteries, more than visible to

---

[14] Other writings about Thomas Morris include, William Henry Brisbane's *An Eulogium of the Life and Character of the Late Hon. Thomas Morris* (Cincinnati: L- Hommedieu, 1845). His son Benjamin Franklin Morris also wrote a book in 1856 entitled, *The Life of Thomas Morris, Pioneer and Long a Legislator of Ohio, and U.S. Senator from 1833- 1839* (Cincinnati: Moore, Wilstach, Keys and Overand, 1856).

[15] Crapsey, *Heretics, p.* 4.

[16] A.S. Crapsey, *Manuscript* pp. 53- 4.

young Algernon in a city teeming with Irish and German immigrants. Their magnificent cathedrals stood in stark contrast to the plain Protestant churches. He considered Cincinnati, the Boston of the west due to its emphasis on scholarship and philosophical inquiry. Moreover, it was the German population who were primarily Roman Catholic that contributed to its reputation as an intellectual and cultural center. Crapsey noted with pride how Cincinnati became the home of America's first astronomical observatory in 1843."[17]

Crapsey associated intellectual achievement with devout religion from his youth. He developed a great love and deep appreciation for the beauty and the mystery of the Roman Catholic Church. Crapsey listened to the calls of the monastery bells from matins to compline and watched as the dutiful friars walked through the graveyards reading their offices. He was overtaken with a deep and lasting sense of reverence and respect for the dedicated priests of the Roman Catholic Church. He respected the devout nature of the Catholic religion, the reputation for erudition and its complicity with art and natural science. He would later write,

> I am sure I owed my future calling to the ministry of the church to the impressions made upon my soul by these devout friars.[18]

Nevertheless, like other young men, the practical matters of life occupied Algernon's mind principally. Due in part to his father's failing practice, he quit school at the age of eleven and secured a job as a cash boy in a dry goods store, much to the consternation of his mother who would not hear of the grandson of Thomas Morris working as a cash boy. His father reacted differently, "You had better let the boy do what he wants to do, Mrs. Crapsey," he said. "As for school, life is the best school of all, and your father, Senator Morris, began his life as a squatter, making his living by the work of his own hands. It seems to me that Algernon has shown enterprise and decision. We had better let him have his own way." He kept the job at the store for two years until his father's practice suddenly recovered. Jacob was hired in a lawsuit (interestingly known as the Whitewater case) that involved millions of dollars. A Colonel West, his only client and a close friend, retained him. Algernon returned to

---

[17] Crapsey was wrong to assert that the Cincinnati Observatory was the nation's oldest. The United States Naval Observatory is actually older. Crapsey, Heretics, pp. 15-16.

[18] Crapsey, *Heretics*, p.16.

school at the advice of his parents only to realize that he was now uncomfortable with his academic surroundings being older than the other boys. Therefore, he accepted a position arranged for him at a hardware factory owned by one of his cousins. Because he was often idle and chided as being worthless, as one of the co-owners soon let him know, Algernon quit and hastened to the call of the military.[19]

Algernon was barely fourteen years old in August of 1862, and he was small for his age. The Civil War was raging and the northern forces were being frustrated at every turn. Algernon was determined to serve his nation for the cause of freedom. The words of his grandfather echoed in his heart, "The Negro shall yet be free!" He would do his part no matter how small he was. He was too little to be a line soldier and he rejected outright the idea of being a drummer boy, but when he suggested that he might play the bugle, they agreed to take him. But there were no bugles to be had, and young Algernon was elated that he was now a part of the regular ranks.[20]

Under General Rosecrans, the Union army pursued Bragg throughout Kentucky. The weather started out warm but worsened as the fall months wore on. The men were exposed to the harsh elements continuously, some without the proper equipment. As the weather turned colder, the marches became a way of maintaining one's body heat and keeping warm. On one long march in freezing weather, Algernon was maintaining the pace on the outside of the formation. An officer spied the young lad, and in an act of misplaced benevolence ordered the young trooper to be seated on his horse while he took his place in the ranks. This was the wrong thing to do for the young soldier, and in due time, he literally froze in place on the horse. He was lowered from his horse, taken to the surgeon's tent and ultimately to the hospital tent where he stayed until Christmas. He was finally sent to Nashville, where they diagnosed him with a "hypertrophied heart." He thought that his real problem was pneumonia, but whatever they wanted to call it was all right with him as long as it meant he could now go home. He was discharged and sent on the long journey back to Cincinnati.[21]

His mother was shocked at his appearance. He recovered slowly but surely. But being so completely bored at the tedium of civilian life and the regimen of the home, when his father offered to have him accompany him to work he jumped at the chance. The boredom of the home was only

---

[19] Ibid., pp. 21-6.
[20] Ibid., pp. 26-7.
[21] Ibid., pp. 32-5.

surpassed by the monotony of his father's office. Nevertheless, with a library in the building below his father's office, Algernon had the opportunity to delve into the world of literature. Through the works of Scott, Dickens, Irving, Macaulay, Thackeray, Prescott and others Algernon received his chance to discover the world through reading. It was by sheer accident that he stumbled upon the book that would lead him into the profession that he would choose for the better part of his life. Ironically, it was this same Bible, which he would later deny in the literal sense that eventuated his deposal from his vocation.[22]

Walking into Christ Church one night, initially to escape the freezing weather, but perhaps with a bit of curiosity motivating him, young Algernon was immediately overwhelmed by the pious ambiance of the place. He had never been in an Episcopal Church before and the environment immediately captivated him. It was Sexagesima Sunday, the second Sunday before Lent. The liturgy, the regalia and the trappings of the church overwhelmed him. The dignified manner of the service, the ministerial garb and the way the priests read the Psalms all combined to make the reading from Jeremiah's thirty- sixth chapter an unforgettable experience. The devout atmosphere created a life long impression on him.[23]

Due to the decorous nature of the church and the ministers, Crapsey could have hardly suspected that the church was actually in an unfortunate state. Christ Church was founded by the missionary efforts of Philander Chase on the eighteenth day of May, 1817. The first rector was the Reverend Samuel Johnston, who served from March 1818 until August 1827. The church at the time that Crapsey attended his first service was probably between rectors, as the previous rector, the Reverend Kingston Goddard, had not been able to get along well with the vestry. He tendered his resignation on the nineteenth of March 1862. The next rector, the Reverend John W. McCarty did not take office until Easter Sunday, April 3, 1863. Crapsey's enchantment with the outward religiosity in the Protestant Episcopal Church betrayed his naiveté at the problems the church was experiencing between the vestry and the clergy.[24]

He became "a devoted disciple of the Bible," in part due to his curious introduction to it on that frosty night. However, his fascination was not with it as a venerated holy oracle, but rather as a great literary work. His

---

[22] Ibid., pp. 38-9.

[23] Ibid., pp.40-2.

[24] William Henry Venable *A Centennial History of Christ Church, Cincinnati: 1817- 1917* (Cincinnati: Stewart & Kidd Co., 1918) pp. 49-54.

favorite book was that of the prophet Isaiah. He could read the Bible and find inspiration, but it was a different kind of inspiration than normally referred to by other converts. The inspiration that Algernon received was more like the enlightenment that one experienced by being captivated with a great novel, or being deeply touched by poetry. Crapsey considered the night he walked into Christ Church, Cincinnati, to escape the onslaught of the cold, as the hour of his conversion. But, unlike the testimonies of other spiritually changed men, there was no deep bewailing of the life he had lived, or repentance for his sin. There was no lifting of his hands towards the heavens for the amazing grace that God had provided, nor kneeling at the foot of the cross in submission to the will of the Father with everlasting gratitude for the work of the Son. Somehow, God the Son was not even present in his initial spiritual experience. If one could consider it a transformation at all, Algernon Sidney Crapsey's was of a very special kind. He was converted to what the early Protestant reformers had disparaged of so adamantly; to formal religion, and organized religiosity. He explained,

> I looked back on that Sexagesima Sunday night as the date of my conversion. The religion of the great prophets became my religion.[25]

With the passing of the seasons came the longing again for adventure. After answering an advertisement in a local paper, he spent the next six months as a storekeeper at a salt yard in West Virginia. The news from Gettysburg and Vicksburg encouraged him. The prospect of his grandfather's words coming true filled him with hopeful anticipation. However, talk of the nation's political situation was so volatile that it was avoided at all cost. Although West Virginia had seceded from the state of Virginia and joined the Union, the provisions of the Emancipation Proclamation allowed for the institution of slavery to continue in states that hadn't seceded. The practice lasted until the passing of the thirteenth amendment. Rude language by the salt workers about the exploitation of black women filled Algernon with a sense of righteous consternation. Thus, Algernon partook in the salt workers community without ever really being a part of it. He related this sense of disconnection in his description of a funeral he observed of a poor white man, who, like the blacks in the area participated in a religious style of worship that he perceived as contemptible.

---

[25] Crapsey, *Heretics,* p. 42.

> The religion of the poor whites and of the slaves was orgiastic, an emotional indulgence ending in a debauch. I recall a funeral conducted by a Baptist minister with a feeling of grotesque horror. The dead man had been killed by a falling tree; he was in his young manhood and was widely known in the mountains. His funeral was held after nightfall. People came from far and wide, lighting their way with tar torches. The scene of the funeral was the mountain- side illuminated by a bonfire; nothing could have been more sublime and nothing was ever more diabolical. The preacher, half naked, jumped and screamed; the mourners filled the air with inarticulate wailings; whiskey was served out of buckets with a ladle, and a drunken orgy closed the scene. I can never think of that night without a chill of horror. It was a degradation of man and the degradation of the gods; below this neither man nor god could go and continue to exist.[26]

By the beginning of 1864, Algernon was back in Cincinnati contemplating his next move. He took a bookkeeper's job at a printer's office and to remedy his lack of mathematical and organizational skills he enrolled in a night school course. While employed there, he walked past many of the theaters playing in Cincinnati. Forewarned of their sinful content he entered them surreptitiously at first, but soon developed an abiding taste for the theater, especially Shakespeare. After watching James E. Murdock in the role of Hamlet he was again truly inspired, and eventually placed Shakespeare in the company with Jesus and Isaiah as his great inspirations.[27]

Shortly thereafter they received word of President Lincoln's assassination. His mother reacted almost as emotionally as she had when Marshall had died and the rest of the family wept as well. His father sadly feared the vengeance that might transpire. The family and the nation mourned for Abraham Lincoln for the next seven days. Crapsey remarked, "by his martyrdom he ascended to the rank of saviour of mankind." After being fired from the job as a bookkeeper at the printer's office, he was asked to fill in for six months for his uncle Franklin in the Dead Letter Office, in Washington, D.C. He was to substitute for his uncle who was in the process of writing a biography about his father, Algernon's grandfather and hero Thomas Morris.[28]

---

[26] Ibid., pp. 47-8.

[27] Ibid., p. 51.

[28] The problem with this scenario, as it is related by Crapsey in his autobiography, is that Benjamin Franklin Morris wrote the book about his father in 1856, not 1865. It is obvious that Algernon at the age of 9 or 10 years old would not have

Algernon identified deeply with the maternal side of his family. His uncle Franklin was a new side Presbyterian minister who had authored several books on social and religious affairs. Two other maternal uncles served in the U.S. Congress, Jonathan David Morris who had spent nearly twenty years of his life as a clerk in the Supreme Court eventually served two terms in Congress. Crapsey realized the successful heights that his two uncles had achieved, and yet it was his other uncle, Isaac Newton Morris that Crapsey considered truly successful. Isaac became a lawyer at the age of twenty-three. At twenty- eight he declined an appointment as the Secretary of the State of Illinois. One year later he became the president of the Illinois and Michigan Canal Company. He was elected to the House of Representatives in 1846. He became a Congressman but eventually left Congress while remaining as commissioner of the Union Pacific Railroad. He considered his uncle Franklin, monotonous and his other uncle Jonathan was rarely mentioned. However, at his young age, he related to the precocious, energetic successes of his uncle Isaac.[29]

Algernon was thrilled to go to the nation's capital but soon found himself in "the morgue of defunct human correspondence." Washington in 1865 was messy and ironic in its character. He observed that the streets were filthy and mostly unpaved and there were ill arranged, untidy houses with the impoverished filth of the Negro quarters befouling the alleys between the streets And yet, in the same area stood the majestic Capitol, the towering Treasury building, the grand Patent Office, the subtle White House and other marvelous examples of fine, classical architecture. He had an easy job, working often a total of five and one-half hours while being paid for eight. His fellow public servants were just as crude as the salt workers of the mountains of West Virginia and he had a hard time adjusting to their tobacco spitting habits and vulgar ways.[30]

As his six-month term came to a close, his uncle Isaac Morris, the man that he truly respected, visited him. Uncle Isaac suggested that he should go to northeast to New York City rather than subscribe to the current popular suggestion to "go west young man." He figured that at the vigorous rate that New York City was growing that opportunity would

---

gone to Washington to work. Crapsey most likely went to Washington to work for his uncle for six months, but his explanation of why he went must be considered suspect to error. Crapsey was 77 years old when his autobiography was published and he probably remembered the reason for his substitution incorrectly.

[29] See Karen Alkalay- Gut, *Alone in the Dawn* (Athens: Univ. of Georgia Press, 1988) pp. 22-4.

[30] Crapsey, *Heretics*, p. 57.

assuredly present itself there. Respecting the advice of his uncle he decided to go to New York and seek his fortune. Algernon had but one hundred dollars in his pocket and the name of a friend whose father was a Swedenborgian minister. When he finally met his friend in New York, his greeting discouraged him. He questioned his uncle's advice calling him "a fool," and with all the newcomers, immigrants and transient men seeking employment in New York City, his prospects for finding a job were greatly compromised. But Algernon persevered, found a decent place to stay and when he was down to his last seven dollars, he finally found a job at a printing office as a bookkeeper and cashier.[31]

Certainly destiny was whispering to young Algernon through his experiences in the great city. He kept company with an Irish woman named Mary at his boarding house, although she was several years his senior. She often took him to Christ Episcopal Church on Fifth Avenue and Thirty- Fifth Street. The rector was the much-heralded Ferdinand Cartwright Ewer. When Algernon started attending he considered Ewer a broad school Episcopalian. Shortly thereafter however, Crapsey noticed that he subscribed to the Anglo-Catholicism of the Oxford Movement, then in vogue.[32] His dynamic preaching style caused quite a sensation especially in the course of presenting sermons on "The Failure of Protestantism." Ewer preached about the majestic character of the church as "the Ark of Salvation," in comparison to the blandness and crass nature of rational Protestantism.[33] Inspired by the poetry of Keats and Keble and the prose of Sir Walter Scott, a revival of medievalism had swept the English countryside.[34] The movement rejected the rationalism of the Enlightenment rediscovering the roots of English culture, including the historical church. By the 1860s, men like Edward Bouverie Pusey were postulating a *via media* or, middle way for common theological ground between the Roman Catholic and Protestant Churches. He wrote his tractates on *Real Presence,* and his *Eirenicon,* in three parts seeking

---

[31] Ibid., pp. 59-61.

[32] There is little written about Ewer that substantiates Crapsey's claim that he once subscribed to the Broad Church movement and subsequently changed his allegiance to Anglo- Catholicism.

[33] Quotations from Crapsey, *Heretics,* p. 68. See also Ferdinand Cartwright Ewer *Four Conferences Touching the Operation of the Holy Spirit* (Milwaukee: The Young Churchman, 1880). In this book, one of the few existing writings by Ewer, one can experience the "Catholicity" of the Episcopal Churchman's thought.

[34] John Keble's provocative sermon, *"National Apostasy,"* created a sensation in the English Church. See, The Rev. John Keble's *"National Apostasy,"* in *Sermons, Academical and Occasional* (Oxford: John Henry Parker, 1847) pp. 129- 148.

dialogue for the commonality of belief between Roman Catholics and Anglicans."[35]

Crapsey became a disciple of Ewer and was overtaken by his preaching style. The young man wanted to preach as Ewer preached. He was later baptized by Ewer and confirmed with the next visitation of the bishop. Ewer persuaded Crapsey to enroll in St. Stephen's College, at Annandale on the Hudson, where he could matriculate in a course of study tailored for the more mature students who had already spent time working. He received a scholarship from the New York Society for the Promotion of Religion and Learning, presided over then by the Rev. Dr. McVickar of Columbia University. Crapsey summarily left his job at the printing company with the conviction that he was called to the ministry.[36]

St. Stephen's at Annandale was situated upon a picturesque bluff overlooking the Hudson Valley on the beautiful estate of John Bard. After a rude reception, Crapsey hunkered down to a special two-year preparatory program. The other students knew him as "a prep." This course of study, unlike that for the regular four-year students, was uniquely structured in anticipation of entering a seminary afterwards. Scorned as a prep, Crapsey soon vanquished any trepidation concerning his scholastic competence. He learned Greek and Latin, was appointed to the Eulexian, an academic literary society and received honors in both Logic and Philosophy. He was also instrumental in establishing a rival society at the campus named Kappa Gamma Chi. He did not graduate, as preps were not allowed such privileges, but he finished his course of study with distinction. Through hard work and concentration he had gained the respect of his peers at St. Stephen's in just two years time.[37]

After a brief summer appointment as a teacher at a parish school in Pennsylvania, Crapsey went on to the General Seminary of the Protestant Episcopal Church, then in the Village of Chelsea, now in Manhattan. At General Seminary Crapsey studied "dogmatic and pastoral theology, Old Testament exegesis, Hebrew, Greek, New Testament exegesis, Church History and Liturgiology." Crapsey considered the seminary a refuge for

[35] See Edward Bouverie Pusey, *The Real Presence of the Body and Blood of Our Lord Jesus Christ the Doctrine of the English Church, with a Vindication of the Reception by the Wicked and of the Adoration of Our Lord Jesus Christ, Truly Present* (Oxford: J.H. Parker, 1857). See also, "Letters in three parts to John Henry Newman, and etc." concerning the reunion of the Catholic and Anglican Churches *Eirenicon* (Oxford: James Parker & Co., 1870).

[36] Crapsey, *Heretics*, p. 69.

[37] Ibid., p. 81.

the multitude of clergymen who would have been considered failures anywhere else in the Protestant Episcopal Church.[38]

To Crapsey, the faculty was wholly inadequate for the courses they taught. Nonetheless, it was an interesting place filled with all the controversy then besetting the denomination. In England, Frederick Denison Maurice and Charles Kingsley were the leaders of the rationalist faction while John Keble and Edward Bouverie Pusey carried the standard for the ritualists. Crapsey noted the antagonism between the two groups.[39] Moreover, as Crapsey realized, all the excitement and contention in the Anglican Church was carried on at the seminary. The divisions were deep and the conflict was intense.[40]

Though insufficient in some ways, the seminary was blessed by its proximity to the major cultural center of the nation. Crapsey traveled the environs of the great city to experience the art, theaters, concert halls, the great libraries and museums and hear the great preachers of the day. Among those he heard were the great orators, Henry Ward Beecher at Plymouth Congregational Church in Brooklyn, and Morgan Dix at St. Paul's Episcopal Church on Vesey St. To supplement his meager resources, Crapsey worked for two hours in the morning at Trinity School, in New York City. He also worked for two summers at Zion Church in Rome, New York. Crapsey's abhorrence of his education at General Seminary was underscored by an incident that happened prior to his final examination before graduation. A certain professor that he felt great affection for told Crapsey what he should specifically study for as his oral examination topic in Old Testament exegesis. Crapsey carried the guilt of his complicity for the better part of his life. He wrote,

> My room in the seminary building was next to the study of Professor Seabury. At the close of my senior year, in examination week, the evening before the examination in Old Testament exegesis, I came home about nine o'clock and, putting my hand to the knob of the door, I found a paper there. Going into my room, I opened it and read: 'Will Mr. Crapsey please step into Dr. Seabury's study when he comes in?' I stepped to the door and knocked. At 'come in' I entered the study and saw the good Doctor sitting crouched up in his chair, the picture of despair. After I was seated and a

---

[38] Crapsey wrote, "I do not think that there was ever an institution so inadequate to its purpose as this seminary when I was under its care." *Heretics,* p. 85.

[39] For a concise and interesting overview of the lives of both Frederick Denison Maurice and Charles Kingsley see Janet E. Courtney, O.B.E. *Free Thinkers of the Nineteenth Century* (Freeport New York: Books for Libraries Press, Inc., 1967).

[40] Crapsey, *Heretics,* p. 88.

little byplay of talk passed between us, he said, 'You know, Mr. Crapsey, that Daniel VIII is one of the themes at tomorrow's examination?' I said, 'Yes, Doctor, I know it.' 'Well, now,' said he, 'I am troubled about that theme; if some of those men get that theme, they'll make asses of themselves and an ass of me, and I wouldn't like it; no I wouldn't like that at all. Now, you know, Mr. Crapsey, I have nothing to do with the assignment of themes, but I was thinking that you might care to look over that chapter before you went to bed and consult South and Louth, so if the theme should happen to come to you, you might do it justice, as I know you can.' I said, 'Thank you, Doctor'; and I rose up and he rose up; he looked at me and I looked at him, and we neither winked an eyelash. I went to my room, took up my Hebrew Bible and read that eighth chapter over and over, until Daniel himself, if there ever were a Daniel, could not have read it more fluently. I went to the library and took down South and Louth and arranged the big horns and the little horns until I could play upon them in a way to shame South and Louth. When I finished with them the grey of the morning had come. I rushed to my room, threw myself upon the bed, fell into a deep sleep from which I was aroused by the ringing of the bell for breakfast. I rose, dressed carefully and went down to my morning meal in a blue funk. If I didn't get that theme, I was lost as a scholar; if I did get it, I was damned as a man.

When the hour arrived I went to the recitation room and saw five examiners sitting in a row on the platform, the professor on the floor to their right. The plan was for one of the examiners to select a theme at random, hand it to the chairman, who would call the name of a student and ask him to discuss the subject of the paper.

The chairman was calling the names in alphabetical order; when he had gotten through the B's, he was handed a theme; he looked at it, paused, looked at it again and said with a smile, 'I think we will skip about a bit.' Mr. Cranston will you please take this Daniel VIII?' With a sinking heart, I looked at Cranston and his face was grey as ashes. Just then professor Seabury was taken with a fit of violent coughing, which lasted half a minute; the chairman rose up and handed him a glass of water. I saw the professor move his lips. When he returned to his seat the chairman said, 'Let me see, whom was I calling- it was Mr. Crapsey, was it not? Yes it was Mr. Crapsey; Mr. Crapsey, will you kindly read for us in the Hebrew Daniel VIII and give us an exegesis of that interesting chapter?' I looked at Cranston and he looked at me with a diabolical grin on his face. But what of that?- my hour had come. I opened the Hebrew Bible, read Daniel VIII as if I were a Jewish rabbi; then explained the meaning of the big horns and the little horns, playing upon them a trenody of judgment on a sinful world.

He passed the examination to the applause of his class and the accolades of his examiners. Crapsey justified his sin in an unrepentant manner. He had been drawn into the situation and he did what he felt was best for all involved. And yet, this climatic incident merely accentuated all that Crapsey felt was lacking in his seminary experience. He wrote,

> This sin has been on my conscience all these years. I have never openly confessed until now. But what could I do? I could not let any one of my fellow students make an ass of himself, much less make an ass of my beloved professor, could I now?[41]

[41] Ibid., pp. 91-3.

CHAPTER TWO

"Neither by Any Oath"

Postulants of the Protestant Episcopal Church applied to the bishops of their dioceses for consideration for Holy Orders. The Bishop of New York, then the Right Reverend Horatio Potter, conferred all orders of ordination. He considered the degree from General Seminary as demonstrative of competence for entrance into the service of the church. In addition, the bishop conferred ordination to the candidate by examination from the Book of Common Prayer as required by the Orders and Canons of the Episcopal Church. The examination consisted of a series of prescribed questions and answers stated by the bishop and reiterated by the candidate. Crapsey would eventually bewail the ordination vows, as taken lightly, by the members of the clergy. He later declared them, "scripturally immoral," submitting that the Bible testified against the taking of oaths by the words of Jesus.[1]

The first vow Crapsey remembered involved his assurance not to teach anything contrary to the Holy Scriptures in matters of salvation. The second vow required that he teach the scriptures as the church had received them, not according to his own private interpretation.[2] The examination was specific in these matters. The vows that Crapsey recounted are contained in the Book of Common Prayer under the heading of the "Ordering of Priests."[3]

Perhaps Crapsey remembered the vows he took as a deacon and substituted them as the vows he took later as a priest. Notwithstanding, Crapsey later repented from what he considered as the juvenile act of

---

[1] Crapsey *Heretics,* pp. 94-5. Crapsey cited Matt. 5: 33- 37.

[2] Crapsey, *Heretics,* pp. 94-5.

[3] Perhaps Crapsey misremembered his vows and the successive procedures in the taking of them, not differentiating between the vows of the office of Deacon or the office of Priest. "The Form and Manner of Making Deacons," and "The Form and Manner of Ordering Priests." *The Book of Common Prayer and Administration of the Sacraments and Other Rites and Ceremonies of the Church, According to the Use of the Protestant Episcopal Church in the United States of America.* (New York: Oxford Univ. Press, 1928), reprinted from 1789 edition. See pp. 529- 548.

giving up his right to think and decide for himself about his conduct in the Protestant Episcopal Church. It is ironic that as a fully persuaded Anglo-Catholic at that time, he must have relished the idea that the church maintained the "ultimate insights into questions of doctrine and dogma."[4]

At the still impressionable age of twenty-five, it is questionable whether Crapsey fully realized all the subtle intellectual nuances that characterized Anglo-Catholic thought. Nevertheless, he must have regarded his ordination as one of the highlights of his young life. He was willing to accept the tenets of the church regardless of his private thoughts or interpretations.

As a disciple of Ferdinand Cartwright Ewer, he perceived the term Catholic in a manner similar to the way Ewer used it, as being part of the universal church. He also considered the word Catholic, in opposition to Protestant, yet, not in accordance with the Church of Rome. Ewer wrote,

> Catholicity is the 'Yea' of Christianity; Protestantism its 'Nay.' Protestantism is diversity without unity; Romanism unity without diversity; Catholicity diversity in unity... Rome regards unity as that of a single person; the Catholic conceives unity as that of a family, He who perverts from Catholicity to Romanism commits the sin of suicide.

In an 1883 answer to the question, offered in his pamphlet "*What is the Anglican Church?*" Ewer considered the description of the Anglican Church as a via media and rejected it by noting that "Anglicanism transcended that portrayal and retained the good from both Protestantism and Rome." In that sense, "Anglicanism was truly Catholic."[5] Crapsey spent his summers while at seminary working under the guidance of Bishop Huntington in upstate New York. After his graduation, Crapsey hoped to be sent to the diocese of Central New York. However, Bishop Potter had other plans for him in New York City. After a short delay he was sent to St. Paul's Chapel, at Trinity parish where Dr. Morgan Dix presided as rector. Crapsey began his parish work by serving approximately one year as a deacon. Crapsey often attended the sick and the poor of his parish, in a way he believed was similar to how the early church did. He did his utmost to adapt St. Paul's protocol to the Anglo-Catholic liturgy. He also became embroiled in a controversy involving the

---

[4] Crapsey, *Heretics,* pp. 94-6.

[5] Reprinted in E. Clowes Chorley *Men and Movements in the American Episcopal Church* (New York: Charles Scribner's Sons, 1946) p. 318.

lighting of candles and praying for the repose of the soul of Bishop McIllvaine, while his body was at St. Paul's waiting to be shipped back home to Ohio. His acts were viewed as impertinent as Bishop McIllvaine was a major figure in the evangelical faction of the church.[6]

Shortly thereafter, the senior assistant at St. Paul's was forced to retire due to health problems. Since Dr. Dix was also compelled to preach at "Old Trinity," Crapsey was ordered to the priesthood in the capacity of "priest officiating," at St. Paul's. He was ordained in St. Chrysostom Chapel by Bishop Potter. Crapsey noted that an African bishop, who he called, "a wild man from Borneo," preached the sermon.[7]

He learned his vocation from two great American ministers, a man, and a woman. The woman, in Crapsey's mind, was superior. Sarah Wisner Thorne walked to work every day at Trinity parish, St. Paul's Cathedral. She made clothing for the poor and employed other women in the parish to serve with her. St. Paul's was, at its inception, in a fashionable section. However, the migration of the wealthy to other parts of the city had left the cathedral in the tenement district. Nevertheless, until virtually the day she died, Sarah Wisner Thorne got off the cable car at the corner and walked to St. Paul's Church to work for those in need. Crapsey knew her for the entire seven years that he ministered at St. Paul's. He intended to immortalize her by writing the story of her life, several years after he left New York City. Dr. Dix also contributed by cataloging the multifarious duties she engaged in. Dix concluded,

> She was not a sister, nor even a deaconess; she was simply a gentlewoman of old and honorable lineage and independent means, who had elected to give her life to the church, Christ and the poor. And withal she was absolutely without pretension or affectation; not one of the usual conventionalisms of dress, speech or manner was ever seen in her; what people did see was merely a cultured, refined, and distinguished lady holding her own place in the world, yet hidden with Christ in God.[8]

Crapsey remembered the grand old woman in a way that was characteristic of his deep Catholic sympathies and Victorian social

---

[6] Crapsey considered that by his actions he did, "wake the bishop." Crapsey, *Heretics,* p. 102.

[7] Obviously, Crapsey's poor geographical skills paralleled his racial insensitivity. Crapsey, *Heretics,* p. 99.

[8] The Rev. Dr. Morgan Dix's description of the life and ministry of Sarah Wisner Thorne. in, A.S. Crapsey's *The Life and Labors of Sarah Wisner Thorne, the Story of a Simple Life* (New York: Thomas Whittaker, 1900).

consciousness. Sarah Wisner Thorne made a life-long impression on the young priest.

> She was the very picture of genteel poverty, that is sweet and clean and shrinking and sad, that poverty does not degrade but elevates and is the kind of poverty never seen except in a women of gentle birth and fine culture.[9]

The senior priest and rector of Trinity Church, Morgan Dix, had a similar effect upon Crapsey. Crapsey characterized him as an Anglo-Catholic who gave freely of his own wealth to assist the poor. He was Crapsey's early mentor and confidant and he admired Dix's sense of Catholic dedication and piety. [10]

Although his title soon changed, Crapsey's job remained essentially the same while at St. Paul's. His work with the poor secured an indelible influence upon his life. Crapsey lived over a grocery store with a barroom in it at 47 Church St. Though once in an elegant neighborhood of wealthy merchants, lawyers and bankers, St. Paul's had become a place for servicing the sick and needy. His work didn't end at night. He organized a club for the young men of the parish above the age of junior Sunday school. His young men's club met weekly. They engaged in fellowship and supported benevolence in the community. He also organized scientific lectures one winter at Trinity Hall. In the evenings Crapsey visited the young men at home. He taught the Sunday school in the mornings before the public worship at the chapel, which he directed as well. On top of all that, he was often responsible to preach on Sunday. It was with gratitude that the young priest acknowledged the aid of Sarah Wisner Thorne.[11]

One job that Crapsey did not hold at St. Paul's was that of the Sexton. As he would later relate, the Sexton dug the graves of the parishioners and held the janitorial responsibilities of the church.[12] A Mr. Weld held the position, a man almost twice Crapsey's age. Every Sacrament Sunday Mr. Weld dressed in a frockcoat and silk hat would take a coach with the finest bred horses to a local bank where he would secure the "Sacred Vessels." The Communion Service used for the presenting of the

---

[9] Ibid.
[10] Crapsey *Heretics*, pp. 103-4.
[11] Ibid., p. 108.
[12] Crapsey *Manuscript* p. 189.

Sacraments was a gift from Queen Anne to Trinity Parish, as were the original lands in and around the parish.[13]

The gift of the royal lands to the American church was known as the Queen Anne Donation. It was through the sale of these lands that the parish maintained its dominant social position in the face of the encroaching industrialization and the poverty of the surrounding neighborhood. Eventually St. John's Park owned by the vestry of Trinity parish was sold to the New York Central Railroad. The railroad immediately erected a freight depot on the old park site. Dr. Dix's rectory, where he could often be seen playing with the neighborhood children, was made into an infirmary under the direction of the Sisters of Saint Mary.[14]

Crapsey greatly admired the Sisters of Saint Mary. He was well acquainted with the order founded February 2nd, 1865, by Mother Harriet and four sisters. Bishop Potter chose the Blessed Virgin Mary as their patroness, and selected the Feast of Purification at St. Michael's Church in Manhattan as the rite establishing the religious community. It was a daring act for the bishop and greatly pleasing to the Anglo- Catholic community. The Sisters of St. Mary was the first Anglican Religious Order founded in America.[15] In 1872, they moved their community headquarters to Peekskill on the Hudson River. They maintained service throughout New York City including the hospital work at the old rectory.[16]

As an Anglo-Catholic, Crapsey was deeply concerned with their success. He visited their community on the Hudson River on day trips and spoke of their setting and the quietude of their lifestyle with great affection. In 1888, he published a Tractate entitled, *Five Joyful Mysteries: Together with a Letter Dedicatory to the Mother Superior of the Sisters of Saint Mary.* All of the proceeds from the sale of the Tractate went to the sisters.[17] Later, Crapsey sent his daughters to Kemper Hall, in Kenosha, Wisconsin, a boarding school run by the Sisters of St. Mary.

Anglo-Catholicism incited passionate arguments concerning the character of the English Church, and the Sisters were deeply embroiled in the controversies. However, the great yellow fever epidemic of 1878 in

---

[13] Ibid., pp. 115-6.

[14] Crapsey, *Heretics,* p. 114.

[15] Private conversation with Mother Miriam, Sisters of Saint Mary.

[16] "*An Overview of Our Life of Prayer,*" Pamphlet, published by Community of Saint Mary, Eastern Province, Peekskill, New York.

[17] A.S. Crapsey, *Five Joyful Mysteries: Together with a Letter Dedicatory to the Mother Superior of the Sisters of Saint Mary.* (New York: James Pott & Co., Publishers, 1888).

Memphis changed all of that. Sister Constance and three others went to Memphis to minister to the sick, abandoned and dying. Many of the afflicted had been spurned even by their relatives and were in various stages of yielding to the disease. The sisters worked tirelessly until they themselves succumbed to the dreaded fever and died.[18] Their critics were less vocal from that point on.[19]

By summer 1873, Crapsey was doing virtually everything of a pastoral function at St. Paul's. He still worked in the capacity of the deacon though promoted to the position of priest officiating. Crapsey's life was one of fervent energy and service. Besides organizing the work at the chapel and directing the young men in the neighborhood, Crapsey organized a mutual benefit society for the older men. To note the extent of his duties he wrote,

> He was celebrating the Holy Communion at seven every Sunday morning, superintending the Sunday school and teaching his Bible class from nine-thirty to ten- thirty, conducting divine worship and sometimes preaching from eleven to twelve- thirty, conducting children's service once a month at three in the afternoon and service every Sunday evening at seven. This priest officiating was reading history, theology and philosophy from eight to eleven, was in his office disposing of twenty to thirty cases from eleven to one every day, visiting the sick and the poor from two to six in the afternoon and on call in the evening till midnight. He was with his workingmen's club and his young men's club on appointed evenings. All this he was doing as a day's work contentedly, happily, for two thousand five hundred dollars a year.[20]

The parish soon hired a senior assistant priest. His salary was ten thousand dollars a year, at the time, more than the governor of the state. Crapsey however, considered that the man was not up to the job. Crapsey noted bitterly how he was not the saintly type. He had little charm of any redeeming value socially and was even a rather lower class cleric in his opinion. He had moved often in his vocation making just the right moves to further his professional life. He came east from a rather posh western

---

[18] For further historical information see, Sr. Mary Hilary *Ten Decades of Praise: The Story of the Community of St. Mary During its First Century: 1865 to 1965.* (Racine, Wisconsin: DeKoven Foundation, 1965).

[19] For further contemporary information concerning the Sisters of Saint Mary see, the pamphlet, *"An Overview of Our Life of Prayer,"* by Community of Saint Mary Eastern Province, Peekskill, New York.

[20] Crapsey, *Heretics*, p. 112.

parish without the insight, experience or the fortitude to deal with the tough urban circumstances in New York City.[21]

According to Crapsey the new senior priest walked up to two hours both to and from work each day for health purposes. He would only stay in his office for a short time and then leave early to get home for dinner. He sifted through a pre-used volume of sermons and selected one for his Sunday selection, which was in Crapsey's words, "too long for a nap, not long enough for a slumber." The vestry didn't take long to realize that there was much work left to be accomplished at St. Paul's."[22]

To remedy this problem the vestry offered Crapsey a junior assistant priest's position at St. Paul's. The offer was an insult to the newly hired senior assistant. For Crapsey, it was an impressive reward and a significant stepping-stone in his professional life. After only twenty months out of the seminary Crapsey was now making four thousand dollars a year. He was suddenly a respectable member of the permanent staff at St. Paul's. He could envision himself in line to become a senior assistant with the same huge salary as the man he now worked under. He further imagined that the office of a bishop was not out of the question in the future.[23]

One event that had a profound effect upon Crapsey was the death of a young man named Hansen whose mother was a widow and a parishioner at St. Paul's. One day Crapsey was particularly sick with "billious fever."[24] He received word that the young man had fallen through a warehouse hatchway and was killed instantly. Miraculously, Crapsey felt immediately better and went to visit the young widow at the tenement where she lived with her two remaining daughters. She just sat and stared at the dead boy and Crapsey sat there with her. They never uttered a word to each other. They sat there all day and through the night and in the early morning the woman suddenly burst into tears. He ministered to her, often writhing in his arms until she finally fell asleep. Crapsey stayed with the family until the funeral. On the following day he rode with Mrs. Hansen to the cemetery. After that, the widow Hansen and Crapsey became great friends, and remained that way, in a pastoral capacity until he left New York City. She was one of the faithful few who attended Crapsey's early, Low Mass on Sunday mornings.[25]

---

[21] Ibid., pp. 112-3.
[22] Ibid., p. 113.
[23] Ibid., p. 114.
[24] Crapsey noted that the affliction came from eating too much meat.
[25] Crapsey, *Manuscript,* pp. 120-1.

Although Crapsey's work at St. Paul's seemed overly burdening at times, he established relationships that lasted his entire life. One of his early friends was George Mumford Coit. After conferring with John Henry Houghton, a deacon at Trinity Church, Crapsey was invited to dinner with Coit where he made a great impression on his children by mysteriously "talking to the imp in the cellar." Coit, at barely thirty years of age, was the Secretary of the Hartford Insurance Company. He was transferred to New York City to increase their share of the insurance market. Crapsey and Coit hit it off famously, and from their first meeting they were the best of friends. Crapsey dined with the Coits at least once a week and every Sunday George would come to St. Paul's for the Low Mass. After the service they would have breakfast at Astor House. While in New York City, George Coit was Crapsey's closest friend.[26]

The best thing however, that happened to the young minister was meeting the enchanting daughter of a Catskill newspaperman, Adelaide Trowbridge. Crapsey met his future wife at the commencement for St. Stephen's College, in June of 1874. The attraction was mutual. Crapsey's love for the beauty of the Catskill mountains was similarly bestowed upon this most ravishing girl from the Catskills. Adelaide was the daughter of Marcus Henry and Harriet Gunn Trowbridge. Marcus was the publisher of the *Catskill Examiner*. Harriet was "tall and Nordic" in appearance according to Crapsey. The Trowbridge family emigrated to America as early as the seventeenth century. The family name derived from the ancient parish of Credition, Devonshire, England. Thomas Trowbridge emigrated from Somersetshire, England in 1636. Adelaide was also a distant relative of Harriet Starr Cannon, Mother Superior of the Sisters of Saint Mary. Crapsey's affection for the Trowbridge family paralleled the love he held for his own.[27]

June 2nd, 1875, was a splendid day for a wedding. Blue skies and a soft breeze and the sweet sound of the songbirds graced the fresh mountain air. Algernon and Adelaide's wedding was quite an event for the village of Catskill. It was a grand affair with the church decorated gloriously and with the "bon ton" of the town attending. It was a beautiful sunny day. Held at St. Luke's Church, the event featured Protestant Episcopal clergy and dignitaries from New York City and the Hudson Valley including Captain John Woodward Philip, one of the later heroes of the Spanish-American War. Adelaide was described as "one of Catskill's fairest daughters" and Crapsey as a "young and brilliant priest

[26] Ibid., pp. 117-9.
[27] Ibid., pp. 163-4.

of the Episcopal Church of New York City." Reverend Robert Weeks, married them and administered the Holy Eucharist afterwards. The newlyweds then traveled by carriage to their reception at the Trowbridge's where they viewed their elaborate gifts and greeted friends and family. For their honeymoon, they took a tour of the South.[28]

Crapsey's marriage to Adelaide Trowbridge caused him to rethink the plausibility of remaining in the tenement region close to St. Paul's on Church Street. Gratified with a suggestion from the vestry, Crapsey moved to Van Dam Street near the Hudson River, where he shared a home and expenses with Philip Brown, a junior assistant minister of St. John's Chapel. Nine months later, the Crapsey's first child was born. He was named Philip after the friend that shared their apartment building, and Trowbridge after Adelaide's family. One year after that, Emily was born. By the time Adelaide, his third child was born, they had moved to a fashionable Brownstone on Orange Street in Brooklyn Heights. From there it was merely a short trip on the ferry and a leisurely walk to St. Paul's church.[29] The Brownstone was close to Plymouth Church, and Henry Ward Beecher often waved to the children as they passed by.[30] It was a dynamic environment for the Crapsey family, and they lived in comfort and style.

One of Crapsey's projects assigned by Dr. Dix was an attempt to renovate a building across from the city jail known as "The Tombs," on Centre Street. The building was to be completely refurbished to accommodate three hundred, providing a restroom for women, a basement restaurant and rooms for children to use as playrooms. It was to be employed for other relief work as well. Crapsey circulated an advertisement in the church to raise the money for the work to commence. In a single week he was surprised they had received more than half of the amount projected to make the renovations. Among the contributions was a large check with a note from John Jacob Astor, a warden of the parish, appreciative of their commitment to the downtown region.[31]

Unfortunately, the country was in the throes of the greenback panic of the 1870s. There were so many needy that at ten cents a bed and an additional ten cents a meal, the accommodations were still not enough to cover all the destitute in the area. Crapsey was particularly concerned for

---

[28] Reprinted from *The Catskill Recorder* in, Crapsey, *Manuscript,* pp. 163-6.
[29] Alkalay- Gut, *Alone,* p. 19.
[30] Mary Elizabeth Osborn *The Life of Adelaide Crapsey* (Bruce Humphries Inc., 1933) p. 8.
[31] Crapsey, *Heretics,* p. 118.

the conscientious, willing to work, poor. He fervently dedicated his energies to the cause of civic reform.[32]

The changes of the parish rectory into a hospital operated by the Sisters of Saint Mary and the renovation of the warehouse providing low-income housing represent only two examples of the social reforms initiated by the Protestant Episcopal Church. The Trinity Church Association developed as a cooperative effort between St. Paul's and Trinity Churches with the purpose of initiating programs to service the poor of the parish. Crapsey credited the Catholic faction of the Protestant Episcopal Church with the responsibility for initiating these reforms, but he could not resist the temptation to take credit for suggesting the work on Centre Street personally. Perhaps Crapsey's statements about starting the Trinity Church Association are true. But in reality, it wasn't until after Crapsey left that the men of Trinity and St. Paul's Churches established the Trinity Church Association. Crapsey's point was to demonstrate that his work was the forerunner of the association and that he was, as usual, ahead of his time in reform work. Nevertheless, the formation of The Trinity Church Association did not officially occur until 1880.[33] The work of the Association in Trinity Parish was later placed under the direct supervision of the Sisters of St, Mary.[34]

In the midst of this dynamic religious environment, Crapsey realized that his only means of advancement was to wait. For him to progress at Trinity Parish depended upon someone else's death or retirement. He figured it might be twenty years before he would move up the ministerial ladder. Subordination was never Crapsey's forte. He was enthusiastic, full of energy and excited about his proposals. He dreamed about implementing plans for his own church. He imagined it to be in a smaller, yet vital and growing city, situated in a working class district. Crapsey believed that he was called to preach and the fact that he could not deliver but perhaps twelve sermons a year was "like starvation" to him. Crapsey's lack of preaching time restricted his opportunity to fundamentally influence his congregation both intellectually as well as spiritually. It also contributed to a spiritual laziness that Crapsey's nature would never countenance.[35]

---

[32] Ibid., pp. 118-9.

[33] Dr. Morgan Dix *History of the Parish of Trinity Church in the City of New York* Vols. I - V. New York: Putnam, 1898- 1950.

[34] Crapsey, *Heretics,* p. 126.

[35] Ibid., pp. 123-4.

With responsibilities and children to think of, Crapsey now considered his position in both the church and society. Tensions grew with his superior at St. Paul's. He was resentful that his new boss had such control over him after he had previously accomplished so much without any interference. Moreover, working as a junior assistant for another twenty years would not be socially reputable. He figured that he should be directly responsible to the people he pastored. He envisioned himself as the servant of those he led. Crapsey's idea of servant-hood was not characteristic of a false humility but rather a complex duality contained in his always-perplexing personality. On the one hand, he had a great opinion of both himself and his capabilities. On the other hand, he chose to serve others and to work for them. For Crapsey, Catholic works were the answer, at least at this point in his career. There was no need to plumb the depths of biblically defined concepts concerning religion or spirituality. Heaven and hell were portrayed before him in the great metropolis in the most realistic of ways daily.[36]

Crapsey held this vision even prior to his college days.[37] When he focused on it, it became more and more clearly defined. He fantasized that this church would be at the center of the community's life. Perhaps, even at this early date, a kind of social radicalism was entering his mind. By the time that Crapsey spoke to George William Douglas, a friend from seminary about a newly established church that his father had built in the Upstate city of Rochester, Crapsey's interest peaked. He was ready to make a change. Within a short period of time, Crapsey was in Rochester speaking personally to the father of his seminarian friend. Previous attempts to establish an Episcopal Church in the same area met with formidable problems. Differences between the rector of the previous church and Mr. William Bradley Douglas, the mortgage holder, led to foreclosure. Although the surviving congregation met independently for a while by moving a short distance away, within a year, St. Clement's, as the dissenters' assemblage was known, was forced to close its doors permanently. Nevertheless, Crapsey's enthusiasm was not swayed by the history of the church in the area nor by the formidability of the mortgage holder. He soon made his intentions to move public.[38]

In a letter written to his friend John Henry Houghton, Crapsey described his reasons for moving to the Rochester area. He wrote,

---

[36] Ibid., pp. 122-3.
[37] Ibid., p. 123.
[38] Ibid., p. 124-5.

> Things have been going from bad to worse for some time, the congregations have been falling off and a general state of dissatisfaction prevails.

However, the frustration that Crapsey described to his friend may have been more characteristic of his own dissatisfaction than that of the congregation.[39]

The relationship between himself and the new rector of St. Paul's brought the situation to a head. Crapsey noted, that there would never be a harmonious working relationship between the two men like there should be in this kind of situation. He was annoyed that whether he worked hard or hardly worked, the attitude of his superior rarely changed. Crapsey wrote, "He thinks I take too much upon myself." And concerning the lack of discretion about the work there, Crapsey noted that he was hearing things that he shouldn't be exposed to and the general state of affairs was deteriorating rapidly.[40]

Finally, with the situation rising to a crescendo he turned to Dr. Dix, for advice. Speaking of the call by Mr. Douglas to come to Rochester to inspect the new church and the area Crapsey noted that Dr. Dix actually encouraged him in his quest.[41] Looking to the future with characteristic optimism Crapsey believed he could do a great work for the Lord in Rochester. He finally made up his mind.

> But I came to see as a call- It was a harder place, unsought, less desirable in a worldly point of view than the one I hold- I felt it was from God, and I could not set it aside without great and good reasons.- So with my return I had a talk with Dr. Dix and when I got through the way was as clear as daylight. I made up my mind then and there and have not changed it since my duty- was to leave Trinity Parish or else hold on to it simply as a good thing- which was the gist of Gen. Dix's advice- If I had done that I should have been degraded in my own eyes forever. I cannot tell you all that Dr. Dix said, but he put before me two propositions. 1st you have not here the place you ought to have to enable you to develop yourself and do the best work for the church. 2nd we cannot make your place any better.[42]

---

[39] Quote taken from a letter from A.S. Crapsey to John Henry Houghton in Arthur H. Crapsey Jr. Collection, Rare Books Dept. Rush Rhees Library, Univ. of Rochester, Rochester, NY. Scrapbooks.
[40] Ibid.
[41] Ibid.
[42] Ibid.

Certainly Dr. Dix spoke directly to his young protégé's heart by clarifying what was not available in terms of professional advancement at Trinity. There was simply not enough available of what Crapsey felt that he deserved. Although he would later state that everyone thought him crazy to be leaving such a plum of the profession, in reality, there was little, if anything at all on the horizon for the enthusiastic young priest with a desire to move rapidly to a place of prominence. Finally, reflecting on his relationships and his work at St. Paul's Crapsey declared there was nothing left for him but to go. He would not remain in a post that was comfortable when he felt called to greater aspirations.

Remembering those he had labored so valiantly with and cared so deeply for, he bewailed the memory of Mrs. Thorne and his best friend George Coit. Obviously both were devastated to see him go. He realized the mutual affection between Coit and himself when he announced his departure and Coit broke down and wept. Adelaide remained faithful to his vision and was a great comfort and support during the time of duress and uncertainty inherent in a move to a new location. Obviously, her sacrifice was even greater leaving virtually everything she was familiar with including the close proximity of her family as well.[43]

Crapsey would later state that General John A. Dix, the controller of the parish, had intimated that the vestry was dissatisfied and there was going to be a change shortly. Although he, and everyone else he consulted, considered that this move would be a tremendous professional blunder, he confided to his close professional associates that there was nothing for him at Trinity Parish but a future filled with frustration and mentally unhealthy working conditions.[44]

Crapsey later wrote that he refused to professionally benefit from any of the imminent changes at St. Paul's. This varies significantly from what he wrote to his friend John Henry Houghton. Dr. Dix his mentor, and the one man who he respected greatly, had in fact laid out all his propositions for Crapsey to consider. The great sacrifice that Crapsey described, was in reality the only door of opportunity that Crapsey might realize for a very long and arduous time. In characteristic style and true to his personality that was brimming with energetic passion, Crapsey once again sought

[43] Ibid.

[44] Crapsey, *Heretics* pp. 124-6.

adventure. After all was said and done, he finally set his face as a flint towards the upstart city of Rochester, New York.[45]

[45] Ibid., p. 125.

CHAPTER THREE

"Prophet, Priest and King"

Crapsey was a colorful, eccentric individual who shared more than just his thoughts with his friend John Henry Houghton. While working at Trinity parish Houghton developed the habit of wearing a cape rather than an overcoat. He had bought a black one with a velvet collar. Finding it too short for him, he realized that it would be just the right size for his more diminutive colleague. He presented it to Crapsey. Thereupon Crapsey embarked upon a life-long habit of wearing capes. It became customary to see Crapsey about in the unpredictable upstate New York weather wearing his cape. This practice continued until his death, distinguishing him from his contemporaries.[1]

Upon accepting the call to St. Andrew's, Crapsey acknowledged the church had experienced an arduous period of genesis and transition. An Episcopal Mission originally opened on Mt. Hope Avenue, in the twelfth ward of the southern part of the city in 1865. The mission established a chapel under the sponsorship of Christ Church, Rochester and the supervisory care of Mr. R.F. Huff. On July 1st, 1870, Reverend Daniel Flack was called to assume control over the Hope Chapel Mission. Flack was a deacon at the time. In the same vicinity, on Bond and Hamilton Streets, at Emanuel Reformed Church, an Episcopal Church School was opened later that month. By December, 164 students attended what was referred to as the German Church. On May 7th, 1871, Flack was ordained as a priest of the Protestant Episcopal Church.[2] On July 6th, 1871, the mission was incorporated as an independent parish under the title of St. Clement's Church.[3]

---

[1] *"The Story of a Cape"* Author unknown, Scrapbooks, In Arthur Crapsey Jr. Collection, Univ. of Rochester, Rochester, New York.

[2] Information taken from *"Historical Time Line"* published by Calvary St. Andrew's Parish, Rochester, NY.

[3] Prepared by the Historical Records Survey Division of Community Service Programs, Work Projects Administration *Inventory of the Church Archives of New York State exclusive of New York City Protestant Episcopal Church (Diocese of Rochester)* (Albany, N.Y.: The Historical Records Survey, June, 1941). pp. 133-4.

Weekly worship services with the Holy Eucharist celebrated on Sunday morning and a children's service in the afternoon commenced at that time. By July 13th, 1871, plans for building St. Clement's Church on a 150 by 150-foot lot began. Mr. William B. Douglas, a wealthy retired banker, purchased the site for $3,000.00. A vestry consisting of Reverend Daniel Flack, Rector, William B. Douglas, Senior Warden and William Dove, Clerk was established. A temporary church opened in a house on South Avenue just north of Alexander Street. However, it wasn't until the spring of 1873 that the building fund proceeded, inaugurated with the amount of $2,500.00 raised by Rev. Flack and other interested parties with a matching gift of the same amount from Mr. Douglas. The cornerstone of St. Clement's Church was laid on July 19th, 1873, at 5:00 P.M. with the Rt. Rev. Arthur Cleveland Coxe presiding.[4]

For whatever reasons, Flack decided by mid- December of 1873 to resign as rector at St. Clement's Church and leave for California. In March of 1874 the church called Reverend David A. Bonnar as the new rector. The same year, the chapel, chancel, and the older part of the rectory were completed at the cost of $13,000.00. Reverend Bonnar remained at St. Clement's for approximately three years until irreconcilable differences caused Mr. Douglas to foreclose on the property on Averill Avenue.[5] The parish was tragically split over the falling-out. [6] Mr. Douglas bought the entire church at the foreclosure sale in 1877. He immediately deeded the church property renamed St. Andrew's, to the Diocese of Western New York. A stipulation in the deed read that if a new diocese formed with St. Andrew's in it, the bishop of the diocese received the privilege of claiming St. Andrew's as his cathedral.[7]

St. Clement's continued by removing itself to another building. But little more than a year later Bonnar resigned. He had been working in the western diocesan region since 1868. His experience with nascent churches had apparently dampened his enthusiasm for mission work. In 1869, he had established a church, St. Mathias', in East Aurora, N.Y. where it had grown by the end of the 1870s to such a sufficient size that it was no

---

[4] *"Historical Time Line,"* published by Calvary St. Andrew's Parish, Rochester, NY.

[5] Ibid.

[6] Crapsey, *Heretics,* p.129

[7] Prepared by The Historical Records Survey Division of Community Service, Work Projects Administration *Inventory of the Church Archives of NY State exclusive of New York City Protestant Episcopal Church (Diocese of Rochester)* (Albany, NY: The Historical Records Survey, June, 1941). pp. 131-4.

longer acknowledged as a mission church. Bonnar however, left St. Mathias' after only two years of serving there.[8] As a young and growing church, they were only able to pay $400.00 a year for his salary and they were experiencing other problems with their building funds.[9]

St. Clement's dissolved and was reorganized on the old site under the new name, St. Andrews Church, on February 7th, 1879. The parish was organized by agreement with the Trustees of the Parochial Fund of the Diocese of Western New York. Under the arrangement with the diocese, the new vestry secured control over the edifice once known as St. Clement's Church. The Reverend Albert Wood presided as *locum tenens,* or, the interim priest- in- charge.[10] Perhaps Mr. Douglas hoped that his son George, Crapsey's friend from seminary, would take the parish for his own. His son decided against the assignment however, procuring Crapsey through his relationship with him at Trinity Parish in New York City. Crapsey answered the call by March of 1879. He started work in person on June 1st, 1879. Ten days later, the property was deeded to St. Andrew's.[11]

Crapsey alluded to his heroic effort of answering the call to a church divided and under the control of one man. According to Crapsey, he carried on, undaunted, establishing the church in the face of considerable odds. The church had failed under the pastoral care of three clergymen prior to Crapsey's arrival. There were only forty parishioners to begin with and Mr. Douglas controlled the property in a despotic manner. Nevertheless, Crapsey entered into his new job with great vigor. Finally, rumors spread as to his incompetence. Why else would he remove to the upstart town in Western New York? He received a drastic reduction in pay, and the possibility of advancing professionally in the largest city in the nation had vanished. Crapsey noted,

> I resigned my position as junior assistant minister of Trinity parish at a salary of four thousand dollars a year, paid the first of every month by

---

[8] Charles Wells Hayes *The Diocese of Western New York: History and Recollections* (Rochester, NY: Scrantom, Wetmore & Co., 1904). p. 309-10.

[9] Paul A. Spengler *A Brief History of St. Mathias' Episcopal Church, East Aurora, New York from 1869- 1994. Part I: 1869- 1936* (East Aurora: St. Mathias' Parish, 1994). Pamphlet.

[10] Charles Wells Hayes *The Diocese of Western New York: History and Recollections* (Rochester, New York: Scrantom, Wetmore & Co., 1904). p. 215.

[11] Information taken from *"Historical Time Line"* published by Calvary St. Andrew' s Parish. W.B. Douglas also had the College Chapel at Hobart built and endowed the chaplaincy of the college. Hayes, *Diocese* p. 238.

> check on the Chemical National Bank, and accepted the rectorship of St. Andrew's Church, Rochester, at a salary of fifteen hundred a year, which, when paid at all, was in the pennies of the collection. This action ruined my professional career. It was naturally concluded that there must be some disgraceful reason for such a foolish step. I learned later that I was given just one year to stay in the parish and the city, if so long.[12]

In reality however, Mr. Douglas relinquished control of the property to the Diocese of Western New York shortly after he purchased it at the foreclosure sale in 1877. Clearly Douglas hoped by his action to underscore his commitment to the parish and to underwrite its success. Only ten days after Crapsey's appointment the property was duly deeded back to St. Andrew's parish in accordance with the practice of the diocese.[13] As the senior warden of St. Andrew's, Mr. Douglas was an integral part of the new vestry, exercising considerable influence over the decision making processes there. However, as a member of the vestry Crapsey retained an equally important say in the business of the church. Mr. Douglas' ability to foreclose on the property, as he had previously, was no longer an option.[14]

It would be hard to believe that Crapsey didn't know that the property was not under the autonomous control of Mr. Douglas ahead of time. He certainly knew this by the beginning of his ministry at St. Andrew's, or at the most, ten days later. Yet he manipulated the facts years later to portray himself in a heroic role. Additionally, although he left Trinity parish sometime in May, Crapsey was paid through September 1st, 1879. Dr. Dix, rector of Trinity Parish, was an Anglo-Catholic of like passions with Crapsey. He mentored Crapsey defending him after his prayers for the repose of the soul of Dr. McIllvaine, the evangelical Bishop. During this time of contention within the Protestant Episcopal Church, men of like passions supported one another. Due to his experience and the great need for clergy there, he probably could have easily secured his old job again or

---

[12] In Richard Greenleaf's "*Algernon Crapsey and the Beginnings of St. Andrew's Parish, Rochester, New York*" Rochester, New York: A Paper Read at the Annual Parish Meeting, November 28th, 1966. Reprinted from Crapsey, *Heretics,* p. 126.

[13] Personal correspondence with and David Sisson archivist, Episcopal Church Diocese of Rochester, NY.

[14] Prepared by the Historical Records Survey Division of Community Service Programs, Works Projects Administration *Inventory of the Church Archives of New York State exclusive of New York City Protestant Episcopal Church (Diocese of Rochester)* (Albany, New York: The Historical Records Survey, June, 1941). pp. 131-4.

obtained a similar one had circumstances not worked out. Taking the job at St. Andrew's was hardly the professional risk that Crapsey depicted it to be.[15]

The salary of $1,500.00 yearly, although a great cut in pay, was almost four times the average salary for clergy in the 1870s. In fact, even by 1920, the average salary for clergy in America was less than one thousand dollars per annum. Moreover, if present circumstances are comparable, life in Rochester was much less expensive than in New York City. Although Crapsey may have concluded that he and his family were suffering, they were in a position of considerable luxury in comparison with other clergy. With the benefit of housing at the rectory on Averill Avenue, the Crapsey's were actually quite well off. Additionally, his income never remained static.[16]

Crapsey left Adelaide and the children in Catskill, New York, with her parents while he went to prepare their new place. As a newspaperman, Mr. Trowbridge exercised his influence in a responsible way. He was involved in abolitionist politics before it was popular, in a manner similar to Crapsey's maternal grandfather. The town of Catskill was in the midst of a grand cultural enterprise in the later portion of the nineteenth century. Great artistic influences pervaded the Catskill region such as the Hudson River School of painting. Trowbridge often published poetry striving for a high literary standard. Mrs. Crapsey's brother experimented with poetry and at least one example of his verse remains. In this belletristic environment, Adelaide, the precocious child of Algernon and Adelaide Crapsey developed into a literary prodigy eventually influencing poets as significant as Carl Sandburg.[17]

Crapsey arrived in Rochester over a month before his family to prepare the way. He made his home in St. Andrew's rectory and dined with Mr. Dove, the vestry clerk, who furnished his meals during Mrs. Crapsey's absence. Crapsey familiarized himself with the pastoral work of the parish, sizing up the challenge involved in his new position. The only congregation available was a "small, inter-related group of English folk."[18]

Adelaide and the children came to Rochester on July 1st arriving in the same way that so many others from the downstate region had, via canal

---

[15] Crapsey. *Heretics*, pp. 125- 7.

[16] William L. Fox *Willard L. Sperry: The Quandaries of a Liberal Protestant Mind 1914- 1939.* New York: Peter Lang, 1991. Clerical salary statistics quoted on p. 4.

[17] Alkalay- Gut, *Alone* pp. 28- 31.

[18] A.S. Crapsey *Heretics* (New York, 1924) p. 126.

boat. They were greeted with a wonderful meal of "spring chickens, butter, cream, milk, cake, vegetables," and he had fresh flowers planted for the occasion.[19] Besides arranging the sumptuous meal, Crapsey soon realized that he had done virtually nothing in Adelaide's absence to prepare the living quarters for the family. There was no bath, no sanitary provisions, and for Adelaide, used to the comfort of suburban Brooklyn and her parents' home, the future seemed bleak. She had anticipated something comparable to what they were accustomed to in New York City. But Crapsey had failed to even notice the lack of basic sanitary facilities. His mind was entranced with his visions. He was torn between images of a complex, wealthy existence with an attending staff and the possibility of a bishopric at the end of an illustrious career and the simple life of a pastoral priest overseeing the plain folk of his parish.[20]

In March of 1879 he wrote to John Henry Houghton expressing what he hoped to accomplish at St. Andrew's. He envisioned St. Andrew's as a people's church, engaged in a great "Catholic work." He explained,

> And it is our intention to carry out the devotional system of the church, a weekly celebration and if possible daily prayers- I shall have a difficult task there- But I hope through God's grace not to fail entirely.[21]

A time of desperate loneliness descended upon the Crapseys. They were used to the excitement of New York City and the young, but burgeoning Rochester was obviously incomparable. Mrs. Crapsey remarked, how a mere wagon passing by the rectory was memorable occasion.[22] They missed their friends and the social life in the big city. They filled their time with visitation, taking care of family matters, reading and dining with Mr. Douglas. Adelaide busied herself with the children and landscaping the grounds so they took on the appearance of an English garden.[23] After noticing the shabby worn out condition of Crapsey's cape, Mr. Douglas presented him with a cape that he politely stated had been made for him, but didn't fit. It was black with a velvet collar just like Crapsey's old one. Perhaps Mr. Douglas was somewhat

---

[19] Reprinted from Susan Smith, "Adelaide Crapsey: Materials for a Biographical and Textual Study," *Univ. of Rochester Library Bulletin 25*, nos. 1& 2 (1969- 70): 5, in Alkalay Gut, *Alone,* pp. 31-2.
[20] Crapsey, *Heretics*, p. 126.
[21] Letter written from A.S. Crapsey to John Henry Houghton March 5th, 1879. Arthur H. Crapsey Jr. Collection, Scrapbooks.
[22] Noted from Mrs. Adelaide Crapsey's diary in Alkalay Gut, *Alone,* p. 32.
[23] Crapsey, *Heretics*, pp. 130- 1.

embarrassed to have his parish priest running around town in a tattered cloak.[24]

Surrounded by Roman Catholics for neighbors, and with the prospect of having an insignificant number of parishioners to deal with, Crapsey realized that he would need to devise more practical means to reach other members of the community.[25] In the heat of the summer, he hit upon an idea. He decided to try to attract men to a society, like the benefit societies he had been involved with in New York City. Crapsey had already established a mutual benefit society at St. Paul's. He called a meeting for the men in the church to share his idea, but only three showed up. He realized he would need a different approach, and "a different bait." His scheme involved hosting a watermelon party. He invited approximately fifty men from throughout the area and this time about forty- five showed up. He offered to open up the benefit society to anyone of good moral character. All denominations were welcome. In that part of the city most of the people were blue-collar workers, and largely Roman Catholic. Therefore, Crapsey felt he had little to lose and everything to gain. Crapsey reckoned, if he could first appeal to their carnal desires he might eventually be able to appeal to their religious ones.[26]

Crapsey called the organization the Brotherhood of St. Andrew's, as it was Andrew who brought Peter to Jesus, but the association between the brotherhood and the church was obvious. Likewise, Crapsey asked only that the men maintain a brotherly spirit. The relationship between the brotherhood and the church at St. Andrew's was thereby firmly established, not only through the name, but also because they originally held their meetings in the church itself. The men paid ten cents a week into a fund. If one became ill he would receive one dollar for the first week, five dollars a week for thirteen additional weeks and two and a half dollars per week after that. In case of a member's death, their widow would receive fifty dollars. If the wife of a member died, the member would receive twenty- five dollars. They waited three years until they received one hundred dollars in their treasury before paying any benefits.[27]

---

[24] *The Story of a Cape* Author Unknown, A.H. Crapsey Jr. Collection.

[25] Crapsey, *Heretics,* p. 128.

[26] Ibid., p. 156. Also quoted from William J. Bailey *St. Andrew's Brotherhood, Organized by Dr. A.S. Crapsey Origin and History from 1880- 1930.* (Rochester: St. Andrew's Brotherhood, 1930). Pamphlet.

[27] Crapsey, *Heretics,* pp. 155- 7.

The Brotherhood drafted a constitution by January of 1880, and by 1881, they elected Crapsey President. On July 11th, of the next year they moved from the church down Ashland Street into Douglas Hall, a building donated to the parish by Mr. Douglas. The first death of a member occurred in 1883, when Brother Henry Ellwanger, an organist who had organized the surpliced choir, died. A stained glass window on the north side of the church was instituted in his memory. By January 1892, Rufus A. Sibley one of the founders of Sibley, Lindsay & Curr Company created "the Sibley Fund." The department store was for many years the largest and finest in Rochester. In January 1894, the Brotherhood moved to Nazareth House directly across from the church on Averill Avenue. With the creation of the Brotherhood of St. Andrew's, Crapsey established a foothold in the community.[28]

St. Andrew's was a one of the first free churches in the area. Although it bordered upon a working- class neighborhood, it was also in one of the wealthiest portions of the city of Rochester. Dr. Dix first planted the desire for a free church in Crapsey's mind when he worked as a young deacon and assistant at St. Paul's Church. Free seating was first proposed for Trinity, in New York City by General J.A. Dix in 1851. He recommended the proposal again in 1854. Shortly afterwards, Dr. Morgan Dix advocated a free church for St. Paul's. In fact, some pew owners and renters voluntarily relinquished their pews to the control of the vestry for the purpose of seating visitors and those less fortunate. Nevertheless, free seating at Trinity Parish was not fully adopted until a resolution was passed in 1919.[29]

In Rochester, First Presbyterian Church had tried to enable equal access for the seating of strangers in the 1850s. Christ Episcopal Church also attempted to establish a free seating plan in 1855. It was a discouraging failure. Finally, Crapsey instituted St. Andrew's as a free church with the advantage of starting the plan from its inception in 1879.

---

[28] The Sibley Fund was an additional fund. William J. Bailey *St. Andrew's Brotherhood, Organized by Dr. A.S. Crapsey, Origin and History from 1880-1930.* (Rochester: St. Andrew's Brotherhood, 1930).

[29] Information concerning General J.A. & Dr. Morgan Dix via personal communication with Trinity Parish Historian Jessica Silver found in Morgan Dix ed. and compiler, *A History of the Parish of Trinity Church in the City of New York Vol. IV.* (New York: G.P. Putnam's Sons, The Knickerbocker Press, 1906). p. 326 Information concerning Morgan Dix found in Leicester C. Lewis ed. and John Dix compiler, *A History of the Parish of Trinity Church in the City of New York Vol. V.* (New York: Compiled for Trinity Parish, Columbia Univ. Press, 1950). p. 29.

Crapsey's introduction of free seating at St. Andrew's, though not original was characteristically innovative for the Rochester region. The next successful free church was not established until 1891, when the Lake Avenue Baptist Church tried the free seating plan. St. Paul's Episcopal Church became a free church after a vote was taken in 1897.[30]

Crapsey's vision was for St. Andrew's to be like the church of the medieval times. He envisioned the church as the center of the community in an institutional capacity.[31] True to the Anglo-Catholic emphasis on works, an interest in social reform through community action materialized. Crapsey purposed in his heart to succeed not only personally but also as a representative of the Anglo-Catholic faction of the church. Moreover, the effervescence of his extemporaneous preaching style started attracting people's attention in the area.[32]

Crapsey felt he was "called to preach." His inability to fully realize his potential while in New York City greatly influenced his decision to relocate to Rochester. Crapsey placed a premium on his ability to communicate effectively. He studied oratory, reading brochures on the subject by John P. Altgeldt and analyzing the introduction of Webster's reply to Hayne. He compared great oratory with the art of architecture. One should come to the subject step by step he suggested,

> as a stairway leading from the street to the porch, and upon the beauty of this entrance lies (sic) very largely the attractiveness of the house. But if the porch is all there is (with) a shabby structure behind it, then the introduction hurts rather than helps what follows. The intellectual architect must have arranged his halls, his drawing rooms, his dining rooms and more especially his stairways as to make them more attractive to the eye and pleasing to the mind. They must have a logical relation one to the other, and he must pay special attention to his conclusion, which is the roof of his intellectual architectural structure. When he has accomplished his task, then the orator has created a lasting building; a great speech lives for ever; it is carried on from generation to generation; it is the mightiest product of the mind of man, and in its proportion such every speech should be, be it made on platform or in pulpit.[33]

---

[30] Edward R. Foreman ed. *Centennial History of Rochester, New York Vol. III* (Rochester Public Library, Rochester, New York, 1933). p. 348.
[31] Ibid., pg. 321.
[32] Personal communication concerning Crapsey's "extemporaneous preaching style," with Arthur H. Crapsey Jr., the rector's grandson.
[33] Crapsey, *Heretics*, p. 133.

Crapsey studied ways to effectively reach people with his eloquence and style. He wrote of how a speaker should be like a painter ornamenting their architectural walls with adroitness and artistic acumen. Crapsey painted with what he called "flowers of speech." He noted how artistic expression served the same purpose that natural flowers did. It attracted attention.[34]

Crapsey coveted the attention and consideration that distinguished oratory provided. He was also concerned with aesthetic art and its effect upon individuals in his congregation and in society at large. Crapsey boasted that he built his congregation through the power of his sermons. He picked a subject for his Sunday sermon in the early part of the week. He would then, meditate upon the sermon all week long by setting his gaze somewhat ahead of him while walking. Crapsey noted that for a clergyman of his stature and notoriety to not notice all those around him as he moved throughout the community was not necessarily a profitable habit. On Sunday, he would delve into his mental files and extrapolate the sermon arranging it by introduction, body and conclusion. His sermons were around twenty minutes in length, remembering the counsel of Bishop Potter who advised, that a brief message afforded mercy. Crapsey unabashedly declared how his sermons established his reputation at St. Andrew's and beyond. However, he never remained content with the sermons and ironically his discontentment contributed to the influence that his ministry had upon Rochester and the world.[35]

In August of 1879, just two months after Crapsey's arrival a contract was let and the ground broken for the completion of the nave and tower of the church.[36] The church was completed in semi- Gothic style. Richard M. Upjohn, the son of architect Richard Upjohn, who had designed Trinity Church in New York, was responsible for the additions to St. Andrew's. Both were known for reestablishing the Gothic style of architecture as the "Romantic craze swept throughout the nation."[37]

Crapsey related how St. Andrew's was a free church in a working class district. His neighbors were primarily blue-collar Irish and German Catholics, and he reveled in the fact that his free church plan established his pastoral credibility through his association with the working and lower classes. Crapsey said, his starting salary (of $1500.00 a year), was paid, if

---

[34] Ibid., pp. 133- 4.

[35] Crapsey, *Heretics,* p. 136.

[36] "*Historical Time Line*" published by Calvary St. Andrew's Parish. Rochester, NY.

[37] Crapsey *Heretics,* p. 130.

at all, by the menial offerings taken on Sundays. It would be impertinent to assume that Crapsey's work did not touch the lives of the poor or the workingman during his tenure at St. Andrew's. The church was located in the midst of a region of the city known as the Southwedge District. The area was also once known as swillburg, because the German population, in particular, often kept pigs in their backyards. One of the large Catholic churches in the area is named St. Boniface after the missionary to Germany.[38] Crapsey wrote,

> We were loyally sustained by the men of our neighborhood who kept us in close relation with the working element of the community, such men as the Baileys, the Lucketts and the Fields, and more especially the farmer, Ambrose Daunton who drove in from his farm ten miles away every Sunday morning to be present at our worship. These men kept us informed as to the thought of their class and they were the basic element in our work from the beginning to the end.[39]

The truth however, was somewhere beyond Crapsey's characterization of the socio- economic situation at St. Andrew's. Obviously, St. Andrew's had an endowment that must have influenced Crapsey's decision to relocate in Rochester. St. Andrew's also bordered upon a very fashionable area of Rochester, the Highland and South Avenue, Mt. Hope District, which, next to the East Avenue section, was one of the wealthiest area of the city. A list of Crapsey's parishioners read like a register of high society in Rochester in the late nineteenth century. It included, the Ellwangers, famous professional nursery operators and contributing donors of Highland Park in Rochester, Judge George P. Humphrey, Samuel Lee Seldon, lawyer, Henry Seldon, Judge of the New York State Court of Appeals, and the father of George Seldon, the original holder of the patent for the internal combustion engine, Elwood Worcester, eventually the rector of Emmanuel Church, Boston, and the leader of the Emmanuel Movement. Both Hiram and Rufus Sibley were also associated with St. Andrew's. Next to George Eastman, founder of Kodak, the Sibleys were perhaps the most prominent businessmen in Rochester. Hiram was one of the founders of Western Union Telegraph Co., and Rufus founded one of the largest department stores in Western New York State. Others included Hobart Atkinson, a leading banker of Rochester,

---

[38] Personal conversations with the Reverend George Exeley- Steigler, ex- rector of St. Andrew's Church.
[39] A.S. Crapsey *Manuscript,* p. 185.

Arthur Coslett, Thomas Montgomery, Frederick Whittlesey, and James Sherlock Andrews, all lawyers with whom Crapsey considered himself as, "one of the boys." Mr. John Rochester, son of Nathaniel Rochester, one of the original founders of the city, was also an intimate friend of the Crapseys.[40]

Crapsey insisted that the wealth of his members didn't matter. Moreover, he refused to belittle or ingratiate himself by extending what he called the glad hand at the end of Sunday's service. Crapsey felt that the rich and the poor came together at St. Andrew's. Except for the forty or so members there at his arrival, all the rest came subsequent to his ministry there. Crapsey declared arrogantly that "he had called the church, the church didn't call him." At the height of his ministry there were over five hundred communicants and one thousand members including the children. St. Andrew's became the fourth largest Episcopal Church in the Diocese of Western New York. The church did not owe anything. At the apex of Crapsey's ministry the operating budget for the year was "only $7,500.00. The curate received $1,000.00 a year, and the choir received $2,000.00, $800.00 for the sexton and $700.00 for church expenses." Crapsey soon secured a raise to $3,000.00 annually, double what he signed on for. He also accepted gifts from his wealthy parishioners, who were personal friends. These gifts, received fairly regularly, supplemented his income.[41]

In 1882 Crapsey's father Jacob died. He was a well loved though relatively unsuccessful man. Crapsey may have despised his father's ineptitude in business but he loved his character and gentility. The composite depths of his soul included both the humanitarian benevolence of his father and the religious passion of his grandfather. Jacob had been admitted to the bar in 1832. The first two years of his work as a District Attorney obviously did not suit his character and he went on to a private practice in Ohio that lasted for forty-eight years. The last sixteen years of his life were caught up with the Whitewater lawsuit case. This sole commission paid his bills providing him with some professional satisfaction although he died before the case was resolved. He was a man of a humble demeanor, a kind and gentle soul. His colleagues were unanimous in their opinions of Jacob T. Crapsey, noting that there was "never an unkind word uttered against him."[42]

---

[40]Ibid., pp. 185-8.

[41] Crapsey *Heretics,* pp. 147-9.

[42] News clipping of Jacob T. Crapsey's obituary in A. H. Crapsey Jr. Collection, Scrapbooks.

In his work, Crapsey envisioned himself as the pastor of his flock. As a pastor he assumed the paradoxical position of both leader and servant. As a High Churchman and an Anglo-Catholic, he sustained an elevated opinion of the role of the cleric in both the church and society. He considered himself one of the elite members of the developing community, intimate with the business, social and political leaders of the city. Conversely, he condescended to the lower classes. He served the poor, as a matter of remaining obedient to the example of Jesus. These varied influences added to his complex and ironic character.

In December of 1888, Crapsey had an altercation with the Bishop of the Western New York Diocese. Bishop Coxe attempted to interfere with the ritualistic lighting of candles and raising the elements during the Eucharist. Crapsey argued that "St. Andrew's was a High Church, church." He defended his position by citing Bishop Doane of Albany and Bishop Potter of New York City as two men who were sympathetic to his position. He also contended that due to St. Andrew's free church status and considering that no class distinctions were apparent in the church, that not even a bishop had the right to interfere with their methods of worship.[43] Perhaps Crapsey had overstated his position. Coxe was no Low Churchman. In fact, he considered himself a proponent of the Catholic Church, and he was an early leader in the Christian Unity Society, which Low Churchman completely disassociated from.[44] Crapsey's penchant for the controversial, his rebelliousness against authority and tendency toward the extreme were manifested both in the controversy over Bishop McIllvaine's remains and now in a liturgical fray with a sound and very Catholic bishop.

Crapsey jealously guarded his autonomy at St. Andrew's. He considered himself ready at any time for any calamity that might befall the church or his parishioners. He once experienced the tribulation of a family of a widower and three children who suffered from diphtheria. Although all three children eventually died, Crapsey was available in their sick rooms to help throughout their ordeal.[45]

Crapsey came home one night in December of 1884, "violently retching." He was placed in bed and the family physician, Dr. Allen B. Carr was summoned to his room. Dr. Carr called in another physician, a Dr. Beigler to assist him. A nurse was also stationed at the home to assist.

---

[43] News clipping A. H. Crapsey Jr. Collection, Scrapbooks.

[44] Charles Wells Hayes, *The Diocese of Western New York,* Rochester: Scrantom, Wetmore & Co., 1904. p. 325.

[45] Crapsey, *Heretics*, p. 138.

Crapsey later related how death came quickly to most experiencing similar symptoms. Nevertheless, though he suffered from several relapses, Crapsey recovered. His good friend George Mumford Coit, after hearing of the situation, came up from Brooklyn bringing with him Sister Harriet, a trained nurse. Crapsey believed the strength of the Anglo-Catholic masses that were offered up around the country, the prayers said for him by his friends, that he might be spared for the church, and the constitutional strength of Sister Harriet was somehow transferred to him. He felt all these factors working together inevitably caused him to recover. Subsequently, Crapsey spent three weeks with Dr. Carr at the ocean side in the warm, healthy climes of Florida while he convalesced and completed his recovery. He later wrote, "prayer set in motion vibrations that traveled instantly all around the globe."[46]

He was convinced that there was something about Christian Science and faith healing that could not be discounted. Crapsey figured that Jesus was a healer of healthy constitution and beyond that he was never selfish in sharing his healthiness. Jesus had the gift and others had it at various times as well. Crapsey noted how a dark and melancholy soul could be made whole through association with one having the gift of healing. But if that healer attempted to profit by his gift he would lose it. Crapsey later rationalized this spirituality. He wrote,

> The giving of life in its fullness is the perpetual miracle. The man and the woman give it by generation to the child. They give it in just proportion as they have it. Healthy parents have healthy children; sickly parents, sickly children. Physical, intellectual and spiritual life are all contagious. Men, women, animals and plants are all life givers and I am sure that Dr. Carr and Sister Harriet had much more to do with my recovery than that one millionth tituration of phosphorus to which Dr. Carr ascribed the cure.[47]

He eventually became interested in the Emmanuel Movement that his friend Dr. Elwood Worcester initiated. Worcester was best known from his work at Emmanuel Church in Boston. He once sat under the teaching of Crapsey at St. Andrew's. He came to St. Andrew's at the age of sixteen with his parents and two sisters. He was then employed as a railway freight office clerk and was very unhappy due to his occupation. Crapsey noted his precocious ability as an acolyte and in the reading of his lessons. Crapsey realized that Worcester was driven to succeed. He graduated from

---

[46] Crapsey, *Manuscript,* pp. 192-4.
[47] Ibid., pp. 193-4.

Columbia University, graduated from Seminary in one year, and studied at Bonn University. He distinguished himself in his ministerial career and eventually took the rector's position at Emmanuel Church in Boston.[48]

Worcester was responsible for starting a movement in Boston that stressed the affinity between physical and spiritual health known as the Emmanuel Movement. He sought a means of procuring both spiritual and physical health and then applying those principles to cure nervous and other physical disorders. Christian Science and other movements were simultaneously hypothesizing about the metaphysical as a means to compliment one's physical health. Dr. Worcester believed that faith healed. As a progenitor of both the positive thinking of Norman Vincent Peale's philosophy, and the later word-faith movement, Worcester stressed not only intellectual assent involved in faith healing, but feelings of trust, confidence and expectation. The Emmanuel Movement sought the holistic development and employment of one's influence over the mind, body, as well as the moral and religious experiences in life.[49]

It is doubtful that the Sister Harriet that Crapsey referred to concerning his illness was the same as Mother Harriet, the first Mother Superior and one of the five founders of the Community of St. Mary. Crapsey would have undoubtedly documented it had he received personal care by the Mother Superior of the Sisters of St. Mary. Crapsey worked together with these nuns in New York City. Nuns often took the names of other distinguished nuns, but rarely, if ever, do they take their names while still alive. Therefore, it makes little sense that Sister Harriet would have taken on Mother Harriet's name if she were from the Community of St. Mary. Mother Harriet did not die until Easter Day, 1896.[50]

Perhaps the Sister Harriet that Crapsey referred to was a member of another Episcopalian Sisterhood. Dr. William Augustus Muhlenberg helped to establish a Sisterhood in New York City as early as 1845. He was however very cautious about providing any association between the Episcopal nuns and the Roman Catholic nuns. There was no consecration by a bishop. No habits were worn. They were kept secretive due to the tensions between high and low factions in the church. They were not a

[48] Ibid. pp. 192-4.

[49] Mark J. Duffy (ed.) *The Episcopal Diocese of Massachusetts 1784- 1984: A Mission to Remember, Proclaim, and Fulfill* (Boston: Published by The Episcopal Diocese of Massachusetts, 1984) pp. 162-6.

[50] Sister Mary Hilary, CSM *Ten Decades of Praise: The Story of the Community of St. Mary During its First Century: 1865 to 1965.* (Racine, Wisconsin: De Koven Foundation, 1965).

true monastic body, but more a philanthropic sorority. There was a split between the order Muhlenberg helped establish and the later Sisters of St. Mary.[51] Many of the Sisters of St. Mary were involved originally with the Sisterhood of the Holy Communion, at St. Luke's hospital in New York City. They were the first Protestant sisterhood in America and "anterior to the first of the English Sisterhoods- Miss Sellon's which did not exist until 1848."[52] Other Sisterhoods or philanthropic bodies of deaconesses were also established during the mid- to late, nineteenth century. Bishop Horatio Potter consecrated the Sisters of St. Mary, the first truly Protestant Episcopal monastic body in America, formally on February 2, 1865.[53]

It is improbable Sister Harriet, the nurse who came up from New York City to help him, was involved with the Sisters of St. Mary. Crapsey conducted a retreat in 1883 at a site that he referred to as St. Gabriel's Chapel. Mount St. Gabriel's was the formal name of the property where the Sisters of St. Mary eventually established their convent community headquarters. In 1888, Crapsey wrote a tractate entitled the *Five Joyful Mysteries.* He addressed the tractate to the Mother Superior of the Sisters of St. Mary. Crapsey dedicated all funds received through his publication of the tract to the chapel fund at Mount St. Gabriel's. St. Mary's Chapel was eventually completed on the grounds of Mt. St. Gabriel's in the 1890s. In lieu of having a formal edifice built on the premises, Crapsey referred to the structure used for the chapel as St. Gabriel's.[54]

During the course of his ministry Crapsey conducted at least five retreats at the convent of St. Mary's. The first of these was conducted in the summer of 1883.[55] During these times, Adelaide and the children spent time with her family, the Trowbridges, in the Catskills. His experience at St. Mary's brought requests from other clergymen from around the country to conduct retreats for them as well. As the conductor, Crapsey gave instruction to the retreatants. He celebrated communion, set times for

---

[51] Ibid.

[52] Rev. Henry C. Potter, D.D. *Sisterhoods and Deaconesses: At Home and Abroad* (New York: E.P. Dutton & Co., 1873). pp. 92, 205-9.

[53] Sr. Mary Hilary, CSM *Ten Decades of Praise: The Story of the Community of St. Mary During its First Century: 1865 to 1965.* (Racine, Wisconsin: De Koven Foundation, 1965).

[54] Personal communication with the Sisters of St. Mary, Peekskill, NY.

[55] A.S. Crapsey *Five Joyful Mysteries With a Letter Dedicatory, to The Mother Superior of the Sisterhood of Saint Mary* (New York: J. Pott & Co., 1888). p. 14. Crapsey's other tractate, *Five Sorrowful Mysteries,* (1885?) apparently no longer exists.

meditation and prayer, and taught that through seclusion, silence and self-examination, others might arrive at the knowledge of their own soul.[56]

Retreats gave Crapsey the opportunity to delve into the devotional customs of the traditional faith. By emphasizing the ancient practices of the Catholic Church, Crapsey rediscovered, among other things, the exercise of meditation. For Crapsey, meditation was more than mental prayer. Meditation was the soul's way of exploring itself and finding answers to some subject God was attempting to show to it. Crapsey explained that apologetics provided explanation, polemics secured defense and dogmatics brought organization to the faith. Similarly, Crapsey placed great significance in the practice of meditation. He believed that the essence of a worthwhile retreat was found in its primary purpose, meditation. Crapsey viewed meditation as a lesson in theology of the most spiritual manner. Spiritual theology contemplates, and actually enters into the place that the other disciplinary exercises previously battled for. Writing figuratively of the meditative process he wrote,

> She mounts upwards as an eagle. On eagle's wings she poises in mid- air, and far above all doubt and mistrust in the clear blue of God's presence she gazes into the heart of the Sun of Righteousness.[57]

Crapsey viewed the meditative study of spiritual theology as among the highest forms of human thought, by which one arrives at truth. Thus, the possession of truth and the steadfastness of mind were the ultimate goals of meditation. He believed the soul was the ultimate beneficiary by knowing, indeed, mastering the truth.[58]

Crapsey also believed that spoken meditation was better than a sermon and was the key to making the mysteries of the faith known to people. Crapsey thought that through a meditative state the priest relates the spiritual verities he experiences in this heightened state. Through this state

---

[56] Crapsey, *Heretics*, pp. 158-163.

[57] A.S. Crapsey: *Meditations on the Five Joyful Mysteries, together with a Letter Dedicatory: To the Mother Superior of the Sisterhood of St. Mary* (New York: J. Pott & Co., 1888). pp 7-9.

[58] Ibid. p. 12. Crapsey believed that the study of "Spiritual Theology was the very best employment of one's faculties." Meditation "fostered steadfastness of the mind" and "the steadfast adherence of the will to the truth was the closing act of meditation." It allowed the "soul to descend from the high place" and gave one the ability to order one's life according to all he experienced at the high place. pp. 7-17.

of the spirit the priest is also prophet and king, and able to address his people's needs in a spiritual manner.[59]

Through celebration of the Eucharist, Crapsey believed, in a Catholic sense, in the functional mediation of the priest between God and man. He was the mediator seeking intercession and forgiveness for the people into the presence of the Lord. From the beginning of his ministry at St. Andrew's, Crapsey focused upon the office of the priest. In fact, he considered himself as holding all three offices, of prophet, priest, and king, as did other ministers in the Protestant Episcopal Church. "The king ruled over the people with the pastoral staff," as he did in the office of the pastor. "The prophet proclaimed the Word of God to the people," as Crapsey did as a preacher. "The priest guided the people in the worship of God."[60]

In the office of a priest, Crapsey envisioned himself fulfilling traditions connatural to humanity from the earliest stages of savagery. He believed that primitive man often reckoned the insane as specially endowed with affinities towards spiritual forces, due to their altered states of perception. He saw political success in ancient times as often consequent to religious accomplishments like Caesar's election to the high priesthood. Crapsey comprehended the state of the priesthood in both historic and evolutionary terms. In the earliest times of the biblical society of the Hebrew patriarchs, the father functioned as the priest. When the patriarchs evolved into the tribes, the priesthood became the responsibility of the elders. When the tribes grew into the nation, with temple worship, the law and all the formalities of organized religion, one tribe, the Levites, were established as the priests of the Hebrews. When Christianity was born all were reckoned as priests. Crapsey recognized the early church as worshiping without the function of the sacrificial and therefore no single priest was called for. When the church further developed into the Catholic religion, it devolved back towards paganism. The spectacle known as the sacrifice of the mass, recalled through imitation, the sacrifices of animals from the old religions. The Anglo-Catholic initiators, Keble, Pusey, and Newman revived the age-old practice and instituted back it into the Anglican Church.[61]

Crapsey made no excuses for his love of pagan religiosity. He felt that highly ritualized Christianity and the Christianity of the heart, or that relationship with God, which was established in the hearts of the people,

---

[59] Ibid. pp. 13.
[60] Crapsey, *Heretics*, p. 143.
[61] Ibid., p. 145.

were reconcilable. He observed the fasts, feasts and the high and low masses. He believed in the office of the priest. He believed the priest was the mediator between God and man.[62]

As an Anglo-Catholic, Crapsey would have then reinforced the significance of the office of the priest in the mass. The very use of the word "mass" by the sect accentuated the disconnection between the high church factions and the rest of Protestantism. Those were the distinctions that Crapsey reveled in. But Crapsey later downplayed the consequence of the atonement in the mass or the continuing sacrifice of the perfect one on the altar every Sunday that Martin Luther decried as disgusting.[63] Later, he would fail to mention the celebration of the mass or the act of communion with God that as an Anglo-Catholic he believed was produced in the inexplicable ordinance through ritual. Crapsey sorted out later what he wanted to present due to his acrimony, as well as for the rhetorical benefit as he evaluated generalities about religiosity. By the time of his autobiography Crapsey wished to present the consequences of religion from a universal, comparative, analytical and highly critical vantage point. He later compared ritual, from a standpoint full of humanistic meaning, value, uniqueness and significance, but devoid of real comprehensive spiritual meaning, even though at this time in his life he would have understood and defended the sacred mystery associated with the liturgical. There may have been some rebellious contention that was part of his nature that crept up now and again, but Crapsey was at this time deeply involved in the Anglo-Catholic movement and orthodox in all his ways. He was much too success oriented then to consider the general consequences of what he would later engage in. At St. Andrew's, at this juncture in life, Crapsey "walked in his calling" satisfied with the status and stature that the Anglo-Catholic movement had restored to the church, specifically, as prophet, priest and king.

---

[62] Ibid., p. 144.

[63] John Dillenberger *Martin Luther*: *Selections from his Writings* New York: Anchor Books, 1951. On the significance and abuse of the mass see pp. 270-3, 278-285.

CHAPTER FOUR

"Old Things Have Passed Away"

By the end of his first decade as the rector of St. Andrew's Crapsey was still firmly in the Anglo-Catholics' camp. He was emerging as a leader in the movement through his work as a parish priest, and as a conductor of retreats for other clergy. His personal life was developing as smoothly as his professional one. Little more than a year after the Crapseys moved with their three children Phillip, Emily and, to Rochester from New York City, Paul was born. Within two more years, Rachel was born. Crapsey's namesake, Algernon Sidney Jr. in 1884, followed Rachel and Ruth Elizabeth was born in 1887. Two more children would be born in the decade of the nineties, Marie Louise and Arthur Hunt. Adelaide was consumed by the task of raising so many children in such close proximity to each other. Although Mrs. Crapsey sometimes received domestic help, in this busy environment, none of the children could expect to receive too much special attention.[1]

Nevertheless, Mrs. Crapsey worked alongside of her husband and helped to establish several institutions that characterized St. Andrew's during its first decade of its life. Crapsey loved his wife and wrote a poem that demonstrated his warm affection and playfulness toward her. He was thankful for her assistance, organizational skills and steadfastness in the ministry. He wrote,

It was seven and thirty years ago
When Catskill hills were white with snow,
There came into this vale of woe
A baby girl.

She grew to be a woman tall;
Her hair was dark, her feet were small;
She had a general smile for all-
That baby girl.

[1] Alkalay- Gut, *Alone,* p. 33.

There came a parson down that way,
In lavender kids and chip hat gay.
She did not dare to say him nay-
That baby girl.

So they before the altar stood,
Where she did tell a great falsehood,
Vowing that she obey him would-
That baby girl.

And now she hath her children eight;
Five pretty girls and three boys great,
Who keep her forever in sad estate
That baby girl.

And she still blooms in early spring
A perfect woman, a beautiful thing;
An angel all except her wing-
That baby girl.[2]

One of the attributes that characterized Crapsey was his extraordinary energy. He found a means to reach his neighborhood with his plan for the benefit society of St. Andrew's Brotherhood within the first months of his ministry. By 1886, Crapsey operated as many as seven benevolent institutions out of St. Andrew's parish. More would follow. Crapsey worked diligently to establish the organizations. Crapsey desired to reach the poor and the needy in the area and to help them to help themselves. He established a night school that was well attended especially in the winter months. The night school had as many as sixty students and functioned as a means of instructing the men, women and children of the area in job related training. The boys learned woodcarving, carpentry and brass engraving. Crapsey boasted that many young men started their vocational career at St. Andrew's night school eventually working in industry or contracting as carpenters, engravers, painters and the like. Crapsey figured that as society caught up to their example he could place his emphasis on other areas of ministry. Crapsey noted how St. Andrew's held the distinction of being the first in the region to produce so many important works that other institutions and organizations would eventually pick up on and advance in. As other night schools were established in the region, the school of the Mechanical Arts at St.

[2] Poem entitled *Adelaide T. Crapsey, March 7, 1855- 1892.* In Arthur H. Crapsey Jr. Collection.

Andrew's suffered in enrollment. But for Crapsey the pragmatist, the real significance lied in the fact that the work was established regardless of who initiated it.[3]

Crapsey established an Industrial School for the women as well at St. Andrew's. The Industrial School also operated at night with paid teachers. The school trained women in knitting, embroidering and sewing skills. Girls and boys were together during the hours of instruction.[4] At one point several young men from the mechanical arts school went into the industrial school to learn sewing for a joke at first, but they later learned to respect the practicality of the art, and the strength needed to just hold the needle in the proper manner. Again, Crapsey lamented that at least three other schools had been established nearby, cutting the enrollment of the sewing school. He commented, "However, our little industrial school goes on its way and we do what we can."[5]

The women of the church established St. Hilda's Guild to provide clothing to those in need. Sewing infant's garments and clothes for the poor accomplished their humanitarian ideals. Eventually the women of the church established a guild in 1912 that became a children's dress business later in the basement of the Crapsey's Averill avenue home.[6] The women of St. Andrew's parish gathered together to bless those in need with their labor of love. Hundreds of women expressed their interest to contribute to the work at St. Hilda's Guild over the years. Many filled the guild room on Wednesday evenings to provide clothing for the poor and needy.[7]

Still, as with most charitable organizations, there was a core of individuals, in this case approximately forty women, who provided the bulk of the labor for the guild. Crapsey hoped to expand the scope of the work so that the women could extend assistance in the form of offering clothing to those in need in the other less fortunate parishes. He pondered, with such a large church as St. Andrew's, and with so many women on the

---

[3] See *Parish Record* (Rochester, St. Andrew's Church publication, Lent, 1886) p. 16.

[4] Crapsey, *Heretics*, p. 153.

[5] *Parish Record* (Rochester, St. Andrew's Church publication, Lent, 1886) p. 16.

[6] The founding of the guild was credited to Mrs. Crapsey in an article summarizing her life's work, "Mrs. Crapsey also organized *St. Hilda's Guild* of St. Andrew's Church and for the women it was a companion effort to her husband's formation of *St. Andrew's Brotherhood,* a non- sectarian society." Obituary notice in *"The Democrat and Chronicle"* Rochester, New York, Jan. 9th, 1950. p. 15.

[7] *Parish Record* p. 16.

list and with so much need, how could they increase the interest and thereby the output?[8]

In an attempt to get more women involved it was reported:

> We hardly think that going to the Guild would be counted an unpleasant duty by so many, if only they could look in upon us some Wednesday evening. Fifteen or twenty women hard at work, and two machines going, make the room full of life and far from stupid. And that there is an utter absence of gossip or ill-will is a cause for great thankfulness. Unfortunately, many live too far away to venture out at night, and many cannot leave their little children, but very many could come that do not; they cannot see that there is any duty connected with the care of the sick and needy.[9]

Two offices were held in the guild, one of treasurer and one of matron. A weekly offering was taken to pay whatever bills they incurred and help with the work of the guild, although on at least one occasion the rector benefited by receiving a new surplice that was bought, and not sewn by the guild. The guild also attempted to cheer the sick through visitation and by bringing to them donations from the congregation of broth, jelly or flowers that were collected at the rectory. In this way, the women's work at St. Andrew's was a significant contribution. Mrs. Crapsey provided an essential addition to the pastoral duties of the rector. Miss Louise Olmstead later carried on the same kind of work called, "Mothers' Meetings."[10]

The young men of the church were also given an opportunity to be involved in an organization benefiting both members and the community. The Order of the White Cross was established for men between the ages of eighteen and thirty to keep them off the streets at night and provide them with decent recreation. The stated purpose was "to promote temperance, purity and reverence, and to this end to encourage attendance at church and to provide innocent amusement and pure reading for its members." In March of 1886, the "Order" numbered thirty men. Business sessions were kept secret on the second and fourth Tuesdays of every month. The members were encouraged to bring friends to play games and partake in the refreshments at the social meetings held every Tuesday night. Crapsey encouraged the older members of the parish to advocate the benefits of young men becoming involved with the Order of the White

---

[8] Ibid. p. 16.

[9] *S. Andrew's Record* (March, 1889) p. 5.

[10] Crapsey, *Heretics*, p. 154

Cross. Crapsey considered this as a method of advancing Christ's cause in the community.[11]

Crapsey also instituted a Parish School at St. Andrew's for the children of the church. By 1886, there were approximately thirty children who attended. Crapsey complained that there was barely enough space in the room set aside for them. Crapsey argued that the work of the school had reached a point where it needed to be one of the parish's permanently established works. Mrs. Baker, the teacher, was loved by the children and respected by the adults at the parish school. Crapsey's children also benefited from the school, especially the older ones. Crapsey appealed to the parish to continue the nascent educational institution. He estimated that the cost would be minimal, only about three hundred dollars, and that the benefits would outweigh the costs many times over. Crapsey noted that the burden of education could be lifted from the mothers who were often over- wrought. Similarly, the children benefited from the expert care and supervision that they could hardly receive elsewhere.[12]

Sunday school also presented a challenge to the parish, not in monetary terms but in the context of commitment. Crapsey appealed to the church to get more involved. He mentioned that although the Sunday School was thriving it would benefit from the assistance of those parents of the children attending, due to the need for some more teachers. He noted that the common misconception was that the school was there to relieve the parents of their duty while they were at church. The fact was, that it was only there to assist them in their responsibility to care for their children. Then in a harsher tone that belied the frustration often involved in administering voluntary organizations, he wrote,

> It will be a blessed day for the church and the world when fathers and mothers come to understand that it is their duty to bring up their children in the fear and admonition of the Lord.[13]

His frustration with Sunday school was not just with the parents, but from an intrinsic lack of fulfillment in the institution itself. Ultimately, Crapsey denounced the ministry of the Sunday school. By the time of the writing of his autobiography he exchanged his conceptions of irrational faith for the broadness of the scientific and fully rational world. In reflecting on the establishment of this institution in his first year at St.

---

[11] *Parish Record* p. 16.

[12] Ibid. p. 16.

[13] Ibid. p. 16.

Andrew's Crapsey wrote acerbically, he organized the Sunday school in the fall but how he hoped God would forgive him for that. He eventually believed, Sunday school was as "futile and immoral an institution as any known to humanity." He criticized the church that, "dared to teach the children their own opinions of the truth, demanding that they believe without question regardless of whether they could comprehend those truths or not."[14]

By emphasizing the truth, Crapsey accentuated his conviction that God was truth. For Crapsey, the highest calling was to seek the truth in the greater cosmology of life. In due course, Crapsey contended that ultimate truth could be apprehended through empirical science. He later considered the complex relationship between faith and the natural world and how the greater issues of life contained in these notions related to the truth. Crapsey demonstrated his sometimes marvelous, sometimes egregiously frustrating ability to reduce very complicated concepts to simple illustrations. He would sardonically write that,

> Once a Catholic priest asked his class a definition of faith. A little girl answered, 'Faith is that gift of God whereby we believe things that are not so.' Not all children, nor even grown folks, have the wit of this Catholic child; what they have learned at that venerable institution, the mother's knee, they think a religious duty to hold for the rest of their lives.[15]

An answer to Crapsey's annoyance with the Sunday school was found through another organization conceived as a companion to the young men's group. The Society of the Silver Cross was formed as both a social and spiritual society. Approximately forty young women gathered together on the first and third Mondays of the month. They provided teachers for the Sunday school, which obviously relieved Crapsey of having to admonish the congregation about their lack of involvement. Moreover, they furnished other social enrichment for the people of the parish. Within just a short time of its establishment, Crapsey considered that the parish was already benefiting from their work. Their interests were primarily in the Sunday school but also in other good works, like orchestrating a concert for the older congregants on a Tuesday night in June.

Crapsey often wrote of the trouble he experienced getting young people involved in the church. But he also remembered working with the youth of the church with nostalgic fondness. They were constantly in and

---

[14] Ibid. pp. 16-17.

[15] Ibid., pp. 151-2.

out of the church scurrying around. He remembered three young men in particular not only for their service with the choir but also their assistance given to Adelaide and the family. The organists Henry Crab, Henry Ellwanger and Harold Kimball did more than simply work in the choir room three times a week. Crapsey remembered them with great affection as they whipped the unruly lads in the surpliced choir into shape, both their voices and their charácter's, without any recompense. Gratitude flowed from the depth of Crapsey's heart.[16]

The association with the church was a positive development in the lives of the young people. Crapsey's shared frustration and fondness for the choirboys of his early ministry was expressed with sentimental passion,

> The one drawback to a boy choir is the boy. Dear reader, did you ever know a bad boy? Well take that boy and multiply him by *x*, and you have a faint approach to a choir boy. These boys drove me to swearing and my wife to tears; they drove the neighborhood to distraction. In the course of our history a large fraction of the male population of our city passed through our choir. As I see them to-day, judges of courts, professors in colleges, physicians of renown, I am lost in wonder that out of such beginnings such endings should come.[17]

Crapsey inspired people in his vision for a better community. He made people feel a part of something important by providing an almost endless amount of institutionally succinct, organizations. Another organization that graced the premises of St. Andrew's was St. Monica's Society. St. Monica's was a subsidiary organization of St. Hilda's Guild, with the purpose of helping the widows of the parish. They met during the 1890s on the first Thursday of the month, in the Parish Building, later known as Douglas Hall. The motto of the society was, "Sorrowful, yet always rejoicing," An anonymous honorary member, started off the year with a gift donation to the society for its operating expenses. Gifts and mite offerings were given to the widows of the parish that totaled for the year 1890-91, only $28.98. In October of 1891, they had only $1.39 for a balance on hand.[18]

The St. Andrew's chapter of the Guild of the Iron Cross was established in 1888. As rector, Crapsey was the chaplain of the society. Others from the congregation presided as its officers. The headquarters of

---

[16] Crapsey, *Manuscript,* p. 188.
[17] Crapsey, *Heretics,* p. 146.
[18] "*St. Andrew's Record*" (Oct. 1891) p. 85.

the organization was located in Philadelphia, where the rules and regulations were instituted. The requirements for entrance into the society were simple; one must be a young man of at least eighteen years old and a communicant and member of St. Andrew's Church. Yearly dues were only one dollar with an additional payment of twenty-five cents for the cross, which was the insignia of the society. Another twenty-five cents was required for reception of a periodical published at the headquarters of the guild in Philadelphia. Meetings were held in the Parish building on the second and fourth Tuesdays of every month at 8:00 P.M. The purpose of the society was to promote the "Catholicity of the faith." Their interest in maintaining Catholic ideals and principles, were furthered in the Western New York region by the high churchmanship of Crapsey and the large following at St. Andrew's. They maintained a library of books written concerning the objectives of the society. At one meeting it was reported that Mr. John Staunton presented a beautiful, leather bound book by Dr. F.C. Ewer entitled, *Catholicity, Protestantism and Romanism* to the Iron Cross Society to be specifically kept in their library. The secretary of the society expressed the gratitude of the chapter for the kind bequest.[19]

Perhaps the greatest organizational achievement was the establishment of a Kindergarten, with the dual function of training both the students and the teachers. Crapsey later described his own introduction to the grade school experience as "conspiratorial, torture, incarceration, despicable and exasperating."[20] In spite of his early personal feelings, Crapsey pressed on and established a kindergarten at the new parish building given to St. Andrew's by William B. Douglas. The building was named Douglas Hall, in consideration of the benevolent gifts that Mr. Douglas bestowed upon the parish. A Dames School had been established there previously employing two elderly women teachers. However the school died out and in its place the following year Crapsey hired Katherine Whitehead, an accomplished kindergarten teacher. With her help, Crapsey started both a kindergarten for young children, and a training school for kindergarten teachers. Crapsey's kindergarten training school was soon instructing approximately a dozen women to the extent that they utilized the entire building for their business. The work was self-supporting, paid for by the fees that the kindergarten pupil-teachers paid for their tuition.

With characteristic lack of humility Crapsey described the endeavor at St. Andrew's as pioneering, and "ahead of their time" as Rochester then had only one rather pathetic kindergarten run by a poorly qualified

---

[19] *"St. Andrew's Record"* (Oct. 1889) p. 35.
[20] Crapsey, *Heretics,* pp. 18-19.

teacher.[21] Reflecting on how important Crapsey felt his establishment of the kindergarten school was, he related the way that the community finally realized the importance of the work:

> We carried on this work for about twelve years, when the community finally caught up to us and the Board of Education established kindergartens in various parts of the city and opened a free class for the training of kindergartners.[22] As we supported our work by the fees that the pupil-teachers paid for their training, we were compelled to abandon our enterprise. Our commencement exercises were always an event in the city; the mayor of the city, or some equally prominent person, would make the address, and the church would be crowded with the friends of the pupils and of the school. Our last commencement was a very sad occasion. I think the mayor made the address, or if he did not, it was some equally important person, and the speaker congratulated the city on the fact that this institution had blazed the way in educational science and practice, which way the city had wisely followed. With many tears, we closed with the blessing of God, and now the city of Rochester has no superior in this field of work.[23]

Indeed, Crapsey's innovation of establishing a kindergarten for the children of St. Andrew's parish eventually benefited the rest of the community as well. Crapsey established the Normal Training School for Kindergarten Teachers, in 1891. His foresight eventually produced a fine harvest of well- trained teachers. As the institutional demand increased throughout the city over eighty of the school's former students were employed as kindergarten teachers in both public and private schools.[24]

Crapsey's vocation, during the first decade of his ministry at St. Andrew's, reflects the passion and energy of a man willing to devote his life to the labor that he envisioned as profitable for God and his community. His vision however was changing, due to his growing socialistic ideals, especially through his idealistic concurrence with the works of various reformers like Frederick Denison Maurice and Charles Kingsley. Crapsey noted derisively that he was "enough of a devotee of Maurice and Kingsley and Rainsford to realize there was more than

---

[21] Ibid., p. 152.

[22] Crapsey used the term "kindergartners" to describe what we would call teachers of Kindergarten rather than what today is colloquially referred to as students of Kindergarten.

[23] Ibid., pp. 152-3.

[24] Edward R. Foreman ed. *Centennial History of Rochester, New York Vol. III* (Rochester Public Library, Rochester, New York, 1933) p. 349.

Sunday school when seeking the knowledge that related to the advancement of mankind."[25]

A transition was beginning to occur by which Crapsey would become increasingly unsettled with his place in the Protestant Episcopal Church. He was becoming estranged from the medieval church he had earlier embraced. Various intellectual developments influenced Crapsey's change. The primary reasons were not solely what Crapsey considered intellectual disillusionment, but as time progressed, practical factors as well. Crapsey's concern about the iniquities in the world led to a passionate hope that he could change societal injustices. Marxism provided a methodology for employing his humanistic considerations. Charles Darwin provided a foundational model for the progression of life and the rational relationship between man and his environment. Eventually, other men would apply Darwin's biological analysis to social models including one of Rochester's leading residents, Lewis Henry Morgan. Rochester was becoming an important center for the social sciences.[26]

Finally, Crapsey's position in the Protestant Episcopal Church made him cognizant of movements occurring elsewhere in the greater Anglican community. The Social Gospel movement adopted a Christian-oriented style of socialism like Maurice and Kingsley had in Great Britain. Walter Rauschenbusch lived in close proximity to the Crapseys. The two men had similar histories of working with the poor in New York City. Both had a heart of understanding for the impoverished and the destitute. For men like Crapsey, there was a gnawing necessity to reconcile new ideas in the economic, social, and political realms with his earlier religious views. Crapsey's new hometown was growing quickly with optimistic leaders willing to embrace innovative ideas and hoping to avoid some of the problems that affected other areas of the nation. In some ways, Rochester became a dynamic center of intellectual progressiveness and social experimentation in the late nineteenth and early twentieth centuries. Crapsey's organizational ability, moral aptitude, social zeal, and energetic persona made for a charismatic combination in a leader who desired to touch the life of his community in an enduring way.

---

[25] Crapsey, *Heretics*, p. 152.

[26] See Rochester Historical Society publication concerning Lewis Henry Morgan A.S. Crapsey "Lewis Henry Morgan Scientist, Philosopher and Humanist." In, *Rochester Historical Society*, compendium Rochester: Rochester Historical Society publication, 1923 pp. 1-27.

Throughout the 1880s and 90s, Crapsey worked hard at being the ideal parish priest. In some ways he became more conventional as he matured in the ministry. He continued to build a sizeable following through the strength of his sermons and his untiring commitment to community involvement.[27] He stood for many of the principles that originally attracted so many people to Anglo-Catholicism. Three standard principles of Anglo-Catholicism were especially central to Crapsey's early ministry. They included the call for the reinstitution of honor among the clergy, respect for the sacraments and liturgy, and the sanctity of the church as a God- ordained institution on the earth.[28]

As the first decade of his employment at St. Andrew's Parish came to an end, Crapsey found merit in cataloguing a list of his accomplishments. Crapsey was never too humble to take credit where credit was due. With the temerity of a politician he characteristically reiterated the history of his achievements at St. Andrew's.

> Ten years ago S. Andrew's Church was the feeblest congregation in the City of Rochester, almost the feeblest in the Diocese of Western New York. It was a little flock in the Great Church. It had hardly twenty families connected with it, and not fifty communicants in good standing on its rolls. At the end of our ten years we find it one of the largest congregations in the City of Rochester, a leading Parish of the Diocese, and a church of the first class in the Church at large. Two hundred and twenty-five families are connected with our Parish. On Easter day, over four hundred communicants received the blessed Sacrament. There are four hundred and sixty communicants now on the list, and forty more are preparing for confirmation and will become communicants so that when ten years are ended we shall have five hundred communicants and four hundred catechumens, or more than ten times the number we had when your Rector entered upon his duties.[29]

Crapsey gave little recognition of the gains that had been made at St. Andrew's to the supernatural work of the Spirit. Although he believed that God had heard him, he contended revealingly,

> All these people had been drawn to us by our worship and our work. We have aimed to give our people a simple, dignified and reverent worship.

[27] *St. Andrew's Record*, (July, 1896) pp. 50-52.

[28] This is obviously a very simplistic definition of Anglo-Catholicism. For a more detailed explanation see W.S.F. Pickering *Anglo-Catholicism: A Study in Ambiguity* London: Routledge, 1989 pp. 15-40.

[29] Ibid. (May 1889) p. 17.

> We have striven to rouse in them a sense of the importance of their lives, and to do among them a work of charity. Our cry has been sacramental worship, spiritual teaching and charitable work; and that cry has been heard and the sheep of Christ have been gathered into our fold, expecting here to be shepherded.[30]

Protestant churches, once the great, comprehensive cultural institution in America, were under extreme pressure as tensions grew on the intellectual horizon. Even the Presbyterian Church, once the bastion of orthodoxy was experiencing assaults from both liberals and fundamentalists alike. Cracks in the dogmatic armor that had held the denomination together, and once even determined the intellectual direction of the nation, could be discerned as early as the 1870s.[31] Dr. Swing of Chicago left the Presbyterian denomination rather than succumbing to further ecclesiastic pressure to modify his views concerning the relativistic value of the creeds, defined in time and space. Crapsey was young then, but obviously deeply concerned with the intellectual developments of the day, especially as they touched the matters of the church as a cultural institution in America.[32]

Although Crapsey aspired to achieve a sense of tradition and history in the Protestant Episcopal Church that pre-dated the English Reformation, his work at St. Andrew's was different from the kind of spiritual gathering that had characterized the church in its earlier times. Crapsey's preference for establishing societies within the church encouraged people to remain and reap the benefits. One of Crapsey's goals manifested itself in an obsession to redevelop the medieval church as an all- encompassing institution holding the community together and incorporating benevolent societies into the church. An attitude of communal benevolence prevailed at St. Andrew's. Many advantages, physical as well as spiritual, were made available to people by belonging to the organizations that Crapsey established at St. Andrew's.

Moreover, Crapsey personally appealed to those he ministered to. Crapsey was a small but vigorously charismatic individual with untiring energy and a magnanimous personality. He attracted those who sought comfort, nurturing, and a sense of belonging in a country that was

---

[30] Ibid. p. 17.

[31] Henry F. May *The Enlightenment in America* (New York: Oxford Univ. Press, 1976) pp. 323-4, 346-7.

[32] Sidney Alstrom *A Religious History of the American People.* (New Haven: Yale Univ. Press, 1972) p. 814.

becoming inordinately dynamic, impersonal and excessively fast-paced. Crapsey, the parish priest, was as assiduous as the young nation itself. With all of his energy, he took the pace of society upon himself to prevent it from affecting his flock in the church. Sooner or later it was bound to catch up with him physically.

Somewhere around the beginning of May 1889, Crapsey became extremely ill. He drifted close to death for several days and then slowly recuperated. One of the consequences of his recovery was a trip overseas presented by his congregation. Crapsey remembered the trip as a transitional point in his life. His love for the cathedrals and the ambience of the Church of England made their decision to send him to the British Isles on a convalescent voyage the obvious choice. Although his health was somewhat restored when he left, the voyage abroad made him feel worse than ever. The accommodations were not first class. The vessel was an American owned, second-rate ship. His room next to the kitchen was extremely hot and filled with insects. The seas were rough. Consequently, he spent most of his time on deck. As a result he met people who remained his friends for life.[33]

Crapsey would have enjoyed visiting other places in Europe but his money and time were both limited. The church had been in debt and at times the rector's salary according to Crapsey, had gone unpaid. Crapsey blamed the fiscal dilemma on the way the church raised their funds rather than on the people. Therefore he constrained himself to taking a tour of his beloved religious institution in the heartland of Anglicanism.[34]

Several influences prevailed upon Crapsey's mind by the onset of his trip. His proximity to Lewis Henry Morgan and Walter Rauschenbusch in Rochester influenced the way that Crapsey intellectually defined the world. Moreover, although dogmatically Anglo-Catholic, his Anglicanism brought him into contact and eventually intellectual repose with several leading figures in the Broad Church movement. Eventually, Crapsey's writings reflected the influences that he absorbed through his readings and personal contacts. Crapsey wrote that he,

> assimilated the principles of evolution and the conservation of energy, and, strange to say these new doctrines did not jostle the old. I still believed, or thought I believed, in the doctrines of the fall of man, redemption by grace, in the miraculous birth, resurrection and ascension of Jesus, and in this I was not peculiar; three-fourths of the Christian world was then and is now

[33] Crapsey, *Heretics*, pp. 182-4.

[34] *St. Andrew's Record* (May & October of 1889) pp. 1, 33

> (in) the same perilous condition: holding with equal tenacity contradictory propositions[35]

If one can sort through Crapsey's autobiography some thirty-five years later, one realizes that by the time of his journey abroad, he was indeed becoming confused. By the end of the decade of the eighties, he didn't know what he believed anymore. He knew that there were contradictions between his Anglo-Catholic beliefs and his emerging, scientifically oriented, intellectual world-view. But as yet, he didn't know how to reconcile the two. Due to this wavering, confused and closet liberalism, he later attempted to claim himself as one of the first modernists.

The extravagance of the Romantic Movement that originally led Crapsey to the priesthood, was becoming less and less romantic to him. Crapsey viewed the pragmatic concerns of the society about him and intended to do something about them. The abject poverty, the dire necessity for the amelioration of industrial life and the acute concern for reform in government challenged Crapsey to reconsider his overall attitude towards the church and society. The Gilded Age of business exploitation was gradually giving way to grass roots populist movements and eventually a Progressive Era of social reform. Crapsey, the parish priest who since his earliest days in New York City consistently worked for the poor and downtrodden, became excited at the possibilities for change.

The rapidity of societal transformation swirled conspicuously in Crapsey's mind. His time of illness and solitude on the ocean voyage provided him, among other things, with rest and time away from the demands of the parish to be alone and ponder the great changes that were taking place in the world around him. Although he had longed to be part of the great Anglican institution, when he finally arrived in Great Britain, his newly obtained, progressive mindset turned his life-long awaited experience into an anti-climatic event. Crapsey was teetering on the edge of intellectual transformation.

Crapsey's love for tradition returned with his arrival at Greenock, Scotland. Happily travelling from Glasgow to Edinburgh and eventually traversing into the old town on Princess Street, he came face to face with his beloved medieval era. A view of the middle ages was still available to the historically interested. For Crapsey, it was the visible proof of the outward manifestations in the world of the Kingdom of God. His perception of "true religion," was reflected in the architecture and

---

[35] Crapsey, *Heretics,* p. 178.

similarly expressed in the attitudes of the sanctimonious divines and chivalrous knights of old. These great men left their legacy through their writings, armor and other relics in the castles, banquet halls and museums of a great society. The artifacts of this medieval period fueled the pride of the people of an empire upon which the sun never set. Crapsey feasted upon the sights, the heirlooms and the traditions that bore witness to the heart of his profession. Ironically however, he was at a critical juncture in his life, as the old was passing away. He later considered that at that particular time. He was in the "last phase of his medieval way of thinking."[36]

By the time he reached the merry old England of his gothic dreams, his disillusionment with the old institution began to surface. As he toured the great cathedrals he was struck by the immensity of the buildings more than their exquisite splendor. He wondered what all this had to do with the message of Jesus. The grandeur and the squalor, coexisting side by side, presented another dimension, which to the mind of the American priest contradicted this well-established, institutionalized religion to the point of embarrassment. He was suddenly astonished at his self-inflicted cultural myopia wondering why he hadn't recognized this discrepancy before. Almost immediately Crapsey began to question both the impetus and the purity of his beloved religious institution. Temporary removal from his own culture allowed Crapsey to see in British culture its starkest dichotomy. The social differentiation was striking. For all their successes overseas, the distinctions manifest in British society were well ingrained in a culture reflecting both the imperial grandeur of the favored classes as well as the squalor of its working class.

Disenchanted, Crapsey heard the bells chime calling worshippers to evensong. Entering to worship one late afternoon, he listened to the canticles from the choir and noted how sensuous and perfected the devotion was. The scriptures were duly read with great oratorical clarity and skill. Then the clergy and the chorus divested themselves of their sacred duty and went home believing they had served God. At that point, Crapsey realized he had been completely and catastrophically converted from his beloved Anglicanism that very day.[37]

Crapsey obviously experienced great emotional trauma with the passing of his nostalgic, medieval, religious world. He was beginning to see things through the lens of the emerging socialists. Crapsey's socialism however was still tempered by the concerns of Christians who saw change

---

[36] Crapsey, *Heretics*, p. 185.

[37] Ibid., p. 187.

without religiously induced moral standards as superficial. Nonetheless, Crapsey had been deeply affected. He noted that he looked at the buildings and even heard the worship from an economic point of view now. He had been converted indeed. He thought incredulously, "where did God get the money to pay for all this?" He wondered "if the laborers where paid what they were worth to produce such mansions and monuments to the faith? The maintenance alone must cost a fortune. Who benefited from it all? The clergy did, at the expense of the workingmen and women" he concluded. "They received the accolades while those who built these cathedrals and supported them with their sweat and blood and waited on them hand and foot called them 'my lord.'"[38]

Crapsey's change of focus was a conversion indeed. In reality however, it transpired incrementally. Initially it caused Crapsey to suffer disgust at the extravagance of the Anglican clergy's overt materialism. As he traveled around England, Crapsey gained more of an aversion to the system that had produced the grandiloquence of the cathedrals and the bishoprics in all their material, worldly splendor. Traveling through York the next day he further noted how the great cathedrals had been built to provide a façade for the society, especially considering that the workingmen and women were still living in wattle huts without even windows or chimneys not to mention any modern conveniences. "The poor were scrounging for a bite of bread to feed their families while the clergy faired sumptuously and lorded over their people." It was a degrading sight after all. He declared that he had lost his respect for the clergy, especially the bishops and the hierarchy of the Anglican Church from that point onward. He despaired of the cathedrals as "they represented the outward manifestation of the obvious iniquitous system."[39]

It would be easy to affirm Crapsey's immediate conversion to socialism. However, his personal history, writings and service to the church betrayed his later ambitions. By the time of his autobiography Crapsey had indeed a bone to pick with the ecclesiastical institution of his earlier life. He also had reason to present his convictions as developing from such an early time period. Crapsey's incentive was one of vying for himself a place in posterity as the "first of the modernists." He noted:

> When I came at last to London, then my indignation passed the boiling-point. I visited the great cathedral of St. Paul's and the Chapel, so called, of Westminster, and was present at their magnificent (time) of worship; and

---

[38] Ibid., pp. 187-8.
[39] Ibid., pp. 188-9.

> then went out into the regions of Shoreditch and Mile End and saw thousands upon thousands of idle men hanging against the wall, hungry and homeless; saw bedraggled women nursing children at empty breasts, and children themselves playing in the streets, having the faces of angels, which I knew would soon be transformed into the faces of these degraded men and women who had brought them into the world. At night I went out and saw other thousands sleeping in the parks and under the arches of the bridges, and I despaired of Christianity.[40]

Crapsey ultimately focused upon the office of the bishop as the prime target of his wrath, although he subsequently included the entire Anglican religion. His later writings divulged a deep-seated antipathy for the office, if not the men themselves. One must remember however that he wrote his autobiography some thirty-five years after his trip. He chose his autobiographical occasion to vent his detestation of the men and office of the church responsible for his subsequent deposal.

Crapsey continued with his travels and his inquiries about the things of the church. He eventually visited a well-known preacher, Canon Henry P. Liddon, and asked his opinion of "why the Bishop of London required a palace to live in?" He was astonished to hear his reply that "without a palace the Bishop would loose his essential dignity." He later went on to hear Liddon preach at St. Paul's. His sermon was on the Virgin Mary and Crapsey remarked that "he had experienced enough. He was through with visiting the cathedrals."[41]

As an acknowledged Puseyite, Crapsey's confession of his dismay over a sermon on the Virgin Mary probably reflects more his estrangement from the church some thirty-five years later, than his personal conviction at the time of this incident. His sympathies towards the Anglo-Catholic movement remained strong even after his return from the British Isles. It would be hard to believe that Crapsey was truly offended at a sermon extolling the virtues of the Virgin Mary at that time. Although he might qualify the presentation as perhaps too Romanish, he would have undoubtedly received it as one of the distinguishing Anglo-Catholic rudiments.

Moreover, through his subsequent writings Crapsey demonstrated that his conversion away from the church into a more secular and socialistic mindset had not happened then. Three years after his return from the British Isles to his duties as rector of St. Andrew's Church, Crapsey ran an

[40] Ibid., p. 189.
[41] Ibid., p. 189.

article from the *NY Sun* entitled, "A Socialist and the Church" in the *St. Andrew's Record.* Socialists were regularly gaining an audience throughout the nation, and in nearby Chautauqua, a socialist from Chicago had belittled the role of the church in society. Nevertheless, the *NY Sun's* author wrote against the socialist lecturer noting that it was unjustifiable to attack the church on the grounds that the clergy were not assisting the workingmen and women to elevate their conditions. Stressing what he obviously perceived as the theoretic basis for the existence of the church temporal, the *NY Sun's* author wrote, how the church existed for exactly that purpose and for the betterment of all mankind, as well.[42]

The church was still perceived as the institution best capable of substantially changing an individual's life. The transformation must be consummated spiritually before it could be accomplished materially. The church consummated this transformation by exhausting all its efforts to that spiritual end. It was an unselfish employment based on the good of all mankind that began with the salvation of the soul under the conditions that God himself set forth. The editor held to the concept of the church as God's instrument on earth given for the betterment of society, be it economic or spiritual.[43]

Speaking of the socialist, Chautauqua lecturer, Crapsey argued,

> He assailed the one institution which is organized and conducted for preserving and propagating the Christian doctrine of the brotherhood of humanity, and which is solely and unremittingly occupied in the effort to elevate the race. As a matter of opinion, he might have denied the efficacy of the means employed by the Church, but he could not truthfully deny that the Church is laboring to improve the condition of the workingmen in the only way which according to its belief, the improvement can come. The Church is for no other purpose than to make men better.[44]

By his recorded words Crapsey obviously challenged the opinions of the socialists. Moreover, he still believed in the efficacy of the church as an instrument of change in the world. Though continuously advocating for workingmen and women, his radical transformation had not really taken place yet.

After a brief stay with the Kennedy's, a family from Scotland that he had met on board the ship during his voyage across the Atlantic, Crapsey

---

[42] Article appeared originally in *NY Sun,* reprinted in *St. Andrew's Record,* (Sept. 1893) p. 5.

[43] Ibid., p. 5.

[44] Ibid., p. 5.

set sail for home to America. He returned to a church that was enthusiastic about the restoration of their rector. After his debilitating illness and long odyssey, Crapsey was also excited at the renewed prospects of his ministry.

CHAPTER FIVE

"And There was War in Heaven"

Crapsey often complained about the poverty that he and his family lived in. However, his definition of their economic situation must be understood entirely from Crapsey's point of view. His perspective was projected against the backdrop of his relationship with the wealthiest denomination in America. Although he was not on a plane that was economically equivalent to many of those in his congregation, Crapsey lived quite well in comparison to other members of the clergy. Nevertheless, he seemed to be forever making appeals to the congregation both in his sermons and through his newsletter for them to give money. In what some may have considered impertinent, his first written statement since his return from overseas emphasized the financial circumstances at St. Andrew's church. He noted that the parish had been making progress, considering that prior to his illness, he had appealed to the members to do whatever they could for the furtherance of the ministry. The results demonstrated a desire to help through "pecuniary assistance" and their munificence was reflected in a general prosperity throughout the congregation.[1]

Crapsey used highly creative methods to achieve his objectives. The need for the work of the ministry was being met. Crapsey's income gained a full one-third more than his beginning salary. Moreover, they now paid an assistant during the summer months and they still had a balance left over. Crapsey noted with pride how a church that had free seating had accomplished all this as a result of his plan of "systematic giving."[2]

Crapsey's concept of systematic giving sought to place the significance of the free church at the highest level in the minds of his parishioners. His success allowed him to share the vision of an egalitarian institution, then somewhat of an anomaly with his congregation. As he put this vision into practice, he noted how rich and poor, young and old were at par with one another. The church was freely occupied with all seats

---

[1] *St. Andrew's Record* (October, 1889) p. 33.
[2] Ibid., p. 33.

open and unassigned. Due in part to this innovative arrangement, the people recognized the ministerial prerogative in the same manner as if they were to visit the store for food or supplies. Crapsey noted with pride how the church was supported by offerings, freely given by the parishioners.[3]

Crapsey figured that about two-thirds of the parish had adopted the systematic giving plan. If the rest contributed, they could expand his concept of the ministry to employ others including women and send them forth with a formal sanction from the church. He noted with enthusiasm how they could employ deaconesses and perhaps even a curate.[4]

Crapsey also rejoiced over plans to put an addition on the rectory. His ever- expanding family required room to live in comfort. The addition was built on the southern end of the rectory providing the Crapsey family with an entranceway and a reception room. They were greatly needed as one room had been used concomitantly as the rector's study, vestry room, and choir room, near the family's reception hall and living room. The project included building a dining room and four new bedrooms, together with a bath and closet space. The old parlor became the rector's study. The choir room remained as it was, and the facilities at the head of the stairs were now open for use by the congregation.[5]

Crapsey eventually remembered his trip to the British Isles as the date of his conversion away from established religion. But in actuality, he came home with a renewed sense of vigor for the work of the ministry. He still employed the terminology and cultural expressions of the Christian skillfully. In a sermon entitled, "The Church and the World," one recognizes both a traditional and a modernist perspective, beginning to clash rather than meld together in the churchman's mind. Crapsey realized that the world and the church were characterized in scripture as antithetical entities. He also noted that the description of the world of St. John, when the scriptures were written, was not the world he experienced in contemporary western society. There had been a change in the concept of the world as a place of evil systems contrary to the Christian's existence. The change had not necessarily been for the integral good of the Christian or society itself because it produced a compromised, distorted Christianity. As Crapsey explained, Christianity did not only change the world but the world had changed Christianity as well. He no longer envisioned the two as stridently contrasting systems, making it easy to

[3] Ibid., p. 33.
[4] Ibid., p. 33.
[5] Ibid., p. 33

choose between them but now rather, as interpenetrating one another. He noted with reprehension the compromise from which only a tiny bit of polluted water mixed with clear water made all the water undrinkable. The result produced either a Christian who was worldly or a worldly person who was a Christian.[6]

In reality, Crapsey was still far from the modernist he wished to portray himself as later. His sermons and writings illustrate the nature of his progressive movement towards the later unorthodox thought. For Crapsey, it did no one any good to be antediluvian in the interpretation of scripture. However, because of what he had just witnessed in England, Crapsey realized that the times were volatile for the Christian. One must be careful about one's relationship with the world and its systems. In this way, Crapsey demonstrated theological complexity. He was not willing to throw away the scriptural foundation that accentuated the integrity of life's experiences. He sought instead to make it correspond with the other intellectual verities of his time. For Crapsey, all truth must be clothed in empirical reality. However, his radical nature deplored the compromise that he would eventually pursue between his religion and the world. He was beginning to show the signs of a man conceptually torn apart. He believed that society had simply toned down the radical nature of Christianity, and Christianity had merely made the world more tolerable. Crapsey argued, that in the old scriptural sense the world meant the "established order." Nevertheless, one could hardly argue that in contemporary society the world hated the Christian. Christianity had, in fact, become the establishment.[7]

At this point, Crapsey vilified Christian worldliness as loudly as a pedigreed fundamentalist might. His answer however, was a world away from the fundamentalist response. Crapsey's experience in Great Britain provided him with personal insight and consequently a troubling quest of one seeking to explore the original meaning of the scriptures. In one of the first sermons he would deliver after his return home, Crapsey was consistent with what he would remember thirty-five years later concerning his disillusionment with the church and those who attained high offices in it. He wrote that one should be apprehensive of any relationships with the world. The individual who lives a true Christian life would never be acceptable for higher office in the church or the state. He would always be

---

[6] Ibid., pp. 34-5.
[7] Ibid., pp. 34-5.

looked upon with distrust and dismay. The consequence of practicing truly faithful Christianity excluded one from general acceptance by the world.[8]

Perhaps Crapsey had somehow foreseen the future with the elevation of his principles. He placed a high value on moral integrity. However, he may have also coveted the position of a bishop to the point that his thoughts about it became a psychological stumbling block in his duty as the rector of St. Andrew's Church. One can only speculate. But his endeavor to gain position and status had not colored his new perspective to the point of causing him to be blind to the duplicity demonstrated in the most extravagant of all the churches in a world full of poverty, pain and suffering. And yet, one can recognize the complexity of the problem between the contrasting viewpoints expressed by the scriptures well within the psychological complexity of Crapsey himself.

Crapsey campaigned vigorously for a bishopric in the Rochester, NY region. There was an obvious need for more Episcopal oversight due to the explosive increase in population both in Rochester and Buffalo. Bishop Coxe himself, apprehended the extent of his duties, by attempting to balance the scope of his responsibilities with the reality of his age. He eventually addressed a committee of fourteen clergymen who met to consider the question of the expanding episcopate. Coxe noted that even a young bishop would have a hard time accomplishing what was required of him due to the growth in Buffalo and Rochester and the other parishes, not to mention all the mission work. Coxe sought ways to achieve greater efficiency and for evangelizing in the region. He also acknowledged the inevitable; leaving little doubt that there should eventually be two separate sees in Rochester and Buffalo. Likewise, he noted the feasibility of St. Andrew's for the use of the bishop of the new diocese in the future.[9]

Crapsey's love for pomp and ritual may have compelled him to covet a diocese in Rochester with the use of St. Andrew's as the bishop's cathedral. He undoubtedly envisioned himself in that role. However, in lieu of setting up another diocese in the near future, the bishop recommended four alternatives. One was the election of a Coadjutor Bishop. The second suggestion involved securing the services of part-time missionary bishops who would provide assistance on a temporary basis especially in the winter months when travel was restricted. The third alternative proposed the setting up of two archdeaconries with two archdeacons who would relieve the bishop of the immense administrative

---

[8] Ibid. pp. 34-5.

[9] G. Sherman Burrows *The Diocese of Western New York, 1897- 1931.* (Buffalo, 1935) p. 432.

duties concerned with the problem of correspondence and other work specific to the bishop in the region. The last suggestion was for supplying administrative deans. Their services would extend to the rural districts allowing them to visit areas where mission works were being established and to provide the guidance needed by the episcopacy.[10]

The age and the reduction of the faculties of the bishop clearly demonstrated the need. The committee however agreed with the bishop that it was not yet time for dividing the diocese. The committee resolved to implement the archdeaconry system. Crapsey however, continued to press the issue making a motion to appoint a committee to propose measures for division. But rather than adopting Crapsey's motion, they adopted another by a Mr. Thomas Montgomery for a special committee of four clergy and six laymen to report on the feasibility of dividing the diocese. Crapsey was duly appointed to that committee, and the recommendations made by the committee at the Diocesan Council of 1891 reflected his desire to have an Episcopal See with a resident bishop established in the city of Rochester. Although the need obviously existed, the decision had already been made. Therefore, the council chose not to adopt the recommendations adding to Crapsey's frustration.[11]

Annoyed, and perhaps in reaction to the decision, Crapsey's revulsion against the materialism and magnificence of the Church of England caused him to view the office of the bishop with distain. However, just exactly when these feelings crystallized is questionable. It may have been only after the last door was unequivocally closed to him for the position. As a man of strong opinions and often-extreme intellectual views, Crapsey was rarely prone to compromising behavior. However, one recognizes the scripturally described conflict between the Spirit and the flesh in Crapsey's quest for the bishopric, paradoxically accompanying his disdain for the worldly church. Through sermons like "The Church and the World," one recognizes the complexity of thought beginning to develop in his mind. While working diligently to change his environment, his latent tendencies included a conscientious withdrawal from the world, which by his own definition included the worldliest of all the churches.

According to Crapsey, the church had compromised its original integrity. In his mind, compromise included association with the unbridled capitalism that created so many contemporary social obstacles. He described those that were pure in heart and mind as being in accordance

---

[10] *Diocesan Journal,* (Diocese of W.NY, Buffalo: 1890) pp. 24-6. Also in Burrows, *Diocese,* pp. 432-3.

[11] Ibid. p. 433.

with the original meaning of the scriptural texts. Both the world and the church would reject them. This once polar dichotomy had been resolved through the intermingling of one with the other. But, Crapsey concluded, like the apostle, that one should "beware of the dogs," who compromised their Christianity. Moreover, one should never "covet the chief seats in the synagogue" as the cost would be levied against the soul. And yet, his mind was clearly upon attaining the office of the bishop. Like the apostle, he noted that tribulations would work patience in Christians and eventually lead them away from a dependence upon the world and towards a more steady reliance upon God.[12]

In some ways one could barely distinguish Crapsey's rhetoric at this point from that of the more caustic of the fundamentalists. Several Roman Catholic orders also held similar views. But Crapsey's understanding of the corruption of the church was beginning to be apprehended historically through a critical vantage- point. This included understanding how the church had abandoned its original ideals emphasized in the scriptural texts. The meaning of the scriptures had become corrupted, according to Crapsey, to the point that the early writings over time had turned into a collection of contrived spiritual ontologisms. Crapsey had taken a mental turn from Anglicanism, due to both the worldliness and practical needs that he experienced so incongruously on his trip to Great Britain. It was not yet the one hundred and eighty-degree turn that would eventually ensue, but it was a decisive turn nonetheless.

However, Crapsey continued to preach in line with the distinctive traditions of the English church. Ironically, Crapsey was at a point in his professional career where he had never before been. Neither would he ever again sound like such an orthodox Anglican. In a sermon entitled the "Barrenness of Example," he defended the Trinity with a vigorous eloquence. Crapsey stated that Unitarians could never experience the true power of God. Christ was not just an example of how good man could be. If that were the case, men would be frustrated continuously by trying to emulate the works of the divine.[13]

After presenting the Unitarian position, Crapsey stated decisively, the perspective simplified theology, negated the testimony of Christian history and belittled the Lord's definition of Himself as presented by the Holy Scriptures. He argued that,

---

[12] *St. Andrew's Record,* (October, 1889) p. 35.

[13] A.S. Crapsey, *The Barrenness of Example* Sermon reprinted in *St. Andrew's Record* (October, 1894) pp. 73-6.

> The Christian Church had its beginning, not in our Lord's example but in his saving power. The angel said of him, he shall save his people from their sins. Our Lord came to this earth not merely to show men what to do, but to give them the strength to do it.

In this most orthodox of sermons, Crapsey specifically affirmed the deity of Christ, the power of the Holy Spirit and the authority of the scriptures.[14]

Crapsey may have left a part of his Anglo-Catholicism behind with his medieval impulses in Britain, but he was in no way estranged from the other powerful conventions of the Anglicanism of the 1890s. He contended, "Christ couldn't have been simply a man. If He only proved the successful nature of a sin-free life what good would His example be, since none could duplicate it?"[15]

Applying the apologetic argument to his own experience, Crapsey remembered when a man asked him "are you not tired of being a good example?" The question fascinated him as he had never realized that it was his job was to be a good example. Crapsey exclaimed. "I an example, God forbid! I was but a poor minister of the manifest grace of God."[16]

If Crapsey was indeed by this time a convinced modernist, he certainly had a strange and traditional way of demonstrating it. It is more likely that he was still hoping for his diocese in Rochester and by articulating strong and powerfully conventional sermons he might secure the coveted mitre and scepter. Drawing on another scriptural example Crapsey considered the rich young man who called the Lord Good Master. He figured that even the Lord's example was not enough to save the world but that they might receive the power from God to live godly lives by "taking human nature up into His divine nature." Crapsey's argument further emphasized the vicarious atonement of Christ and the power of God unto salvation, quite the historic orthodox interpretation indeed.[17]

Though spiritually orthodox on the outside, Crapsey was being intellectually torn on the inside. He refused on the basis of faith alone to disavow the Darwinian theorists. He endeavored desperately to bring the theory of evolution into compliance with his shaken but established belief system. He attempted to incorporate the concept of the survival of the fittest into a contrived description of heaven. In an article entitled "The

---

[14] Ibid., pp 73-6.
[15] Ibid., pp. 73-6.
[16] Ibid., pp. 73-6.
[17] Ibid., pp. 73-6.

War in Heaven," Crapsey defined the spiritual warfare waged by the Kingdom of God. He viewed the war as serious and sacred. He argued for the concept of justifiable warfare, conceivably remembering the war that had once liberated the slaves. He believed that war was a necessity and at times we must wage it. Our effort to attain perfection as a species depended upon it.[18]

He presented the theory of evolution as a hard fact of life. It was one that must be dealt with intellectually and that meant religiously. Crapsey did as competent a job as anyone in attempting to make evolutionary theory compatible theologically. He presented his argument by providing examples among the plants and the animals of the earth, demonstrating how they must wage their own warfare of survival. This warfare however, was not due to the sinfulness of the world as the scriptures contended, but rather to the fact that the strongest and the best must flourish. Crapsey presented a convoluted version of heaven, with the supposition that heavenly warfare was continuously waged in a way sometimes analogous to and sometimes in opposition to the evolutionary struggles on the earth. Concerning that warfare Crapsey stated, "we must embrace it after all, because even in heaven the struggles between the better and the worse and the better and the best will continue."[19]

For Crapsey, the question about the war in heaven was never whether one should fight at all, but one of logistics. Crapsey took for granted that the survival for the fittest would continue and that warfare was part of the grand scheme of natural processes. He threw up his arms rhetorically noting interestingly that, "one's hope involved choosing one's method of engagement. One could make war through destruction or by creation."[20]

Contrasting the evolutionary development of mankind with the means of making creative warfare Crapsey noted that, mankind's warfare has been "horrible brutality, and wasteful destruction, where men have acted out in their passions like dreadful beasts." Crapsey's opinion of war varied little with time. Yet, he noted, there was a

> different kind of warfare that exemplified the work of God, Christ, the angelic host and flowers. This kind of warfare allows creation to prevail through perfection. In this sense, the flower strives to become the best of

---

[18]A.S. Crapsey, *St. Andrew's Record*, (Nov. 1894) pp. 81-4.

[19] Ibid, He wrote, " So we must not hope to be rid of it- not now nor forever. There is no heaven where the better will not be struggling with the worse, the best with the better." pp. 81-4.

[20] Ibid., pp. 81-4.

> flowers possible, not through defeating an obvious enemy but by simultaneously making the lesser flower fade while the favored one grows stronger producing better seed and moving ever onward towards perfection.[21]

It all sounded so right, at least for the moment. The process of perfectionism would assist in bringing creation to its highest point simultaneously destroying the weaker vessels while benefiting the ever evolving whole. If he could demonstrate in a religiously meaningful manner how God employed the survival of the fittest for the greatest overall benefit, Crapsey could successfully explain evolutionary theory, at least tentatively, from a theological perspective. He worked hard to make it all fit and correspond. With the incorporation of all of the diverse elements, including evangelical revivalism and holiness perfectionism, he contented himself with the fact that his paradigm simply had to work. And yet, the concept of evolution continued to plague him like a jigsaw puzzle with a piece that looked right but never truly fit unless it was squeezed and forced out of shape.[22]

In December, Crapsey wrote of the sovereignty of man's will. He despised the doctrine of election considering himself comically, "fully Armenian" (sic). The recipe for success involved responsible choices and hard work. Crapsey believed that God chose men according to His foreknowledge because "God foresaw that they would be good." Moreover, Crapsey believed that men shared with God in the power of election. The world bore witness. Both God and men based the realities of life upon personal choices and work. The works of men in compliance with the leading of God were the key. Crapsey the unashamed Pelagian, tried to intellectually tie it all together. Crapsey argued, "When God or man chooses, He chooses for service and not for reward, and there can be no thought of reward until the service is done." This statement clearly portrayed Crapsey's belief in works righteousness and the choices of God and man working together for the salvation of mankind. Man had a choice. He could wage war like worldly men or he could chose to wage the heavenly war that would lead to mankind's perfection. The species would evolve naturally due to the choices of man in compliance with the leading of God. Salvation by grace through faith was no longer an issue for

---

[21] Ibid., pp. 81-4.

[22] See chapter VIII, of George M. Marsden's *Fundamentalism and American Culture* (New York: Oxford Univ. Press, 1980). For an index of writers of Keswick perfectionism see pp. 246- 250.

Crapsey. Crapsey was on to something from which he would never intellectually turn back. In his mind, society would progressively evolve into a perfected state through works righteousness and the correct moral choices.[23]

[23] Crapsey, *St. Andrew's Record,* (Dec. 1894), pp. 89- 92.

CHAPTER SIX

"Train up a Child in the Way He Should Go"

With all of the organizations that Crapsey established at St. Andrew's Parish, there was not enough space for the work to be done. The house at the corner of Hickory and Ashland Streets was willed outright to the parish with the death of Mr. William B. Douglas. But considering all the organizations and programs that had developed at St. Andrew's it was inadequate. On a clear Sunday afternoon, the 20th of August 1893, ground was broken and a cornerstone set on the north-eastern corners of Averill Avenue and Ashland Streets for a new building, named Nazareth House. Rev. Dr. Anstice, the senior presbyter of the city of Rochester, who acted as surrogate for the bishop, laid the cornerstone. At four P.M., after a brief historical message by the rector, the choir and a procession advanced to the building site singing *The Church's One Foundation Is Jesus Christ Her Lord.* Inside the cornerstone were copies of the *Journal of the Diocese* for 1890- 91- and 92, a copy of *The Churchman, St Andrew's Record*, "Our Church Work," St. Andrew's cross, an engraving of the bishop and a picture of the rector.[1]

Some opposition to the naming of Nazareth House came from those who were afraid that the name was, too Catholic. Crapsey responded in typical fashion by praising Rome for preserving nearly two thousand years of church history. Crapsey's ongoing Catholic sympathies were revealed in a column written for the *St. Andrew's Record.* He stated emphatically, that though he was willing to "defer to Rome," in some things, in others the Catholic Church had obviously erred. Therefore, those points of departure must not be tolerated. Nevertheless, Crapsey felt a deep and abiding affinity with the Roman Catholic Church and as members of the English communion whether it be in Great Britain, America, Australia or Africa, he felt that they "maintained the same traditions and venerated the same Christ, the same great saints including Chrysostom, Augustine, Boniface and Bernard and the same familiar political and literary figures,

[1] Crapsey, *St. Andrew's Record,* (Sept., 1893) p. 4.

including Burke and Fox and Shakespeare and Milton."[2] Crapsey's inclusion of political and literary figures for veneration along with the classic examples of the saints is instructive when considering his developing liberal state of mind.

By 1894, Nazareth House was paid in full. This was no small feat considering that the outstanding debt totaled over seven thousand dollars. It was also impressive because the country was still recovering from an economic downswing. The depression of 1893 caused significant pressure upon Crapsey's ability to continue to support the private education of his children. The parishioners' weekly donations to the church were the first casualties of the economic upheaval. Nevertheless, Crapsey persevered, and with his three oldest children in private schools, he looked to mission work and writing for further means of supporting his growing family.[3]

In October of 1894, Crapsey took on the added responsibility of being the Minister in Charge of St. John's Church. The Rev. Dr. Masey founded the church on Hawthorne Street. After several additions the church was moved to the corners of East Avenue and Vick Park B. Unfortunately, the church was left with an excessive amount of real estate. St. John's vestry planned to sell the old property on Hawthorne Street to pay off the new. To compound matters a downswing in the real estate market depressed the sale of expensive properties in Rochester. Church members became discouraged and sent a representative to St. Andrew's to seek help from Crapsey. With Dr. Masey gone the church needed both a minister and an economic plan to bail them out before foreclosure. Crapsey was eventually persuaded to take on the fledgling church.[4]

Crapsey secured an arrangement through his relationship with those in the financial community to restructure the plan for the repayment of the loan. As Minister in Charge, St. John's also paid Crapsey enough money for him to hire an assistant to conduct services on Sunday mornings while Crapsey preached at St. Andrew's. Crapsey taught the Sunday school at 3:30 P.M, preached at 4:30 P.M. and conducted the evening prayer service. He also made himself available at the rectory of St. Andrew's for counseling and pastoral care to both churches. He worked with the new church to help it grow and to bring it into the Episcopal community in Rochester. Coupled with his responsibilities at St. Andrew's, his studies

---

[2] Ibid., p. 4.

[3] Alkalay- Gut, *Alone,* p. 47.

[4] *St. Andrew's Record* (Oct. 1894) pp. 72-3.

and his planning for the missions work that ensued, his work load must have been immense.[5]

By the time of the youngest, Arthur's birth in 1896, Philip, the eldest, was already twenty years old and busy at St. John's Academy approximately four or five miles east of Syracuse, New York.[6] Emily was a year younger and Adelaide was seventeen. Both daughters were enrolled at Kemper Hall, a boarding school in Kenosha, Wisconsin. Run by Episcopal nuns, the school was associated with the extended ministry of the Sisters of St. Mary.

By 1896, Crapsey had nine children in all. He was becoming well-known as an educational innovator. The older children were provided with some public education before the opening of the parish school at St. Andrew's Church. His children all benefited from his resourceful leadership at the parish with the development of the parochial institutions. One of their first educational experiences was in the Saturday classes that Crapsey conducted for the children in the parish. Bored during his first summer at St. Andrew's, Crapsey gathered the children in the fields and taught them about the natural world around them. They considered the functions of the roots, the seeds and the leaves of the trees, and they gathered various plants studying their diverse structural similarities and differences.[7]

Crapsey's provision for his eldest daughters' education demonstrated his disregard for the traditional role of women in society. There is a wealth of information about Adelaide's education and life because she was such a gifted poet. Contrary to prevailing cultural beliefs that "women were mentally inferior, their brain capacity was smaller, and too much education created physical problems," Crapsey believed they deserved the opportunity to achieve their utmost in life.[8] In this, he was in line with his heritage. His great-grandmother Rachel Davies had rode on horseback

---

[5] Ibid., pp. 72-3.

[6] Crapsey sent his son Philip to St. John's Academy. The academy was founded by Episcopal Bishop F.D. Huntington and Judge George F. Comstock in 1869. It became St. John's Military Academy in 1881. The school became the Manlius School in 1923, still a military academy. In 1970, Manlius School and Pebble Hill School merged to form Manlius, Pebble Hill School, a private non- military institution. Private conversation with Margaret Barclay director alumni relations Manlius, Pebble Hill School.

[7] Crapsey, *Heretics*, p. 151.

[8] Alkalay- Gut, *Alone,* pp. 65-6.

through the wilds of Kentucky. Crapsey's hero, his maternal grandfather, championed the cause for female education as early as the 1820s.[9]

Crapsey sat on the board of the private school established by Mother Superior Harriet. He reveled in the fact that the first Mother Superior of a cloistered community in the Episcopal Church since the Reformation was a distant relative of Adelaide Trowbridge Crapsey. Crapsey sent his children to Wisconsin providing both opportunities for the girls' personal growth and support for the sisters' institution. Adelaide received her educational foundation and proved her immense talent there later inspiring literary luminaries like Carl Sandburg to dedicate verse to her.[10]

Emily was also a gifted student, though her interests tended more towards marriage and domesticity. Adelaide withdrew from school for a short time to be with her grandfather at the time of his death. Another time she became extremely sick. Both intervals set her schooling back. Both girls were homesick but they took consolation in the fact that they were together. [11] In 1896, Emily received the honor of valedictorian at Kemper Hall. One year later, Adelaide received the same award.[12]

At home and away from the school, Adelaide kept her literary talents to herself for the most part. And yet, fluid originality and stark beauty characterized her prose. Adelaide developed her talents to some extent through her volunteer work as editor of the *Kemper Hall Kodak*. Not

---

[9] ...."The advancement of the female character, and the instruction and cultivation which woman receives, has always been justly viewed as evidence of the improved state of society where it exists. It is therefore, an indispensable duty to provide for female education; for knowledge is the handmaid of virtue, prudence, and economy; and where female virtue, knowledge and intelligence abound, man can never be degraded or a slave".... Benjamin Franklin Morris *The Life of Thomas Morris* (Cincinnati: Wilsatch, Keys and Overend, 1856) p. 43.

[10] "Carl Sanburg wrote a poem to Miss Crapsey's memory in 1908 (1918?). "She is acknowledged as the originator of the verse form cinquain, a five line poem." Adelaide was also mentioned as one of Rochester's immortals in *Rolli's Immortals Nominated."* June 11, 1934. (Source of column unidentified) "Adelaide Crapsey whose poetry has been favorably compared with that of Swinburne." They also included Algernon Sidney Crapsey as among the immortals of Rochester. Quoted from Bill Beeney, columnist of *"The Hometowner"* Rochester, *Democrat and Chronicle* April 22, 1960 p. 13.

[11] Alakaly- Gut, *Alone,* p. 46.

[12] Ibid. p. 62.See also "Kemper Hall Origins," As published in "The History of Racine and Kenosha Counties" Chicago: The Western Historical Co., (1879) date probably incorrect as reported on, Frank and Michelle Laycock and contributing volunteers W.J. Gen Web "Kemper Hall"
http://www.rootsweb.com/wikenosh/kemper.htm

many examples of her early writing are available. However, one or two remain as a testimony of her extraordinary abilities.

In January 1896, Adelaide wrote a short historical piece entitled, *"War Songs."* In it she documented the evolution throughout the centuries of, and the cultural differences expressed in, various war songs. She believed that early tribal peoples used war songs to encourage one another prior to a battle. She thought of the *Chant de Guerre* as a perfect example with its booming, triumphant tones that excited men to passion. She documented how *Yankee Doodle Dandy* must have driven the enemy crazy because it was, like the nation itself, so completely self-assured and so terribly insolent in its rebelliousness. She went on to mention how George Frederick Root had contributed to the Civil War effort so magnanimously through the distribution of his war songs like *Tramp, Tramp, Tramp, Marching Through Georgia*, and *The Battle Cry of Freedom*. Root was given a standing ovation in Chicago at a War Songs concert that included a large number of Civil War veterans. Speaking of Root, Adelaide noted how his music had the power to stimulate people. The songs stirred the patriotic passions of the men motivating them to face the inevitable dangers and often death associated with battle.[13]

The *Kemper Hall Kodak* published in June 1897 recorded the valedictory address by Adelaide entitled, "The Open Road." In this address the budding genius of the young writer is portrayed with stark clarity. The valedictory referred to the old Oxford legend of Glanvil. Adelaide referred to the timeless conflict associated with adolescent maturation while retaining the youthful allure of the freedom of the open road. She wrote,

> The road stretches out before us and our feet are set therein. The wind of the morning blows against our foreheads, and with buoyant steps we renew the journey. Deep into our hearts has sunk the image of the land we are leaving, in all its serenity and beauty. Deeply loved voices still float up to us calling 'God speed,' and full of their inspiration we press on, bravely, cheerfully, hopefully. The farewell to a life loved, serene, beautiful and blessed. A wistful hello to that which awaits around a bend down the road.[14]

---

[13] Adelaide Crapsey "War Songs" In *Kemper HallKodak* Kenosha Wisconsin: (January, 1896).

[14] Adelaide Crapsey Valedictory "The Open Road" In *The Kemper Hall Kodak* Kenosha, Wis.: Vol. IV No.9 (June, 1897).

She also considered Ulysses, Camelot, and Hiawatha as legends that addressed the subject of the adolescent allure with adventure against the backdrop of childhood and familial security. Her use of symbolism and allegory fortified her already colorful and natural use of the language. Adelaide looked out to the horizon at the crest of a new century and expressed an optimism characteristic of her generation. Vistas would open on both the physical and the spiritual plane. Like her father and her peers, Adelaide looked to the new century as a time when the world would progress and the great problems plaguing humanity would finally be solved. Adelaide's valedictory expressed both the poetic sentiment and the practical assurance of her youth. Like the young country she lived in, she was filled with an intensity ready to explode into the world.

But the poet in her, like her father, expressed herself in universal terms that hinted at an open and free belief in the kinship of the human soul. One might scoff at her youthful idealism as being naïve. However, one can't help considering that the youthful culture simultaneously felt what was happening was clearly unique. They were at the threshold of their lives. Not only were they at the portal of the century, they believed that they were at the very brink of human evolution.[15]

Adelaide received many honors for her writing ability. However, due to her unassuming character, it wasn't until quite late in her life that her own mother realized what a gifted poet she was. To be fair, her mother had other pressing concerns to consider with nine children to raise, a rectory to keep in perfect order and with the duties of a pastor's wife. Adelaide's relationship with her family and sister Emily in particular, remained quite intimate. Certainly the general atmosphere at home and St. Andrew's contributed greatly to the development of their intellectual aptitude. She demonstrated a literary precocity derived from her visitation to her father's study and developed through the classical courses crafted by the devout Episcopal nuns.

Adelaide's surviving letters home are filled with both love for her mother and father and despondency at the constraints caused by their economic situation. Obviously, many of her acquaintances were unhindered by the realities of economics. The Crapsey family was close. Adelaide wished she were there to help her mother with the birth of the new baby Arthur, and in the cleaning of the home. She readily acknowledged her domestic incapacity in favor of her older sister. Emily

[15] Ibid.

sought the domestic life. Adelaide was more concerned about her place in the world. In that way, she was closer to her father.[16]

Eventually Crapsey believed the conventional patriarchal family was an anachronism. Although he was the traditional breadwinner and Mrs. Crapsey was employed as the typical housewife, during the 1890s, both vocations were matters of familial practicality. Additionally, Adelaide Trowbridge Crapsey was the manager of the family's business at the rectory, and an essential participant with her husband in the work of the church, especially the women's ministries. She was a perfectionist at her housework, physically attractive and charismatic.[17] She respected each of her children and allowed them to flourish. Adelaide Trowbridge and her husband encouraged individual growth through the development of the unique qualities in each of the children's characters. One of Adelaide's biographers would later write that "she was given great independence and freedom in the method of shaping her destiny."[18]

Crapsey's childhood experience influenced his democratic comportment in the raising of his children. His father refrained from raising his voice in the presence of his family or others. Discipline was the sole responsibility of his mother. Crapsey's busy schedule in the ministry, coupled with the size of his family clearly demarcated the responsibilities within the home. However, as a social innovator Crapsey was interested in freeing women from the bondage of domesticity. He noted that "society needed radical readjusting concerning the liberation of the woman." Moreover, one could hardly estimate the "amount of damage that had been done to the human race by isolating women from the significant matters of life." Concerning the gender roles related to the financial responsibility of raising children, Crapsey believed that "providing the main source of income was never exclusively the dominion of men." In fact, according to Crapsey, "women possibly provided as much as two-thirds of the labor necessary for the family's provision."[19]

Crapsey also expressed interest in securing for children the opportunity of fulfilling their own lives without the oppression of the parents. Speaking of the freedom of the child in the modern family, Crapsey later

---

[16] Alkalay- Gut, *Alone,* pp. 70-2.

[17] Adelaide wrote letters extolling her mother's physical attractiveness mentioning how others remarked about her beauty and how she had changed her hairstyle to look more like her mother's. Ibid., p. 43.

[18] Ibid. p. 42.

[19] All quotes are taken from A.S. Crapsey *The Rise of the Working Class* New York: The Century Co., 1914. pp. 72-91.

wrote, "the time of parental authority had passed." He felt the parents of the modern era needed to use tactics of persuasion rather than authoritative domination. Moreover, it was the parent that needed to conform to the desires and will of the child in most cases. The best way for parents to rule their homes was for the parent to ascertain what the child desired and then request the child to do it. Crapsey related the story of the master whose dog habitually went under the bed to lie down. After several instances of disobedience the man "commanded the dog to go and lie under the bed." He wrote, "the master's will ultimately corresponded to the will of the animal." Likewise, Crapsey believed that recognition of the child's will was vital for peace to be established in the home.[20]

Just how unconventional this attitude was for the time is clear. Crapsey however, may have been writing with a great deal of reflection and with the intention of shocking those staid conservatives that continued, in his estimation, to stifle the development of a progressive society. Nevertheless, Crapsey never realized the depth of opposition to the kind of social experimentation and standards that he advocated. He failed to discriminate between loving persuasion and having the will of the parents bend to the will of children. It was one thing to develop a machine to drive without the aid of beasts of burden. It was quite another to profess ideas that would directly challenge the social conventions regarding gender distinctions and the modes of raising children outside the time-honored family structure and traditions of western society.

As the Crapsey family grew and their income steadied, they were able to find time together, especially in the summer months at various locations in the eastern states. Most of their vacation time however, would be spent in close proximity to the Rochester area. In 1890, the electric trolley replaced the horse drawn streetcars. People were flocking from the business district downtown to State Street and then to Lake Avenue where they would board the trolley to Ontario beach at Charlotte.[21] The Crapseys often took day trips via the trolley to the lake. They eventually secured a summer residence at Guilford Farm, in Charlotte. They also spent overnight or weekend stays at a cottage at Charles Point, at the bay in Sodus, east of Rochester. On other occasions the family would vacation to the south of the city in the beautiful Finger Lakes region. They spent time at Hemlock Lake and at Vine Cottage on Canandaigua Lake. Canandaigua

---

[20] Ibid. pp. 93-4

[21] Smith, Henry Bradford and McKelvey, Blake "Rochester's Turbulent Transit History" In *Rochester History* Blake McKelvey ed. Vol. 30, No. 3 (July 1968) pp. 1-24.

was the same lake where Crapsey's father had been sent to school as a young man. Ironically, it was there that Jacob decided against the ministry.[22]

In Canandaigua, Crapsey spent time at Cook's Point, a favorite place for other churchmen and intellectuals to vacation. One such seasonal visitor to Cook's Point was the Davies Professor of Theology at the Rochester Theological Seminary, Augustus Hopkins Strong.[23] Strong was an extraordinary intellectual presence at the Baptist Seminary and a colleague of Walter Rauschenbusch. There were also extended stays over the summer months. The Crapseys spent time one summer in Spenser, Massachusetts in a lovely pastoral region between Springfield and Worcester. Crapsey conducted a mission in the area.[24] They also spent time at a farm in Conway, Massachusetts. Their favorite place however was at their grandparents, the Trowbridge's, in Catskill, usually while Crapsey was in New York City on church related business. Adelaide Trowbridge Crapsey kept a journal of one such visit to her mother's in August of 1888.[25] Marcus Trowbridge had sold his newspaper in the 1880s. He subsequently passed away in January of 1891. His father James survived him. Grandma Dottie, as she was affectionately called, left the ancestral family home at that point to live with her son. Thereafter, days of summer visitation in Catskill, New York were forever over for the Crapsey family.[26]

---

[22] A. H. Crapsey Jr. Collection Scrapbooks.
[23] Alakalay Gut, *Alone,* p. 131.
[24] Alkalay- Gut, *Alone,* p. 42.
[25] A. H. Crapsey Jr. Collection, Box 2.
[26] Alkalay- Gut, *Alone,* p. 44.

CHAPTER SEVEN

"Do the Work of an Evangelist"

Like the nation, the Crapseys were becoming more and more mobile. Crapsey rose rapidly within the ranks of the Protestant Episcopal Church. With the success of St. Andrew's presumably well assured, he turned to wider matters within the denomination. He entered the second decade of his ministry busily writing tractates and conducting retreats throughout the eastern United States. Crapsey's leadership qualities, extemporaneous preaching style, and successful ability at leading retreats provided him with an opportunity to expand his ministry. The Episcopal administration sought increased membership nationwide. They termed their endeavor to gain patronage a mission to maintain their distance and dignity from the more revivalistic denominations.[1]

Crapsey recognized the purpose of a mission as separate from the work he had been doing. Rather than simply edifying the saints through his preaching he would now be seeking to convert the sinner and bring him or her into the fold. The ultimate end was to bring the new believers to an understanding of the Episcopal Church's traditions, doctrines, organizational structure and mission and to confirm them into the greater body of Christ. Crapsey viewed the work as one of "making saints out of sinners." He believed that "the faithful should support the work of missions, as the work was commissioned by Christ and ordained by God." The work of the missioner was perpetuated by the support of the greater body. After all, it was the faithful saints who made the mission work possible through financial support and prayer.[2]

Crapsey believed that after one's prayers and alms God would call a man to the mission field. Then the mission must be proclaimed throughout the receiving parish before the actual work began. In secular terms, the coming of the missionary was to be advertised. Crapsey placed a high degree of significance on the preparation for the missioner. He noted that

---

[1] Crapsey, *Heretics,* p. 151

[2] A.S. Crapsey "What is a Mission?" *St. Andrew's Record* Vol. V. No. 10 (Oct. 1893).

the people should go from house to house inviting others to the event. The greatest effort should be undertaken in anticipation of the missioner's arrival to ensure that non-church members would be able to hear the word of God.[3]

Crapsey was not willing to leave much to the work of the Holy Spirit. He concocted a formula dependent upon the expertise of the missioner. His work was to be initiated, regulated and continued by the faithful of the church. He also encouraged advertising in the public press. For Crapsey, the missioner brought fire to the people who he considered the fuel. The historic Christian concept of the burning presence of the Holy Spirit confirmed his rationale. He believed that "the fuel must be made ready for the fire to come" and Crapsey himself would provide the fire. It was Crapsey's job to not let the expectant, eager newcomers down when they came into the mission. Crapsey would be ready for them. For his part, he brought experience in both study and meditation for the inspiration of those at the mission event. Crapsey believed that the missioner needed to "awaken the soul and make it conscious of both itself and God." Neither ordinary standards nor laws would bind the missioner. All the knowledge of the missioner's lifetime through his work, writings and sermons was brought to bear during the event.[4]

The mission work continued for hours out of the day and for several days straight. When finished, the time for the gathering of the newcomers into the fold began. Though not necessarily diagnostic of the success of the mission by the numbers of those added to the church, some results were expected to follow. Crapsey believed that both outward and inward indications of the success of the mission should be left on the churches in the area as a result.[5]

As a missioner, he was on leave from St. Andrew's. His assistant or others filled in for him in his absence. Crapsey's first assignment was to St. Philip's Church in New York City. The congregation was exclusively black. Crapsey's abandonment for the racial conventions of the time added to his success. He noted how he started off on the right track with the wardens of St. Philips Church. Crapsey and his traveling companion, Mr. Rochester, met with the wardens of St. Philip's Church in the morning. Both wardens were black, one a fine looking, tall and slender West Indian with a genteel manner and the other an American who exuded an air of one who had been controlled his entire life. Crapsey instinctively

[3] Ibid. p. 5.
[4] Ibid. pp. 4-5.
[5] Ibid. pp. 4-5.

walked together with the West Indian gentleman and laid his hand on his arm to make a point and noticed the reaction of the man. He was gratified that he was being treated both equally and with dignity and later he commented on Crapsey's attitude. Crapsey attributed his instinctive ability to treat everyone evenly as the reason for his success at St. Philip's Church.[6]

Crapsey's pattern of hard work bolstered by his resourcefulness also led to his success at St. Philip's. He conducted the mission work with the same enthusiasm he employed in establishing his work at St. Andrew's. Crapsey departed from the traditional preaching of sermons. He started with doctrinal instruction. After fifteen or twenty minutes he would ask the choir to present a hymn. Then he taught on how to apply the previous teachings to one's life practically. He then called for another hymn to give the newcomers a break, to regain their attention and keep them interested. He followed the same method as long as he remained as a missioner.[7]

Before finishing, Crapsey conducted over twenty such missions. In 1893, the Episcopal Church sent him to Omaha, Nebraska. Once again, he worked tirelessly. He taught throughout the day, providing instruction to various groups. The mission began on Thursday February 23rd, and culminated on March 5th, 1893. On a typical day he would celebrate communion at 6:30 and 8:00 AM. He held morning prayers and gave doctrinal instruction at 10:30. At noon he held a luncheon at the New York Life building for various businessmen in the city. By 4:00 PM there were more prayers and an address to the women. After dinner he gave a mission sermon for all of the parishes in the city at 7:45 PM.[8]

Trinity Cathedral Parish's newspaper in Omaha detailed Crapsey's itinerary even more succinctly, demonstrating Crapsey's full schedule and his untiring energy at his work.

Morning Instructions	*The Noon Addresses*	*Evening Instructions*
1st The Fullness of the Times, Providence.	*1st God Manifest in the Flesh, Love.*	*1st The Fullness of the Times, Providence.*
2nd God; His Power, Wisdom and Unity.	*2nd Justified in the Spirit, Righteousness*	*2nd God; His Power, Wisdom and Unity.*
3rd His Fatherhood as	*3rd Seen of Angels,*	*3rd His Fatherhood as*

---

6 Crapsey, *Heretics*, pp. 164-5.

7 Ibid. p.166.

8 News clipping, no title, only heading is "Nebraska" A.H. Crapsey Jr. Collection Scrapbook # 7.

seen in the Divine Sonship of Christ, The Incarnation.
4th Redemption, Christ for us, The Doctrine of Sacrifice.
5th Redemption, Christ in us, The Doctrine of Grace.
6th The Nature Office and Work of the Holy Ghost.
7th The Holy Catholic Church as the Sphere of the Operation of the Spirit.
8th The Communion of Saints,
9th The Doctrine of Faith and Works.

Spirituality.
4th Preached unto the Gentiles, Truth
5th Believed on in the World, Order.
6th Received up in Glory, Justice.
7th God's Light in the Home.
8th God's Highway in the Heart.

seen in the Divine Sonship of Christ, The Incarnation.
4th Redemption, Christ for us, The Doctrine of Sacrifice.
5th Redemption, Christ in us, The Doctrine of Grace.
6th The Nature Office and Work of the Holy Ghost.
7th The Holy Catholic Church as the Sphere of the Operation of the Spirit.
8th The Communion of Saints,
9th The Doctrine of Faith and Works.

The aforementioned itinerary concludes before chronicling the evening sermons.[9] He usually worked well into the evening expounding on such themes as "The Human Soul, its Nature and Value," and "The Laws of Sinfulness, Hiddenness,(sic) Palliation, Degradation and Enmity," and "For Men Only, Personal Purity."[10] One newspaper noting Crapsey's short stature and energetic demeanor described Crapsey as "resembling Napoleon." The paper characterized him as being a "remarkable man." He worked tirelessly at his commission.[11]

Crapsey experimented with his preaching style feeling comfortable to move around in front of his audience. Crapsey revealed the efficacy of fluidity, candor and enthusiasm. He found freedom apart from the austere,

[9] "The Cathedral Chimes" *Trinity Cathedral Parish,* labeled March, 1893. A.H. Crapsey Jr. Collection, Scrapbooks.
[10] Ibid.
[11] News Clipping Source unknown, from Scrapbooks Arthur H. Crapsey Jr. Collection.

high-church deportment that limited movement or the intonations of the preacher in favor of decency and decorum.[12]

One paper reported that Crapsey was obviously a "born missioner." The article considered him novel and inventive while holding fast to the acceptable liturgy of the church. Crapsey would preach from the pulpit and then speak at the chancel, he would even sit "reverentially" in a seat at the rail of the chancel while completing his discourse. He broke up the sermon into various parts between which he would interject worship and prayer, allowing the service to flow while maintaining an air of continuity throughout. Crapsey reminded the reporter of "an instructor from another age, at whose feet the wise men would gather to expropriate the wisdom of his teachings."[13]

Crapsey hammered home his version of the Protestant Episcopal religion. He believed in the free agency of mankind. He believed that with the proper guidance and encouragement we could make the correct choices to free us from the depravity that afflicted our lives. Crapsey's understanding of the capability of the soul is telling. Unlike the Protestant reformers who would stress that the soul was not only depraved, but utterly so, Crapsey considered the soul as a rich part of the human being. It was for Crapsey, the inner-self that contained all the faculties that were essential to the human being like the memory, personal identity and the storage place of all the important information that comes into the individual's life. But, other faculties included the emotional realm where one experienced the passions of both love and hatred.

Crapsey argued that one should take Christ's words literally when attempting to overcome the darker passions of the soul. Christ's words should be contrasted against one's maladies of profanity, pride and covetousness to allow the Great Physician's words to doctor the soul. Crapsey believed the character of Christ's words could be applied to combat the depraved soul. The biblical distinction missing from Crapsey's analysis was the contrast of the spirit with the flesh. Crapsey lumped the work of the soul with the regeneration of the spirit. Crapsey found efficacy, as well as depravity in the soul. But he left the responsibility to refine oneself to the individual soul, rather than to the regenerated spirit. The biblical perspective spoke of replacing the old heart with a new one. The work Crapsey proposed was more a work to fix and repair the old. In that way it wasn't merely a work of the spirit. For Crapsey, the individual

---

[12] News clipping entitled *"Episcopal Mission Begun"* Source unknown , from Arthur H. Crapsey Jr. Collection.

[13] Ibid.

must overcome by applying the principles of that which he had learned and therefore, it was a work, in the Roman Catholic manner, in conjunction with the Lord. The work of the soul, or the inner-self must prevail.

Crapsey was known as a walker. He took long walks whenever time permitted. While in Omaha, Crapsey walked throughout the city. His walks took him to some of the less amiable places. He spoke of the lodgings afforded to women of the red- light district. He noted that the higher-class women lived with fine accommodations, in nice houses and he assumed that they were treated quite well. The lower-class prostitutes lived in isolated districts in tenement-like edifices that were simply long, strung out, one-story structures. Rich or poor, both classes of prostitutes were licensed by the municipality. Whether Crapsey approved of such a practice remains undisclosed. Crapsey did mention however, that he would do whatever necessary to facilitate any women who wanted to attend his mission work. His mission work in Omaha and elsewhere was always intended as pragmatic, as well as spiritual work. He extended the lofty hand of the Episcopal Church to those who were less fortunate as a means of helping them to reform in a religious, but also very practical way.[14]

During the Omaha mission people crowded the aisles and there were seats set up wherever space permitted. It was crowded for blocks in both directions outside the church.[15] One of Crapsey's sermons was taken from John 10: 16, concerning Christian unity. Quoting the text about how Jesus said, "Other sheep I have which are not of this fold, them also shall I bring, and there shall be one flock and one shepherd," Crapsey preached about how that scriptural metaphor denoted Christian reality. Crapsey spoke of how he had traveled through the city and experienced the sinful districts. He appealed to the faithful of Omaha to find it within themselves to establish a chapel and to support a priest and a sister of charity to look after these lost sheep of God.[16]

The press raved about his work in Omaha. One article entitled "Episcopal Mission Begun," described Crapsey as "an interesting personality." All of Omaha seemed to be under his spell. The press also marveled at the multitudes that came to hear Crapsey. Beginning on

---

[14] Crapsey *Heretics*, pp. 168-9.

[15] Ibid. p.169.

[16] Article entitled "Episcopal Mission Begun," subtitled "Mr. Crapsey Draws a Lesson From the Burnt District." News clipping from. A.H. Crapsey Jr. Collection Scrapbooks.

Thursday evening February 23rd Trinity Parish Cathedral was crowded to capacity.[17] By the last evening there were over 4,000 in attendance and the traffic was blocked off for a half a mile. It was estimated that thousands were turned away.[18]

After pleading for the moral work to be done the citizens of Omaha responded. The results of the mission included the expressed desire for the building of a chapel and a shelter for prostitutes in the "burnt district." By the time Crapsey left Omaha, the funds for the purchase of the lot and for the construction costs were beginning to accumulate.[19]

The effort expended in Nebraska was not without benefaction. Crapsey had expressed his hopes for a Christian presence in the burnt district. His supplication successful, Crapsey could rest after realizing that his work had borne fruit now that the good citizens of Omaha had responded. Crapsey returned to Rochester after spending a day at the Columbian Exposition.[20]

Crapsey embarked on other missions for the Protestant Episcopal Church as well. In 1894, he traveled to Bermuda. He took Mrs. Crapsey and his friend and mission work companion, John Rochester, with him. Crapsey stayed at the Vicarage with the rector of Paget parish while Mrs. Crapsey and Mr. Rochester stayed at the Hamilton hotel. Crapsey immediately abolished the color line that ran across the church. No white man would sit behind the line and no black man in front of it. Within a short period of time black and white sat together throughout the church.

Once again, due to his disregard for the conventions of the day, Crapsey gained a reputation for reform. Moreover, Crapsey found ways to minister to the downtrodden regardless of race, gender, or objectionable profession. For Crapsey, all kinds of people, everywhere, needed help.

While on the island of Bermuda, Crapsey found the time to visit Pembrooke and Smith parishes. The Crapsey party went sight seeing to Mt. Langdon and Harrington Sound and spent time taking pictures of the inhabitants. One picture of an old black woman was labeled "Auntie." Although Crapsey worked diligently for the equal treatment and cultural acceptance of the black race, he and Mrs. Crapsey were obviously still

---

[17] Ibid.

[18] News clipping entitled "Looks like Napoleon" A.H. Crapsey Jr. Collection Scrapbooks.

[19] News clipping no title, labeled only, "Nebraska." A.H. Crapsey Jr. Collection Scrapbooks.

[20] *The Cathedral Chimes* (Trinity Cathedral Parish, March, 1893), A.H. Crapsey Jr. Collection Scrapbook s.

prone to the deeply imbedded prejudices that under-girded the culture of the late nineteenth century.[21]

Great throngs of people around the church almost prevented Crapsey from entering the chancellery when he presented his summation sermon. The parishioners finally noticed him and called out, "here is the little man." They proceeded to convey Crapsey over their heads to the front of the church. Undaunted, he finally stood at the altar with the bishop at his side.[22]

On the return trip home the Crapseys encountered a storm that he remembered as a terribly unnerving experience. Crapsey related that his wife suffered tremendously from seasickness. The storm was so rough that Mr. Rochester was thrown across the saloon against the wainscoting on the wall. He received a huge gash over his eye. The Crapseys feared for Mr. Rochester's life the rest of the trip home. Even after their return, the Crapseys worried about his deteriorating health and realized that he would never be the same. It was devastating for Crapsey to lose the fellowship of his close friend and traveling companion after such a distressing experience.[23]

Crapsey became well known throughout the Protestant Episcopal Church as a successful missioner. The people of Nebraska invited him back, extremely enthusiastic about his work there. Crapsey graciously accepted, this time traveling to St. James Church in Fremont, Nebraska, about thirty miles northwest of Omaha. Once again, Crapsey succeeded in getting the attention of the press.

An article in the local newspapers noted once again that he "Looks Like Napoleon." Ever the exhibitionist, Crapsey held their interest by unbuttoning one of his shirt buttons and inserting his hand upon his breast.[24] The press further characterized Crapsey as an "eloquent speaker." One article related that "he was a man of power," comparing him to president-elect McKinley. Enchanted by his oratory powers one

---

[21] Picture in A.H. Crapsey Jr. Collection, Scrapbooks.

[22] Event chronicled in news clipping from Omaha, Nebraska, newspaper, dated February, 22, 1897. Article entitled "Makes Every Word Tell." Subtitled, "Dr. Crapsey Conducting Mission Services at St. James Church." A.H. Crapsey Jr. Collection.

[23] Crapsey, *Heretics*, pp. 172-3.

[24] Picture of Crapsey in his Napoleon pose exists in A.H. Crapsey Jr. Collection.

report stated, that his eloquence put him at par with some of the great politicians of the time.[25]

Since first coming to Nebraska, his perspective had broadened considerably. His views hinted at his growing secularism. Unlike the sermon comparing the world and the believer, Crapsey now related that, the world, not the spirit of God alone, held the hope of the future. He preached on the scripture, "To every one that hath shall be given and from him that hath not shall be taken away even that which he hath." Crapsey reckoned that many in attendance held the general opinion that the present life was so hard and in some cases so depressing that one could only find hope in the future. But Crapsey demonstrated how this was an erroneous view of life. Crapsey noticed the good in the life around him and concocted a philosophical formula to make his point apply. He contended that life was best realized from the context of the excellence of the present. Even one's hope for the future relied on the measure of what we can experience in this present good. In Crapsey's mind, a poor man needed to overcome poverty before he could hope to be rich. There was nothing credulous about that.[26]

For Crapsey, the world was good and one could experience that goodness daily. If there were nothing but devastation and despair then there would be no hope. But that simply was not the case. The world was not only good, but it was very good. Therefore, there was not only hope in the future but one could have confidence and an expectation that it will get even better. Either Crapsey was demonstrating the paradoxical nature of God's truth or, just as likely, Crapsey's heart had turned truly progressive. He no longer defined himself as the religious radical at odds with the systems of the world and the religious systems of men. Rather, he recognized the good of this world and expected to win the promise of the next. He explained that our future hope of heaven depended on the good life we live now. In pure, Thomist theology, Crapsey related that God gives grace and if we do not squander it but use it wisely He gives more. Therefore, we should make the most of what we have been given in fact it is our duty. Furthermore, from an obvious works righteousness perspective, Crapsey noted that if men hoped for a future promise of heaven without God's enabling grace and power in their souls they were deluded. All of mankind's anticipation of heaven was but a delusion if not

---

[25] News clipping dated Feb. 22nd, 1897. Entitled, "Looks Like Napoleon," subtitled, "Dr. Crapsey, Conducting a Mission at St. James, an Eloquent Preacher." Scrapbooks A.H. Crapsey Jr. Collection.

[26] Ibid.

based on the reality of this present good. Crapsey argued unequivocally that any man's future hope for heaven depended on what he did to achieve it today.[27]

It would be impossible to read Crapsey's statements and downplay his works righteousness mentality since the earliest of his Anglo-Catholic days. In reality, Crapsey embraced both Arminianism and perfectionism. Rather than simply rebelling against the Protestant reformers' emphasis on grace and the sovereignty of God, he was conforming to other standards of the Protestant Episcopal Church. In that way, Crapsey sought a *via media* of his own. For Crapsey, the world was good and worth winning and heaven would assuredly follow. One gained heaven by properly applying the grace that God bestowed. God continued to grant it, but only if we used it wisely. For Crapsey, grace was conditional depending on what you did with the last batch of it. To Crapsey the soul warred against itself, between the good and bad parts of it. The good must prevail and overcome the bad through a conscientious effort by the individual and the proper application of the grace conferred by God.

Crapsey's missionary effort in Nebraska produced a groundswell of popular support for him as the next Coadjutor Bishop of the Diocese of Nebraska. Bishop Worthington of the Nebraska Diocese reportedly needed a coadjutor because of his failing health. In all likelihood, the coadjutor would succeed Worthington as Bishop of Nebraska. Before Crapsey could contain the press, lines were being drawn for the election. The parties considered as having the greatest chance of succeeding were the ritualists, in the majority in Nebraska, and the moderates, in a position to affiliate themselves with the anti- ritualist minority. Crapsey now associated himself with the moderate party. The press considered him as one of the leading candidates for the job. The other candidate considered to have the best chance was Father Huntington of New York City. Others considered, though less prominently included, Dean Fair of Omaha, Rev. Dr. Williams of Chicago, Rev. Dr. Codman of Boston, and Rev. Dr. Greene of Cedar Rapids, Iowa, a recently defeated candidate for bishop in Iowa.[28]

The press played upon the great impending battle between the ritualists and the anti- ritualists. For the first time in his career Crapsey was

---

[27] Ibid.

[28] News clipping entitled "Coadjutor- Bishop of Diocese of Nebraska." Subtitled, "Rev. Algernon S. Crapsey, Rector of St. Andrew's Church, May be Appointed to that Position by Episcopalian Diocesan Council of Nebraska." Scrapbooks A.H. Crapsey Jr. Collection.

considered as the middle party candidate. Crapsey, of all people, was being billed as a moderate, or at least one who was tolerant of both the extreme faction of high churchmen as well as the liberal, broad churchmen. Therefore, it was postulated that Crapsey had a good chance of prevailing. They reasoned that after one or two ballots without result, the anti- ritualists or the low church faction would realize that they would not have the votes to defeat the ritualists. They would then throw their support behind a moderate candidate who was tolerant of the low church, anti- ritualists and the broad church factions, as well as the extreme ritualist faction. According to the analysis of the press, Crapsey would have prevailed. The position of Coadjutor-Bishop carried a salary of $4,000, not to mention the prestige and the means to order the future affairs of the church in Nebraska. Interestingly, the anti- ritualists desired a liberal with an aspiration to work amongst the western people. Crapsey was considered perfect for the position due to his mission experience in Nebraska and in other western states. His popularity as a missioner placed him in the minds of Nebraska's Episcopalians as one of the foremost churchmen of the country. The press portrayed him as one they would appreciate as coadjutor and eventually the next bishop of Nebraska.[29]

Crapsey found no satisfaction in the position of an assistant as demonstrated by his untimely departure from Trinity Parish in New York City. In May of 1899, Crapsey forbid his name to be placed on the ballot in the Diocese of Nebraska. According to the local press in Rochester, Crapsey was surprised that he had been considered as a candidate and he straight away telegraphed the convention to withdraw from the ballot. Once more Crapsey shunned the conventional advice of those who counseled others to go west. He was quoted as saying that he chose to continue with the work in the east rather than moving west.[30]

While Crapsey had withdrawn from the position of coadjutor, he was actively trying to persuade his diocese of the need for a bishopric in the Rochester region. No doubt Crapsey welcomed that position. His views had changed considerably as he aged. His move towards the moderate camp was confirmed through his writings. Crapsey wrote that he was still in sympathy with the Catholic movement in the church. He wanted that work to continue. However, he now portrayed himself as a moderate believing that was what was needed to satisfy his political ambitions of gaining the bishop's mitre. He added however, that he did not want the

---

[29] Ibid.

[30] *The Post Express,* "Mr. Crapsey to Stay." May 5, 1899. In Scrapbooks. A.H. Crapsey Jr. Collection.

movement to grow too strong. If it did it could engender a fierce reaction. In a tone almost assuredly foreign to Crapsey he related, that he wanted enough space for the interplay of ideas and the freedom for a diversity of responses. Crapsey went on to state colorfully but ambiguously,

> As the good old divine said of his hat, that it was a shovel hat, but not too shovel, so I wish the church to be Catholic, but not too Catholic.[31]

Crapsey had arrived at a point where he was beginning to make peace with his broadening views. Undoubtedly, that peace was influenced by his desire for the position of a bishop. Nevertheless, he recognized the place for the Protestant resistance to the errors of the Roman Catholic Church. Moreover, Crapsey now considered there were influences inherent in Protestant concepts, which had an important place in life. For Crapsey, Catholicity meant recommended, established religion and continuity. In contrast, Protestantism stood for change, engagement and the unconventional. But God provided for both and used both in His economy. Crapsey distinguished his commitment to a broader perspective through his embrace of Anglicanism. He asserted that his denomination was not only inclusive, but according to Crapsey, "Anglicanism believes everything."[32]

One writer criticized a statement Crapsey made about the election of Phillips Brooks as Bishop of Massachusetts as the best possible thing for the Protestant Episcopal Church. The author objected to Crapsey's statement as "wholly supportive of liberality in the church." The author went on to state satirically, concerning Brooks' irresolute perspective, that "one could not tell these days what broad churchmen like Brooks believed pertaining to any particular subject." He went on to complain that "that kind of latitude to promote unity was done so at the expense of the historic doctrines of the faith and the timeless necessity of dogma." Swelling to a climax the author continued sarcastically that men would soon need to "see around corners rather than to take a straightforward view of things." He looked at the Episcopal Church's aptitude for ecumenicity as the opposite of acceptable, civilized behavior.[33]

---

[31] A.S. Crapsey "Massachusetts Episcopate," *St. Andrews Record* Vol. 5 No. 2 (February, 1893) pp. 2- 3.

[32] Ibid.

[33] He wrote, "Men might as well fly the flag of Christian Unity over a circus tent and menagerie of wild animals as over a Protestant Episcopal Church or any other kind Protestant Church in these conditions, though one has seen such a thing as a

Crapsey answered by building on the theme of a prophecy in Isaiah. He contrasted God's present creation with the eventual experience of the wolf someday laying down with the lamb. Crapsey declared his agreement with both the moderate faction and his growing ecumenicity by noting someday all factions of the church would dwell together in safety and unity when the Great Shepherd will lead them.[34]

Crapsey referred to Isaiah metaphorically but not without application. He recognized the growing controversy in his own thoughts with an honesty that was characteristic of the man. What was uncharacteristic of the man was his newfound sense of moderation. Crapsey was given to extremes, even in the exaggerations of his later sense of recall. And yet, another thought bedeviled him. Because his sympathies needed to be with all the factions, he feared he could not find true acceptance in any one. He wrote that he couldn't possibly want any one of the factions of the church to be driven out because

> I go to bed a Catholic and I wake up a Broad Churchman; when I think of God in my own soul, I am a Low Churchman; when I think of God among my own people, the English, I am a High Churchman; when I think of God among the nations of the earth I am a Catholic; when I think of God in His infinite universe, I am a Broad Churchman.[35]

Perhaps more than being sympathetic to all, Crapsey noted with apprehension that he had come to the point where he could not participate fully with any of the factions. Therefore to a certain extent he felt excluded by all. This was more than mere rhetoric for Crapsey because he felt bound to believe in all that he declared.

He considered the controversy over the Episcopal election of both Brooks the Broad Churchman, and Grafton (a Catholic), a grand thing. There was now the possibility for resolution of the prolonged factionalism that had plagued the church. It is tempting to postulate again that Crapsey was deliberately mellowing in his views for political reasons, that he might gain a newly created episcopate of his own someday. But just as likely he was honestly confused and seeking an intellectual *via media* of his own where he might find comfort amidst all the different perspectives he now desired to subscribe to. His one hope for escape from intellectual

---

'happy family' even in brute creation." From January, 1893, *Eclectic,* reprinted in February, 1893 *St. Andrew's Record*, p. 5.

[34] *St. Andrew's Record*, Vol. 5 No. 2, (February 1893).

[35] Ibid.

bewilderment was to follow the example of Phillips Brooks along a path of what he described as "richness." As a friend of Brooks once explained, Brooks never "defined his position lest he would have to defend it." Brooks downplayed the doctrinal arguments in favor of the richness of the love of God, which he hoped to champion. Thus Crapsey stated about Brooks, he conceived of God as being rich in all things good, especially in love. For Crapsey that was the essence of truth because it ministered not only to life in general but to his personal situation of how to reconcile all the disparate intellectual divergences in the church. But it also provided Crapsey with a means of becoming a bishop, because he saw in Brooks the success of ambiguity and he realized that it was that which was becoming more and more politically expedient in the Protestant Episcopal Church. He believed that was what he needed to attain his aspirations.[36]

Crapsey also saw that Brooks' example was characteristic of the loving godliness he desired. He recalled the controversy at St. Andrew's in 1885, when he used the columns of the *St. Andrew's Record* to dispute a point about lighting candles in the church. He reconsidered his reply to his bishop who found his Catholic practices odious. He used the pages of his parish newspaper as a sounding board to air his opinions. He now realized that he had erred in his acerbic reaction that must have been hurtful to the bishop. Moreover, he once defended a colleague against the attacks of others. He again used the newspaper combatively to defend his friend. Crapsey wrote humbly that now he too would use the gospel like Brooks, from the perspective of love. Therefore, he sought forgiveness for his earlier combativeness. Moreover, he wished to bring it all out and into the open to eliminate any residual bitterness for the health of his soul. Crapsey believed that he had sinned by making his defense of his friend a public issue as he had done over the lighting of the candles. Therefore he figured his penance would be to start over doing what was right beginning with a public confession.[37]

Brooks died prematurely, without making the difference that he might have. But the mere fact that Massachusetts' Episcopalians had elected him spoke volumes about where they were headed. Brooks stood for the Broad Church. He did so without defining his positions beyond calling for the broad and somewhat vague concepts of love and toleration. In a special way, his election was a call to unity in the church. It was a call to put away the dogmatism of the past and to look to the richness of the church's future. Crapsey finally recognized the efficacy of that position. He greatly

---

[36] Ibid.
[37] Ibid.

respected Brooks. Like Frederick Denison Maurice in Great Britain both stood posthumously for the higher calling of love. Crapsey found revelation in Brooks' life concerning the direction for Christendom in the world. Thereafter he would advocate the integrating force of unity through peace and love.

In Brooks' fate, Crapsey realized the odd, yet sovereign ways that God worked. In retrospect, Crapsey noted that Brooks had been called once more to a higher mission. Crapsey eulogized the man in a way that defined his own thinking. He never considered Brooks a profound theologian but his personality and articulation of thought were certainly inimitable. Brooks didn't solve the larger problems that confounded mankind but he had encouraged multitudes through the definite sweetness of his spirit.[38]

Finally, Crapsey warned those in his church not to judge the providence of God in His taking of Phillips Brooks' life. Noting the prevailing opposition to broad thinking even in his own parish, he advised, that no one should question the providence of God by saying that the Lord took someone for whatever reason. Crapsey considered such presumptions as, "an officious intrusion into the affairs of God." Crapsey counseled to "let him rest in peace."[39]

---

[38] Ibid.
[39] Ibid.

CHAPTER EIGHT

"The Beginnings of Sorrows"

As a leader in the Episcopal missions movement, Crapsey incorporated social activism and reform into his evangelism. He particularly sought interaction with the lower classes of society. His aspiration of developing a more loving and gentle character like Phillips Brooks mellowed his dogmatic Anglo- Catholic tone considerably in the decade of the nineties. Nevertheless, Crapsey remained provocative in his writings about the role of the church. He still held the prevailing opinion of Christianity as the great and civilizing influence in the world, even as he grew more radical and perhaps more secular all the time. Likewise, he still refused to define the church Catholic, by fully separating out the Roman Catholic Church. He applied the toleration he received from Brooks to the Roman Catholic Church, while refusing the doctrinal limitations of his evangelical contemporaries in the Episcopal Church.

Coupled with his success as a missioner Crapsey's reputation as a leading high churchman imparted considerable prestige. As the 1890s unfolded, he focused his influence on a movement brewing since at least the 1870s towards the building of an universal body Catholic. Broad churchmen, to whom Crapsey was moving considerably closer in his views, believed that true salvation for a global society required western leadership and a form of Christian ecumenicalism. Anglo- Catholics enthusiastically agreed. They imagined a bridge from the Protestant Church to the great Roman Catholic masses through their liturgical relationship. They considered themselves culturally superior to the teeming Irish and darker, southern European masses who insisted upon maintaining their Roman Catholicism.

Crapsey, like the Broad Church Episcopalians, attempted to forge his own way. He sought to prove himself an original thinker without bondage to the different sects. He held a vision of society fused with religious unity and socio- political equality. Nevertheless, a paradox seemed to bedevil the broad churchmen. The greater the effort at expended towards obtaining unity, the greater the division that seemed to result. Their efforts resulted in schism, intellectual estrangement and religious polarization.

In 1896, Crapsey received an opportunity to travel to Europe again. St. Andrew's now enjoyed the status of a well-established institution in Rochester. The church's decision to send their minister to Europe once more indicated the high esteem that they held him in, as well as the institutional success they enjoyed. Crapsey arrived in Antwerp in the summer of 1896 after a ten-day journey across the Atlantic. He appreciated the "Catholicity" of the city, the first such European municipality that he had ever been to. He visited the cathedral and was enchanted by the construction and trappings of its interior design including Ruebens' *Descent from the Cross.* The devotion of the Belgian people impressed him but he figured that they were stuck in a medieval stage of evolution. Crapsey also commented on the problems with the traditional Roman Catholic Church practices such as the collection of alms for those caught in purgatory. He noted in caustic Protestant style that God's justice was not for sale and the practice of indulgences had destroyed the unity of the church since the fifteenth century. Crapsey assumed that the practice continued in the more traditional sector of the church because it was so lucrative.[1]

As he traveled through Europe and on to southern Italy he noted the dire poverty of the land and the inordinate amount of priests and nuns. Crapsey thought their poverty could be alleviated if the money spent on the clergy and in support of their superstitions was put to practical use through the physical deliverance of the populace. He traveled to Florence and as he venerated Savonarola, he visited the Duomo, Santa Maria del Fiore, that he might partake in the customary acts of worship, while absorbing the ambiance of the place. The great churchman stirred his soul. Inspired by Brunelleschi's dome of the Cathedral, he admired the baptistery and the bronze doors by Ghiberti, and simply adored the Campanile of Giotto. He soon realized something that would stick with him to the end of his life as he marveled at the work. He realized as he beheld the work of the great artist that it was the soul of the great Giotto that was actually immortalized in his enduring work. For Crapsey this was more than mere inspiration. Work truly expressed the immortal soul of the individual. He reckoned that hard labor and good works were his key to immortality also.[2]

Crapsey eventually traveled back to London where he commented on the heart-wrenching situation of Piccadilly Circus with its red-light

---

[1] A.S. Crapsey *The Ways of the Gods* (New York: The International Press, 1921) pp. xiii- xviii.

[2] Ibid.

district. He ended up in Scotland staying with his aristocratic friends, the Kennedy's, whom he met on his previous trip. He remarked on the widespread drunken debauchery of Edinburgh after dark. He wondered why the next day in church the preacher failed to mention the scene he witnessed the night before. Donald Kennedy explained that what they observed was the result of human depravity. Crapsey blamed the social organization. He came away from his tour of Europe convinced that Christianity everywhere was doomed if social repentance and a political remedy were not forthcoming.[3]

In the same year, the Right Reverend Arthur Cleveland Coxe died. Immediately the diocese of Western New York sought a replacement. The diocese was huge. It consisted of fifteen counties and 11,353 square miles. By 1905 it contained 127 Episcopal clergymen, 151 parishes and missions and 23,520 communicants. It was a large, wealthy and highly prestigious diocese.[4]

Bishop Coxe previously opposed Crapsey's audacious displays of Anglo- Catholicism during the 1880s. At one point he considered the lighting of candles and other "Catholic displays, as repugnant." Coxe remained conservative in his administrative role in the diocese. The election of the next Bishop of Western New York subsequently developed into an event full of political maneuvering, as Crapsey and others sought the opportunity for the establishment of a separate diocese for the Rochester region.

Concerned with the proceedings to elect a new bishop, Crapsey wrote to protest the appointment of a committee of laymen under the direction of a clergyman, which would meet to discover the needs of the diocese, and to discuss the qualities desired of a new bishop. Crapsey's wrote the letter to the editor of *Our Church Work*, a publication of the Diocese of Western New York saying that, "it was his desire that nothing would be done that might prejudice the council that held the final say concerning the appointment of the bishop." He commented, "the whole matter for the present time should be consigned to prayer."[5]

Others shared Crapsey's concern for a separate diocese in the Rochester region. However, they viewed the process of electing a new bishop as unrelated to the creation of a new see in the city of Rochester.

---

[3] Crapsey, *Heretics,* p. 216.

[4] Article in *Rochester Democrat & Chronicle* entitled "Annual Council of the Diocese Opened at Corning." Wed. May 17, 1905.

[5] Burrows, *Diocese*, p. 4.

At the convening of the council to elect the new bishop, Crapsey abruptly offered resolutions calling for the immediate division of the diocese. He proposed a commission consisting of seven clergymen and eight laymen constituted for the carrying out of this charge. He also recommended that there should be no election without a resolution concerning the division of the diocese in place. The council denied the proposals on the basis that their sole purpose was to elect a bishop. Furthermore, the canons specifically forbade the division of a diocese of any Episcopate that was vacant. Finally, the diocese elected William David Walker in October 1896.

In early 1897, after Walker's election, Crapsey gave a series of lectures at the Connecticut Club, which met at Trinity Church in New Haven. The president of the club prescribed the subjects of "The Primitive Church, the Greek Church, the Roman Church, the English Church and the Protestant Episcopal Church" for the lecturers. He allowed the speakers to choose their own subjects within the superstructure he provided. A book resulted from the issues raised at the lecture series. The book, a compilation of the lectures, addressed the various stages of the historical church. Crapsey wrote a short prefix addressed to the bishops of the Anglo-Catholic Communion. He then gave his "Interpretation of the Quadrilateral: A Scheme for the Reunion of the Church offered by the Bishops of the Anglo- American Episcopate to the Various Communions of Christendom."[6]

The Quadrilateral provided for ecumenical unification based on four principles. The Episcopal Church offered full communion,

> 1). to anyone accepting the Old and New Testament as the Revealed Word of God;
> 2). to anyone professing the Nicene Creed as the essential faith;
> 3). to anyone receiving the two Sacraments ordained by Christ;
> 4). to anyone submitting to the Historic Episcopate.[7]

Crapsey called the Quadrilateral, "The scheme of the Anglo- American Episcopate for the readjustment of the Church." With the episcopacy's acceptance of the Quadrilateral, Crapsey realized his need to tailor his dogma if he expected to become a bishop. He also found it necessary, to reaffirm his ordination vows and publicly affirm his belief in "the

---

[6] *Five Lectures Upon the Church Delivered in Trinity Church, New Haven, Connecticut before the Church Club of the Diocese of Connecticut.* (New Haven: The Tuttle, Morehouse & Taylor Press, 1897).
[7] Ibid.

inspiration of the Holy Scriptures" and that he held them "to be the Word of God." He also professed his conviction, "explicit and implicit, in the Apostles' and Nicene Creeds as setting forth in language, the best that man can speak, the truth that is in Jesus." He further affirmed his, "use and veneration of the Sacraments as the means of union between the soul and God." He was ready, "confessing past failure, to follow, with glad mind, the Bishops and others who are set over him in the Lord."

He also asserted,

> that Scriptural inspiration without personal inspiration, that intellectual creed without faithfulness of heart, that sacraments without holiness, and episcopates without oversight are but dead and useless things that hinder the work of the Spirit of God in the Soul of Man.8

Why did Crapsey reaffirm his vows? Because in light of his sectarian past he wanted to declare his orthodoxy, and set forth his qualifications as aligned with the newly proposed ecumenical conventions of the church, especially in case of the creation of a new bishopric of Rochester. These affirmations brought him fully in line with the Anglo-American episcopacy's Quadrilateral declarations.

Lest the issue of a new bishopric in Rochester be dropped, Crapsey wrote another short book in 1897, again based on the lectures at the Connecticut Club. This time he added a second section pertaining to the office of a bishop. Crapsey dedicated the book to the Bishop of Central New York reviving the ancient custom of securing a sponsor for his literary endeavor. Realizing the unfavorable position of the new bishop towards the establishment of a new episcopate, he deferred to the judgment of another bishop. It was a smooth move considering the controversial nature of the subject. Whether the newly elected bishop of Western New York considered his act impertinent is speculative as Crapsey eventually noted that he had strongly supported Walker early on for Bishop of Western New York. But Walker fully opposed a separate see in Rochester.[9]

Crapsey addressed his book to the bishops, as they alone could create the new bishopric. He presented his understanding of the office and place of a bishop in the Anglo-American communion in the second part of his treatise. He argued publicly for the splitting up of the Diocese of Western New York, and he addressed his concerns to Bishop Walker. Crapsey had

---

[8] Ibid. p.72.

[9] Burrows, *Diocese,* p. 4 cf. 4.

lived in Rochester for eighteen years by then. He desired to remain in the Rochester area, undoubtedly believing he should receive the position of bishop in the new see of Rochester. He felt that to consider the city of Rochester, being the cultural, intellectual, and economic center that it was, as simply an outlying region of the city of Buffalo was ridiculous. Nevertheless, campaigning for the bishopric could not have endeared him to those colleagues who considered his methods imprudent.[10]

One thing clearly indicative of the growing population in Rochester was crime. In May of 1897 a man was murdered on the corner of Ashland and Averill Avenues. The murder took place directly outside the church. Called to testify as to what she had heard, Mrs. Crapsey stated that even though she had been up late that night, she had neither seen nor heard a thing.[11]

To Crapsey, the unprecedented growth of the city warranted a see of its own. Conveniently utilizing Protestant rhetoric he declared that it was just as unreasonable to have the churches in the Rochester sphere subject to those in Buffalo, as it was to have the church in New York subject to the church of Rome. Crapsey related how the past bishop once wrote him that with his coming the sadly disorganized state of the church in Rochester would hopefully change. Crapsey obviously irritated his clerical brethren with his unabashed desire to elevate himself. He stated that though his house and church were in order the fact was that the church in Rochester was in a sad state of disorganization.[12]

Focusing on the source of the Episcopal office provided the answer for Crapsey. The authority for their pastoral office derived from Christ Himself. Crapsey noted how the energy of things spiritual were preserved by the office of the bishop. He affirmed the Apostolic succession of the episcopate through time, tracing its authority from Christ to the apostles and eventually residing in the office of the bishop. Crapsey declared that Christ provided the authority, the apostles subsequently ordered it but it is through office of the bishop that it is realized onto salvation for men. In a theologically revealing, albeit ironic footnote, Crapsey argued that salvation meant belonging to and continuing in the church that was the visible representation of God's spiritual and moral order.[13]

---

[10] A.S. Crapsey *A Voice in the Wilderness, Being a Plea for the Restoration of Primitive Christianity*. (New York: J. Potts & Co., 1897).
[11] Column dated May 17, 1897 in A.H. Crapsey Jr. Collection.
[12] A.S. Crapsey *'A Voice in the Wilderness'* (New York: J. Potts & Co., 1897).
[13] Ibid.

Conversely, Crapsey argued that the acceptance and institutionalization of the bishops brought a worldly decadence into the church. He could not resist the opportunity to declare the wayward nature of the current arrangement. As a solution, Crapsey contended that the episcopate needed to return to an uncomplicated time when the bishop was the primary overseer and spiritual leader as well as the major influence in maintaining the unity of the church.[14]

Crapsey called for a bishop to pastor the clergy of the city of Rochester. Some critics believed a bishopric in Rochester would be too small. Crapsey answered, "the territory in consideration encompassed more than the upper and lower Galilee regions that constituted the Lord's Episcopal jurisdiction." Critics also claimed there should be no bishopric until enough money was received. Crapsey considered that viewpoint, "the great apostasy!" Regarding that perspective he argued, "one could not compare the work of the kingdom with the business of the world." Crapsey's practical plan included his personal campaign for the diocese. He would carry the banner for the new see to the outlying towns and region. He would personally organize a campaign of education while stirring up the people for the new office. He would personally make the institution a passion in the hearts and minds of the people of Rochester by the convening of the next General Convention in Washington in 1898. Crapsey crusaded openly for the office of bishop. Moreover, he would do it all himself if need be.[15]

The end of the decade of the nineties, filled as it was with professional success for the Crapsey, was also the beginning of sorrows for the Crapsey family. Emily decided to remain in Rochester concerned with domestic issues and romance, while Adelaide entered Vassar. The family read the news about the rumors of war with Spain. Philip, who previously attended an Episcopal Church sponsored, military school at St. John's, later known as Manlius Military Academy, enlisted. Philip put his military training into action by working at the adjutant General's office in Albany, New York. He lived in what Mrs. Crapsey described as "solid comfort" at number forty- two, Eagle St.[16] He subsequently joined the Tenth Battalion of the National Guard in Albany. He was later made a corporal in the New York Infantry Company A, and then quartermaster. The unit was activated and before long Philip was sent to Hawaii for training and further

[14] Ibid.

[15] Ibid.

[16] A picture shows Philip's living quarters at Eagle St. in Albany, N.Y. labeled "solid comfort." A.H. Crapsey Jr. Collection.

assignment. The unit called themselves the "Catskill Boys" and the "Spaniard Hunters."[17] While on active duty in the Hawaiian tropics he fell ill. He never seemed to recover completely. Nevertheless, Philip eventually rose to the rank of second lieutenant in his extended service back at home.[18]

Only a few days prior to the famous battle of San Juan Hill, Crapsey's young daughter Ruth contracted a terrible fever. Ruth had been named for the Sisters of Mary Episcopal nun, Sister Ruth, who died in the yellow fever epidemic in Memphis, Tennessee. The sacrificial deaths of the nuns helped to establish the order of St. Mary and gained them the popular support needed to keep alive their vision of a cloistered sisterhood within the Protestant Episcopal Church. As Ruth's condition grew worse, the children were called home to their summer residence at Guilford Farm in Charlotte near Lake Ontario. Adelaide came home from Vassar, and Philip from the army. Ruth dictated poems to her nurse articulating with clarity of mind what was happening to her withering life amongst the surroundings.[19]

As the younger children played outside her window, Ruth died on an early summer day in June 1898. After her death, an unimposing memorial notice read that she had gained an "intellectual and spiritual plane beyond her years." The family noted that even on her deathbed she had composed poems, which demonstrated her exceptional command over her mind.[20]

Earlier, Ruth composed a patriotic poem to commemorate the sinking of the Maine. Later, she wrote of a wildflower. Precociously comparing her life to that of a "little flower that had been cut down in the garden before its time," she expressed herself with optimistic abandonment of the material life. Devotedly, she declared, "I grow for God."[21]

Ruth's death devastated the family. Their pain was such that they would virtually refrain from referring to the sweet, talented young child in their correspondence or public addresses. The pain of loosing such a child at eleven-years-old was unbearable. In times of great stress and heartache Crapsey became somewhat eccentric. A picture of Guilford Farm in

---

[17] A.H. Crapsey Jr. Collection Scrapbooks.

[18] The disease was either typhus or malaria. Both have been described as the culprit in the later death of Philip. A.H. Crapsey Jr. Collection, Scrapbooks.

[19] Alkalay- Gut, *Alone,* pp. 80- 1.

[20] "In Memorium, June 23rd, 1898, Ruth Elizabeth Crapsey" In *The Churchman* A. H. Crapsey Jr. Collection, Scrapbook #9.

[21] Ibid.

Charlotte, the summer Ruth died, captioned "On Lake Ontario" also states "shockingly, Algernon went swimming nude there."[22]

Fortunately, he got away and remained busy. The same summer he accepted a temporary position as a professor of dogmatic theology at Peterborough in southern Ontario, Canada. While at Peterborough he would get up early and take the Eucharist daily, eat breakfast and take his daily walk. The classes met from nine in the morning to one in the afternoon. While there, Crapsey stated that he taught men who were well established in high places in the church. He related that to such men he dared to make Christian dogma comprehensible. The death of Ruth triggered something mordant in his already drifting mind about the feasibility of the historical doctrines of the faith. Accompanying his burgeoning frustration at the bishop's unwillingness to bend to his will concerning the partition of the diocese, a growing sense of cynicism began to manifest itself visibly in Crapsey.[23]

The Canadians summoned Crapsey to Peterborough assuming they had invited a famous high churchman. In his dogmatic theology classes Crapsey proceeded to rationalize the very tenets of the faith that steadfastly refused logical explication. As an Anglo-Catholic Crapsey had previously defended these same concepts from what he had considered as the limited capacity of man's rationale alone. Subsequent influences prodded Crapsey to now explain the historic doctrines of the church reasonably. Before long Crapsey found that his new sympathy for rationalism still held plenty of resistance with the clergy of the Protestant Episcopal and Anglican Churches. Opposition to his teachings came first from high churchmen that had misconstrued Crapsey as a ritualistic colleague.[24]

Using what he considered as "Butlerian analogy," Crapsey attempted to illustrate the major doctrines of the faith by using natural analogies to his students.[25] First, he described the Trinity, using the father, mother and child analogy. He saw the father as singular but unproductive without the union with the mother. As the two become one another proceeds from that union and this characterizes the union of the three in one.[26] Crapsey's

---

[22] Scrapbooks Arthur H. Crapsey Jr. Collection.

[23] Crapsey, *Heretics,* pp. 195-6.

[24] Ibid., p. 198.

[25] Crapsey's understanding of Butler was reductionistic. See Joseph Butler *The Analogy of Religion* London: Knapton, 1736.

[26] See Crapsey, *Heretics* pp. 195-198. Crapsey wrote it this way, "The father is one but, as long as the Father is an isolated unity he is barren. It is not until his

explanation was obviously far from the high church's concept of the eternality of the Godhead or the mystery of the faith. Moreover, his understanding of the Trinity re-kindled passionate arguments within the church regarding the *Filoque*, which in Episcopalian circles were considered bad form to re-ignite.[27]

When he came to the doctrine of grace he explained,

> I used the analogy, the air and the lung. Theologians speak of the grace of God, which is the power of God, as prevenient grace and sacramental grace. Grace that goes before and grace that follows after. Thus before the man can breathe the air, the air must be there to breathe: The air is always there waiting on life; but before a man can appropriate the air, he must have a breathing apparatus, and his lungs are that device; they take in the air and transform it in the blood. The air goes before and follows after the act of breathing.28

Speaking of the Incarnation, Crapsey demonstrated to his class the analogy of the "thought and the brain." He stated that the thought process was entirely spiritual as it was

> without form, shape, sound or smell, nor was it measurable. Only when thought incarnates itself in the brain is it available to the corporeal world to accomplish what it is there for.[29]

Crapsey inferred that the effectiveness of God was subject to His creation. His attempt to make doctrine fit into material or rationalistic analogies was offensive to the high churchmen. Finally, Professor Clark of the Theological Seminary of Toronto, who had brought a sizeable contingent of students to the summer school, could no longer countenance what he considered error. Crapsey's analogies were certainly not what they had expected. Seated for a few days in the back of the classroom, Professor Clark finally rose up and confronted Crapsey, to the great pleasure of the students, who according to Crapsey, reacted less maturely than he had previously described them. Clark accused Crapsey of "expressing his concept of the dogma of the church through his own

---

unity is merged with the unity of the woman and these two become one that the third member of the Trinity emerges from the union of the two; this is the union of three in one."

[27] Ibid., p. 196.

[28] Ibid., pp. 196-7.

[29] Ibid., p. 197.

limited and quite fallible rationale." Crapsey was taken aback, but responded by declaring "if the human brain must appropriate Christian dogma, must not the human mind explain it?" Clark cried out, "Sir, such teaching as yours has no place in the Church! You are worse than a Ritschlian." To which Crapsey replied, "he didn't know who or what a Ritschlian was." The class was by then in an uproar, especially when the Professor stormed out of the room after stating that he was "unable to believe that a man sitting in a chair of dogmatic theology did not know what a Ritschlian was." Crapsey's ignorance of Ritschlian theology underscored his growing problem. Unable to grasp the depth of significant theological argument due to a lack of education and other reasons, Crapsey relied upon his own contrived analogies and convoluted reasoning to understand the timeless, often paradoxical doctrines of the church.[30]

Crapsey attempted to resign his post at Peterborough, but his students prevented him as they were obviously amused by him. His summer school activities ended shortly afterwards. But Crapsey continued to make waves in the denomination. Back in Rochester, he made an observable breach in the Protestant Episcopal Church's decorum and discipline by preaching at Third Presbyterian Church. His bishop attempted to stop him by even visiting his rectory in person, but Crapsey ignored his wishes, by this time embarrassed by his previous parochialism.[31]

Crapsey's rebellious side had been loosed. Although he ultimately lost the battle for the separate episcopate, he redirected his energies to other points of controversy. Crapsey disdained hypocrisy. To be broad mentally and not practice it outwardly would have been atypical of the man. His rejection by the episcopate provided fodder for his hatred of duplicity.

In the midst of this inner struggle, Crapsey eccentrically preached against unqualified rationalism in the church at Third Presbyterian Church. Crapsey would not be presumed upon as a mere rationalist either. After all, the unabashed rationalism of the early reformers had been fodder for the Catholic cause. Therefore Crapsey took on a new and different persona. Like Maurice, Kingsley or Brooks, he preferred ambiguity in his new role prohibiting others to categorize him.

Conversely, Crapsey characterized dogmatism as another of the scourges of the modern church. The Jewish religion was, according to Crapsey, "communistic and pacifistic." Notwithstanding the association with monotheistic rationalism, Crapsey viewed the defeat of Arius, as an

[30] Ibid., pp. 197-8.
[31] Ibid., pp. 198-201.

overthrow of the primitive, pure, communistic-pacifistic champion. He believed the subsequent adaptation of the Athanasian doctrinaire system created an imperialistic Catholic Church. Crapsey argued, that the church and the world far before the time of Constantine had wedded. The uncontaminated religion of Jesus of Nazareth had subsequently become an adulterated theology of men. Crapsey pointed back to the thought that the early church held of Jesus returning to judge the rich and to lift up the poor and needy.[32]

Similarly, Crapsey now considered the "ritualization of Christianity a scourge to the church" as well. Unable to compete with the philosophizing capabilities of the Greeks, the Roman Church adopted primitive religious practices. Crapsey noted that the true power of the Roman Church was through the liturgical superiority it maintained over the people. The people were taught that austere observance of the rituals provided them with salvation through the church.[33]

According to Crapsey, "the priesthood subjugated the people from that point forward. The nobility held power over the people in the present world while the priests held the power over their hope for eternity." Crapsey contrasted the historical resurgence of Catholic ritual in the church against the growing industrialization of the world's system. He observed how the church ignored the evils of society. "Enmeshed in pedantic rituals, they couldn't even recognize glaring social problems as they developed."[34]

Crapsey concluded his sermon at Third Presbyterian Church with the "Socialization of Christianity." Crapsey insisted that true Christianity was a "social order." Nonetheless, as long as society was filled with elements at variance with one another it would certainly not be orderly. He considered that, the rich and poor were at enmity with one another. Societal peace was impossible under such conditions. He looked around him and compared society to his concept of the ideal Christian civilization. Crapsey noted that

> Jesus was a true Master of social science. Jesus saw that society must be composed of equal elements. Each individual should have an equal right to a place in society and a place to work as a dutiful means of obtaining order. Moreover political equality was a clear necessity. There should be no division between the classes, either in the aristocratic or in the

---

[32] Ibid., pp. 201-4

[33] Ibid., p. 205.

[34] Ibid., pp. 205-7.

> capitalistic sense. These economic, social and political divisions have produced inherent disorder in societies.[35]

For Crapsey, becoming more and more radical every day, these factors have been the cause of tragedy throughout history. Crapsey based his conclusions on what he assumed Jesus would prefer as a social structure. He took into consideration what he felt were the prevailing consequences of the time. Biblical accounts however, document that Jesus chose not to spiritualize the economics of the world's system, but taught his disciples to realize who was in control of it. He wasn't stating that the systems had to necessarily be separated, simply that they were. Concerning the poor, Jesus said, "The poor you shall always have with you." These were not crass pronouncements of judgment upon the lower classes but rather prophetic insights into the chronic baseness of human nature. Social Gospel spokesmen saw in these statements the clamor to a higher calling. If, "thy Kingdom come on earth as it is in heaven," then the responsibility falls on Christians on earth to make it like it is in heaven. To the Social Gospel leaders, this presumably meant without caste or gradation of social position. Christians, as Crapsey complained, "married the world instead of the Kingdom," and the result had become a tragic espousal of the catastrophic.

Social Gospelers pushed forward to do a similar thing. The paradigm of socialism seemed to fit the contemporary occasion well. The only difference was that they inserted a specially contrived system for the one in operation. Social Gospel leaders often trumpeted socialism as God's best for earth. They heralded it as in concordance with God's social order in heaven. But pure, secular socialism lacked a moral construct to guide it on earth. A religious system should complement the social system, a didactic economic, political and social system would then all function together for the greater good. The Social Gospelers believed that just as individuals could be saved the same could be true for society.[36]

The church needed to come together before considering itself a viable force in the world. Crapsey viewed the historical position of the Anglican Communion as unique in its ability to draw together various strains of dogmatism and piety. With these thoughts in mind, Crapsey entered into a period of intense writing. He published several Tractates and papers and traveled to various churches lecturing on the merits of reuniting

---

[35] Ibid., p. 210.

[36] Richard Hofstadter, *The Age of Reform* (New York: Vintage Books, 1955). p. 11.

Christendom. In 1897, Crapsey delivered a lecture in Philadelphia securing his passage into the broad camp. Annoyed at his assault on traditional doctrine and his departure from the high church one writer mused that he had succumbed to "attacks of his peculiar prophesying in outlying regions."[37]

The death of young Ruth truly brought the beginnings of sorrows. Something dreadful happened at the peak of Crapsey's life and it shook him. He was the same man but profoundly changed. Ruth's death engendered a sense of cynicism that grew with time. He moved from forever scurrying after success, towards disparagement, eccentricity and then, rebellion. Perhaps Ruth's death was the first thing that he couldn't actually control. God had demonstrated His sovereignty in the most final of all acts. Perhaps it caused him to rethink his theology and relationship with God. The result ironically strengthened his theological opinion about the sovereign will of man.

Crapsey never received the bishopric of Rochester for which he lobbied so intensely. The new bishop refused to succumb to Crapsey's strong will. The affair provoked a profound sense of dissatisfaction in Crapsey with the hierarchy of the church. Finally, a sense of pessimism about the direction of the church produced an overwhelming negativity about his future within the organization. Crapsey's sovereign will was shaken once again. Nevertheless, the response that Crapsey would make was never to capitulate to the will of others but to fortify his determination and fight back.

---

[37] Rev. Arthur Ritchie *Catholic Champion* Vol. XII No. 5 (New York: April, 1900). Reference to this lecture was also stated in a column entitled "Spindrift" dated April 7, 1900. In Scrapbooks, A.H. Crapsey Jr. Collection.

CHAPTER NINE

"Till We All Come in the Unity of the Faith"

In May of 1899, Crapsey preached at Vassar during Adelaide's sophomore year. His invitation to Vassar indicated his growing status throughout the nation. He was becoming a well-known figure in the Protestant Episcopal Church and the media.[1]

His attention now centered on unity in the church. In November 1899, Crapsey went back to Canada to read a tractate before the Canadian Society of Christian Unity in Toronto. As his most widely read tractate, it examined the problem of disunion within the modern church and considered how it could be remedied. The Lord would be greatly disappointed because Christ's hope and prayer for harmony had not been answered, Crapsey argued. The problem, he continued, was that the children of God were not in concordance, with one another. Crapsey referred to the prayer of Jesus recorded in John, chapter seventeen. The Lord's plan was to attain unity in the body of Christ through God. Crapsey noted that the early church was in unity but since the fourth century there has been virtual disorder. Crapsey laid the cause of the failure on two false assumptions that disregarded the Lord's concerns for unity. Crapsey laid the foundation of his future heresies upon his planned resolution of these erroneous theories.[2]

The first presumption stated, "the unity of the Church centers in her own organization." Perhaps ridiculing those who stood against his wishes for a bishopric Crapsey criticized those that believed that unity in the church centered in the authority of its leaders. The concept of apostolic succession actually produced the mistaken belief that their official status provided plenary organizational and governmental power over the church. Crapsey compared the hierarchy of the church with the divine right of kings, and found similarities that needed addressing. Despotic behavior carried over into the church. Focusing on the Roman Catholic, the Anglican and Orthodox systems, he criticized the authoritarianism of one

---

[1] Alkalay-Gut, *Alone,* p. 90 cf. 24.

[2] A.S. Crapsey *The Disappointment of Jesus Christ* Tractate No. 1 "Causes and Remedy of the Disunion of Christendom." (Rochester, 1902) pp. 4-10.

or several men that was antithetical to the unity of the church. Applying his hypothesis to sensitive contemporary political issues Crapsey mused that the Roman Catholic Church of the Reformation was as great a political machine as Tammany Hall ever thought of being. He appealed to the public to stand behind contemporary reformers. He believed this power could force rulers to capitulate and likewise affect the destiny of the church. Crapsey labeled this power the "unofficial power of the church." He called for real "evolutionary" change.[3]

Frustrated over his rejection for the bishopric he warned, that church needed true bishops rather than Apostolic Succession. Moreover the true church would find such as ordained by God in the "wilderness," rather than in the established cathedrals and fine places of worship if the church refused to change. In effect, Crapsey declared his own Apostolic succession. The whole thing was all-wrong anyway. If the church would not recognize him as a bishop or a leader of note he would declare himself one, like a prophet crying out in the wilderness.[4]

The second false and inadequate theory was "that the unity of the church centers in her own formal doctrine." Crapsey noted how men who questioned the doctrines of the church were historically executed for their beliefs. He argued, that "the early church sought to discipline themselves to bring out their best. But since the fourth century the church has attempted to discipline men's intellects. The dogmatic church in fact undervalued men's intellectual ideas to control what they thought in a uniform manner. Thus, they would repeat the same liturgies and ultimately think in the same way." Crapsey argued that the church hierarchy believed they now had the right to think for the rest of the body of Christ. He decried the loss of the pious life in favor of the intellectual. Piety produced from discipline had been damaged by the church's acceptance in the world. A distraction resulted from one's responsibility to a live godly life due to all the developing intellectual diversions including dogmatic assemblages. The result was that church's discipline was "now intellectual rather than truly spiritual."[5]

Intellectuals, even during Crapsey's day, had noted how important economic, social and political concepts like capitalism and republicanism developed from the Reformation. They eventually drew important suppositions about the revolutionary transformation of western society in

---

[3] Ibid., pp. 14-15.
[4] Ibid., pp. 14-15.
[5] Ibid., pp. 16-19.

the process.[6] But the Reformation was never the panacea for Crapsey that it was for other thinkers. For Crapsey, the Reformation created a new bondage of the intellect personified by the dogmatic austerity of the Puritans. Both Catholics and Protestants shored up their intellectual defenses and waged an intellectual war that in the case of Protestantism simply exchanged one form of intellectual tyranny for another.[7]

Regarding man's quest for freedom since the Reformation, Crapsey noted how "sovereignty over the intellect was not gained without a great cultural battle. Scientific truth gained ascendancy at the expense of both Christian piety and doctrine." Crapsey believed that scientific dogmatism has gained its liberty completely by "defeating the church's organizational power." Prophetically contemplating how power corrupts, Crapsey realized that "science could ultimately become a cultural tyranny itself. "[8]

Nonetheless, Crapsey recognized little of substantial intellectual freedom anywhere in the contemporary religious situation. He considered that if things were different one might gladly submit his life to a great institution like the church. But regardless of whether it was one of the denominational factions of Protestantism or the Roman Catholic Church, the entire Christian system was opposed to intellectual, as well as spiritual freedom.

Nevertheless, Crapsey had developed a misguided sense of allegiance, certain to alienate those in official positions over him. He felt that the Anglican Church due to its structure and traditions was the only church presently available that was conducive to freedom. However the only reason for that was because it was also "out of order." Crapsey mused that the "machines that didn't work were the safest because they weren't used as much." The picture Crapsey painted was hardly a flattering portrait of Christendom let alone the Anglican Church.[9]

Crapsey had made his point concerning unity, but only by bringing the bondage of the intellect and the repression of official organizationalism sharply into focus. The answer for Crapsey was to simply "unify the church in God and in humanity." Crapsey declared, "the scientific revolution had freed men from official bondage by the church. The two false theories had lost their battles of centering the unity of the church in themselves." With a misconstrued sense of triumphalism, Crapsey figured

---

[6] For example see Dirk Kasler's *Max Weber, An Introduction to his Life and Work.* Chicago: Univ. of Chicago Press, 1988 pp. 74-141.

[7] Crapsey, *Disappointment,* p. 23.

[8] Ibid., pp. 20- 21.

[9] Ibid., pp. 23-4.

that, "due to science, man's mind had been liberated once and for all. You might be able to keep someone from Christianity but you couldn't keep the same from thinking freely." Embracing the role of the prophet Crapsey declared, "God had a word for the people and they might never know through whom the word might come." Therefore, and because truth must be personally discerned Crapsey warned his readers "not to deny the truth because it may be adverse to some organization." Moreover, Crapsey stated,

> Let us not stone the speaker of the word, lest we be stoning the messenger of God, let us not kill the watcher, lest, with him, we kill the truth of God.

In his own, as of yet, subtle way, Crapsey equated the truth of science with the new message that would be forthcoming from God. It was an important message to be embraced indeed.[10]

Crapsey prophesied that the Christians of the twentieth century would come together in one accord, unified under the banner of popular democracy and scientific protocol. His language signified the message of the evolutionary perspective of the social and biological sciences. He was concerned with higher and lower scientific forms of all types and classifications, social as well as biological. From his new systematic, evolutionary standpoint he envisioned the inclusion of all contemporary types into a greater superior type.[11]

Crapsey realized the difference between the late nineteenth century and earlier times when people were stuck in their churches from birth to death. The scientific revolution brought real mobility. Transportation, urban lifestyles and other developments allowed people to go from one church to another to explore the distinctions of the faith while realizing that they are, in effect, maintaining overall beliefs common to the faith in general. He contended that whether they knew it or not "there was already a great deal of commonality between the various denominations. However, real unity for Christians was to be found in God regardless of the size or the relative obscurity of the denomination or sect." Moreover, Crapsey declared that "the godliness of men like Savaranola, Keble, Wesley, or John Henry Newman was shared with others like WilliamWadsworth or Ralph Waldo Emerson ."[12]

---

[10] Ibid., p. 24.
[11] Ibid., p. 24
[12] Ibid., p. 25.

Obviously Crapsey's new definition of godliness held an extremely broad meaning. Similarly, his understanding of God broadened as well. He now started questioning the necessity for subscribing to the basic doctrines of the historical faith. He developed a subtle double-mindedness in his concept of Jesus as the Christ. His argument had not yet culminated in the intellectual impasse that it would in the future. In conclusion, he boldly but ambiguously wrote that,

> It cannot be that the love of the Father will forever disappoint the expectation of the Son. Unless all signs fail, a belief in Jesus Christ as the Spiritual head and center of the human race is the goal of human thought; and a union, through Him, with God, the end of human life.[13]

Crapsey proposed a manifesto to insure success in answering the problem of Christian disunity. He anticipated seven steps for the Church to guarantee the development necessary for the completion of his theory. The first vaguely proposed that the official hierarchy of the church should become subordinate to the "Church itself." The next proposed a "pastoral rather than the priestly conception of the ministry." The third called for "a uniform doctrine that would correspond to the factual, empirical universe."[14]

The fourth argued for inclusion in that doctrine of the basic concepts of humanity including "justice, mercy and truth." In the fifth step Crapsey demanded "Absolute intellectual freedom within the Church." The sixth committed all of Christian history and tradition both oral and written, to well-trained researchers who would determine the "content, value and meaning" involved. The last precept declared that "the moral discipline of the church must be restored as the true basis of its spirituality."[15]

Crapsey gained support for his views throughout the Protestant Episcopal Church, and elsewhere. Those who approved of the tractate *(The Disappointment of Jesus Christ)* and the argument that Crapsey brought forth included, "Dr. William R. Huntington, of Grace Church, New York; Dr. S.D. McConnell of Trinity Church, Brooklyn; Dr. William M. Grosvenor, of the Church of the Incarnation, New York; Dr. Elwood Worcester, of St. Stephen's Church, Philadelphia, and Rev. Floyd W. Tompkins of Holy Trinity Church, Philadelphia. The Bishop of Western Virginia demonstrated his appreciation by ordering a copy of the tractate

---

[13] Ibid., p. 25.
[14] Ibid., Tractate No. 2, "The Royal Priesthood ," See Appendix.
[15] Ibid., Appendix.

for each of his clergy." Crapsey also garnered support from the lay community. Such men as Seth Low, President of Columbia College; Mr. Hamilton W. Mable, of *Outlook* a contemporary issue-oriented magazine and the Hon. David Jayne Hill, LL.D., First Assistant Secretary of State, supported his publication. Hill wrote:

> I find myself in hearty sympathy with your generous conceptions of Christian truth and moral aspirations. It seems to me you reconcile all the great elements of human nature in your conceptions of truth.

Crapsey received letters from all over the country encouraging him to continue with his cause. They inspired him to dedicate all of his extra time and energy beyond his pastoral duties to the new work. Shortly thereafter, Crapsey hoped to kick off his lecturing crusade in Philadelphia where he believed that he would be well received.[16]

Others reported on the tract without an opinion on either side of the question.[17] However, one publication noted acerbically that his concept of the unity of the church ultimately eradicated any of the doctrines absolutely necessary to salvation, including those pertaining to "faith and obedience to authority." Crapsey's argument was so broad that it rendered the creeds "indifferent." He demonstrated an altogether "tolerant spirit." The great questions of the centuries were left unasked without resolution and nothing was left in which the "wearied soul can rest as on the fiat of God." The author noted Crapsey's conception of Christ as, 'the centre of humanity.' But who is Christ and what? Who can tell us anything about Him which we can be sure is true? Where is 'the unity of the Faith and of the knowledge of the Son of God.' The author stressed that "without the stability of the dogmatic truths, the truth held no sure definition. Without definition it was meaningless to call Christ the center of humanity, and that was the real truth of the matter."[18]

The author added his own sense of irony. Inspired by Christ's prayer for unity he noted how men attempt to achieve it. He declared that

> one should never compromise because of man's inability to grasp the truth of God through faith and divine revelation and bring those who remain outside God's divine city within as the problems involved were

---

[16] *The Public Ledger* (Phila. Pa., March 8, 1899). A.H. Crapsey Jr. Collection Scrapbook #7.

[17] *New York Daily Tribune* (New York, Nov. 20, 1899). A.H. Crapsey Jr. Collection, Scrapbook #7.

[18] News clipping A.H. Crapsey Jr. Collection Scrapbook #7.

insurmountable. Should one then simply allow the outsiders in by breaking down the walls and destroying the foundation?

The author replied disdainfully, "We are told that the 'movement will come from below, not from above,' and in a profounder sense than that intended, we fear that that statement is true."[19] In other words, the author suggested the unity Crapsey sought from below came from the very pit of hell.[20]

The *New York Tribune* however, was kinder to the Crapsey tractates than the previous author. Noting that a further publication entitled "The Answer to Pilate," would without a doubt provide further controversy especially from a "representative High Church Episcopalian." The editor welcomed the coming storm.[21] The new tractate's title referred to the biblical question Pilate posed concerning "Art thou a King?" In it Crapsey simply demanded exactly what Jesus Christ demanded for himself and for his people in terms of applying one's sovereign intellect to religious truth.[22]

Crapsey conscientiously disregarded the other famous question of Pilate's concerning "what is truth?" The former question of Pilate's provided Crapsey with enough leeway to play with the answer that Christ gave. Crapsey noted that, Christ was correct to call Himself a king and contend that He came into the world to "bear witness to the truth." Crapsey concluded, "Christ had beneficently restated the truth. To do so was to consecrate human intelligence, while taking that process away destroyed the intellect and sets the soul adrift toward a place of superstition and fear." Moreover, he asserted,

> The Lord may have committed the keys of the Kingdom of Heaven to Peter (of which more by and by), but the keys to the Kingdom of Truth He committed to the sovereign mind of man.[23]

For Crapsey, the providence of truth resided in the "sovereign mind of man," not merely with God. Crapsey emphasized the need for truth in Christianity to coalesce with the truths of scientific thought. He stated that the present employment of intelligent men was to demonstrate through

---

[19] Ibid.

[20] Irony is no stranger to the Bible. See John 8: 23, 11: 49- 52,.

[21] *NY Daily Tribune* Feb 7, 1900.

[22] Crapsey, *Disappointment,* Tractate No. 4, "The Answer to Pilate."(Rochester, 1899) p. 31.

[23] Ibid., p. 33.

scientific methodology how "religious beliefs" and "acts of faith" could corroborate with scientific truth. Crapsey believed unity in the church could succeed if unanimity of thought preceded it. But it required faith in the preeminence of the scientific as the supreme representative of the truth. Then reconciliation between scientific truth and religion would ultimately result in an intellectual harmony that would sustain the welfare of human life. Crapsey hoped for the time when of "faith and reason could come together with each contributing in its own way to uphold man's love of God."[24]

Agreeing with Crapsey's argument, the editor of the *New York Tribune* emphasized that the powerful "spirit of scientific investigation" alone would throw off the dogmatism of Protestantism. It was time for the church to take their heads out of the sand and to stop forcing others to leave their heads in. Science would lead the world into a system of understanding bringing unity and edification to humanity. The author concluded, "Churchmen could no longer deny the verities of science. The scientific had become the very essence of human thought." He perceived futility for any poor theologian who dared to come against the progressive nature of science. It was like throwing "chips against the wind." Moreover, the editor claimed real spiritual significance in scientific truth. He claimed that "science had wrested infinity and eternity from the realm of the theological placing them squarely within the grasp of human consciousness." What he meant by that was a complete mystery, but it sounded rather good.[25]

As others commented on Crapsey's tractates it became apparent that his purpose for their publication had not been accomplished. Crapsey naively hoped to encourage unity through his publications, but he created antagonism. Realizing the departure of one of its brethren, the Anglo-Catholic faction mounted a particularly acrimonious attack. Rev. Arthur Ritchie, the editor of the *"Catholic Champion,"* and militant Anglo-Catholic rector of St. Ignatius Church in the upper west side of Manhattan wrote a long and scathing article about Crapsey entitled, "Mr. Crapsey's Attack Upon the Church."[26]

---

[24] Ibid., p. 34.

[25] *New York Tribune* February 7, 1900.

[26] Rev. Arthur Ritchie "Mr. Crapsey's Attack Upon the Church" In *Catholic Champion* (St. Ignatius Guild: New York City, April, 1900). Column entitled "Spindrift." A.H. Crapsey Jr. Collection. Scrapbook #7.

The paper, nicknamed the "Catholic Scorpion," for its biting and stinging character lived up to its reputation.[27] Ritchie wrote, "The *'Catholic Champion'* finds that Mr. Crapsey's mind has a hopeless and ungodly twist." Ritchie continued, "Mr. Crapsey attacks or supposes he attacks the church. But as a matter of fact, he has no conception of what the church is." Rev. Ritchie decried the fact that Crapsey was "as yet one of our own clergy, and is allowed to use some of our pulpits in which to ventilate his crude notions." Apparently not realizing Crapsey's success as a rector of a very large upstate church and missioner, Ritchie noted, "we are mistaken if he ever succeeds in attracting any considerable following." Criticizing Crapsey's rhetoric and use of hyperbole Ritchie continued, "He makes attacks on everything we believe- everything which in God's goodness has come down to us and offers us nothing instead but vague promises based upon his own alleged gift of prophecy." Turning to Crapsey personally Ritchie wrote, "He is a dreadful example of what broad churchmanship may lead a man to, and such an example properly shunned may be of service." Further elucidating about Crapsey's broad churchmanship Ritchie continued, "because he has not the subtlety to clothe his attacks in some semblance of sound religion, he serves the good purpose of laying bare the falsehood of that school of thought to which he has become a detrimental adherent."[28]

Noting the vitriol of the *"Catholic Champion,"* another publication sarcastically commented,

> The 'odium theologicum' has long been a proverb, and if one wants to find 'hatred, malice, and uncharitableness' there is no surer place to go for them than to the so- called 'religious' papers. The daily papers in their bitterest strife are models of gentleness compared with these 'champions' of the gospel of love and peace.[29]

Ritchie's fury highlighted the intensity of the debate. Another editor wrote, "By talking as he is now doing in these 'attacks,' our dear brother is rapidly destroying his capacity for ministering to souls." He portrayed Crapsey's indiscretion as "dreadful," and a "wretched thing." As an "anointed minister of Christ," Crapsey told people that they "needed no

---

[27] Personal communication with Rev. Stuart Hoke, Church Historian and administrative secretary of St. Ignatius Church, March 3, 1999.

[28] Rev. Arthur Ritchie "Mr. Crapsey's Attack Upon the Church" In, *Catholic Champion* (St. Ignatius Guild: New York, April, 1900).

[29] Author unknown A. H. Crapsey Jr. Collection Scrapbook #7.

propitiation because God has never been angry. This doctrine Mr. Crapsey has preached, and it is in harmony with the rest of his lucubrations." Building his sarcasm, the author of *"Spindrift"* stated that Crapsey started an "ecclesiastical fire" that needed putting out. But the engines and the equipment needed were out of date and the fire-fighters' skills had been quelled by their lack of use.[30]

Ritchie's points were inadequately served by the duplications of the article by the author of *"Spindrift."* But, Ritchie considered that "the doctrine Crapsey preached would cause a penitent who heeds such a message to say, 'They have taken away my Lord and I know not where they have laid Him.'" The point was clear, Crapsey's call for abstinence from dogma of any meaningful sort meant Christ's life and death could be interpreted in whatever way necessary for satisfaction of an individual's conscience. If as an allegory or an example solely to live the good life, then, there was no compelling need for a savior in the first place. Thus, Ritchie pointed to the rational problem with the rational church. By promoting individual interpretation without the guidance of the church one risked error. Ritchie wondered logically, "we suppose that Mr. Crapsey means to deny that our Blessed Lord offered a Propitiatory Sacrifice. Why should He have done so if God requires no propitiation?" Ritchie pointed to the glaring problem of departure from Catholic principles.[31]

Crapsey indeed started a fire burning in the Episcopal Church community. He quickly succeeded in alienating the dogmatic Anglo-Catholics. Alarm reached even those whom Crapsey had joined earlier in intimate communion. Men separated unto the "mysterium of the Catholic Church," called for a joint effort in standing against the "guile of the Crapseys of the world." Ritchie qualified the acceptable unified church. He argued that if any unity was to exist it had to be according to the necessity to return to a complete devotion to the church on earth, and that included the Roman, the Anglican and the Eastern Orthodox communions uniting in one accord over the voice of the church. Ritchie found unity between the various Apostolic communions in the very concepts that

---

[30] *"Spindrift"* dated April 7, 1900. In Scrapbook #7 of the A.H. Crapsey Jr. Collection, A spindrift is "the blinding drift of salt water blown from the surface of the sea during hurricanes." Definition taken from *Webster's Encyclopedic Dictionary* (Publisher's Guild Inc.: New York, 1941).

[31] Rev. A. Ritchie *Catholic Champion* (New York, 1900).

Crapsey advocated abolishing, by affirmation of the historic doctrines of the faith.[32]

The modern ecumenical movement in the Protestant Episcopal Church began in essence in the 1870s with William Reed Huntington's famous book *The Church Idea.*[33] The church subsequently adopted several of Dr. Huntington's principles at the Chicago General Convention in 1886. Shortly thereafter, the bishops revised and adopted the recommendations of the General Convention at the Lambeth Conference in 1888.[34] Huntington advocated his concept of church unity in publications throughout the 1890s.[35]

Crapsey acknowledged William Reed Huntington's leadership in the movement. He credited Huntington with his changed perspective. In a letter to Huntington about the publication of another tractate, Crapsey called Huntington a pioneer in the field of Christian unity. He credited Huntington with helping him formulate his outlook about the unity of the church. Crapsey noted his tardiness in coming to terms with all that the unity movement espoused. He explained to Huntington that his outlook had developed slowly over time through a somewhat unwilling manner. Crapsey justified his earlier Catholicity by arguing that he had always longed for continuity and membership in the church. His basic ideals had not changed. However, Crapsey's intellect both broadened and expanded. He wrote to Huntington, that "he now belonged to a greater household of faith with more continuity than he had ever imagined." Unfortunately, Crapsey failed to realize the extent of the opposition to the unity movement, which necessarily required broadness and liberality of one's intellect. He wrote naively to Huntington, "I think I can truly say that I am not in controversy with any school of thought in the church."[36]

---

[32] Ibid.

[33] William Reed Huntington *The Church Idea* (New York: E.P. Dutton & Co., 1870).

[34] Several books and journal articles have been published concerning the Chicago-Lambeth Conferences. See Louis August Haselmayer's *Lambeth and Unity* (New York: Morehouse- Gorham, 1948). See also J. Robert Wright ed. "Essays on the Centenary of the Chicago- Lambeth Quadrilateral 1886- 88- 1986- 88: Quadrilateral at One Hundred." In *Anglican Theological Review* Evanston, Ill.: (Supplementary Series # 10, Forward Movement Publications, 1988).

[35] William Reed Huntington *The Peace of the Church* (New York: Scribner's Sons, 1893).

[36] A.S. Crapsey, letter dated Christmas Tide 1899 preceding Tractate # 4, "The Answer to Pilate" In *The Dissapointment of Jesus Christ* (Rochester, 1899) p. 1.

Huntington was then in the midst of a successful career. Recognized as a leader of the broad school, as one of his biographers stated, he was "above all partisan narrowness or exclusiveness." As the rector of Grace Church, New York he was considered a true leader of the Protestant Episcopal Church.[37] Crapsey wrote to Huntington, "In our own communion I have long ceased to be a party man." Crapsey believed that he had the support of all the broad churchmen, Dr. Huntington in particular. However, Huntington later disclosed in a private letter that even he had become extremely disillusioned by Crapsey. He wrote,

> Mr. Davies' letter I enclose. It is interesting as showing that even a typical Broad Churchman finds it impossible to follow Brother Crapsey all lengths. I certainly cannot, and his last 'Tractate' has remained undistributed, though I sent out 100 each of all others.[38]

Crapsey incited opposition in those who argued, "his views were simply destructive." Others criticized his historical accuracy, took issue with his interpretation of the unification that Christ proposed and found his argument about the organization of the church as deriving its authority from men and not Christ as subjective. Crapsey's contentions might be true for the Roman Catholic Church but in the "Oriental and Anglican Churches, Christ alone was indeed the 'centre of the of unity.'"[39]

One author accused Crapsey of "having no unchanging form of belief, doctrine or creed whatsoever." In fact, there was "no inference of divine origin or sanction either." Following Crapsey's line of logic he considered that there was therefore "no authoritative measure involved with religion or any revelatory significance to it at all." The author corrected Crapsey's assumptions that the abuses in the church really started only after the fourth century when the organized church began to flourish. Without directly calling Crapsey a heretic, the author noted that disputations and disunity did not date from the fourth century. A wide

---

[37] Hughes, W.D.F. "Agreement on the Fundamentals: The Huntington- Manning Correspondence on the Crapsey Case." In *Historical Magazine of the Protestant Episcopal Church* 25:3 (1956: Sept.) p. 263.

[38] Letter from Dr. William Reed Huntingtonto a friend dated Dec. 31, 1900, recorded in John Wallace Suter, *Life and Letters of William Reed Huntington : A Champion of Unity* (New York and London, 1925), pgs. 304- 305. Later recorded in Hughes, W.D.F. "Agreement on the Fundamentals: The Huntington- Manning Correspondence on the Crapsey Case." In *Historical Magazine of the Protestant Episcopal Church* 25:3 (1956: Sept.) p. 263.

[39] "Emancipated Unity" In Scrapbook #7, Arthur H. Crapsey Jr. Collection.

range of groups called themselves Christians without the sanction of those who laid the foundations of the historic faith in the first and second centuries. However, even gentle spirits like St. John, well known as the "apostle of love," was similarly "known for his steadfastness against heterodoxy and he remained inflexible to his death." The author wrote sharply, "The greater his love, the deeper his hatred of heresy."[40]

Conservatives found nothing new in Crapsey's writings. They recognized a strain of heretical teaching that went back as far as the church itself. The author of "Emancipated Unity" stated, that they had heard all this before. What surprised them was that "they were now hearing it from one of their own members of the clergy." The author associated Crapsey with the heresy of the past categorizing him with the liberals of the present, "It is precisely the 'liberal' platform, as illustrated by the 'Mid-continent Congress of Religions' in Chicago the other day."[41]

Crapsey and the liberals did not simply attack the organization and the doctrinal underpinnings of the Church innocently; they attacked those who had placed their faith in the efficacy of the institution itself. For the conservatives, Anglo- Catholic or evangelical, Crapsey's writings were not creative insight into contemporary problems. Instead, they were a reversion to the age-old errors rooted in individual aggrandizement. Meanwhile, Crapsey pointed to Jesus Christ conveniently declaring he placed himself under His authority. But he skirted the issue of just who Jesus Christ was. Though he once had railed against the Unitarian concept of the second person of the Godhead, Crapsey found himself formulating notions of Jesus more as the Son of God and less as God the Son.

Crapsey seized every opportunity to put his developing intellectual perspectives into practical action. While raising so many eyebrows attacking both the organization and the dogma of the church, Crapsey also defended several highly visible social causes demonstrating his approach towards complete toleration. Though previously repentant over the contention he had once caused by coming against his clerical brethren in print, he obviously now reveled in the new controversy his writings engendered.[42]

By 1901 he was busy defending the Negro, the Roman Catholic Church in the Caribbean and the Philippines and his manifesto on church unity. Crapsey entered new and dangerous territory, suitable for only the

---

[40] Ibid.

[41] Ibid.

[42] Column of no title, labeled as appearing in the *New York Daily Tribunal* dated only 1901. A.H. Crapsey Jr. Collection, Scrapbooks.

most cautious, diplomatic thinkers. His activism highlighted the controversy swirling around him. Rather than shunning attention, Crapsey made himself the epicenter of contention. With the publication of the seventh tractate in his series entitled *"God's Winnowing Fan,"* he now stepped onto a wilderness path familiar to only a select few. Bishop Colenso of South Africa had been lost on that path. Few dared to tread the reaches of this wilderness Crapsey hazarded to call the truth.[43]

In his final tractate of the series, Crapsey presented his concept of the utility of historical and biblical criticism. He also attacked two historic doctrines of the church, that of the Virgin Birth, and the role of Satan on earth. Crapsey's elucidation of these doctrines now verged on definable heresy.

Crapsey began by ridiculing those who held fast to the doctrine of the inerrancy of the scriptures, superstitiously worried that they might loose their salvation if they gave it up. The time of the writings, places involved, the events described and the authorship of the scriptures were all in question.[44] Crapsey believed critical methodology applied to the Holy Bible in the same way it did to other books of antiquity. He refused to entertain any other explanations, especially those supporting apologetic or traditional perspectives. In reference to the plenary inspiration of the scriptures he concluded, "As all books were written so were these written." For Crapsey, "each book stood" and was "judged by itself." Crapsey considered, Job "a sublime philosophical novel. Isaiah, could not have "lived and wrote in the days of the Babylonist Captivity, mentioning by name Cyrus the Persian who was not born until a century and more after the prophet was dead." According to Crapsey, no explanation existed for "a writer in the days of Darius the Median, to imitate the language and the literary style, which came into existence and allude to events that happened in the days of Antiochus Epiphanes, two centuries later."[45]

Crapsey failed to grasp any relevance in the conservative response calling for a change in perspective from a natural to the supernatural when reading prophecy or the Bible. To conservatives, the answers were both timeless and clear, Isaiah was able to name Cyrus because God inspired him and the ability to name the person centuries before he became king demonstrated the supernatural validity of the scriptures. He also failed to answer the persistent questions the conservatives asked. What about Jesus, who was He, and why did He have to die? What did He die for? What did

---

[43] Crapsey, *Disappointment,* "God's Winnowing Fan" (Rochester, 1902) pp. 1-48.
[44] Ibid., pp. 24-5.
[45] Ibid., p. 28.

the scriptures say about themselves? What did the scriptures say about Christ and what did Christ say about the scriptures? Crapsey contended that the scriptures had finally passed to sound scholarship that would eventually unravel the questions that the texts provoked. For Crapsey, academics held the future to "the intellectual, moral and spiritual life of man."[46]

Crapsey emphasized that biblical criticism would scientifically answer the age-old questions of the bible unhampered by superstition or external interference. He assumed that eventually a new generation would learn to read the scriptures in the light of the scientific truth. This enlightenment would alone bring Christians, Catholic or Protestant together as Protestants especially were divided over their petty, unempirical misunderstandings of the scriptures. Once the authority over the texts had passed into the hands of the academics any impediment to Christian unity should pass as well. Crapsey concluded that "unity could be achieved by impartially understanding the intellectual barriers that separated them while emphasizing the virtues that they all shared."[47]

Tradition, according to Crapsey, caused many of the problems that lingered on in the contemporary church, including the Catholic concept of the Virgin Mary. With an audacity sure to alienate both the Roman and Anglo-Catholic communities, Crapsey boldly stated,

> The Catholic Virgin is purely traditional. She has no basis in history at all. She is a mythical and legendary character created out of the slightest historical material.

What was worse, Crapsey compared her to Diana, the Greek goddess, believing the legends of Mary developed because the great triune God of the Bible was so huge, impersonal and mysterious, that people needed something more human to relate to.[48]

Crapsey endeavored to explain the Virgin mother in rational terms.

> As the Virgin she inspired love, as a mother veneration; as a woman she was the consoler of human sorrow, as Queen of Heaven and Mother of God she was the dispenser of divine favors.

---

[46] Ibid., p. 29.
[47] Ibid., p. 31.
[48] Ibid., pp. 32-3.

Crapsey now regretted the turn away from rationalism producing such myths and legends. Nevertheless, he still identified with the romanticism of his earlier medieval perspective considering that the Virgin mother was the "very incarnation of the emotional nature of man." With a characteristic lack of discretion, Crapsey continued,

> In the worship of the Virgin and the saints the pagan world avenged itself for the loss of its gods and goddesses. The Virgin as she has been worshipped in Catholic countries for a thousand years and more is as mythological as any of her pagan predecessors.[49]

Crapsey pointed to dogma as the villain. Explaining how it encouraged obstacles to unity he blamed Pope Pius the IX's decree of the Immaculate Conception in 1854 as the doctrine that turned the myth into fact. Crapsey refused any ground to the supernatural dogma of the Roman church by declaring "the decrees of the Vatican council were antithetical to modern scientific thinking and thus to modern progress."[50]

Conversely, Crapsey exalted the doctrines of science as genuinely empirical. He argued emphatically, "neither historical events nor factual occurrences could be instituted by the decrees of a Pope. Arbitration of these matters depended upon substantial evidence, and there was absolutely none at all for the assumption of Mary that could stand up to a test of scientific examination."[51]

In Crapsey's mind, Catholicism retained its myths but so did Protestantism. All needed dispelling for the sake of unity. Protestant myths were perhaps even more destructive. To stir the coals of passion and incite the flames of intellectual insurrection Crapsey wrote, "If the Catholic worships his Virgin, the Protestant fears and in a manner worships his Devil called Satan."

Jumping on the bandwagon of anti- Puritan diatribe rampant in the contemporary literature, Crapsey blamed the "gloomy imagination of the Puritan" mind for inventing the myth of Satan's personal involvement in human affairs and allowing it to develop historically. Utilizing the scriptures to prove what he wanted while discarding those that disagreed with him Crapsey resolved, "The Devil or Satan is of necessity mythological." Crapsey considered the Hebrews' ignorance of Satan

---

[49] Ibid., pp. 33-4.
[50] Ibid., p. 34.
[51] Ibid., p. 34.

conspicuous. Completely disregarding the argument about the reference to Lucifer in Isaiah he wrote,

> In the Hebrew scriptures the Devil plays a very subordinate and variable part. The earlier Hebrew writers, such as Amos and Isaiah know nothing of him. Isaiah especially has no place for such a being as Satan in his philosophy.[52]

Crapsey considered the devil as "the truly significant piece in the Calvinist scheme of salvation." Crapsey's designation of redemption by the vicarious atonement of the Lord Jesus Christ as a "scheme" could not have endeared him to those who sat in authority over him. Neither would he gain the commiseration of his peers in the ministry, let alone the sympathy of unassuming believers who relied on sacerdotal influences to help guide them in their faith. In his contempt for conservative theology Crapsey argued that "the whole purpose for the incarnation as they understood it, was so Christ's work would undo that of Satan's. The conservatives posed a balance of power in favor of Satan to purposely justify their dogma that began with Satan defeating God in the garden and receiving the entire world from that time forward until the advent of the Lord. And now, according to the evangelicals Christ has only been able to save a small portion of humanity from the grip of the devil. The rest of the world is still in the hands of the enemy and his unholy angels." Therefore, if Satan were taken out of the equation the entire "scheme" of conservative salvation would utterly fall apart.[53]

Crapsey credited "Milton's muse" of *Paradise Lost* for securing Satan's place in the popular imagination. Crapsey went so far as to intonate that, in the book, as well as in the resulting dogmatic scheme, Satan's role was not only equal to God but actually superior. Nevertheless, for Crapsey that proved nothing at all. In the end, "Satan would have to leave the minds of modern man because a God who was subservient to the devil was simply not worth believing in."[54]

Crapsey concluded that the God that he believed in was more likened unto a concept known as truth. The way to get to this God was not necessarily as the Christian Church had traditionally taught, through the reception of the grace of God through faith in the sacrifice of the Lord Jesus Christ on the cross, qualifying one for entrance into the family of

---

[52] Ibid., pp. 35-6.
[53] Ibid., p. 37.
[54] Ibid., pp. 37- 8.

God. Rather, the reception of hard historical fact, attained through vigorous scientific endeavor was the real way to God. He contended,

> The trained intelligence which is explaining and so resolving into its elements the great Catholic myth of the Virgin and the great Protestant myth of Satan will continue to work until it has resolved all myth, legend and tradition and brought all men to the sober solid ground of historic truth and reality and upon that ground all parties not only may but must meet; for there is the meeting place of truth and God is truth.[55]

On the other hand, Crapsey lauded the scriptures for their continuing utility. Crapsey saw in the Christian and Hebrew scriptures legends containing the richest treasures of spiritual truth available. By spiritual he now presumably meant allegoric or symbolic. Crapsey perceived the operational significance of the scriptures as "striking deep into the heart of humanity compelling men to personal piety and society to righteousness." Although the scriptures may not have been literally true they were in this way, inspired by God. But the "inspiration of the Old Testament had passed and a time of social commentary and tradition had been superimposed on the religion of the Jews, so much so that by the time of Jesus the true meaning of the Hebrew Scriptures had been all but lost." Jesus arrived assuming the role of the true Rabbi or Master. With his "winnowing fan," he, in fact, separated out the chaff from the grain and brought new life to the scriptures. Nevertheless, the process of accumulating social commentary and tradition through literary legends continued unabated up to modern times.[56]

This new scripture confined the old to its original setting while liberating the new texts from their narrow surroundings. They ultimately became the "revered literature of the western world and have inspired the west to realize the greatest civilizations known to the history man." Crapsey respected the scriptures for their spiritual content, but made an important distinction between literal and literary truth. He praised the depth and beauty of the literature as unparalleled in history due to its inspirational quality. He especially loved Isaiah. Quoting the fifty-fifth chapter,

> As the rain cometh down and the snow from heaven and returneth not thither, but watereth the earth, and maketh it bring forth and to bud, so

[55] Ibid., p. 38.
[56] Ibid., p. 45.

> shall my word be that proceedeth out of my mouth; it shall not return to me void, but it shall accomplish that whereunto I sent it."

The prophet spoke of how God's ways were so much more awesome than our ways. For Crapsey, God did not just give the world a book with all necessary truth in it and was then done with it all. There was continuing revelation of God's truth to man. Crapsey believed that revelation to both the sinner and the saint through God's Word was like a "passionate storm." Criticism could not dispel the kind of truth it imparted. Criticism could only describe the processes involved. Crapsey believed the Bible was woven into "mind and soul" of mankind without which human consciousness itself would be destroyed.[57]

For Crapsey, the "Word of God" was a metaphor. God's revelation applied to all of human life, not only to the scriptures. Dispensations never precluded the direct revelation of God to men. Crapsey figured himself as a modern day prophet. In a similar way to the others throughout time, God spoke in and through him. He concluded that God's manner of speaking through the prophets would never end as long as the world existed and the Holy Ghost moved in men. [58]

Crapsey's defense of the established ministry was gone. He had lost all confidence in the foundational doctrines of Christianity. On one hand, Crapsey defended the metaphoric content of the scriptures as truths imperative for humanity. But, he now considered them nothing more than allegory. Eventually, he elevated the status of other writings, literary, historical and scientific to a place of inspirational equity with the scriptures. While doing so, he envisioned a special place for himself as a prophet of God. He also envisioned suffering for his courage to bring his own revelation of the "word of God" forth. With the publication of his tractates Crapsey entered upon a course he considered necessary to the advancement of civilization. He called for the proper understanding of myth and legend. He realized the determination of the opposition and welcomed the oncoming conflict. He would not shirk from his responsibility. Interestingly, Crapsey never mentioned how prophecy played out in his life, like in the way he had been named before he had been martyred though he must have thought about it constantly. He was certainly willing to receive a prophet's reward by paying a martyr's price for his conviction about the truth, just like his once ostracized grandfather had, just like his namesake had received at the hands of the restorers of the

[57] Ibid., pp. 45-7.
[58] Ibid., p. 47.

kingdom. One wonders if he ever saw the irony in that, or if he ever considered whether he had been born to a special kind martyrdom himself with the prophetic appellation of his name.

CHAPTER TEN

"Greater Love Hath No Man Than This"

While he was writing additional tractates, Hobart College invited Crapsey to the graduation ceremony in the spring of 1900. Crapsey preached the Baccalaureate Sermon at the commencement and for the seventy-fifth anniversary of the founding of the college. Geneva Academy was founded in 1796, but it wasn't chartered as a college for men until 1825 when it became known as Geneva College. In 1852, the school was renamed Hobart College for the Episcopal bishop.[1]

Crapsey arrived on Wednesday, June 20, 1900 to receive the prestigious award of the STD.[2] He would no longer need to correct those who referred to him as "Dr. Crapsey" with embarrassing regularity. Nevertheless, the press continued to mistakenly refer to him as "D.D." for the rest of his life. His extraordinary work as a missioner and the twenty plus years of successful service at St. Andrew's Church in Rochester apparently qualified him for the honorary degree. Perhaps his growing status hastened some in liberal circles to recommend an honorary degree to forestall opposition to his controversial writings.

Forever energetic and prolific, Crapsey declined an opportunity for intellectual repose with the completion of his tractates. His new opinion about the inspired nature of literature written with a didactic or prophetic message motivated his first literary endeavor. Crapsey completed his only work of fiction by 1902. The novel's characters are based on people Crapsey knew while working in New York City. He admitted that while he was working as a teacher at the Duane Street Lodging House for Boys he had actually met the heroine.[3]

---

[1] *Hobart College Catalog: 1998- 1999.* (Geneva, N.Y.: Hobart and William Smith Colleges, 1998).

[2] Personal communication with Charlotte Hegyi, archivist and associate librarian Joseph Chmura, Hobart and William Smith Colleges, Geneva, NY. *Echo Yearbook of 1902,* p. 29- 30.

[3] Review "The Library: Within It and Beyond It." June 28' 1902 A.H. Crapsey Jr. Collection, Scrapbooks.

Unfortunately, during the writing of the novel his oldest daughter, Emily Margaret died suddenly from appendicitis. Emily received credit for her beauty and intelligence during her short life. But instead of going off to college as Adelaide did to Vassar, Emily opted to stay at home and work in Rochester. Engaged to a young man, Channing Moore, she took a job as a stenographer in the office of attorneys Remington, Gifford and Willey, at the Lincoln Alliance Bank Building in Rochester. She left her work one day in early April, and died after a brief illness on April 13, 1901.[4]

Tragic sorrow engulfed Crapsey delaying the completion of his novel. In his dedication for the book he mentioned how he regularly deferred to Emily's criticism. He wrote,

> Now that he is about to submit his creation to the colder impartial judgment of the reading public, the writer wishes to say, that, whatever may be the fate of his book, he has already been amply repaid for any labor and anxiety it may have cost him, by the fact that it gave some pleasure and added some interest to the last days on earth of Emily Margaret Crapsey; who was both the loving daughter and the judicious friend of the writer, and to whose blessed memory and pure spirit, as an act of gratitude for all that she was to him and of all that she did for him, he now dedicates this book.[5]

Beginning with the death of young Ruth, further sorrows now complicated the personal life of the rector. The illness and sometime incapacitation of his eldest son and now, the sudden death of lovely Emily brought depression and deep personal anguish. Crapsey and his family struggled to find meaning in such a horrendous event. A wealthy benefactor from St. Andrew's Church, Mrs. Watson, endowed a bed at the Homeopathic Hospital in memory of Emily. Some of the women of the church furnished one of the rooms at the church home in Emily's memory also.[6] Adelaide, who had gone off to school with her to Wisconsin was overwhelmed. She was Emily's loving mate separated by only one year. After Vassar she took a teaching job back at Kemper Hall. She reminisced about her sister and tried to relax in the security, strength and mental adroitness of the Episcopal nuns.[7]

---

[4] Letter to Dr. John Lowe, October 8, 1948, Adelaide Crapsey Papers, Rochester Public Library. Also in Alkalay- Gut, *Alone* pp. 110-1.

[5] Dedication from A.S. Crapsey *The Greater Love* New York: Abbey Press, 1902.

[6] Crapsey, *Manuscript,* p. 174.

[7] Alkalay- Gut, *Alone,* p. 114.

Beset by emotional depletion, Crapsey found refuge in his work. He returned to the privacy of his study to complete his novel. But the book became an emotional albatross for Crapsey as Emily had read, edited and provided useful criticism for its publication. *Greater Love,* received good reviews for an initial novel, although Crapsey later mused that the novel "spawned a diverse assortment of opinions."[8] One review announced the novel as "powerful" and sure to arouse widespread interest locally. The reviewer considered it a straightforward kind of "social study" of the 19th century.[9]

But overall, Crapsey figured it a failure. He completed the latter part of the book quickly after Emily died. He felt the section about London was particularly poor. He wrote, "The book was the work of an amateur; it was a mistake, a bad mistake to carry Dr. Suydam to London." He blamed poor judgment for releasing the book instead of revising it while he was in a traumatic state due to the death of his daughter. He later wrote that he would have changed the novel and published another edition if not for the advent of his heresy trial and the collapse of the publisher.[10]

The book exposed Crapsey's prevailing fantasy. Subtitled, *A Story of Modern Martyrdom,* it provides insight into his developing psychological state. His hero exemplified the type of Christianity that Crapsey advocated. Dr. Suydam is a kind man of both piety and action. Crapsey's words reveal a glimpse into both the tragic Victorian romantic style as well as his own psychological composition. He wrote,

> The reader of this history will find out why it was that a clergyman, who up to his fortieth year was irreproachable in his calling, honored as a scholar, and almost worshipped as a preacher, suddenly fell from the high place which he held in the world, was divorced by his wife and deposed by his bishop, and passed the rest of his life in obscurity, and was buried in a nameless grave.[11]

The protagonist is a woman named Keturah. In the Bible, Keturah, the concubine, became the wife of Abraham after the death of Sarah. The children of Abraham and Keturah were not heir to the promise of God, or their father.[12] The children of Keturah became desert tribes like Ishmael,

---

[8] Crapsey, Manuscript.

[9] Ibid.

[10] Ibid.

[11] Crapsey, *Greater,* p. 11.

[12] *Harpers Bible Dictionary* Paul J. Achtemeier, Gen. Ed. San Francisco: Harper & Row, 1985 p. 524. The scriptures designate six tribes as descending from

the child of Hagar, literally fulfilling the prophecy that Abraham would be the father of many nations. Employing the contemporary method of using biblical names as a metaphoric tool, the symbolism is both provocative and rich.

He attempted to answer the question, "what of those who are not heir to the promise either from the beginning or now?" He realized that life was not easy for most of humanity. And yet, one could separate the moral from the material when evaluating the quality of life. He believed the quality of life was attained through hard work and sacrifice. Crapsey even questioned Christianity's exclusive hold on the moral quality of life now. His theme centered on meaningful, moral experiences both inside and outside the body of the believers.

In Crapsey's novel, Keturah descended from "native Yankee stock." Keturah's father was beaten each Sunday for his insufferably happy and presumably irreligious ways as a youth. Her father, Joshua Bain, finally left home for being beaten once too often by his Puritan father after kissing his beau on a long Sunday afternoon at church. He eventually fled to New York City with his child bride where in due time they set up a thriving trading business. As time progressed, Joshua had three children. Keturah was the oldest. They owned a nice cottage by the river where Joshua's boat was docked. His business took him throughout the coastal region of the Atlantic where he piloted a trading vessel, the Falmouth.

Inevitably, he contacted so many drunken traders that he became one himself. His estrangement from religion of any kind, due to the harshness of his father's Puritanism had left him exposed to the barren meaninglessness of life. One day, Keturah watched from the shore as her father drunkenly piloted his craft. Subsequently he crashed into a prison vessel sinking it. In the process three prisoners and two of the guards died. Respect for her father evaporated. He was sued and lost everything. Her mother turned to opium and they were forced to sell their cottage and shamefully rent the same home. Meanwhile, a millionaire developer built a brownstone row house in front of their cottage blocking their sunlight and their once treasured view of the river.

During the draft riots of the Civil War, her brother Benjamin was pushed down the stairs of a hotel as he watched the proceedings. He was left for dead until someone finally took him to Bellevue Hospital. Keturah eventually found him there. His injury crippled him physically and

---

Keturah and Abraham's offspring. They were from the sons Zimran, Jokshan, Medan, Midian, Ishbak, and Shuah. They settled to the south and east of the Hebrews. See Gen. 25: 1- 6, and 1 Chron. 1- 33.

mentally. Keturah's hope for his help with the family income instantly vanished. She provided for her younger sister alone. She also cared for the children at an Irish woman's orphanage. At Mother Magrath's, the abandoning of unwanted babies coupled with horrendous conditions caused the children to die like flies. But through doting nurturing, Keturah helped to save one of them and eventually set him up as a bootblack. He worked in front of Mike Cronin's saloon all day and night making just enough money to keep him alive. Because he had no name, they called him "Shinar," for the "shiner of shoes."

Keturah worked day and night in a sweatshop-sewing establishment for a Jewish entrepreneur, Mr. Rosenthal. Because of her character, derived from her native Yankee blood, especially compared to the other immigrant girls, she was promoted to supervisor of her shift. Crapsey's liberal nature did not hide his social Darwinism or his native bigotry and arrogance. As supervisor, she had to inform the poor girls when their wages were cut ten percent or more at times, and was sometimes made to fire them outright. Through all of these problems Keturah selflessly supported a physically and psychologically incapacitated family.

Keturah represents the virtuous, hard- working poor. Interestingly, she is one of the native poor. Crapsey demonstrated little or no sympathy for the immigrant stock in his novel. Keturah's one hope is to provide an escape for her sister from the tenements. Her father gains prestige in the neighborhood by bringing in votes for the local political machine. The Irish boss-run machine maintained ties all the way to the top of the political venue in New York.

Keturah forsakes all hope for personal happiness even though her beau remains ever faithful. She never understood the ways of God because her alcoholic father hated religion due to the abuse he suffered at the hands of his fanatic, misguided father. He refused any kind of religious association for his family. One moral malady after another resulted from his lack of character. Nevertheless, Keturah represents the virtuous, yet pagan, working poor. Crapsey disseminated the opinion that some poor people were deserving of help. Society should contribute to their economic well-being and foster a sense of decency in their lives.

In desperation Keturah enters an Episcopal Church during a rain shower one day and listens to the stirring message of a priest. She eventually develops a sacerdotal relationship with him. She learns through conversation and by witnessing his piety that God touches the lives of ordinary people. Dr. Suydam's deep social roots, independent wealth and position of high standing as the rector of a prestigious church makes him a target for rich women. Nouveau riche widows especially try to trap him into matrimony to gain higher social status. To escape the scandal of publicly kissing a manipulative woman in a moment of emotional indiscretion, Suydam decides to do the honorable thing and marry her. He summarily becomes the stepfather to two grown but spoiled rich children. The children seek a place in high society at the expense of whoever gets in their way. His step-daughter, schemes to marry a member of a noble but financially depleted family from England. Meanwhile, she compromises her latent quest for love in marriage. Her independent wealth bails the royal family out and establishes an important position in high society for herself. Representing the wealthy, virtuous and hereditarily ingrained element of the traditional Episcopal Church, Suydam is trapped by marriage into the crass, compromising and quasi-pagan world of the ambitious nouveau riche.

As the plot thickens one finds that the rich and powerful, Crapsey's antagonists, are members of Suydam's congregation. They control the graft and vice all the way from the neighborhood bosses to the top of the city government. Keturah's father plots with some small time crooks to topple a neighborhood boss. When the political intrigue runs its course, the mayor, himself one of Suydam's parishioners, flees the city to avoid prosecution. Keturah opens Dr. Suydam's eyes to the graft around him. He finally realizes his role as an isolated figurehead, a dupe of sorts, once unwilling to recognize the dire corruption of those all around him. In a way, Crapsey was now railing against the very church he had been employed by for two decades. Not only the leadership but now even the laity came under his symbolic criticism.

Meanwhile, Keturah's sister is the only one with any real hope of leaving tenement life. Keturah paid for her to get the best education possible. She works long, extra hours to provide a fine dress for her graduation and enough money for a night out afterwards. She believes in her sister's ability to escape the tenement existence due to her education, cultivation and beauty. Nevertheless, Abigail, Keturah's sister, naively allows a wealthy suitor to prey upon her. Ironically, she meets him in Suydam's church. Flattered to be offered a seat with the elite in his private pew, he entraps her, eventually using her as a kind of showpiece demonstrative of his cavalier existence. He leaves her pregnant, shamed, ruined and penniless abandoning her abroad in London. Dr. Suydam is deeply grieved by the information he hears from Keturah.

Eventually Suydam realizes his wealthy step-son caused this travesty to befall Keturah's family. Against the will of his wealthy, social climbing, manipulative wife, he goes abroad to do the honorable thing. He intends to correct the wrong done to Abigail. But wealthy British gentlemen recognize Suydam in the red- light district of Piccadilly Circus as he searches for the young woman. They irreverently and erroneously expose him as a partaker of the vice. He innocently endures the criticism returning with Abigail and another ex-prostitute whose life was also shattered by decadent British peers. Sued for divorce, his bishop begs him to expose the scandal and uphold the good name of the church. Suydam however opts to do the honorable thing again, refusing further exposure of his estranged family. He endures his own cross, sacrificially allowing for his divorce without contestation. Dr. Suydam is eventually excommunicated from the church. He continues however with his own type of ministry. Keturah introduces him to the street people and he ministers to them with his own resources.

Keturah's sister marries Shinar the poor orphan boy. He becomes the heir to mother Magrath's, scant fortune. The inheritance is just big enough to get them started on a farm in the Ohio Valley where no one will ever know their past. They raise a large family and become wealthy landowners. Keturah finally marries her beau who waited for over a decade for her hand. She was however, well past her prime by then. She has a baby in her middle age and it dies in infancy. The strain of losing her child becomes too much for her and she slowly ebbs away.

Keturah dies in the arms of her lover, without experiencing all the benefits of life and love. She is buried on a hill overlooking the great city of New York. Her life, like Dr. Suydam's, is a superlative example to others. Although there was no indication that she ever had any real relationship with God, Keturah's tombstone reads, "Her life was a Sacrifice of Sweet Savour unto the Lord." Dr. Suydam dies after contracting a fever from the poor sheep he went out to pastor. He is buried without any enduring legacy other than the love of the people whose lives he touched. He is buried at the foot of Keturah at a right angle to her casket.

As friends and relatives gather at the gravesites of Suydam and Keturah twenty years later, they realize the inspirational testimony of their friends' unfortunately shortened lives. The woman who Dr. Suydam retrieved from England, granting her a new start in life in America, states to Keturah's widower, "'Look John look,' said the woman pointing to the great city that lay in the growing darkness of the night, 'the dead do not need us; we can do nothing for them; down yonder are the living, crying for help; let us go to them.'"[13]

[13] Ibid., p. 453.

The lesson is clear, money, influence and power were not the way to escape the depravity of life. Neither was contemporary religion. In its then, present-day form it was only a shadow of the reality of one's inner goodness. Hard work and depth of character was the key to a good life especially when that meant adversity and sacrifice. Crapsey refused to concede that American social strength was based on the dogmatic foundations of the Puritans. However, he forwarded the notion that hereditary factors like "pure Yankee stock," rather than Slavic, Irish, Jewish or southern European blood, provided Keturah with a distinct, moral advantage. It characterized her sacrificial deportment. Though portrayed in Victorian fashion somewhat as victims, the women of Crapsey's novel were also strong and progressive enough to realize their possibilities. Like Suydam, the country needed loosening from its old religious moorings. Once set afloat, a sea of possibilities attended one with a broadened mindset and a strong work ethic.

One reviewer quoting the novel wrote, "It is not strange that an ordinary Protestant minister should be ignorant of the spiritual condition of the people under his charge." But in affect, "there came a time when Dr. Suydam's eyes were opened." The reviewer noted that Dr. Suydam, "began to look upon himself and the social class to which he belonged as vampires, who were sucking the life-blood of the poor." The reviewer recognized Crapsey's anxiety about how the people paid deeply, sometimes with their very souls, for the luxury of a few. Their honor and purity were often relinquished and sacrificed on the altar of materialism shared by the elite few. The Episcopal Church, which denied Crapsey his bishopric, was being portrayed as thoroughly hostile to Crapsey's ideal version of the gospel of Christ.[14] Crapsey's social message spoke clearly through the novel about the failure of contemporary Christianity. Simply;

> The religion of the Master had been betrayed by its own disciples. The power and success of the world had laid hold of the machinery of the Christian religion and were using it for their own advantage. They were keeping the people quiet by the hope of a world to come, while they themselves were seizing and enjoying the world that now is.[15]

For Crapsey the highest calling was still the selfless example of Christ-like sacrifice. Crapsey's heroes were feminine as well as masculine. Dr.

---

[14] Letter to editor of *Post Express* from Jane Marsh Parker in Crapsey, *Manuscript,* pp. 266b, c & d.

[15] Quoted from letter to Chicago newspaper in Crapsey, *Manuscript,* p. 265.

Suydam represents both Christian virtue and nativistic heritage. But Keturah Bain never makes a profession of faith. Each one gives of their selves, fulfilling their responsibilities. The trait of sacrificial giving, or what Crapsey considered as modern martyrdom, was worthy of honor. It was not one's faith alone necessarily, but their work that proved their character and that distinguished them. Or perhaps as James considered the most "Catholic" of all the writers of scripture said, "one's works proved their faith.[16]

The rich especially the tactless, crude, nouveau riche are the villains in this story. Crapsey obviously had them pegged. He disdained the haughtiness of the Protestant Episcopal Church. He despised the hypocrisy of those sitting under his teachings week after week, year by year but never showing the fruits of a life given over to God. Keturah and Suydam were similar in their heritage, natives for many generations. Moreover, both held similar moral values. These went beyond the character traits of the various "races" then pouring into the nation by the droves. Crapsey expressed his socialistic sympathy through religious discontent, moral purpose and social Darwinism. Crapsey's mind teetered on the edge of religious frustration, social and economic consternation and political activism.

A fellow priest praised Crapsey's style as "Simple, direct, nothing lyrical or over-wrought in diction or detail, yet every sentence vibrates with the force of moral passion or conviction that inspires the work."[17] The metaphors are clear also. The greater love is the sacrificial love that Christ spoke of when he stated, "Greater love hath no man than this, that a man lay down his life for his friends."[18] In an interesting twist from the scene at the tomb of Jesus, where the angels of the Lord asked the women "why seek ye the living among the dead," the characters at the end of the book that remain realize that they also must not seek the dead, but the living.[19] As Christ had counseled, "let the dead bury the dead, but go thou and preach the Kingdom of God."[20] The remaining characters finally understand the examples of sacrifice and then they also seek to help the poor and needy. Crapsey called for greater commitment to emulate Christ,

---

[16] Martin Luther once remarked tellingly, that James should not be in the modern canon.

[17] Letter from R.R. Converse to the Editor of the *Post Express* Rochester, June 30, 1902 Crapsey, *Manuscript* pp. 266a & b.

[18] Jn. 15: 13.

[19] Luke 24: 4.

[20] Luke 9: 60.

through the inspirational example of his fiction. Those with wealth and power would come and go but "the Kingdom of God would remain forever." For the sake of the Kingdom, men and women of valor must perpetuate the greater love.

On a different level, Crapsey called for individual commitment and social responsibility. He deplored the graft running rampant throughout the urban areas around the nation. A true distinction between the prosperity of Western society and the ultimate aim of the Kingdom of God remained. The Kingdom must be established in righteousness and provide blessings for society in principled ways. The Christ Crapsey now described was not the same as the one he had sermonized about in the past. Crapsey was moving ever closer to conceiving of Jesus as the Unitarian archetype he once deplored.

Crapsey actually knew the characters that he attempted to immortalize of Keturah and Dr. Suydam. One reviewer wrote, "The acquaintance of the writer with this remarkable woman ripened into friendship that lasted as long as she lived." The reviewer continued, "There will be much speculation as to the identity of this clergyman; and already the rector of a great church, who left the ministry and went abroad many years ago has been suggested as the original of the character." [21] Another reviewer wrote, "To the many admirers of the author, it will be good news that he has found time, among his charitable enterprises, his discussion of social topics, to do something distinctly literary."[22] A different reviewer wrote, that the book was, "a study of social conditions in New York in the middle of the last century." Crapsey's illumination of the time was important because, "The period is one of intense interest and significance and furnishes a scarce-touched literary field." Furthermore, "Rev. Dr. Crapsey's first novel is likely to prove both interesting and influential."[23] The press knew of Crapsey's ventures at seeking unity by attacking the traditional organization and doctrines of the church. Subsequently, one portion of the press rallied around Crapsey and his liberal causes. They embraced the provocative nature of the novel. Another reviewer wrote, "The readers of *'The Greater Love'* are sure to disagree in deciding whether Dr. Suydam was a saint and a martyr or one of those who are so easily misled by the buzzing of a bee in the bonnet. A book that leaves

---

[21] Review from *"The Library: Within It and Beyond It."* June 28, 1902 in A.H. Crapsey Jr. Collection, Scrapbooks.

[22] News clipping in A.H. Crapsey Jr. Collection.

[23] Article in A.H. Crapsey Collection Scrapbooks.

something like this for its readers to discuss with considerable spirit has in it the element of success."[24]

Critical acclaim abounded, but numerous detractors surfaced as well. Speaking of the publication Crapsey wrote, "By some it was hailed as the greatest novel of recent times; by others it was set down as an amateur, indecent production." Delving as it did into the world of harlotry while sharing its pages with the life of a decent, pious churchman was obviously provocative for its day. Crapsey noted ironically that, "The book shared the fate of its author; it had bitter enemies and enthusiastic friends."[25]

Crapsey's decision to unilaterally present a pagan woman in similar moral context with a male clergyman was notable for its time. Their native cultivation makes them similar, perhaps even comparable. This evolutionary component championed by another Rochesterian, Lewis Henry Morgan, brought society into focus for the maturing clergyman. Darwin's theories of stratified biological life systems were readily adapted to include ethnic categories, social systems, societies, and individual people. The scientific adaptations resulted in endless classifications. Meanwhile, white, Anglo- Saxon, western- European society prevailed at the top of the comparative ladder. Crapsey's emulation of Morgan and Darwin resulted in his depiction of Suydam and Keturah as morally superior through the production of his didactic novel advocating ethical, as well as social evolution.

And yet, neither the religious reviewers nor the literary critics actually would get what was truly at the core of Crapsey's one and only novel. He was giving the world a glimpse of what was on the horizon for him. His thoughts that prophecy and continuous revelation could be brought about in a contemporary sense had likewise motivated Crapsey to foreshadow his own great venture into sacrificial martyrdom. Crapsey tellingly saw the fictional world of Dr. Suydam as a prophecy in its own right. In his mind, he would eventually fulfill that prophecy thereby establishing himself as a true prophet of God.

---

[24] Letter from Jane Marsh Parker to the editor of the *Post Express* Rochester, July 8, 1902.

[25] A.S. Crapsey *Unpublished Manuscript* p. 263.

CHAPTER ELEVEN

"Go Ye Into all the World"

The lore that grew up concerning Algernon around the Crapsey family in the later years of his life was that "he was no great intellectual, just a simple parish priest."[1] Though ignorant of Ritschlian theology, he embraced Anglican developments that paralleled continental theologies. He was especially interested in historical criticism. Moreover, he assumed that man's moral development could correspond with his technological progress by applying scientific methods.[2]

While writing his novel, Crapsey engaged in another controversy within the church. Americans considered what to do with the recent acquisitions resulting from the Spanish-American War. The Episcopal Church contemplated whether as the new administrators of the Philippines, Cuba and Puerto Rico they should evangelize the native people into the Protestantism of the United States. An argument arose in the Episcopal Church over whether they should send a bishop to the Philippines to aid in the conversion process. Evangelicals maintained a strong presence in the Protestant Episcopal Church in spite of the break-off and formation of the Reformed Episcopalian Church.[3] Moreover, the consistent gains of liberals in seminaries and academic institutions in the American church brought further pressure to bear upon the evangelicals.[4]

The battle in the Episcopal press seemed to be between the Anglo-Catholics and the evangelicals over missions to the Philippines. However, the true antagonism to evangelical plans for mass conversions came from

---

[1] Personal communication with Arthur H. Crapsey Jr.

[2] Although Crapsey denied knowledge of Ritschl while teaching theology in Canada he obviously soon learned of him and adopted precepts like relying solely upon the "factual, historical basis of the New Testament." *The Westminster Dictionary of Christian Theology* Alan Richardson and John Bowden eds. (Phila.: The Westminster Press, 1983) p.326.

[3] Allen C. Guelzo *For the Union of Evangelical Christendom: The Irony of Reformed Episcopalians* (Univ. Park, Pa: Penn State Univ. Press, 1994).

[4] J.I. Packer "The Oxford Evangelicals in Theology ," in J.S. Reynolds *The Evangelicals at Oxford.* (Oxford: Marcham Manor Press, 1975).

the broad-church faction. While Crapsey's emotional ties were still strong towards the Anglo-Catholic portion of the church, his social, economic and political interests had broadened considerably. Crapsey's dismay at the church's decision to send a bishop to the Philippines was based on principle. He envisioned the War against Spain as altruistic. His eldest son Philip served in the military. Prior to the war with Spain, Crapsey sermonized about American imperialism with optimism. Short of outright support of the war, Crapsey was confident about the valor and ethical standing of the military, as well as hopeful for a capable civil administration to be instituted after the war.[5]

But Crapsey eventually saw Dewey's defeat of the Spanish in Manilla Bay as an opportunity for American businessmen to expand and exploit the native population. He argued that what was happening in the Philippines wasn't what the popular political rhetoric was maintaining about freeing the natives from the oppression of decadent Spain. In reality, it was our turn to oppress and Crapsey would not countenance it. In relation to the Filipino situation Crapsey wrote that he deplored the change in what he and many others saw as an altruistic policy. Many saw the war as an aid to free Cuba from Spanish oppression. Nevertheless, in Crapsey's mind it had degenerated into an outright plan to conquer the Philippines. Crapsey became indignant regarding the turn in events viewing them as treacherously betraying American ideology, and all that America stood for. When the question was finally posed to the Episcopal Church of what their part would be in relation to the Philippines, Crapsey could no longer remain quiet.[6]

The majority of Filipinos were Catholic. In the popular press, laymen and clergy alike called for the Protestant evangelism of the newly acquired lands.[7] Evangelicals rejoiced that the people of the Philippines now had the opportunity to become true Christians. Crapsey thought this presumptuous, considering the long history of the Catholic Church in that region. The evangelical attitude was paternalistic. They desired to bring the Filipinos under the banner of conservative Protestantism.

As the controversy deepened about the Episcopalian bishopric, Crapsey entered into the fray. In an open letter to the Rev. Charles H. Brent, rector of St. Stephen's Church, Boston, the man chosen by the

---

[5] Column from *NY Times* "Imperial Power of America" Aug. 6, 1898? 6:5. In A.H. Crapsey Jr. Collection.

[6] Crapsey. *Heretics* p. 238.

[7] Caption of newspaper article appearing as letter to the editor, by D.B. Lyon "To the editor of the Democrat and Chronicle" Nov. 5, 1901.

church for the job, Crapsey opposed the movement to create a bishopric in the Philippines. Crapsey believed that the attempt to maintain religious jurisdiction over the islands conflicted with the work of the Catholic Church. Crapsey considered the Philippines already Christian. They had been Christian for generations. Regardless of what they thought of the Spanish administration, Crapsey believed that they loved the Catholic Church.[8]

Crapsey exploited Anglo-Catholic sympathies while encouraging a rift between the conservatives of both factions of the church. Under the guise of standing for Catholic values, Crapsey exercised his liberality. In the published letter he wrote that he was not pleased with Brent's election as bishop of the Philippines because it was not the place of the Protestant Episcopal Church to establish ecclesiastic administration there. Besides, they already had Christian bishops who maintained oversight of their churches. Therefore, the endeavor was not only intrusive, but futile and potentially hazardous.[9]

Crapsey's identification with the broad school provided him with an enigmatic stance on issues and dogma. Conversely, he envisioned the broad school as the vehicle to unify the faith. Crapsey simply ignored the fact that some considered Roman Catholicism as defiled. He disparaged those who judged Catholicism as corrupt believing they should be careful to judge themselves first. In his new notion of Christianity, Crapsey conceded that a great gulf still existed between Christian denominations, and he felt compelled to narrow it. Nonetheless, unable to contain his dissatisfaction with his own denomination, he then attacked the materialistic aspects of the Episcopalian church. He noted sarcastically that the "commercial religion" of the Episcopalians was not untainted enough to criticize the Roman Catholic religion. Moreover he felt that the only reason Americans remained in the Philippines was due to our overt power and that was not a good enough reason to be there.[10]

There was no unanimity among the experts about the administration of the islands. In reality, the situation presented a genuine dilemma for the government to deal with.[11] Crapsey argued against complicating the already tenuous political situation with religious competition and

---

[8] Crapsey, *Heretics,* p. 237.

[9] A.S. Crapsey *"Should Not Create Philippine Bishopric"* A published "Open Letter" written to Rev. Charles H. Brent, dated, Oct. 11, 1901, in A. H. Crapsey Collection.

[10] Ibid.

[11] Ibid.

contention. He noted if the floodgates were open to all of the denominations to go in and proselytize, the already dangerous situation could get much worse.[12]

Had Crapsey left the argument in a defensive posture he might have garnered more sympathetic support, especially with the clergy, who held the key to Crapsey's future. But Crapsey attacked the group within the Episcopal Church he recognized as his persistent adversary. Crapsey knew the evangelicals would retaliate, as they perceived their own future in the church as extremely tenuous. Crapsey felt that the people of the Philippines had enough problems without forcing sectarian Protestantism on them. Crapsey traduced the spirit of the Protestantism since the reformation, considering that it had never truly taken root in any land "under the influence of the Latin race." He criticized the Protestants' inability to penetrate anywhere Roman Catholicism had been established, calling all previous attempts at proselytizing unproductive, indeed futile.[13]

In contrast, Crapsey's proposal included toleration and constructive development for the Philippines. He felt that education and other positive agencies should provide a civilizing effect on Filipino society, but beyond that, the indigenous people should be left alone to worship according to their traditions and history.[14]

Crapsey held a deep and abiding love for his nation and for the American example of freedom. His conception of the American ethos was of the legendary type, one that held in mind that we had also wrested our liberty from colonial oppressors not too terribly long ago. The same democratic philosophy would someday reign supreme throughout the world bringing together all peoples through shared moral beliefs. Crapsey expanded his concept of Christian unity to encompass the secular and to discover areas of shared beliefs. In light of the thought that American style democracy, the kind that every schoolboy believed to be part of our unique, personal heritage, would someday be the overriding ethos of the entire world, Crapsey perceived the endeavor in the Philippines as abhorrent and shameful. Even if the Americans improved the basic conditions of sanitation and education, they had taken away the one thing that was important, the right for Filipinos to govern themselves.[15]

While elevating secular concepts that individuals might share that could subsequently unify diverse groups, he similarly attacked the old

---

[12] Ibid.

[13] Ibid.

[14] Ibid.

[15] Crapsey, *Heretics,* p. 238.

religious values he perceived as separating and isolating people. He played upon the wealth and status of the Episcopal Church. He attacked a sensitive area in which the church would respond. The use of their wealth belied their intentions, especially where missions were concerned. If the support for mission work was not forthcoming then Crapsey felt obviously was there was a lack of interest. He related that there was a deficiency of $100,000 with the board of missions. He wondered, how a corporation that was in debt to such an extent could assume new obligations by establishing an episcopate in the Philippines? He believed the conspicuous lack of funding reflected the tenor of the laity towards missions.[16]

Crapsey pointed to his own country where the Protestant Episcopal Church contained less than 2 per cent of the population. They had not even effectively engaged the American Negro of the south or the multitudes of the cities living in paganized districts with the doctrine and discipline of the church. Crapsey wondered cynically, how one could justify going to the Philippines, Africa, China or Japan while the work at home was barely even begun. Then "why not consider going to Europe as well?"[17] Crapsey's inclusion of Europe in his argument was obviously meant to shock his readers, as he was demonstrating the sanctimonious nature of going abroad with the task at home left undone. He likewise answered the objection that Episcopalians in the Philippines might be in need of the services of the church. Crapsey figured the spiritual needs of Episcopalians could be met by military chaplains and if they eventually desired a bishop to preside over them, they could subsequently elect one. In conclusion he warned,

> I hope my dear Mr. Brent, that you will not leave the great work you are doing in Boston, to become the private chaplain of a few transient residents in a foreign land, and still less that you will give yourself to the hopeless task of trying to change a form of Christianity which does not need changing- only betterment. Let us leave to our Roman Catholic brethren the work that lies upon them of readjusting their church to its new conditions.[18]

The Archdeacon of the Diocese of Western New York, Rev. Dr. Louis Washburn took exception to Crapsey's comments, responding diplomatically to the "Open Letter," written to Brent. Washburn hinted

---

[16] A.S. Crapsey "Open Letter" addressed to Rev Charles H. Brent, Oct. 11, 1901. A. H. Crapsey Jr. Collection.

[17] Ibid.

[18] Ibid.

that something had happened to Crapsey in the not so distant past to turn him against the church and cause him to become a spokesperson for dissension. Washburn assumed that Crapsey had published this letter to create a public issue. Episcopalians customarily remained discreet and outside of the public forum. He noted that the question of a Philippine bishopric had already been decided. Therefore, the arguments that Crapsey presented were undignified and self-serving. He noted that even the simplest schoolboy realized that the ordinary Filipino was "a heathen who lived by the basest means." If that was the legacy of the Catholic Church in the islands then something indeed was wrong. Certainly only a minute percentage had been won to the church. According to Washburn the rest were "pitiably in need of the regenerating power of the Gospel of the Lord Jesus Christ."[19]

Washburn further ridiculed Crapsey's inference that because of one's human weaknesses one should retract from aiding others, especially those in dire spiritual need. The mere thought contradicted the underlying principles of their religion. The notion that one could only help another spiritually when one had attained perfection was unchristian. Washburn assured Crapsey that the church would continue to facilitate unity, and that entering the Philippines would only hasten it. Moreover, the mission work in Mexico and South America could not be impugned by Crapsey simply because he came to different conclusions from those involved. Quoting the declaration of their mission convention Washburn further assured Crapsey that the Mexican missionary work had not only been a success, but it had surpassed what they had anticipated. Washburn similarly stated, "the God appointed duty of the reformed church was not only to inform pagans but to purge and bring life to the dispirited of Latin Christianity."[20]

Crapsey had called the unwillingness to support his separate see without the money ahead of time, "the great apostasy." Washburn likewise dismissed Crapsey's contentions about mission finances as merely a lack of faith. Episcopalians had never been so eager about supporting this vision of the church abroad. With the missions conference just a short time in the future Washburn didn't want public opinion tainted by the defiance of an influential churchman like Crapsey. The missions needed the support of the community and he hoped that it would continue unabated.[21]

---

[19] In *Rochester Democrat & Chronicle* dated Oct. 21 1901. "Open Letter" by Archdeacon Washburn to Rev. Crapsey.
[20] Ibid.
[21] Ibid.

Crapsey refused to bury his head in the sand over matters he felt were of the greatest social concern. He responded to Archdeacon Washburn,

> You consider the vast majority of our fellow citizens in the Philippine Islands 'as the most depraved and debased of mankind.' I think of them perhaps with school boy ignorance as, on the whole, a gentle, peace-loving people living up to their own light and acting in accordance with their inherited character and historical development. Even the savage must have the virtues of the savage.[22]

Crapsey considered the "Latin races" as primarily spiritually minded, even though the Filipinos were still stuck in the developmental stage of savagery. He referred to St Francis of Assisi and St. Francis de Sales as being examples of great saints both prior to and after the Reformation who were devoted like no others.[23] Crapsey noted the irrationality of the evangelical contention, that one needed to go to South America or Asia to convert Catholics when a huge proportion of the population of Rochester, New York belonged to the Roman Catholic Church. [24]

However, Crapsey was ethnocentric enough to see the efficacy of the American presence in the Philippines. He believed in the white man's burden, a moral mission of social, economic and political benefits for native people. His contention was not with the Christian religion. It was with sectarian religion that caused people to question the effectiveness of the universal church. He considered the development of the Philippines on a comparative scale. However, he refused to extend his prejudice to the Roman Catholic Church. He figured that since the Roman Catholic Church had been there for centuries they would know how to deal with the native population better than outsiders would. Crapsey saw the American role as "governmental and non- sectarian." He believed that supporting health related and educational civic institutions were the way to morally and physically elevate the people of the Philippines. He saw nothing but confusion and harm in the competition of various sects vying for their own denominational ascendancy amongst the native people.[25]

Crapsey extended his religious toleration to what he viewed as inter-denominational peace. Meanwhile, he developed a mature sense of doctrinal heterodoxy as well. To the Protestant Episcopal Church, his

---

[22] A.S. Crapsey "Open Letter written to Archdeacon Louis C. Washburn D.D. ," dated Oct. 23, 1901, in A.H. Crapsey Jr. Collection.

[23] Ibid.

[24] Ibid.

[25] Ibid.

great indiscretion was his inability to remain confidential and private on controversial public matters. Philosophically, he now adopted the insight of the moralistic humanists. Crapsey explained to Archdeacon Washburn the key to his entire mode of reasoning over the Filipino issue.

> We approach the subject of missions from opposite points of view. I do not believe that there is anywhere an utterly debased, depraved and outcast people. We are all children of one Father. We have each something to give to the other, can each learn from the other. Having such thoughts I am not in a hurry to convert others to my way of thinking, but am anxious to confer with them as to what we shall do to be saved. I know this is not the orthodox way of thinking, but I have long ceased to be orthodox on the doctrine of exclusive salvation.[26]

Thus, Crapsey exposed himself to the oncoming storm. Salvation, from a traditional standpoint was at the heart of the issue to every evangelical. But he carried out something publicly that other liberals had wisely shied away from. There would be a showdown. And like his maternal grandfather, Crapsey was not one to back down from a good fight. His unwillingness to compromise sowed dissension in the ranks. He also knew that the Episcopal clergy typically protected their own. But the shielding umbrella of the church only applied if one chose to come under its authority.

Crapsey argued from a position that betrayed his lack of faith in the decisions of the missionary board and the general convention. Because they were in debt for the previous year's work they needed every cent for the current year. Crapsey similarly overstated his point that if they were to send a bishop to the Philippines they should bar no expense in the endeavor. He would need 100 helpers at a cost of 150,000 dollars a year. After erecting his straw man he decided to cut it down as well. He wondered where the money would come from? He noted that although the board might be able to affirm its jurisdiction it couldn't generate the funds to continue it. Further unsupported work was sure to alienate churchmen by setting aside resources towards charities they did not wish to sustain.[27]

Addressing Washburn's assurance of missionary significance Crapsey pointed out contentiously that he must have overlooked the details concerning the Latin American missions' fiasco. He reported,

---

[26] Ibid.

[27] A.S. Crapsey "Open Letter written to Archdeacon Washburn," Oct. 23, 1901. In A.H. Crapsey Jr. Collection.

> We now maintain the form of a church there without the substance. We report six clergymen at work, 124 children in our school and no communicants (though there may be some not reported). In Brazil we have a bishop and a staff of clergy and report 400 communicants; in Cuba we report 250 communicants. Among all the millions of the Latin race in Central and South America we report 650 communicants, who have about as much influence as a similar number of Buddhists would have in North America. If the general convention and the mission board look upon that as a brilliantly successful work then the general convention and the mission board are easily satisfied. But I am one of many who refuse to give either money or aid of so futile an effort to override the laws of religious life and growth.[28]

Crapsey had done his homework on the issue but his willingness to vocalize the politics of the church publicly caused more personal scrutiny by leaders in the church. As Crapsey became visibly more contentious, local opposition began to fester and boil. Rev. Andrew J. Graham, rector of Christ Church, Rochester, noted that Crapsey had denigrated the Lord's directive to "Go ye into all the world and preach the gospel to every creature." Graham accused Crapsey of encouraging the complacency of good people in a sinful world through the selfish "egoism" of a leading figure of the Episcopal Church.[29]

Graham obviously lacked faith in the Roman Catholic religion in the Philippines or anywhere else for that matter. Nevertheless, he directed his attack at Crapsey in a personal manner bordering on the malevolent. Graham wrote,

> It seems a rather strange coincidence that, on the eve of the great missionary conference soon to assemble in this city, you should smite the whole missionary effort of the church in the face; sneer at her administration; seem almost to rejoice at her stress and declare that you will have no further part or lot in her evangelizing movements. A color-bearer is supposed to occupy the honorable position of bringing the regiment up, not trailing the flag in the mire; the ambassador of Christ has pledged himself to deliver Christ's message to a suffering and dying race, not to throw to fickle, selfish galleries, sweet, nauseating crumbs, which float about in the feeble wash of his own imagination.[30]

---

[28] Ibid.

[29] Rev. Dr. Andrew J. Graham "For a Bishopric in the Philippines" Letter labeled Christ Church, Rochester, NY, Oct. 26, 1901. In A.H. Crapsey Jr. Collection.

[30] Ibid.

Graham pulled no punches in his attack upon Crapsey. Herein lay the seeds of the further discontent. To his critics, Crapsey's faith was increasingly of his own definition. From their vantage point he had moved consistently away from historically defined orthodoxy and the canon of scripture. But Crapsey now sought ways to utilize the canon by acknowledging its spiritual authority without completely discountenancing its supposed literal inconsistencies. That required scholarly reinterpretation of the canon and delicate political maneuvering. Phillips Brooks might have provided help had he not died so suddenly. Crapsey however lacked Brook's discretion, sensitivity to detail, or his political acumen. He debated the necessity for modernistic interpretations of the scriptures. He sought new modes of understanding about the universality of the church. He advocated bringing Christendom back together in unison. He wanted to direct the church away from its parochial moorings and expand it into a more ecumenical framework. Crapsey believed a liberal interpretation of scripture would bring the church into the twentieth century. Socialism and evolutionary theory could not be ignored any longer. They deserved inclusion in the church's worldview. Crapsey visualized himself as a leader of the modernistic church into the new century.

But as Graham noted,

> The question as to whether the ancient canons of the undivided church are violated by sending the Anglican episcopate to the Philippine, where the Roman episcopate already has jurisdiction, is one which may be fairly discussed, and an honest difference of opinion is allowable. But the Anglican communion has long since settled its policy and law and conscience on that subject.

Then turning upon Crapsey as a dissident, Graham expressed the depth of his personal distaste. He wrote maliciously,

> And your puny beating of the air is simply a sign of the 'time-spirit,' that individualism rebelling against the organism, which in the state is civil anarchy and in the church, ecclesiastical anarchy.[31]

But Crapsey and Graham were not on the same page. The election of Brooks as Bishop of Massachusetts demonstrated that the church desired to meet the challenges of progressive culture head on. Furthermore, the

---

[31] Ibid.

Anglican heritage of Christian Socialism epitomized by Frederick Denison Maurice, Charles Kingsley and John Ludlow once again emerged as a possible method for achieving the ancient Stuart dream of reuniting Christendom under the banner of Anglicanism.

The onslaught led by Graham characterized the depth of personal distaste and the sense of urgency that conservatives felt necessary to reclaim lost ground. Graham stated,

> You say: 'I am not in a hurry to convert people to my way of thinking.' That is an encouraging statement for 'your way of thinking' and my 'way of thinking' are of no moment when it comes to eternal salvation:
>
> "Our little thinking has its day
> "It has its day and ceases to be
>
> You and I were ordained to convert people to 'God's way of thinking,' not our own, and failure to do it borders closely on rebellion.[32]

Graham continued by answering every point and hammering home the tenets of the historic Protestant Episcopal Church. But Crapsey viewed the technological and intellectual developments as revolutionary for western society. He entered his career a confirmed Anglo- Catholic, but cultural developments led him to reexamine his views. He became a "lover of science." His faith in the scientific produced optimism about man's role in society. Consequently, he expressed a sanguine sense of hope about western civilization.[33]

Crapsey's detractors denounced his passion for the progressive. His humanism appeared to them as a compromise of their "great commission." Graham wrote bitingly that to confer with people as to how they should be saved was a joke. He wondered, "did Jesus Christ come into the world to check with the authorities about what was the best way to save the world?" He advised one should consult the records. The record of course, was the bible. The record that Crapsey had increasing problems with from a literal point of view.

Graham perceived the issues in oppositional terms. In biblical terms he viewed the world's ways as enmity against God. He upheld the faith. Chiding Crapsey, he noted,

---

[32] Rev. Dr. Andrew J. Graham "For a Bishopric in the Philippines" Open letter labeled Christ Church, Rochester, NY, Oct. 26, 1901. In the A. H. Crapsey Jr. Collection.

[33] Crapsey, *Heretics,* p. 178.

> Again Dr. Crapsey, imagine yourself, with all your learning and culture and with the inherited light of nineteen Christian centuries shining in your face and eyes, imagine yourself, pursuing the fierce Geronimo through the dark places of Florida, or Sitting Bull along the Dakotas, or the lawless boloman, with his short shirt and stuffed club, and having come within hailing distance craved the permission to get their judgment as to the way of salvation. The suggestion is an insult to Jesus Christ, who has given us a perfect revelation of all things necessary to salvation and certainly no heathen is now able to better that revelation.[34]

Graham even addressed the contention that the seed of the Reformation was unproductive in the Latin lands. He provided seven witnesses to counter Crapsey's assertion. Graham concluded that Christianity would have died out along time ago in Jerusalem had there not been a "missionary anointing." In fact there would not even be any charitable institutions in existence if not for the body of Christ. Pointing accusingly at Crapsey, Graham declared, "the pessimists of the world were the destroyers of it."[35]

In his own way, Crapsey rationalized about the place of ritual and mysticism in the church. As he had started to take a broader view of religion in general, Crapsey realized that the ritualistic expressions of the Anglican liturgy held very cogent places in the continuing traditions of the church. Crapsey's decision to remain in the Protestant Episcopal Church as an Anglo- Catholic when others had defected to Roman Catholicism said something about his Anglican ethnocentricity. Crapsey would have echoed the sentiments of Phillips Brooks in his writing about the distinct religious niches of both Anglicanism and Romanism. Brooks once stated, "Anglican Protestantism, attempting to rival Rome on her own ground, to do for the world what Rome claims to do, to live by the method of authority, must always be a nonentity, a failure."

And yet, Brooks contended,

> Anglican Protestantism, attempting to do another thing, to treat the soul in another way, to provide for the world another culture, to educate and appeal to the human conscience, has before her the power of immense usefulness and power.[36]

---

[34] Graham, "For a Bishopric in the Philippines" A. H. Crapsey Jr. Collection.

[35] Ibid.

[36] Phillips Brooks "Essays and Addresses," pp. 105- 118. Reprinted in Raymond W. Albright *Focus on Infinity: The Life of Phillips Brooks* (New York: The Macmillan Co., 1961) p. 274.

Some of Crapsey's defenders were Roman Catholics. One encouraged Crapsey's opinions ironically submitting that the proselytizing of the United States was of the utmost importance for the Roman Catholic Church. He noted the shortcomings of the Spanish system but also the inadequacy and irresponsibility of Americans dealing with their own indigenous populations. Hopefully, due to God's grace and excellence in statesmanship, Americans would not repeat a similar venture elsewhere.[37]

At the Missionary Conference of the Protestant Episcopal Church held shortly afterwards in Rochester, several anti-Catholic remarks entered the discourse. Bishop McQuaid of the Roman Catholic Diocese of Rochester later spoke out in defense of the Roman Catholic Church by going on the offensive. McQuaid wondered rhetorically who could promote the interests of the people and lift up the ecclesiastic state of affairs in the Philippines better than the Catholic Church? McQuaid pointed to American history and the way European Protestants had "civilized the native Americans off the face of the earth." He noted how when missionaries first arrived in Hawaii there were over a quarter of a million inhabitants there. Now there were less than 30,000 and the lands they once enjoyed were now the property of the sons and grandsons of those that went to civilize them. These were not Catholics who were responsible, but Protestants.[38]

Whether McQuaid was right to associate the possible genocide in America and the Hawaiian Islands with the Protestant church was a question worth addressing given its rhetorical value. Indeed, should not those who extolled the virtues of American civilization own the realties of it as well? McQuaid inquired loudly, "was what had resulted in American and Hawaiian native populations the legacy of Protestantism as well?"

---

[37] James H. Dormer, Entitled, "Another Open Letter" Subtitled, *James A. Dormer, of Buffalo Catholic Truth Society, in Sympathy with Dr. Crapsey.* Oct. 30, 1901. In A.H. Crapsey Jr. Collection.

[38] Bishop Bernard J. McQuaid. Letter telegraphed to the New York Tribune "Bishop McQuaid Replies." Dec. 9, 1901. In A.H. Crapsey Jr. Collection.

A different missionary meeting took place at the Park Avenue Church, in Rochester. Under the direction of Rev. C.H. Moss of the Federation of Churches and true to liberal form Moss called for "a study of the position taken by Dr. Crapsey." Crapsey had gained an audience with local liberals. Whether he would gain their support was another question.[39]

[39] Letter to editor of *Rochester Democrat & Chronicle* from C.H. Moscrip "Dr. Crapsey and Missions" Rochester, Nov. 8, 1901 In A.H. Crapsey Jr. Collection.

CHAPTER TWELVE

"For it is the Jubilee"

Crapsey continued to preach as a missioner throughout the country. He conducted large and enthusiastic affairs in Detroit, Michigan, and Philadelphia, Pennsylvania. He also composed sermons on a variety of social issues. On October 17, 1901, Crapsey delivered a sermon suggesting three recommendations for prison reform. His sermon satisfied a fact-finding request by the New York State Prison Association. He expressed a compassionate liberalism through the sermon. Crapsey identified the reasons why people turned to crime. He isolated four causes contributing to the development of prisoners, including, "inheritance, environment, personal neglect and bad laws." Crapsey then considered how the state might change the present system for the good of society. He argued that the criminal was a victim of society, often of disease and personal circumstances. Rather than punishing and demeaning the prisoner, which contributed to his adverse behavior the exact opposite should take place in a civilized society. He also called for the elimination of the inmate's uniform. He argued that it degraded the prisoner and it was undemocratic in its social separation. The sole benefit involved recapturing escapees.[1]

Crapsey outlined three basic principles for reform. The first required fair treatment for prisoners including extending respect to them. The second called for meaningful employment for prisoners encouraging the importance of work in order for them to gain respect for themselves. He considered employment a positive addition to a person's life, not a negative one. He believed that employment was therapeutic for the mind and body. Finally, he called for professionally trained personnel who would not mistreat prisoners.[2]

One of Crapsey's final missions was to the black congregation of St. Luke's Church in Washington, D.C. St. Luke's provided a base for

---

[1] News article entitled "Dr. Crapsey's Protest." Oct. 20, 1901. In A.H. Crapsey Jr. Collection.

[2] Alkalay- Gut, *Alone,* p.112.

affluent blacks in Washington, D.C. According to Crapsey, the church's parishioners also included successful businessmen, judges and high government officials including the Secretary of the Treasury of the United States.[3] Crapsey lectured on "The Race Problem; National Ideals versus National Practice, and our Relation to the Negro and the Filipino."[4] His lecture also described how the early church was created through martyrdom and passive resistance.[5]

After completing his mission work at St. Luke's, Crapsey received an invitation to speak from the large Metropolitan AME Church in Washington, D.C. The letter said,

> Appreciating deeply your able and courageous sermon on 'National Ideals versus National Practice,' delivered last Sunday morning in St. Luke's Church, we are desirous that a greater number of the citizens of our community be given an opportunity to hear you. We therefore most respectfully and earnestly request you to preach to a mass meeting of citizens next Sunday at 3:30 o'clock P.M., at the Metropolitan A.M.E. Church, M street, northwest, this city.[6]

Crapsey titled his speech delivered on December 15th, 1901, "The Constitutional Defense of the Negro." His advice was clear; if black Americans refused to safeguard their liberties, they forfeited the liberties of all. Crapsey exhorted them to forfeit their lives if need be, but not their political rights.[7] Crapsey noted that forty years after the Civil War, the nation was still struggling with basic human rights, legal integrity and the power of government. The grave of Abraham Lincoln testified to intensity of the rebellious spirit that had invalidated the power of the United States government.[8]

---

[3] Crapsey, *Heretics,* p.174. These statements could not be corroborated with St. Luke's, Washington, DC.

[4] News clipping entitled "There in Interest of Advent Mission, but Speaks on Race Problem." A.H. Crapsey Jr. Collection. Scrapbooks.

[5] Crapsey, *Heretics*, p. 174.

[6] News clipping entitled "There in Interest of Advent Mission, but Speaks on Race Problem." A. H. Crapsey Jr. Collection, Scrapbooks.

[7] A.S. Crapsey, *A Constitutional Defense of the Negro, by A.S. Crapsey Delivered at a Mass Meeting of Citizens in the Metropolitan A.M.E. Church, Washington, D.C. December 15th, 1901.* (A.S. Crapsey, 1901).

[8] News clipping entitled "Dr. Crapsey in Washington" subtitled, "Says the United States is Still Struggling With the Slave Power." A.H. Crapsey Jr. Collection Scrapbooks.

Crapsey believed the great guarantor of Americans' rights was the constitution. But shamefully, it had not been properly enforced due to the high price that still needed to be paid. Therefore, the magnificent document was tarnished. The law had been discarded. People were denied due process. He railed against continuing racial subordination achieved through conspiracy, anarchism and murder. Crapsey was incensed by the continuing campaign of terror waged against black Americans in the south with the proliferation of lynching and mob rule.[9]

Crapsey pointed to the historic example of Christian martyrdom. He advocated passive resistance as being necessary even if it included sacrifice. Crapsey foresaw martrydom in stark, yet hallowed terms. He advocated laying down one's life for the ultimate cause of gaining the franchise. It made little sense to resist forcefully. That would only provide an excuse for evil men to justify genocide. While he counseled against taking up arms he also called for courage and sacrifice. With stirring passion Crapsey cried,

> God forbid that you should lift up your hands save in defense of the rights of man and the lives of women and children. Do not kill but be killed; be killed until your blood becomes as a river defiling all the land, until like the blood of Abel it cries from the ground for vengeance. Be killed until you have lost from your veins the last drop of the slave and can stand up as free men in a free land.[10]

Drawing on his Civil War service and near death experience in the just cause of freedom for the Negro, Crapsey noted that over a million white men's lives had been sacrificed, including Abraham Lincoln, for the cause of political freedom.[11] He figured that a million more black lives might need to be given for the cause of racial equality to be settled forever.[12] In conclusion, Crapsey noted that the political difficulties of the nation would only be resolved by extending the franchise to black Americans.[13]

Crapsey's provocative speeches in the nation's capital produced rebukes from the editor of *Harper's*, and the Episcopal Bishop of Washington, D.C. After being shunned at the door to his palatial home, Crapsey later received a letter from the bishop, Henry Yates Satterlee,

---

[9] Ibid.
[10] Portion of his speech recorded in Alkalay- Gut, *Alone*, p. 113.
[11] Crapsey, *A Constitutional Defense of the Negro.*
[12] Crapsey, *Heretics*, pp. 174- 5.
[13] Ibid. p. 175.

upbraiding him for contentious preaching in his diocese.[14] Moreover, no other white clergymen in the Washington area supported or participated with Crapsey in his efforts there. Crapsey regarded the Negro as the South's great source of labor. His growing socialistic perspective persuaded him to conveniently lump the church's attitude about race relations in America with the working class. He felt it obviously benefited capitalists to exploit the black race both economically and politically.[15]

Concerning Crapsey's speech before the AME Church in Washington, the editor of *Harper's* wrote that Crapsey considered the Negro cowardly in their capitulation to the situation in the southern states. He stated that Crapsey urged them to form an organization to set them free from their insufferable circumstances. Contrasting Crapsey's opinions with those of Booker T. Washington, the editor sarcastically mentioned that "Washington was also quite well informed about the Negro situation," reckoning that "he probably thinks about it regularly and without diminishing its significance as the primary social problem in America," Washington still believed that American blacks were "far better off in comparison to any others." The editor figured that if African-Americans were the "best lot of negroes on earth, their 'intolerable condition' must have considerable mitigations."[16]

The editor noted that Washington wasn't overly worried about the franchise. According to the editor, Washington was more concerned that black Americans were prepared and ready to vote. Citing Washington at Montclair, he declared,

> We must seek those things which are high, we must learn as a race to dwell away beyond race and sectional hatred, and the mere temporary success of to-day or failure of to-morrow. Fundamentally and permanently we should not be so much concerned as to whether we are to ride in a 'Jim Crow' car as with the question as to whether one will find in the inferior car a superior man, not a beast, but one who- in body, mind, and soul is a man. We cannot as a race make stronger our cause by depending too much upon mere law.[17]

---

[14] Crapsey failed to identify the bishop in his autobiography. Identification of the Right Rev. Henry Yates Saterlee from personal communication with Diane Nye, Records Manager of Washington National Cathedral Archives, Washington, DC.
[15] Ibid. pp. 175- 6.
[16] Article in the A.H. Crapsey Collection without title, author or date. Crapsey refers to the author as Mr. Sanford of *Harper's Weekly* Scrapbooks.
[17] Ibid.

The editor noted, how refreshing to find a notable black layman who was urging patience and persistence to demonstrate one's worthiness in opposition to a white clergyman and "supposed man of God" who was advising the Negro to "shed rivers of blood." Focusing on the irony of the opposing opinions between the black layman and the white clergyman the editor vilified Crapsey's call for rage, death and retaliation while Washington sought education both of the mind and soul and peace and common assurance between the races. The editor noted that, "The white minister says, 'sweep away purse and dinner-pail;' the black layman says, 'gain property!' Truly the black race has made progress."[18]

The editor however, slipped into ethnocentric arrogance in stating that Crapsey made the mistake of "offering strong drink to babes." While he assured his readers that both he and Booker T. Washington were in one accord concerning the issue of fairness, he figured that the south had nearly been ruined by radical reconstruction, primarily through black votes. He assumed that the black voter had been given the franchise prematurely, considering them unfit to vote. The result brought colossal damage to the south. He considered the restriction or abrogation of black voting rights unfortunate but not as unfortunate as the resultant carpetbagger governments constituted through black votes. Moreover, he contradicted Crapsey's premise about what the Civil War and Reconstruction were all about. The editor, somehow unable to make the connection between freedom and social and political liberty, contended that white men were not killed by the multitudes to secure for the Negro civil and political rights. For the editor, the war was about maintaining the integrity of the union and freeing the slaves. Gettysburg and Lincoln's assassination were not about the civil rights of the black man. It was slavery in and of itself that threatened the union and it had to end. Black suffrage evolved from that tumult. But the time was not right yet. Therefore, suffrage had simply failed as a social experiment.[19]

Perhaps, sometime in the future, the time would come for the experiment to succeed, the editor figured. Declarations of racial retribution and hatred and bloodshed however, from men like Crapsey, would never make it succeed. It would only succeed through the "patient, sustained efforts of godly men and women of both races working and praying together."[20]

---

[18] Ibid.

[19] Ibid.

[20] Ibid.

Nevertheless, Crapsey contended that "maintaining one's political rights were fundamental to success in the social and the economic realm."[21] Indeed political rights protected one's economic rights. Washington held that the maintenance of industrial rights and certain economic privileges would compensate for the social indiscretions shown to the black race. This would unfortunately continue until such time as society came to terms with the issue of real equality in the political realm. But to Crapsey and others patience meant to compromise one's beliefs, even if it was impractical to act. One must act upon their convictions. He would never concede that point.

Crapsey advocated the free agency of man's will. He called for immediate action. His advice contradicted the acquiescent rhetoric employed by Washington. To the Bishop of Washington, it was completely irresponsible. To others, it was extremely dangerous advice. But Crapsey thought more like W.E.B. Dubois and Frederick Douglass. Douglass counseled a younger generation of blacks to, "agitate, agitate, agitate." DuBois represented an intellectual antithesis to Booker T. Washington in the black community stressing education, political solidarity and civil rights. But like Washington, Douglass also advocated,

> the gospel of wealth, holding that 'Negroes would never be respected until they respect themselves, and that they would never respect themselves until they had the means to live respectably.'[22]

Crapsey however, doubted if capital gain held the answer at all. For Crapsey, politics, economic gain and social standing were all tied intrinsically together. Neither was religion merely a separate entity. All areas of the human experience were interrelated and they functioned best when they worked together.

Crapsey considered himself prophetic in his vision of social and political parity for the American Negro. However, it was one thing to advise others. It was quite another to ask an entire generation of people to lay down their lives for voting rights. Black Americans had had just about enough of whites asking them to lay down their lives for any reason by then. Institutionalized apartheid under the banner of "separate but equal" was now the standard of southern politics, backed by hardened legislation

---

[21] A.S. Crapsey *Heretics* (New York, 1924) paraphrased p. 176.

[22] Quote originally taken from *Frederick Douglass's Life and Times,* p. 670. Recorded in Benjamin Quarles's *Frederick Douglass* New York: Athenium, 1969 p. 335.

and judicial support. Crapsey could only imagine what it must be like to live under such repressive conditions, with little hope of achieving political liberty in the south of the late nineteenth, early twentieth centuries. Crapsey probably inspired the black men and women who he spoke to in Washington, D.C. And yet, it is also obvious that he had failed to incite them. Black men and women, likely considered Crapsey's statements with a grain of salt, as a well-meaning outsider. African-Americans would follow their own paths. They would forge their own future. These considerations were forever before them as a people. They alone were forced to deal with the situation and similarly persevere.

Crapsey succeeded however in once again estranging yet another portion of the Protestant Episcopal Church, this time in the reactionary South. The snubbing of Crapsey, the missioner, in Washington, D.C. was obviously not uncalculated. The Bishop of Washington, D.C. was held in high esteem in the Protestant Episcopal Church. Indeed, if Crapsey were to be shunned he certainly found no small satisfaction that it came from such a venerated and official place. Perhaps he even associated his treatment with the scorning of his maternal grandfather by the political entourage in Washington, D.C. He envisioned the coming commotion realizing his need to hold fast against the whirlwind of the reactionary elements of his church. Meanwhile, he would desperately grasp onto a staff of his own construction, holding it high as the blowing desert sands tore away at his tattered clothing and exposed flesh. He would act indeed, but he would never concede.

CHAPTER THIRTEEN

"Walk Honestly as in the Day"

Crapsey was fifty-two years old as the nineteenth turned into the twentieth century. His influence grew, especially as he became more vocal on social issues. His popularity throughout the Rochester region was well established and his notoriety in the press was growing to the point of national recognition. Crapsey had pastored a successful church, conducted missions, been involved in community reform, lectured about prison improvement, and preached around the nation. He had spoken out boldly about the race issue in the south, traveled to Europe twice, written a moralistic novel, caused controversy in both the Protestant Episcopal Church and in the press, received an honorary doctorate from Hobart College and lost two children.

He had come a long way from the young combative Anglo- Catholic priest who had worked the slums of New York City and prayed for the repose of Bishop McIllvaine's soul. He had passed through a medieval stage, an Anglo-Catholic stage, a high church phase and an evangelical phase of sorts (without the encumbrance of the biblical literalism that attended so many other evangelicals). He had eventually come to a broad-church stage in his life that was expressly Pelagian, socialistic, Darwinian, progressive, modernistic and ecumenical. His participation in social reform naturally inclined him towards the social gospel. But as time progressed, Crapsey grew more radical in all his ways. He never remained lukewarm about an undertaking he embraced. As a consequence of his character, he inevitably took matters to their logical extent. In the process, he often pushed issues beyond culturally acceptable limits.

He took an unsuccessful church and saw it grow and prosper. He successfully administered a Kindergarten, a primary school and a vocational night school at his parish. He started brotherhoods, sponsored sisterhoods, and led progressive reforms on the local and national levels. He had a bishopric tentatively offered him, and had immersed his local church in societal involvement. Had he remained the consistent Anglo-Catholic that he had started out as, or even the broadened modernist that he eventually became, he might have retired within a decade, a very successful and prominent churchman.

Crapsey's engagement with his community developed from his view of the medieval church. Ironically, a trip to Great Britain and his nascent American pragmatism mitigated that view in favor of a socialistic outlook. Nevertheless, the utopian aspect of this communally oriented vision remained consistently intact.

Just how much Crapsey influenced his daughter in her growing socialistic perspective is not clear. Perhaps Adelaide influenced him as well, with her support of Eugene Debs while at Vassar and her likely participation in editing a socialist journal entitled, *Here and Now.* Her interest in applying socialistic principles to literary endeavors and visa versa, motivated her to interpret both classical and contemporary literature through a socialistic lens. It certainly affected the way she utilized her own creative abilities. She eventually developed a sort of scientific methodology that was applied to her poetry and literature. She would go on to develop an innovative form of poetry in five-line refrain that came to be known as *cinquain.* Her father whole-heartedly endorsed her interest in utilizing the scientific method for poetry, just as he advocated it for the study of religion. Whether Crapsey influenced his daughter in her socialism and promotion of the scientific method or visa versa cannot be readily determined. Both undoubtedly influenced each another.[1]

In 1898, a chapel altar was erected at St. Andrew's to provide a sense of decorum in the ever-expanding church. Two years later a parishioner, by the name of J.S. Andrew, provided a gift for the erection of a high altar for the church.[2] A short time afterwards George M. Haushaltar, the artist who painted St. Andrew's memorial altar, designed a new marble altar. Mrs. Henry M. Perkins provided the gift for the new altar, which cost $6,000.00 to complete. The base was struck in Rochester while the reredos were developed overseas in Florence, Italy. Suddenly, there was a deluge of new and expensive altars at St. Andrew's Church.[3]

The new marble structure was to be the main altar and the showpiece of the church. Obviously Crapsey's love for the formalism of the church and the propriety of its architecture had not diminished with his intellectual skepticism about high church Anglicanism. In Crapsey's eyes,

---

[1] Alkalay- Gut, *Alone,* p. 139.

[2] Chronological record courtesy of Calvary St. Andrew's Church. Averill Ave. Rochester, NY.

[3] Article originally from *Post Express* handwritten date of May 15, 1899 on the top of the postscript in Arthur H. Crapsey Jr. Collection.

the decorum and the rich accouterments indicated how far the culture had advanced along the social evolutionary scale.[4]

By1902, the Rochester City School District took over the parish Kindergarten. Led by its principal, Mrs. Catherine Whitehead at St. Andrew's Parish, over eighty women had graduated taking jobs in public and private schools throughout the Rochester region. The same year, a new sanctuary at St. Andrew's was dedicated.[5] By 1903, an Epiphany altar mural would grace the church, as would other window murals of beautifully colored stained glass. The proliferation of expensive trappings and possessions like the marble altar imported from Italy and the paintings, murals and fine stained glass executed by an artist from Paris, suggests that the church had matured into a highly successful religious establishment. Crapsey was at the height of his ministry.[6]

Crapsey continued to press for community reform and work with the poor, though he was well known in the upper crust of Rochester's high society as well. On Friday, October 20, 1902, John Rochester, Crapsey's good friend and the man who had accompanied him and his wife on the mission trip to Bermuda died. Crapsey perhaps took upon himself some of the responsibility for John Rochester's demise since their trip to Bermuda. The hurling of Mr. Rochester into a wall during a rough sea voyage home in Crapsey's mind precipitated his steady decline in health.[7] With John's death the male lineage of the Rochester clan ceased to exist in the city that bore their name. As one of the founding members of St. Luke's Episcopal,

---

[4] Another account states the altar gift was taken from a brochure published at "the dedication of the new sanctuary" it stated, "In the year 1900 a parishioner of St. Andrew's Church (Maria L. Perkins Willard) asked permission of the Vestry to place in the Church an altar which she wished to give as an expression of gratitude for blessings which she had enjoyed in that holy place.

"In course of time, permission having been given, an altar and reredos of pure marble, of exquisite design, was built and duly consecrated.

"In the year of our Lord 1902, the same parishioner completed the enrichment of the Sanctuary by gifts of a painting and mural decorations.

"The work has been executed by the same artist, Mr. George Haushalter, of Paris, France, to whom we are also indebted for the beautiful altar- piece and windows of the Andrews Memorial Chapel." Richard Greenleaf *"Algernon Crapsey and the Beginnings of St. Andrew's Parish Rochester, New York"* A Paper Read at the Annual Parish Meeting- November 28, 1966.

[5] Ibid.

[6] Chronological Record courtesy of Calvary St. Andrew's Church. Averill Ave. Rochester, NY.

[7] Crapsey, *Heretics,* p. 173.

John Rochester remained a member there until his death, but he continued to support other Episcopalian works like Crapsey's at St. Andrew's. They had remained close friends. Rochester shared several of Crapsey's social concerns and served on boards sustaining many of the institutions that Crapsey supported. Rochester devoted much time to his interest of establishing a park system in the greater Rochester region.[8]

Two of the wealthiest women in the city also attended St. Andrew's and personally supported Crapsey's work at the church. One of these women, Mrs. Elizabeth Maria Tinker Sibley, was the wife of Hiram Sibley, the founder of Western Union Telegraph Company. Elizabeth Sibley, a devoted Episcopalian, had at least two churches built by her endowments, one in Honeoye Falls, NY, just south of Rochester, and one in North Adams, Massachusetts, the town of her youth. Mrs. Sibley served as the president of the board of supervisors for the Homeopathic Hospital, and was the first vice president of the board of managers of the Church Home in Rochester. Although her home on East Avenue in Rochester was closer to some of the other Episcopal Churches she also attended and supported the work at St. Andrew's for over twenty years until her death in the summer of 1903.[9]

When Mrs. Sibley died, the same artist that painted the J.S. Andrew altar and subsequently designed the marble altar given by Mrs. Perkins, was commissioned by Mrs. James Watson Sibley, to paint a picture for the walls of St. Andrew's of *"The Magi and the Christ Child."* The painting was an imitation of the Italian fresco style in wax-like colors. The work was started in Paris and completed eventually in Brittany.[10]

The other female benefactor of St. Andrew's was Cornelia Brooks Ellwanger. She was the wife of the prominent nurseryman George Ellwanger, who eventually gave Rochester its most unusual and beautiful south park, where rare breeds of trees and plants continue to grace the landscape. Highland Park eventually became the scene of a unique spring ritual when thousands in the area would come to see the Lilac Festival. Her son, Henry Brooks Ellwanger had, since 1881, been the vested choirmaster, who helped to train the choirboys at St. Andrew's.[11] Henry

---

[8] News article "Death Comes To J.H. Rochester" Friday Oct. 21, 1902. In A.H. Crapsey Jr. Collection.

[9] Crapsey, *Manuscript,* pp. 178- 182.

[10] "In Memory of Mrs. Sibley" In *Rochester Democrat & Chronicle* in A.H. Crapsey Jr. Collection.

[11] Richard Greenleaf *"Algernon Crapsey and the Beginnings of St. Andrew's Parish."* Paper Read at the Annual Parish Meeting- Nov. 28, 1966.

along with Harold Kimball and Henry Crab, were the organists at the church. Both Cornelia Brooks Ellwanger and Mrs. Elizabeth Maria Tinker Sibley died in the summer of 1903.[12]

Crapsey wrote a pamphlet dedicated to George Ellwanger. Crapsey and other distinguished citizens such as George Eastman of Eastman Kodak fame and Col. Henry Alvah Strong who eventually bequeathed to Rochester its teaching medical center in conjunction with the University of Rochester in the southern sector of the city, dined with Ellwanger regularly. As a member of the prominent Rochester Club, Crapsey rubbed shoulders with the rich and famous on a regular basis. Prior to Rochester's death, Crapsey dined almost every Saturday evening with the Rochester family.[13] His conspicuous popularity brought him into frequent social contact with the other distinguished personalities of Rochester.[14]

In the summer of 1903, Crapsey's third daughter Rachel married Arthur M. Clark, an heir to a fortune. Rachel was an uncommon beauty. They were married at St. Andrew's Church on June 24th. Soon after their marriage they went to live in South River, New Jersey close to Arthur's mother who controlled the family assets.[15]

St. Andrew's Church was a dynamic place full of life. Young people rushed about for choir practice, always busily involved in the numerous societies, brotherhoods and sisterhoods, as well as the various educational facilities around the grounds. The parish took on the industrious character of its rector. Several young people held an especially fond place in the rector's memory long after he retired from his work. Samuel Lee Seldon, the son of the very prominent justice of the New York State Court of Appeals, whose uncle, according to Crapsey, was the one who invented the gasoline engine, was, as a youth, Crapsey's helpful handyman around the grounds. Lee, as he was affectionately known, died of a fever after becoming a promising lawyer and having a crippling gun accident.[16]

Crapsey also remembered a young man named Lansing Humphrey, the son of Judge George P. Humphrey. Crapsey influenced the young man to

---

[12] "In Memory of Mrs. Sibley," *Rochester Democrat & Chronicle* in A.H. Crapsey Jr. Collection. Crapsey, *Manuscript,* pp. 178 – 183.

[13] Crapsey, *Manuscript,* p.187.

[14] A.S. Crapsey *"Das Mann frum Gross-heppach, by the Ghost of Hans Breitman."* (Rochester, 1901).

[15] Alkalay- Gut, *Alone,* p. 240.

[16] Crapsey, *Manuscript,* p.188. George Seldon has been cited as the one who developed the gasoline engine. See Mary Beth Norton et. al. *A People and a Nation* 7th ed. Vol. 2, Boston: Houghton Mifflin Co., 2005.

the point that he felt called to the ministry. But he died while in the course of his preparation for it. Crapsey loved the young people and they were always running in and out of the church and around the grounds. Coupled with the vibrant activity of his own children, St. Andrew's was a lively and bustling place.[17]

1904 began hazardously for the city of Rochester, as a fire destroyed almost two acres in the heart of the retail district. The fire occurred on a particularly cold February day, hampering the efforts of the local firemen. Close to three million dollars worth of damage resulted. St. Andrew's escaped the tragedy fortunately situated far enough from the business district.[18]

The new Archbishop of Canterbury, Randall Thomas Davidson, came to the United States for the Triennial General Convention of the Protestant Episcopal Church of the United States and Canada in 1904. Grand pomp and circumstance greeted him. The personal guest of Theodore Roosevelt, the President of the United States, he visited with such dignitaries as John Pierpoint Morgan and others. The significance of the occasion prompted Crapsey to consider presenting a series of historical lectures at St. Andrew's on the topic "Religion and Politics," culminating with the contemporary relationship of the church to the state. Because only two women habitually attended the Sunday evening service. Crapsey wanted something that would spark the attendance.[19]

By June of 1904, Crapsey celebrated his twenty-fifth anniversary at St. Andrew's Church. Special services were held. The grounds were prepared specifically for the illustrious event. Roses, lilies and other flowers graced the rectory's parlors and the grounds were ceremoniously lit with Chinese lanterns for the occasion. The guests included "Mr. and Mrs. Hobart F. Atkinson, Mr. and Mrs. Ernest R. Willard, his old friend, and his wife, Mr. and Mrs. George Field and George Foster Peabody of New York City."[20]

---

[17] Ibid. p. 190.

[18] News article entitled "One and Three=Quarters (sic) Acres In the Retail District Destroyed." Newspaper unknown, Saturday, February 27, 1904. In A.H. Crapsey Jr. Collection.

[19] Crapsey, *Heretics,* p. 239. Perhaps Crapsey misremembered the occasion for the archbishop's visitation at the Triennial General Convention of the Protestant ant Episcopal Church of the United States and Canada, as well as the date as he wrote that Davidson came in 1903.

[20] News article entitled, "Gifts for the Loved Rector of St. Andrew's Church" In A.H. Crapsey Jr. Collection.

Gifts from the church included a cup engraved with the inscription, *"Dr. A.S. Crapsey from St. Andrew's congregation and vestry, St. Andrew's Sunday -school, St. Monica's Society, St. Andrew's Parish Aid Society, St. Andrew's Women's Auxiliary Society, the Girls' Friendly Society, St. Andrew's Brotherhood and St. Andrew's Young People's Society."*[21] The cup contained gold and silver coins. Crapsey also received a check for $2500.00 from a parishioner. The congregation further presented Crapsey with a letter of commendation.[22]

During the evening, Dr. Elwood Worcester of St. Stephen's Church in Philadelphia gave tribute to Crapsey, who, after a quarter of a century had so faithfully and successfully served his parish at St. Andrew's. He compared Crapsey to Luther and Savonarola. Crapsey, signifying his true veneration of the saint respectfully declined the honor of his likeness. But as for Luther, Crapsey considered himself quite as aggressive and truculent.[23]

Worcester reminisced about a time when Crapsey visited Philadelphia. Judging that the sophisticated audience in Philadelphia would appreciate an erudite sermon, Crapsey decided to speak on a learned and theoretic subject. Worcester advised him to give one of his regular folksy-style sermons like he customarily gave from his own pulpit instead. His Crapseyish sermon resulted in the congregation being "crazy about Crapsey."[24]

Worcester paid homage to the simple parish priest who inspired him in his own successful, big-city ministry. His relationship with Crapsey continued and deepened after his departure from Rochester. He extolled Crapsey for remaining faithful in his commitment to his parish while achieving great personal success in his ministry. Worcester eventually founded the Emmanuel Movement in Boston, a movement relating to religion and health.[25]

Appreciation and recognition poured in from outside the parish as well. A short editorial in the *Evening Times,* summed up the mood of the city. It stated,

---

[21] Ibid.
[22] Crapsey, *Heretics,* p. 233.
[23] Ibid. p. 233.
[24] News article entitled, "His Anniversary. Dr. Crapsey Twenty- Five Years with St. Andrews." A.H. Crapsey Jr. Collection.
[25] Ibid.

> There is one simple thing to be said on the anniversary of Dr. Crapsey's coming to Rochester. He has been a power for good in the community for twenty-five years. He has preached strongly; he has sympathized strongly and he has wrought strongly; and he has influenced the private and public life of the city without going beyond his sphere as a clergyman. He has kept clear of political entanglements and movements for reform by the mere agitation of the surface of things, but day by day the circle of his personal power has been widening here and elsewhere. He is a bold man and a positive man, but it may be said that his personality has been a source of religious peace; for even where he entered into controversy, it was in the cause of liberality, and he has ever been disposed to welcome him as a brother who works sincerely toward the betterment of the individual and of society.[26]

Obviously Crapsey's liberality was, by this time, well known. He received recognition for being more than just the simple parish priest he assured everyone he was. People started listening closely to Crapsey. As his radical thinking increased, his lectures drew him farther beyond the pale of orthodoxy.

Though now in his mid-fifties, his vigor and tireless drive had diminished little. By approximately this time, the parochial school employed twenty teachers and enrolled one hundred and fifty students. Membership in the church had grown to three hundred and forty-two families with six hundred and fourteen communicants.[27] His church and related organizations had become eminent establishments in the city of Rochester. As the president of the Citizens Political Reform Association and contrary to the assertions of the *Evening Times,* Crapsey had become a major leader of social and political reform in the rapidly growing city of Rochester, NY.[28]

Shortly after the twenty-fifth anniversary festivities, Crapsey left on the Canadian Line for his third trip to England. This time he took a walking tour of Wales. Crapsey's stamina astounded many that knew him. He could sometimes walk thirty or forty miles a day and then go out for a short walk after dinner. Perhaps this was his adaptation of the sporting mentality of Theodore Roosevelt's manliness movement then sweeping the nation. Crapsey embarked with John Warrant Castleman, a prominent

---

[26] Reported in the *"Evening Times."* Mentioned in Crapsey, *Heretics,* pp. 233- 4.

[27] Edward M. Shepard *Argument before the Court of Review upon Appeal for A.S. Crapsey.* Oct. 19, 1906. Reprinted in Karen Alkalay- Gut's, *Alone,* p. 147.

[28] Reported in Blake McKelvey's *Rochester on the Genesee* Syracuse: Syracuse Univ. Press, 1973.

judge in Rochester. While walking through the Welsh mountains and moors Castleman encouraged Crapsey to press for further religious reform. By this time, Crapsey was already considering giving a series of lectures dedicated to "bringing the church into the twentieth century."[29]

The Protestant Episcopal Church had never been notably dogmatic. Its intellectual history is inseparable from the Anglican Church of England. Anglicanism, as an Erastian body in England and as a voluntary organization in America, recognized a variety of factions within its ranks. It diligently incorporated them through a methodology that might best be described as a *"via media."* There were High Church and Low Church factions, Anglo-Catholics, Evangelicals, Ritualists, Rationalists, Memorialists, Broad Churchmen, Liberal Catholics, and even Evangelical Catholics. Within the church some groups remained as insulated as denominations themselves.

By the 1870s a split occurred within the Protestant Episcopal Church as an evangelical faction refused to concede any further to the growing Catholic and alarming liberal directions of the church. Their position was expressed in the name they chose, the Reformed Episcopal Church. Considering the other schisms that had occurred, by the 1880s the Protestant Episcopal Church was moving steadily towards a broadened scope of the *via media* while embracing growing ecumenical concerns.[30]

In 1886, William Reed Huntington presented a doctrinal statement for a "national church" to the House of Bishops. With the adaptation of Huntington's statements concerning unity and reconciliation among Christians, the Chicago Quadrilateral officially embraced the prescribed concerns. The first point of unity stemmed from the declaration of the Bible as the "revealed Word of God." The second point avowed the Nicene Creed as a "sufficient statement of the Christian Faith." By the Chicago Lambeth Quadrilateral of 1888, the points presented by Huntington for a national church had become even broader. Modified to points A and B, they affirmed "The Holy Scriptures of the Old and New Testaments, as 'containing all things necessary to salvation,' and as being the rule and ultimate standard of faith." Point B now recommended "The

---

[29] Crapsey, *Heretics,* pp. 234- 5.

[30] See Diana Hochstedt Butler's *Standing Against the Whirlwind: Evangelical Episcopalians in Nineteenth- Century America* (New York: Oxford Univ. Press, 1995).

Apostles Creed, as the Baptismal Symbol; and the Nicene Creed, as the sufficient statement of the Christian Faith."[31]

Crapsey's sense of Catholicity included the broadest forms of interpretation. His latest collection of tractates, *The Disappointment of Jesus Christ* presented a means for incorporating all the various Christian groups. He soon became a darling of the broad camp establishing relationships with men who would later defend Crapsey's divergence from the creeds. He also continued to break unwritten Episcopal Church tradition by preaching and lecturing outside the denomination. As a consequence, Crapsey soon began to receive opportunities to lecture before other liberal Christian organizations. At one such lecture Crapsey presented visual imagery of the "unorganized forces of religion." He collected certain refuse from the streets and some apple seeds and then vividly pointing to the sky spoke of the ministry of heaven providing sunlight and rain. His ability to achieve the most dramatic affect was emblematic of Crapsey's ingenuity. He was a great hit on the liberal circuit making friends of individuals in high social places like George Foster Peabody, Spencer Trask and his wife the author, Katrina Trask, and Edward M. Shepard.[32]

Unfortunately, he simultaneously estranged the one who ordained him, Bishop Potter, and probably more troubling to Crapsey, the man whom he earlier looked to as both a mentor and a friend, Dr. Morgan Dix.[33] But to Crapsey, Catholicism had become a way of pushing the limits of orthodoxy by redefining dogmatic boundaries. To be Catholic, was to belong to the one great Christian church indeed. This true Catholic Church could embrace all of the possibilities that had escaped the grasp of both Roman Catholicism and Protestantism.

Anglicans in England were limited legally by their liturgical subscription to the historical tenets of the faith, and to the Athanasian and

---

[31] Armentrout, Don S., and Slocum, Robert Boak (eds.) *Documents of Witness: A History of the Episcopal Church, 1782- 1985* (New York: Church Hymnal Corp., 1994) pp. 224- 7.

[32] Peabody and Spencer Trask were business partners in investment banking at Spencer Trask & Co. The company sponsored Thomas Edison and financially resurrected the *NY Times* in 1896. Katrina Trask was an author and wife of first Trask and later of Peabody. Both men were philanthropists. Katrina donated her mansion in Saratoga Springs, New York "Yaddo" to aspiring artists. Biographies by David O'Donald Cullen Vol. 17, and Barbara L. Ciccarelli Vol. 21 in *American National Biography,* John A. Garraty and Mark C. Carnes eds. Oxford Univ. Press: New York, 1999.

[33] Crapsey, *Heretics,* pp. 226- 231.

Nicene Creeds. Crapsey was not the only one to struggle with such intellectual restrictions from the past. Others wrestled with discerning to what extent scriptural interpretation could be thought of as symbolic. Some wondered where the limits of intellectual orthodoxy were. They recognized their inability to subscribe to what they felt were outdated creeds. By the turn of the century a movement was well under way to restate the language of the creeds in light of more recent scientific evidence. Some argued that empirical science contradicted what they were forced to subscribe to. Recitation of the creed each Sunday was a necessary part of the liturgy, clearly representing subscription to the creeds. In Great Britain, it was a constitutional imperative.

The issue had become, not a ritualistic question of proper form as before, but wholly theological and ethical. When Bishop Gore reprimanded a Rev. C.E. Beeby for writing an article in the *Hibbert Journal,* that criticized the doctrine of the Virgin Birth, the bishop's point was rational and clear.

> How can a clergyman who consistently quotes the words of the creed in a manner that is intended to lead the flock of God in their devotion, continue to do so unless he believes in what he is leading others to believe?

The words of the creed were explicit, "Conceived by the Holy Ghost, born of the Virgin Mary." The Bishop therefore felt that he was bound to reestablish the confines that governed the offices of the clergy in the Church of England."[34]

Shortly thereafter, Beeby resigned his office in the church. The question might have been resolved had not broad churchmen taken up the issue on his behalf. They quickly made their feelings known. Canon Henson in particular, vocalized his disgust by accusing the bishop of bigotry. The bishop had responded to Mr. Beeby's resignation diplomatically, without agreeing with him, by relating how the church would be better off due to his low-key departure. In an outpouring of support, a former parishioner of Beeby's wrote him a letter with a check enclosed for one hundred pounds. The letter relayed the fact that Beeby's opinions were shared by many clergy and educated laity alike, and if the Church of England continued to persecute those who held such opinions they would cease to represent the beliefs of the English people.[35]

---

[34] Article in *Outlook Magazine* Vol. 76, Jan.- April, 1904.

[35] Ibid.

The waters had been publicly stirred by the Beeby affair. The problem of creed subscription was not going to disappear. Now the question of personal ethics had to be addressed as well. The church represented by Bishop Gore brought the question to the forefront. For those in the church that agreed with Beeby the question was how could they remain and submit to the continual recitation of a creed which they did not believe in. Was it unethical to do so without qualification? On the other hand, it was untenable to have pastors who did not believe what they were supposed to be leading others in believing. It was unethical to keep them in a perpetual state of hypocrisy. Subscription was central to the issue of faith itself.

Speaking of the scarcity of clergy applying for Holy Orders in the Anglican Church, a contributor in the *Hibbert Journal* stated that the shortage could be clearly realized as an incongruity between contemporary ideas and the ancient formularies. There was a true reluctance of young men to compromise their principles by acquiescing to the ancient beliefs. The contributor contended the practical way out of such a situation was to simply amend the creeds. That however, would take an act of Parliament due to the establishment of the Church. It was doubtful that would happen. But if the church were disestablished the doctrinal revisions could possibly take place without too much social, religious or political upheaval. However, in his political approach to this problem the author refused to fathom the depth of ingrained traditions that the Anglican Church inspired in the hearts of the ordinary population. This was true for its counterpart in America as well, where disestablishment was certainly not a problem.[36]

By the end of 1904, lines were being drawn for the social and religious battles to commence. Crapsey's impetuous statements had alienated a large portion of the church. Questions concerning the orthodoxy of members of the clergy quietly surfaced in Episcopal circles. The bishop of the diocese felt the heat of the mounting controversy. He recognized the responsibility of maintaining order and integrity in his flock. He perceived this charge as his duty under God. In his Council Address at Niagara Falls, Bishop Walker grew anxious about the ruminations of certain members of his clergy without mentioning any particular names.[37]

It would be difficult not to recognize the clear implications of the bishop's statements considering Crapsey's standing and high visibility.

[36] Ibid.

[37] G. Sherman Burrows *The Diocese of Western New York 1897- 1931* (Buffalo, 1935) p. 121.

[38] Ibid. p. 121.

Walker's primary theme was one of honesty and secondarily loyalty. He stated,

> It is with a deep sense of my responsibility as your father in God that I undertake to address you on the grave subject which shall occupy the short time that I shall give to this charge. I have asked for guidance from above.... It is a day of reckless and unconsidered speech in too many pulpits.... There is a natural sense and a non- natural sense in which Bible doctrine may be stated. The one is 'as this church hath received the same,' the other is as the individual man warps it to suit his personal fancy. The one shows honest loyalty, the other manifests obvious dishonesty.... Brethren of the Clergy, what is my closing word- not only take heed what ye hear- but take heed what ye speak. God help us all to do our duty now and ever.[38]

Crapsey disdained hypocrisy. He realized he needed to "walk honestly as in the day."[39] He could accomplish that in only one way. He needed to be open and forthcoming about his opinions. He would be heard and he would not compromise.

[39] Romans 13:13.

CHAPTER FOURTEEN

"Knowledge Puffeth Up"

Well aware of the conflict within the church Crapsey sought to remain at the forefront of the ongoing controversies. With this in mind, he embarked upon his most serious intellectual enterprise to date. After returning from his walking tour of Wales and with the prompting of his friend John Castleman, Crapsey considered presenting a series of lectures at St. Andrew's. The lectures were widely reported upon in the local press. He later gathered them into the book entitled, *Religion and Politics.*[1]

By this time Crapsey had considered the consequences but boldly chanced alienating the rather insulated upper-class who had supported him for over a quarter of a century. Crapsey's lectures began on Sunday evening December 4, 1904. He presented his version of the historical relationship between Christianity and government. He was proud of the fact that he habitually delivered his sermons extemporaneously. However, for the first time in his career, he spoke from notes prepared for the lectures. The new method provided him with the source material needed for a book.[2]

In his initial analysis, Crapsey traced the historical rise and fall of the Roman State from republic to imperial power. He found that several conditions contributed to the decline in morality from the time when Cicero declared that although others exceeded them in numbers, strength, cunning, the arts and natural intelligence, the Romans were noteworthy for their piety and religion.[3] Crapsey postulated that the great success that Roman Republic achieved created immense wealth. Eventually, slave labor replaced the industrious character of the citizens of Rome. Society stratified, with fewer citizens controlling more and more. A similar occurrence transpired with the management of the government. Things went slowly downhill from that point on. Caesar became both the law and

---

[1] A.S. Crapsey *Religion and Politics* New York: Thomas Whittaker, 1905.

[2] Crapsey, *Heretics,* p. 243.

[3] Lecture by A.S. Crapsey in *Rochester Democrat & Chronicle* Monday Dec. 5, 1904.

religious head of the state. Ultimately, he became a god, a symbol of the power and authority of the state. He was perhaps the most important deity to the Roman citizen in their polytheistic system. Crapsey argued that Caesar usurped all other gods, setting himself up as the only god. The state brought order by preventing anyone but itself from robbing, suppressing and dominating the peasantry and the poor. For Crapsey, the contemporary state was built on the same coercive tendencies. Crapsey attempted to show that the interaction between the empire and its religiosity corrupted both. The state substituted itself as the one thing that deserved veneration. Crapsey believed the Roman subjects were made to worship the one they feared the most, Caesar.[4]

In his second lecture, Crapsey considered the attitude of Jesus to the state. The Jews sought a militant Messiah. Crapsey, like those who sought to crucify Christ, ironically contended that the Messiah must have come to demolish the state. He asserted that the state was born out of fear. Crapsey argued that after fifteen miserable years of Tiberius Caesar's reign, Jesus entered upon his radical mission to destroy the state. Jesus' attitude toward the Roman State was one of contempt and hatred. He envisioned the system as inspired by the devil. He was not interested in curing the malevolence or transferring its power. His mission was to put an end to the evil system and tear down the state.[5]

Crapsey now embarked upon developing his own history of religion. For Crapsey, the Old Testament was materialistic and temporal; the New Testament was spiritual and eternal. He elevated the role of man. In arguing about Jesus' attitude toward mankind, Crapsey contended that man was divine rather than the state. To Crapsey, it was now the divinity of humanity instead of the humanity of divinity that would save the world.

For Crapsey, the Roman state began in fear with the city surrounded by hills and walls due to their dread of invaders.[6] Nevertheless, Crapsey expressed optimism in mankind stating that Jesus looked for the best in men and taught others to do likewise. Man did not have to naturally fear or consider one another as enemies, but they could be friends. He added that Jesus was anti-war, and that the fielding of armies was damnable, and atheistic. Crapsey also related that Jesus also had little or no regard for the

---

[4] Ibid.

[5] Lecture by A.S. Crapsey reported in the *Rochester Democrat & Chronicle* Monday Dec. 12, 1904. The headlines read "His Mission to Destroy State," and "Military Armaments and Courts of Law had no Place in the Plan of Jesus, Says the Rector of St. Andrew's Episcopal Church."

[6] Ibid.

legal system of the day. He felt Jesus held the lawyers and the courts equally in contempt.[7]

Crapsey's Jesus was a true radical. He had little use for private property and he pitied those who spent all their time accumulating wealth. "A man's life," He said, "does not consist in the abundance of the things He possesseth."[8] Moreover, Crapsey stated that Jesus despised the wealthy and those who held high offices in society. Jesus considered them insolent and vain and parasitic politically. To Crapsey, Jesus completely denied the power of the corrupt state. Crapsey asserted that Christ's reticence before Pilate revealed that, he denied the jurisdictional validity of the court that presumed to try Him. To Crapsey, Jesus refused Pilate the right to sit in question of His guilt.[9]

For Crapsey, Jesus' death was the ultimate remonstration against Rome. Certainly the Jewish leaders saw it that way. He argued that the symbol of the cross struck at the very foundation of society. Jesus was dangerous to the state as was demonstrated by His execution. In Crapsey's estimation, Jesus radically revolutionized the world by changing the hearts and minds of its inhabitants. He believed that the Kingdom Jesus spoke of was well within the capacity of humanity.[10]

By the time of the third lecture, the church was filled with people interested in Crapsey's perspective. University professors, judges, and a wide variety of individuals attended. The lectures were widely reported in the press as far as New York City and elsewhere.[11] Crapsey taught next that the state became even more wicked with its persecution of the early church. [12]

Crapsey then inferred that Christ Himself, as well as the early Christians, erred in their understanding of the establishment of the Kingdom of God. Crapsey concluded that Jesus anticipated the destruction and recreation of the world immediately. Therefore, because the Kingdom had not yet been realized, Christ's assertions were mistakes. Crapsey had taken a bold step indeed. It was one thing to question the inerrancy of the scriptures, quite another to infer that Jesus had made a mistake.[13]

---

[7] Ibid.
[8] Luke 12: 15.
[9] Ibid.
[10] Ibid.
[11] Crapsey, *Heretics,* pp. 242-3.
[12] Crapsey, *Religion* pp. 56-60.
[13] Column in *Rochester Democrat & Chronicle* Dec. 19, 1904.

He went on to state that the church began as a small group of Jewish believers holding confidence in the immediate Second Coming of Christ. Without that belief the church would never have come into existence. Although men sought the purity of the Jewish God, the belief that He was a universal God of all men prevented Israel and the Jews from spreading their faith throughout the world. But when men like Paul, Barnabas and Silas taught that the God of righteousness could be found in the belief in the power of the blood of Christ and how Jesus embodied the wisdom of God, men flocked to them to hear the good news. The new religion spread rapidly.[14]

Furthermore, Crapsey believed that Christianity brought a radical message of brotherly love and equality before God into a disorganized and disconnected world. In an original, entirely secular way, Crapsey now attempted to equate early Christianity with democracy as the highest form of human achievement in government. Crapsey stated that, in Christian countries churches existed for the rights of those that were in them and the ancient spirit of the Greeks was reestablished in the Christian communities. Like others, Crapsey perceived the early church as communitarian and socially pristine. The church was there to bless the people, not the other way around as had eventually developed with the elevation of the clergy. He argued that the immortal words of Abraham Lincoln embodied the spirit of the early church when he related that the United States was a government "of the people, by the people and for the people[15]

Crapsey extolled the early democratic church prior to its subsequent corruption. Crapsey undoubtedly knew that the government of Abraham Lincoln was not the government of the Protestant Episcopal Church or of the first century church. His description of the service of the office-holders of the early church obviously did not correspond with the contemporary Protestant Episcopal Church. He nonetheless realized the expediency of involving the audience's emotions by provoking their love of their heritage and quoting Lincoln's expressed legacy.[16]

Crapsey contrived a dichotomy to demonstrate how Christians formulated the doctrine of the Second Coming of Christ. In Crapsey's mind, only hostility reigned between the church and the state due to their oppositional characteristics. The one was imperial, while the other democratic. The imperial government despised the church and considered

[14] Ibid.
[15] Ibid.
[16] Ibid.

them as rebellious to the religious-state system. The church viewed the government as in open rebellion to God expecting it to be destroyed by His wrath. Wickedness pervaded all. According to Crapsey, annihilation of one or the other was entirely expected.[17]

For Crapsey, the Second Coming was a fantasy caused by the evil of the imperial state. Viewing eschatology from an amillennialist perspective alone, Crapsey assumed that was how the early church imagined it and he equated the Second Advent with the destruction of the world, not with a millennial reign like the fundamentalists. Regardless, he considered the end of the universe due to the sin of man, an illusion. Crapsey ultimately understood it all as a grandiose mistake, although there was metaphoric truth to it. He saw a new world embodied by the church emerging through the ashes of the old world's wickedness and that in itself justified their belief in a new world.[18]

Crapsey presented his next lecture on Christmas Eve. He compared the methods of Jesus with that of the rebellious Jew, Coziba. (Bar Cochba?) He noted how few recognized the name of Coziba in their daily speech. And yet almost no one failed to recognize the name of Jesus. The methods each employed historically accentuated the difference between the two. The teachings of Jesus were universally embraced while no one even remembered the teachings of Coziba.[19]

However, few people embraced the uncompromising saying of Jesus, "resist not evil." Crapsey considered it as a great stumbling block to modern Christians. He thought that many considered it to mean submission to that which was evil, even cowardliness. However, he explained that it was really a great contribution to the history of mankind by developing one of the great social doctrines of all time, that of passive resistance. Crapsey advocated the doctrine with variations for the remainder of his life. Crapsey noted that Jesus taught us to "return not evil for evil, but to return good for evil." Crapsey figured that in the end, Caesar was the weaker of the two because though he could kill the body of Jesus he could never stifle the spirit that remained.[20]

Crapsey believed that Jesus changed the course of human history through His method of passive resistance. The problem was that the ordinary man did not believe in the moral life of the spirit. Crapsey

---

[17] Ibid.

[18] Ibid.

[19] Lecture by A.S. Crapsey in *Rochester Democrat & Chronicle* December 25, 1904.

[20] Ibid.

contemplated how if a man recognized the ever-lasting life of the soul, that death then does not become an impediment or an end, but a means by which further influence could be exerted and ultimately a powerful tool to lead one to victory. Crapsey ignored the question of the afterlife. But the calculated process of death as a way of achieving something fascinated him. He portrayed the crucifixion as a method of extending Jesus' power and influence.[21]

Perhaps remembering his grandfather's political martyrdom, while sensing his religious martyrdom on the horizon, Crapsey felt a natural compassion, or perhaps better yet, a compulsion for the martyred. He perceived martyrdom as the ultimate means of gaining the greatest influence possible. Martyrdom provided meaningful inspiration for those left behind. Jesus limited the power of evil through His death since evil can only accomplish so much through the use of force. Whereas,

> through passive endurance He was ready not to kill, but if need be to be killed and the Christian world has in doctrine admitted the wisdom of Jesus, by finding in His death the salvation of mankind.[22]

Crapsey declared boldly that theologians had subsequently obscured the real meaning of Jesus' death. Theologians asserted that Christ died to satisfy the justice and therefore the wrath of God. Crapsey considered that as taking vengeance, and that concept was simply foreign to the idea of God or Christ. He stated that Christ's death couldn't satisfy God's vengeance because God had none, but it exposed the wickedness of men. For Crapsey, Jesus' death was a victory of the human spirit considering all the forces that were brought to bear against Him.[23]

Crapsey elevated Jesus' methods to those of the greatest humanitarian ideals while reducing His death to the mere gaining of power and influence. The traditional spiritual meaning of His death was ignored. Crapsey reduced it to metaphoric worldly significance. Crapsey considered the statement of how the blood of martyrs was the seed of the church from his humanitarian perspective. The use of arms by the zealot Jews would bring death and further enemies but the work of the martyrs brought life and fellowship to the church.[24]

---

[21] Ibid.
[22] Ibid.
[23] Ibid.
[24] Ibid.

Crapsey celebrated the methods that Jesus employed by noting that you had to win one's heart to win one's mind. Crapsey believed that those that lived by the sword died by it. It was God's universal law of how like begets like. Likewise, love would ultimately beget love. The principle of how like begets like that Crapsey quoted, was a principle more akin to paganism, and the primitive practice of universal magic than to Christianity. Crapsey's understanding of what Christ did on the cross now held the same natural, moral applications that Unitarians had long asserted.

Applying Christ's passive resistance to the nations of the world, Crapsey decried the stockpiling of weaponry as destructive and the nations indeed had to fear the damage that the weapons could inflict. But, if they disarmed themselves they would have nothing left to fear from one another. Crapsey figured naively that one's more hostile neighbors would never destroy such a nation, instead it would become like a "monastery" and as such it would set the standards that would eventually rule the world.[25]

Crapsey further applied Jesus' teachings to the criminal justice system. He thought that the way to end criminal behavior was to make the criminal honest. One must reach even the most degenerate somewhere within the deep expanses of his soul instilling within him the desire to be good. Applying the law of how like begets like again, Crapsey noted that if one were first good to another the other would necessarily return the favor. Crapsey considered this the "doctrine of Jesus," and if it was diligently adhered to society would no longer apprehend the need for incarceration or execution.[26]

Shortly after Christmas, 1904, a group of eight clergymen from the Rochester area, including Crapsey, circulated *A Primer of the Peace Movement.* The pamphlet was distributed to those who would hopefully use it to promote peace including six hundred teachers and two hundred pastors regardless of denomination. Lucia Ann Mead of Boston prepared the pamphlet. With her husband Edwin, they previously hosted the International Peace Conference in Boston. Mrs. Mead lectured at the Universalist Church on Sunday, January 8, 1905 under the sponsorship of the Political Equality Club in the city of Rochester. The pamphlet detailed the labor of the peace movement. It also provided a brief history of recent accomplishments including legal undertakings, tribunals started, lists of articles and books on peace and it forwarded suggestions of how to

---

[25] Ibid.
[26] Ibid.

abolish war both individually as well as corporately. The establishment of the World Court at the Hague in 1901 received considerable attention. The pamphlet also mentioned the desire for the establishment of the "Stated World Congress." The World Congress would at first be advisory, but would hopefully grow in its influence progressively. The pamphlet further explored the need for ongoing disarmament amongst nations, the need for treaty arbitration by the World Court and the introduction of an international police force. [27]

The pamphlet asserted that people of various occupations and responsibilities could help. Businessmen needed to know that over half of the nation's revenue was on armament expenditures for defense rather than allocated to fight poverty. Editors could help by accentuating the truth regardless of its unpopularity. They could help by editing fake reports, emotional and disingenuous headlines, and by suppressing the cynics and those who flippantly tarnished the case for peace. The pamphlet presumptuously advised editors to realize their responsibility to think for the masses.[28]

Ministers could help by preaching the Christ of peace as stated in the New Testament rather than the God of war associated with Joshua and others in the old. One should carefully explain hard to understand verses about how Christ stated that He came to bring a sword or division to a home. In addition, one must never sanction boys' brigades in one's church. Finally, parents could help the cause of peace by, abolishing toy guns or playing war in the home. It made no sense to allow that kind of behavior. One might as well give a child a rope and have them play hanging as to allow them to go around shooting one another. [29]

Crapsey's fifth lecture dealt with "The Rise of the Imperial Church." He lectured on the conversion of Constantine, who unified the empire through his vision of the cross with the words "by this conquer." But Crapsey denied the validity of such a vision, as it was in his mind, a moral contradiction. The Jesus of heaven would never contradict His teaching on earth.[30] Rather, Crapsey attributed Constantine's conversion to astute, skillful politics. Men were being drawn to the church who wanted to live better, more productive lives. They also desired a sense of fellowship with one another that provided unity while the world struggled under the

---

[27] Reported in the *Rochester Democrat & Chronicle* Sunday, Jan. 1, 1905.
[28] Ibid.
[29] Ibid.
[30] Lecture by A.S. Crapsey. Reported in *Rochester Democrat & Chronicle* Monday, Jan. 2, 1905.

burden of a class structured system. Crapsey perceived a spirit of democratic equality in the early church that inspired a common bond and vision.[31]

The episcopate came into existence, according to Crapsey, because in every town and village throughout the empire a body of believers chose a leader, advised by a body of elders. At the beginning no real distinctions between the clergy and laity existed. To Crapsey, the rise of the Episcopal order was the by-product of the exemplary lives lived by the early bishops. He described the lives of St. Nicholas, and of Polycarp as examples of how Episcopal benevolence originally worked toward the good of the people. Christianity triumphed through its revolutionary morality over the raw power of the empire. But the church lost its simplicity during its eventual integration with the Imperial State. There resulted a structured system of wealth and intellectual controversy and ultimately the church acquiesced to the state.[32]

As the Christian ministry returned to positions similar to the ancient priesthood, the place of the bishop then became one of power and social honor. Crapsey noted, "the very temples of the pagan Gods became the churches of Christianity and the bishop of Rome became the Pontifex Maximus." Crapsey argued that "by one hundred years after Constantine the church had become imperial in its administration, and it has been so ever since."[33]

The lectures appeared in the newspaper every Monday morning. With all probability Bishop Walker would have heard about them through his associates in Rochester or by following them through the Rochester newspapers. When the media recognized someone in the clergy, the bishop soon found out. Crapsey referred to the hierarchy of the church in unflattering terms. However, Walker and the other clergymen who believed in the church hierarchy patiently endured the criticism leveled at them. To complicate matters, within a week a presentment was being made against Bishop Talbot in Pennsylvania due to the controversy created by his alleged harassment of a priest of his diocese. The case may have encouraged Crapsey to continue with his bold commentary.[34] The Irvine-Talbot case demonstrated the kind of heated ecclesiastic litigation that could occur due to strained relations between a bishop and one of his priests. The bishop received anecdotal evidence impugning the character

[31] Ibid.
[32] Ibid.
[33] Ibid.
[34]Talbot case reported in the *Rochester Democrat & Chronicle* Sat. Jan. 7, 1905.

of one of the priests of his diocese. Disciplined for what he considered false accusations, the priest responded through an ecclesiastical court presenting the bishop.[35]

At the same time Dr. Lyman Abbott, Congregationalist minister at Plymouth Church Brooklyn, came under fire for an address he gave at Appleton Chapel at Harvard. Abbott had stated he no longer believed in God as a "first cause." Abbott mentioned that because of this many might consider him heretical. He found the concept illogical as he wondered, where then did the first cause come from? Apparently disavowing the validity of the Genesis account Abbott stated, "the theory was unscriptural." As far as he was concerned, it wasn't taught until the most recent millennium. Dr. Abbott thought of God as an omnipresent force rather than the bearded being sitting on a cloud with a thunderbolt in His hand.[36]

One of Crapsey's contemporaries, Dr. Murray Bartlett, rector of St. Paul's Episcopal Church on East Avenue in Rochester rushed to Abbott's defense. Bartlett considered that mankind was becoming progressively enlightened regarding the ultimate question of God. Ideas changed over time causing men to perceive things differently in light of the changing times. Bartlett stated, "his understanding of God was through the light of Jesus Christ as he believed Abbott's was also. Therefore, one must be cautious about using the term heretic. In a progressive sense, what was considered heresy in the present-day might become the orthodoxy of the future."[37]

At the next Sunday evening lecture at St. Andrew's Church Crapsey spoke on "The Church, a Function of the State: The History of the Eastern Church." Crapsey hoped to expose the origins of dogmatic oppression within the church and demonstrate how the church and the state collaborated in their attempt to control men. The church restricted men's minds, while the state enslaved them physically. He used the dramatic example of the desecration of St. Sophia's church in 404 AD.[38]

---

[35] William S. Price Esq. *The Irvine- Talbot Case, With Notes on the Presentment of Bishop Talbot.* (Phila.: John R. McFetridge & Sons, 1902).

[36] Reported in the *Rochester Democrat & Chronicle* Monday, Jan. 9, 1905. Lyman Abbott succeeded Henry Ward Beecher at Plymouth Church, 1888- 1899 and was also an editor of *Outlook*, a liberal, New York magazine publication from 1893-1922.

[37] Ibid.

[38] A.S. Crapsey's lecture reported in the *Rochester Democrat & Chronicle* Monday, Jan. 9, 1905.

For Crapsey, the problems started when the church and the state came together to impose religion. He saw the Edict of Theodosius as the point of departure between the original teachings of Jesus and the state sponsored orthodoxy that attempted to control the people's minds and persecute its own populace. Men were now imprisoned and executed for heresy. Romans considered the Christians as rebels but the church now condemned men and women for misconstruing scripture. It all started with the edict of Theodosius, which according to Crapsey apprehended cultural advancement in the eastern empire for a millennium. After experiencing the physical hazards of well-coordinated, mind control, the Eastern Church declined rapidly.[39]

Speaking of the Russian intelligentsia, especially Christians like Tolstoy, Crapsey argued, "they felt betrayed." The Russian reformers had become estranged from the dogma of the Eastern Church especially with reference to the teachings of Jesus. Crapsey stated, "Tolstoy gave up his brilliant career for his love of truth." He considered Tolstoy a true revolutionary fighting against the doctrine, ceremony, and tyranny of the church.[40] Crapsey realized political change was on the horizon, especially in Russia, commenting that Russia was by far the closest to revolutionary change. He stated prophetically, "the revolution to come would be even longer lasting in its influence than the Reformation."[41] He stated emphatically,

> The doctrine of passive resistance and communistic living have a stronger hold in the great empire than anywhere else in the world. The bomb throwing Nihilist is simply retarding the movement that is at last to make Russia the most Christian and democratic of the nations.[42]

Times were changing. In Rochester, for the first time Rabbis shared pulpits with clergy from Presbyterian churches as well as from other denominations. Liberal churchmen and rabbis alike challenged the historical accuracy and literary salience of the ancient texts. Liberal religious scholars believed the Jews adopted their belief in life in the hereafter from the religiosity of the Persians, the Babylonians and the philosophical contemplation of the Greeks, especially Plato. The original concept had been that the nation of Israel was to be eternal, not the

---

[39] Ibid.
[40] Ibid.
[41] Ibid.
[42] Ibid.

individual soul. Clergy and laity alike pondered whether the scriptures actually supported the traditional beliefs or did the Bible teach them merely as concepts.[43]

Crapsey's next lecture dealt with "The Rise of the Roman Church to Imperial Power in Europe." He detailed the power of the Vatican, concentrating on a few popes of exceptional ability like Leo I, the great organizer of the church, and Gregory The Great, the missionary pope. Through Gregory's missionary efforts much of Northern Europe and England converted. Incredibly, Gregory had more pastoral influence on Europe than any Pope up to his time. Crapsey noted how "the plethora of letters that remain confirm his industrious ministry."[44] He equated the monastic life with the attempt by men to literally fulfill the words of scripture. By such means the popes extended their control over Europe. The monasteries established the power of the church. The monks were the foot soldiers of the pope who intended to make the state subservient to the church.[45]

In Crapsey's eyes, the temporal power of the church started when Charlemagne increased the papal territory. On Christmas Eve in the year 800 AD, Pope Leo III crowned Charlemagne Holy Roman Emperor. The empire consolidated by Charlemagne eventually broke up after his death causing tragedy for Rome but conversely creating a revival at the grass-root level of the monasteries. Eventually Hildebrand, who became pope Gregory VII, succeeded to the papacy vanquishing the ineptitude of the previous popes and determining the policy of the church for a full 66 years. Hildebrand worked to stamp out several abuses in the church. He used the power of excommunication and the interdict. He sought to eradicate concubinage, simony and the benefice. Hildebrand sought to reinstate the authority of the church by reforming it of its abuses. Crapsey viewed the submission of Emperor Henry IV to Pope Gregory VII as one of the most dramatic episodes in church history. The power of the papacy had returned.[46]

For Crapsey, the zenith of the papacy came with the assumption of Innocent III, from 1198 to 1216. Crapsey declared that the power of the popes exceeded even that of the Caesars. Crapsey now believed the state

---

[43] Lecture of Rabbi Max Landsberg in the Third Presbyterian Church of Rochester reported in the *Rochester Democrat & Chronicle* Monday, Jan. 9, 1905.

[44] Lecture by A.S. Crapsey reported in *Rochester Democrat & Chronicle* Mon., Jan. 16, 1905.

[45] Ibid.

[46] Ibid.

had become a true functionary of the church. The nobility remained subservient to the priests and the pope was elevated to the position of vicar of the King of Kings.[47]

The next lecture explored the subsequent "Fall of the Papacy." Beginning with Boniface VIII, the papacy fell from its lofty heights. The pope had ascended through underhanded manipulation and political maneuvering. His arrogance led to a conflict with Phillip IV of France. Boniface VIII's problems included confronting a growing spirit of nationalism, along with a tide of secular education coupled with the power of the world's wealth. Emboldened with worldly power, King Phillip confronted Boniface, thereby symbolizing the conflict of the secular state against the church. This eventuated further problems throughout society including confrontations between lawyers and clergymen, merchants and monks as so on. Phillip's victory, from Crapsey's point of view, was the triumph of the secular over the church, the temporal over the spiritual.[48]

After the papal bull Unum Sanctum Ecclesiam, partisans of the King of France imprisoned the pope. That Crapsey argued, was "the end of the power of the papacy over the political affairs of the Europe."[49] The papacy moved to Avignon, France with the election of the puppet pope Clement V. Popularly known as the seventy-year captivity of the papacy, Crapsey termed it, "the papacy's self-imposed exile of seventy years." Martin V became the first of a long line of purely Italian popes after Constance. Crapsey contended that these Italian popes were solely interested in personal profiteering and bringing resources back into Rome. Eventually the papacy became, in Crapsey's words, "the plaything of pig and worldling."[50]

Crapsey's next message concerned "The Establishment of National Churches." This subject was close to home considering the relationship between the Church of England and the Episcopal churches. Crapsey began with a radical reevaluation of the Reformation. He stated, "Luther has been misunderstood and over-rated." He was never the champion of freedom when it concerned freedom of thought. The Reformation was not about freeing the intellect. The Reformation was about reinstituting the old, written values of antiquity and investing power in the localities rather than in the universal church. The Reformation allowed the princes of each

---

[47] Ibid.

[48] Lecture by A.S. Crapsey reported in *Rochester Democrat & Chronicle* Monday, Jan. 23, 1905.

[49] Ibid.

[50] Ibid.

individual German state to become the head of his own church, regardless of whether they were Catholic or Protestant, and the subjects meekly followed their rulers.[51] In contrast to scholars like Max Weber who later contended that the extraordinary influence of the Reformation promoted a "spirit of capitalism," that eventually transformed western civilization, Crapsey figured, "it was the princes and nobility who really benefited from the Reformation."[52]

The national church establishments were the products of the Reformation. The English model exemplified the complicity between church and state. Crapsey lectured that Henry VIII found willing accomplices within the upper echelons of the church in his attempt to break away from the authority of Rome. The collaborators were merely submissive to the will of the king. The Reformation was different in England historically from the rest of Europe because Henry maintained a traditional form of continuity in the church, unlike the churches on the continent. The ancient practices were conserved in the vernacular and the Prayer Book became the precious inheritance of the English people. Crapsey noted that Henry became the head of the church through an act of Parliament. Elizabeth eventually established a church that excluded none but the extremists on both sides, Catholics and Puritans. Though tested for a time by Cromwell, Crapsey felt that it was the Elizabethan church that maintained the love and respect of the English people.[53]

Although the English church was subjected to the state it was both progressive in thought and conservative in form. Crapsey noted,

> The English church will freely allow every clergyman to deny the damnatory clauses of the Athanasian creed in his sermon, but will compel him to say them in the service. Canon Henson, the radical, and Canon Newboldt, the ritualist, are equally devoted to the liturgical worship of the church. It is the strength of the church of England that men of widely differing opinions are of one mind in worship and in work.[54]

Crapsey coveted that freedom and those British character traits for the Protestant Episcopal Church. He respected the special prelates who were simultaneously devout and politically endowed and he considered their

51 Lecture by A.S. Crapsey reported by *Rochester Democrat & Chronicle* Mon., Jan. 30, 1905.
52 See Max Weber's *The Protestant Ethic and the Spirit of Capitalism* translated by Talcott Parsons (New York: Scribner, 1952).
53 Ibid.
54 Ibid.

commission a phenomenally superb arrangement. He regarded the present Archbishop of Canterbury as that sort of man. His visit to the Episcopal convention brought class and decorum as Crapsey noted how he had risen from the humblest of origins to the top of his field. He respected how the Archbishop must subsequently satisfy the requirements of both the church and the state in Great Britain.[55]

Crapsey felt that in the Protestant Episcopal Church, the clergy were evaluated by their salaries. This unfortunately translated into how much a rector was worth spiritually to the people he served. Crapsey concluded his lecture by expressing his dissatisfaction with the diocese and the Bishop of Western New York. Still disturbed over his loss in the battle over the bishopric, Crapsey assumed the bishop's avarice as it related to his professional status and social standing. Ultimatelly he prevented the City of Rochester from having its own bishop. Crapsey argued,

> The city of Rochester for instance is not a see city of the Episcopal church, as it ought to be, because in the opinion of many of the leading members of our communion the dignity of the episcopal office depends upon the extent of territory over which the bishop presides and upon the wealth of the church as expressed in property and contributions.[56]

Crapsey's next lecture was entitled, "The Relation of the Church and State in the United States." He spoke of how the Pilgrims shaped the political and spiritual destiny of the new nation since their intent was to have the church and state in mutual accord. Eventually, the settlement at Plymouth attracted the Puritans, who were growing increasingly agitated at the policies of the English establishment.[57]

Puritan theology was antithetical to Crapsey's, but he was American enough to own the legendary exodus. Crapsey noted that the strength of the Puritan ideal was in their concept of their theocracy modified with English common law. Crapsey however, agreed with the progressive scholars in criticizing their intolerance. He disparaged their myopia in considering it treason to question the dogmatic inspiration of the scriptures. The Puritans attempted to secure their experiment through

---

[55] Ibid.

[56] Ibid.

[57] Lecture by A.S. Crapsey at St. Andrew's Church reported in *Rochester Democrat and Chronicle* Mon., Feb. 6, 1905.

political limitations by keeping the power primarily in the hands of the church members.[58]

But in the Puritan experiment, Crapsey also saw far reaching implications for government. The election of men coming together as a covenanting nation of saints provided a formidable concept of a God-sanctioned state. According to Crapsey, the concept remained in the national conscience because of its high ideals. He believed the experiment failed institutionally but American culture held on to the enduring ideal nonetheless. In fact it predominated as the primary American ethos until the time of the Civil War.[59]

Crapsey envisioned a contemporary spiritual conflict between commercialism and the "spirit of Puritanism." He believed a new warfare was being waged between the capitalist and the minister. Merchants merely envisioned men as outlets for their merchandise while ministers saw men as people. Crapsey concluded that his study of history clearly demonstrated how the church was necessarily in subjection to the state or the state was in submission to the church. It had to be one way or the other. But Crapsey broke it down even further into simple dualistic terms. He figured either the spiritual or the material would reign supreme. He noted how explicit, spiritual interests distinguished the great periods of history. The great periods of moral decay and depravity were characterized by the struggle for material gain. Therefore, the church needed to maintain its high calling and positional role of being the "conscience of the state." For Crapsey, it was the departure from that calling that caused the church to become a functionary of the state. Subsequently they both fell.[60]

Crapsey's love for the dramatic in his presentations made him a great oratorical success in Rochester. His store of knowledge was general and his analysis simplistic. His prophetic utterances consisted of vague predictions. One wonders what Walter Rauschenbusch, Crapsey's "intimate friend," then at the Rochester Theological Seminary as a church

---

[58] Ibid.

[59] Ibid.

[60] Ibid.

historian, thought about these wide-ranging lectures. The record is unfortunately silent.[61]

[61] Quotations indicate Sharpe's words. Dores Robinson Sharpe *Walter Rauschenbusch* New York: Macmillan Co., 1942.

CHAPTER FIFTEEN

"For There Must Also be Heresies Among You"

On February 20, 1905, Crapsey presented a bold socialistic statement on the relation between church and state in America. It created a stir in the commercially- oriented, lay sector of the Protestant Episcopal Church. Formerly, Crapsey dealt with historical information considered harmless. His next lecture on "A Commercialized Church in a Commercialized State," hit closer to home.

After the denial of his request for the separation of the diocese, Crapsey's ministry took a decided turn. He rejected the power and authority over him. He took the offensive against the hierarchical church and the offices of the clerical order. He openly and visibly demonstrated distaste not only for the bishop but also for the highly successful, business and commercially oriented laity, whom he served. As his disillusionment with the church deepened, his passion for modern science intensified. Science would pervade society with, political, economic and religious applications. Like Belshazzar, Crapsey believed he could see the "handwriting on the wall."

In his lecture, Crapsey described a meeting he attended in which the Mayor of Rochester read a paper before the Ministerial Association of Rochester. The mayor opened by stating that there was no natural relationship between the church and the state. The only thing that tied the two was the rather vague expression concerning God in the oath of office required of those who enter into public service. According to Crapsey, the mayor subsequently sought to elevate the religious aspect of this solemn act, and use the oath of office to consecrate his endeavors. He figured that he was by his solemn utterance, now in the service of God. Crapsey declared, "When an officer of the state takes his oath of office seriously he makes the state a religious institution; it rests not only on the consent of the people but also upon the will of God."[1]

---

[1] Lecture by A.S. Crapsey, in the *Rochester Democrat & Chronicle* Mon., Feb. 13, 1905.

But Crapsey derided the gullibility of elected officials who thought that all the ministers of the city were interested in was the other-worldly existence of things. Crapsey reckoned cynically, that the mayor displayed a conspicuous sense of naiveté when he figured that those in attendance were solely interested in the influence that government had upon their religious experience like the blue laws.[2] The mayor thought that ministers took no interest in pressing social concerns. The opening of saloons on Sunday alone held the clergy's interest, as that would directly affect their occupations. Conversely, Crapsey ridiculed the clergy's lack of interest in anything but that which paid the bills for them on a weekly basis. He noted rhetorically, "if a minister could not defeat a bartender for the attendance of his constituents then where was the real authority of God over his creation?"[3]

Nevertheless, Crapsey increasingly considered the profession he had labored in for over twenty-five years as a farce. He would take the criticism due any prophet that dared point out the hypocrisy of the ministry. To Crapsey, the greatest evil was the clergy's monetary attachment and that needed addressing immediately. He saw both the ministerial and the political administrations operating in the realm of materialism. Although their paths only intersected on Sunday due to the establishment of censure laws, both were simultaneously immersed in an environment of commercialism that ultimately corrupted their occupations[4]

Crapsey gave a short review of recent American history attempting to identify exactly how and when this evil surfaced. Things had changed considerably since industry was centered on the family farm and people knew the merchants who handled their commerce. Once upon a time in America, merchants were personally responsible for both their products and their service. He viewed historic American society and the church as coterminous entities with the church providing spiritual guidance through a highly respected member of the community as its minister. Crapsey portrayed the early era of American history as vigorous and fit. He equated moral and physical wholesomeness with commercial and agricultural propriety extolling the purity of the English race, the prolific nature of the expanding nation and the familial aspects of local governments. He noted how society developed like individual families, without the problems of divorce or infertility.[5]

---

[2] Ibid.
[3] Ibid.
[4] Ibid.
[5] Ibid.

As the nation grew it became physically and morally complex. He considered the Jacksonian period as an age of political selfishness. Immigration increased and industrial capabilities were augmented by steam and machinery. Remembering his maternal grandfather, and the time when abolitionists were regularly excommunicated, he spoke scathingly of the church's failure to understand the ethical imperative behind the anti-slavery campaign. Crapsey believed that men of the utmost quality and character were disassociated from the churches at that time. Crapsey's antipathy towards the church was justified historically by his family's early experience. He noted that such moral men as Whittier, Emerson, Garrison, Phillips, Brown, Sumner and even Lincoln were outside the communion of, and in some cases even banned from orthodox churches.[6]

The country changed dramatically after the Civil War. Crapsey believed that after the war the nation's merchants grew great with power. Crapsey tied the corruption of the latter period to the men who had personally profited by the war's devastation. The merchant class received possession of the bonded debt and with it, enormous revenue. Crapsey considered that the age of industrial proliferation and organization was characterized by vice so widespread it threatened the nation's freedom. The railroad wielded immense power and the administrations of both Johnson and Grant were horribly stained with corruption. The Tweed scandal in New York City exemplified the vice in government. Crapsey mentioned how Tweed's real employment was intrinsically tied with the businessmen of the city. In Crapsey's mind things didn't have to be necessarily unbalanced and dissolute. Crapsey blamed the problem on business practices void of any moral or ethical constraints that challenged the representative system of American government.[7]

While the problem was not as bad in Rochester as in the rest of the country, the common man had all but capitulated. Times had changed dramatically from when a man could rise from the ranks to own a shop or industrial enterprise. The economy had become so impersonal that the great shops and factories simply bought labor and skills in the same manner in which they bought or sold raw products.[8]

But the men Crapsey spoke of paid his salary. They listened to his sermons weekly and they supported his ministry and family with special gifts like trips to Europe. They held high positions in the government, sat

[6] Ibid.
[7] Ibid.
[8] Ibid.

in judgment and wrote the laws. More numerous in the Episcopal Church than in any other, these men were being tainted by profiteering merchants with commercial interests impervious to moral convictions. Crapsey certainly realized that he was alienating more than just the hierarchy of the church with his injudicious statements. He spoke against the system itself, obviously realizing how it was sustained by the wealthy and powerful who supported the Protestant Episcopal Church. Indeed, those who Crapsey railed against were the system, pure and simple. The wealthy commercialists he ministered to and patronized for so many years were intensely interested in what Crapsey was now saying from his pulpit on Sunday evenings. The system that placed the worker entirely at the mercy of the buyer and seller created a conflict between the classes. The settlement of that struggle would establish the nature of the American society of the future.[9]

Crapsey came to the climax of his analysis. The issue concerned was one of democracy. Would the people govern themselves or would the commercialists rule them? Crapsey believed the commercial class definitely ruled. They ruled the government and made the laws. They exploited the workers, controlled the utilities and were even capable of levying taxes without the public's approval.[10]

Commercialism corrupted society. It took possession of the press, with its advertising agents. The streets became hideous with poles and wires. It even affected travel. Americans were considered vulgar and extravagant on the continent of Europe. Its wealth built churches, while its patrons listened to the gospel. They insisted on orthodoxy, but carefully kept the ministry tucked away in a duplicitous place considered hallowed thereby preventing religion from having any profound effect upon their lives.[11]

In conclusion, Crapsey further deplored the exploitation of women in various vocations. With a revolutionary's spirit, his voice rising, he equated the state sponsored church with the establishment of wealth and vested interests. As Crapsey knew from personal experience, they were the final arbiters of the system. Grasping the attention of the audience with the voice of the skilled orator he derided the power of the state church proclaiming,

> You can believe in any one of the one hundred and forty creeds of Christendom that you please; you can belong to this or that party, but there

[9] Ibid.
[10] Ibid.
[11] Ibid.

> is one thing you must do or die; you must go to the plain of Dura, and at the sound of the coronet, flute, harp, sackbut, psaltry, dulcimer, and all kinds of music you must fall down and worship the golden image which this modern Nebuchadnezzar has set up.

Moreover, Crapsey left them with the question, "What are you going to do about it?" Would they like Shadrach, Mishach and Abednego go into the fiery furnace or would they bow down? Crapsey left them stirred with passion.[12]

Crapsey had finally reached the point of no return. He exposed the commercial system for what it was and alienated himself from its benefactors in the process. But Crapsey lived in their midst. He rubbed shoulders with the captains of industry, took walking tours with judges and hobnobbed with lawyers daily. Something beyond a question of scruples drove him to rail at the church. Perhaps he was obsessed with martyrdom and sacrificing himself on the altar of modernistic religion, evolutionary theory and socialism. Perhaps he was enraged by the inability to further his career. Perhaps he was simply fed up and sincerely impassioned with his cause.

Crapsey's next lecture tipped the scales, giving his critics all the ammunition they needed to relieve him from his post. Crapsey began where he left off. He bemoaned the fact that the clergy's influence was waning in society. The intellectual direction of the nation had turned and the clergy was losing its authority. The clergy must agree with the new scientific evidence to regain a legitimate intellectual standing. They should also stand for egalitarian progress. The churches were both undemocratic and unscientific in spirit. Unless that fact changed they were doomed to intellectual ambiguity. In essence, they would be devoid of any intellectual status at all.[13]

Looking back into the nineteenth century Crapsey wistfully noted that education had been a primary function of the clergy. The presidents of both the larger universities and smaller colleges were almost without exception ministers. People took for granted that the teachers and administrators were clergy. But, the church's influence had receded over the past fifty years. Now, the presidents of most universities and colleges were laymen. Institutions of higher learning sought their faculty from an emerging professional class of laymen. Moreover, the public schools had

---

[12] Ibid.

[13] Lecture by A.S. Crapsey in the *Rochester Democrat & Chronicle* Mon., Feb. 20, 1905.

actually become hostile to churchmen of any religious persuasion. Crapsey noted how nothing was as antagonistic to the public as the intervention of the religious sector into the nation's public school system.[14]

To Crapsey, the clergy were summarily forced out of the important matters of life. He wondered where the clergy truly fit into the social regimen of the day. He believed that separation from the practical matters of society produced a psychological question of value in the clergy's worthiness in vocation and society. For all practical purposes, religion had been effectively removed from both the public life of American society and the modern world. Depicting this modern calamity of complete separation between the spiritual and the mundane, Crapsey noted how there would be little value to life and desperation would ensue if that were completely true.[15]

Out of that desperate situation Crapsey advocated a new form of pragmatic religion. He enthusiastically proclaimed how religion didn't need to fade away but how it could rather evolve to survive in the modern world. A new kind of vital religion would eventually become a part of every aspect of modern life. It would be socially pervasive, expressed in public as well as kept in private. It would be in the home, in the streets and in the marketplace as well as in the political arena. The loss of religious influence evolved from the fact that contemporary religion needed to gain a wider scope than the former doctrinal interpretation permitted.[16]

For Crapsey the answer for the church was in establishing a democratic spirit and thereby reestablishing its intellectual validity in society, even if the cost meant denying the power of the supernatural. He believed the new church must incorporate democracy and science into its dogma to regain its intellectual legitimacy. He noted how the modern universe of thought substituted the laws of nature for the mystery of the miraculous. Men once filled the world with spirits that portrayed their hopes and fears. The ancients based their beliefs upon spirits who could manipulate nature for their own purposes.[17]

Crapsey boiled religion down to the universal human conception of gods made in human images. He believed that the gods were merely "deified men" who could use disease or natural disasters to convey their power or their authority. Crapsey ascribed the control of worldly

---

[14] Ibid.
[15] Ibid.
[16] Ibid.
[17] Ibid.

kingdoms to the conspiratorial power of men, be they kings or gentry or lawyers or merchants. He considered his religious analysis a theoretic rendering of the miraculous. The theory of the miraculous pointed to events in nature as having a supernatural reference.[18]

Crapsey saw a great conflict between the imagination of men and the rationality of scientific thought. He recognized how the scientific revolution had changed the world. Therefore, science and the miraculous simply could not exist in the same universe of thought. Because Christians found no credence in any religion besides Christianity, they never bothered to consider comparisons between their religion based on the miraculous and the primitive superstitions of the ancient mind. Protestants especially expressed annoyance at both the Catholic Church and the Christian Scientists for their belief in the miraculous. Their beliefs were considered either psychologically beneficial or mere fantasy. Despite their rejection of the miraculous the Protestant church's dogma was based on the miraculous as well. Protestants however believed their concept of the miraculous as the exception because it stayed true to the course of the scriptural rendition. But according to Crapsey, the Bible was not a miraculous book. It was simply fine literature containing profound spiritual relevance.[19]

Crapsey might have left his argument there but he seized the opportunity to compound the sum of his heresy. The crux of his transgression needed to be completely delineated, exposed, and expressed in its entirety by his denial of the deity of Jesus of Nazareth. Crapsey boldly stated:

> In light of scientific research, the Founder of Christianity, Jesus the Son of Joseph, no longer stands apart from the common destiny of man in life and death. He is in all things like as we are, born as we are born, dying as we die, and both in life and death is in the keeping of that same divine power, that heavenly Fatherhood which delivers us from the womb and carries us down to the grave. When we come to know Jesus in His historical relations, we see that miracle is not a help- it is a hindrance to an intelligent comprehension of His person, His character, and His mission. We are not alarmed, we are relieved when scientific history proves to us that the fact of His miraculous birth was unknown to Himself, unknown to His mother and unknown to the whole Christian community of the first generation. We are relieved I say, because we are no longer compelled to look upon the scientific movement as irreligious, but are able to see in it a

[18] Ibid.
[19] Ibid.

> new and greater religion, a religion based not upon the sporadic miracle, but upon the eternal law. We are no longer compelled to look for our God in some obscure event of the past we have but to lift up our eyes to see Him in the outgoings of the evening and morning, of all the days of our pilgrimage.[20]

In one bold statement, Crapsey had stepped over the line. However, he refused to trouble himself over the immediate effects of his open heresy. For him, the wider-ranging force of the scientific movement was overwhelming. Similarly, Crapsey believed that the seminaries of the nation were remiss because as institutions of higher education they should necessarily teach the truth according to the new scientific method.[21]

Crapsey felt that the church was resisting the truth established by science. He attacked the hypocrisy of a nation that proved every day of the week that nature was rational. But then, for a half an hour a week, people with absolutely no qualifications whatsoever taught the nation's children that the universe was conceived by the miraculous. It all seemed so incongruous in light of all that was happening around him and Crapsey refused to remain silent any longer.[22]

The answer could only be found in the unifying force of science. Where religion had failed to unify mankind science was already succeeding. God did not play favorites between the various peoples and religions of the world. He was a God of all mankind and beyond. In Crapsey's mind the scientist knew God in a special way. In his work he came before God moment to moment. Crapsey then applied this new theology of science, democracy and socialism to the age-old questions about one's soul, salvation and the propitiation for sin. For Crapsey, the scientist had unlocked the furtive mysteries of the universe, relegated to their clandestine places by the superstitious dogma of religion. In this way, the scientist was a liberating champion of the human soul.[23]

---

[20] Ibid. Also in Crapsey, *Religion*, pp. 288-9.

[21] In the preface of his book Crapsey qualified this statement. He made the exceptions of Union Theological Seminary in New York, Harvard Divinity School, Yale Divinity School, The Divinity School of Chicago University, and the Episcopal Divinity School of Cambridge, Mass., as being "all schools of scientific as opposed to scholastic theology and are doing a work of a very high order." Crapsey *Religion*, p. 8.

[22] A.S. Crapsey lecture reported in *Rochester Democrat & Chronicle* Monday Feb. 20, 1905.

[23] Ibid.

Crapsey simply disallowed the uniqueness of the gospel of Jesus Christ, asking rhetorically what the requirements of God's salvation were?

> He requires of me, answers the man of science, that I shall abide in His presence and keep His law. As long as I do this all that He has and is, is mine. If I go out of His presence, I am in misery. If I break His law, I suffer the exact penalty of that law and nothing more.[24]

Considering the doctrine of the propitiation for one's sins, sacrifice and how one would pay the price for sin and satisfy the anger of God, Crapsey, must have appeared to the orthodox of the faith entirely supercilious by unabashedly asserting his own merit. He broadened soteriology immeasurably by declaring that he brought himself to the altar of God as an offering for His service. Crapsey had always accentuated the human element in man's relationship with God, but the difference now was his dogma was without qualification and therefore completely out of balance in the eyes of the orthodox.[25]

Crapsey considered truth itself as meritorious, and he turned the tables on the traditionalists. For Crapsey, the creature required the creator to demonstrate and answer all that was expected. Crapsey asked God to show him His truth first, then to define his duty in it for the satisfaction of his soul.[26]

Crapsey had done something Phillips Brooks or other broad churchmen would never have dreamed of. By declaring his life's works as an offering to God, completely unlike the offering the Apostle Paul spoke of, Crapsey declared himself worthy, confirming the righteousness of God in himself, outside of Christ.[27] Furthermore, he continued to define his proposal of the new religion by denying that the man of science was any less faithful than the ordinary Christian. In fact, Crapsey envisioned the man of science as enlightened and realistic about his religiosity. The man of science was not an unbeliever as the average unenlightened Christian might think, his faith extended beyond that of even the greatest saints.[28]

---

[24] Ibid.

[25] Ibid.

[26] Ibid.

[27] See this in contrast to Romans 12:1-2.

[28] This brings to mind the statements made by the great anthropologist Alfred Kroeber who once mused, "Anthropology is my religion."

Science was not simply a philosophy; it was dispassionate religiosity. Moreover, it had the capability of unifying the world.[29]

Crapsey's quest to unify Christianity led him to science. He equated the loss of the influence of the clergy with the fact that the churches were outside of the great scientific revolution that would unify the world. The churches were scattered and disorganized. Each held its own notion of the truth delineated through formularies that remained at variance with the scientific world. Crapsey detested the dysfunctional, disunity of the church. He observed how Catholics and Protestants considered each other satanic. The whole thing was counter-productive. Crapsey believed a loss of influence also resulted from the schismatic behavior. The lack of unity lessened ministerial influence. Ministers could not be true servants of the people while they served their individual formularies. Moreover, the formularies could not all be true. Therefore, Crapsey argued, some, if not all, were false. The only way the formularies could be tested as truthful was by the scientific method. Since the official denominations absolutely refused to use this method they would continue to be divided and lack legitimacy in the world's eyes.[30]

Crapsey summed up his revolutionary statement with a candid consideration of the state of the ministry and the ministers. It was a wasted effort according to Crapsey. It was the sum total of his treatise which would have to be answered. The answer would, of course, come from his estranged brethren. Therefore, Crapsey would beat the clerical opinions to the punch. He contended,

> As long as we ministers are desperately holding on to the waning miracle and to the crumbling denomination difference, we are in no condition to fight for eternal truth and justice. We are trying in a piteous way to get back into real life through what we call the institutional churches.[31]

Crapsey avowed his right to articulate the sum total of his religious experience for over a quarter of a century with the voice of the prophet. He contended for modernity and reform. The only problem was, his argument entailed the complete dismantling of the traditions and spirit of the church. He supplanted his earlier view that the church was an organism known as the body of Christ, requiring now nothing less than the

---

[29] A.S. Crapsey lecture reported in *Rochester Democrat & Chronicle* Feb. 20, 1905.

[30] Ibid.

[31] Ibid.

church to come under the hegemony of the secular. He asked the church to self-destruct and if it would not, he would, as an example that others might follow. Crapsey concluded with his voice in the wilderness,

> Hear now, O ye churches, the sum of the whole matter. There are three great spirits at work creating the world that is and that is to be- the spirit of scientific investigation, that will know nothing but the truth; the spirit of democratic revolution, which will trust no one but the people; the spirit of social evolution, which will call no man common or unclean. If the churches wish for influence in the world that is and is to be, they must master these spirits and make them their own; the churches must become scientific, democratic and socialistic. And if they do so, then the churches will merge into the church, and then the church will no longer be separate from the state nor the state from the church, but these two will be one flesh.[32]

The response from the church was cautious, but immediate. The church's answer was interdenominational, though the clergy of the Protestant Episcopal Church felt most responsible to reply. Of the fifteen clergymen contacted by reporters about the lecture, only three decided to speak out freely. Two others spoke haltingly in response. Although others agreed with some of Crapsey's views only one, Rev. Nelson Millard D.D., approved of Crapsey's position openly. Millard characterized Crapsey's address as competent, straightforward and sincere and called upon the church not to criticize but to weigh out the message rationally.[33]

All save one of Crapsey's brethren in the Episcopal Church chose to keep quiet hoping the situation would somehow resolve itself. Crapsey's old nemesis however, Dr. Andrew J. Graham, rector of Christ Church, would not remain silent. Graham had taken up the position of the traditional church in previous public arguments. Graham felt compelled to respond, disturbed that a clergyman of the Protestant Episcopal Church would make such incongruous statements. Graham refused to quibble about whether men had the right to speak out about their opinions. That was a not the issue. Crapsey was a leading representative of the Protestant Episcopal Church. Therefore, his statements were not only at variance with the doctrines and creeds of the church but dishonest. Graham noted that Crapsey's statements were inconsistent with the position of the church

---

[32] Lecture of A.S. Crapsey reported in the *Rochester Democrat & Chronicle* Mon., Feb. 20, 1905.

[33] Column reported in the *Rochester Democrat & Chronicle* Tues., Feb 21, 1905. Millard was then the retired pastor of First Presbyterian Church, Rochester.

and as a leader in that church therefore tinged with duplicity. One could not explain away the foundational miracle of revelation or the incarnation as mere foolishness.[34]

Dr. Graham viewed Crapsey as "clearly a Deist." However, he didn't criticize him for that reason alone, but rather because he maintained his office and taught in a Christian Church. Others had held similar opinions in the past but at least they had the decency to leave the church. Graham would not argue about the efficacy of science in modern life. But he maintained that those who taught "the religion of science" focusing on the natural rejected the realm of the soul and turned their followers from the "creator to the creature."[35]

Graham directed Crapsey to Moncure D. Conway's memoirs, written in 1903. In them, Conway stated in part, men like Hebert Spencer were already decrying the death of the religious era due to the replacement of science. Graham repeated the words of Moncure D. Conway that he felt were essential to the procurement of a decent, civilized society. These facts were as important as they were simple. The Protestant concept of a personal God was the primary key to understanding the character of western society. The knowledge of a personal God procured a sense of "responsibility and accountability" that generated moral fiber in men. Science was cold and made for an icy relationship. No love was generated from such a connection. Furthermore, one could not ascertain God like one could science, God was a revelation, a person, love in the truest sense. Understanding God and all that God has for men such as, love, grace, unity, communion, etc., came not by an act of empirical observation or scientific consideration but by the miracle of revelation. Graham warned the young and old alike of being seduced by iconoclasts who sought to change the truth of the cross into fiction. He warned his readers not to follow Crapsey's system of science and socialism as their religion.[36]

Others warned of further inconsistencies in Crapsey's statements. Rev. MacLaurin D.D., of the Second Baptist Church reckoned that Crapsey had created a "straw man" and was in the process of tearing it down. The questions Crapsey brought up were already settled in academia. Crapsey was at least fifteen years late in coming out with his opinions. MacLaurin dispelled the question of miracles by not considering them as primary themes of church doctrine but secondary concerns. MacLaurin saw the problem as a question of focus. Even the newest thinking in theology still

---

[34] Ibid.
[35] Ibid.
[36] Ibid.

considered the personal relationship of man with God. But MacLaurin had a crimp in his armor as well. He also questioned the miraculous birth. He noted how great theologians were concurrently attending the issue. However, the charge that the church was against scientific investigation was patently false. Theologians in Germany, England and America were investigating the efficacy of scientific methodology. At the same time, scientists were daily shifting their positions. MacLaurin was obviously better apprized at the revisions in theories of science than Crapsey was. He noted perceptively that in the ever-changing world of science, scientists were questioning and negating this and that aspect of evolutionary theory continually. "The church was not in the market for absolutely everything that happened to come along."[37]

Other clergymen found much to object to in Crapsey's statements. Rev. N. J. Conklin stated that the Bible proved itself through the life a man lived. A life given over to a biblical perspective shed light in the world; conversely there was darkness where this never occurred.[38] Even the more liberal of the pastors of the community viewed Crapsey's perspective on the church as unsettling. Hardly a conservative, Rev. Paul Moore Strayer of the Third Presbyterian Church noted how Crapsey's view of the modern church was too pessimistic and virtually hopeless[39]

Few of Crapsey's colleagues found much to commend in the Crapsey's lectures. By the end of the week the papers were carrying other stories of men who attacked Crapsey's positions. MacLaurin gave a speech stating that the inability to perceive the possibility of the miraculous was "bewildered judgment." The problem with the conservative Christian is that he also confuses his own thinking when someone comes against the perfection of the Bible by believing that they are trying to take away their Christ in the process. The Bible came from Christ not the other way around. However, if there was a power that was supreme in the universe would it not be His right to reveal Himself and even demonstrate the miraculous if He chose to? Concerning Crapsey, MacLaurin stated bluntly that Crapsey's lectures provided nothing new even though they were billed as such. In conclusion, Crapsey's thinking had simply become confused.[40]

---

[37] Ibid.
[38] Ibid.
[39] Ibid.
[40] Speech before the Dewey Class at annual banquet in *Rochester Democrat & Chronicle* Fri., Feb. 24, 1905.

Other prominent clergymen also criticized Crapsey's lectures. Dr. Barbour asserted that he could not worship a Christ who was not divine. Barbour quoted the famous cleric who Crapsey's children once waved to while walking past his home. He provided a very clear analogy;

> Beecher used to say about the Bible, comparing it to the Hudson river and also to the mighty mountains behind his home, that he could go to sleep without being afraid that some child would come along with a quart pail and dig up the mighty Hudson and that he did not worry that some child with a toy wagon would remove the lordly mountain while he slept.[41]

By the time that Crapsey delivered his last lecture the community was eager to hear what would be next. He didn't disappoint them. Crapsey contended, "true politics was religion." He opened his last lecture by relating how the Mayor of Rochester had told the Ministerial Association that if they wanted to have any real influence in government they needed to attend the primaries of their parties. The political primary was the source of the politics of society, by which the community demonstrates its wholesomeness. But a minister could only be involved to the point where he would not have to abdicate his religious standing or moral character by partaking in the desecration, profanity and obscenity of the political world.[42]

Crapsey described the primary as a place where ordinary citizens, and ministers especially would have little or no understanding of who they were voting for. People were easily coerced into voting for whomever the bosses wanted through bribery by money, the promise of employment or by providing liquor. In reality, moral considerations had little to do with the political process. Crapsey illustrated his point by contrasting politics with prostitution considering that when the functions of the state became mercenary they were worse than the personal prostitution of a woman. One should no more participate in that kind of environment than in a house of ill-repute. However, the reality of the situation in its purest sense was that politics was religion. Crapsey quoted Woodrow Wilson's treatise *The State,* and affirmed that politics were indeed from ancient Greece to present-day America, essentially religious in character. He presented a litany of examples through history to corroborate his treatise. Crapsey maintained that the national conscience sought justice. Man appeals to

---

[41] Ibid., Dewey Class banquet.

[42] Lecture by A.S. Crapsey reported in *Rochester Democrat & Chronicle* Mon., Feb. 27. 1905.

God for justice today just as Moses and the prophets asked that righteousness be done then. God is righteousness and He would not establish His Kingdom outside of it. The righteousness of God must be translated into justice for men.[43]

Crapsey quoted the Preamble to the Constitution depicting it as a "description of the kingdom of God on earth." Through the disestablishment of religion the government ironically established the holistic, transcendent nature of the American people concerning religion. Crapsey went on to extol the homogenizing effect of the public school system. Crapsey noted that in his neighborhood Italians had assimilated in a single generation. It was the genius of the public school system that allowed it to happen. Crapsey thought that if it hadn't been for the public school system the United States would have been a disastrous hodgepodge of the various races.[44]

The schools had taken the lead in bringing all sorts of people together under a common ethos. The schools were already implementing this new form of religiosity. Although people considered the public schools as devoid of religion, in fact they were the very essence of it. Crapsey defined religion as "love and joy and peace," so therefore the public schools were truly operating in a purer sense of religion than the churches. Conversely, the denominations were doing their utmost to prevent what the public schools were accomplishing. Crapsey viewed the public schools as providing unity through a common religious experience. His concept of this new religion was based upon science, which identified God in rational and empirical truth, and socialism, which was entirely democratic and as a public beneficiary controlled by the people regardless of class or status.[45]

Crapsey's enthusiasm for the government run school system was evident. He endorsed it as the vehicle that would bring all of society together into this secularized religiosity for the common good. Crapsey transposed his original perspectives of community religion, once medieval and historical in his mind to the modern era. He noted how the public school system was guided by the principle of molding individuals through intellectual, physical and ethical means. All these practices needed to continue and increase in importance in America's collective conscience.[46]

Crapsey pondered the ways in which the young from every spectrum of humanity might come under the public school system's banner and

---

[43] Ibid.
[44] Ibid.
[45] Ibid.
[46] Ibid.

influence. Religious denominations would eventually be cut off "like Goliath's head." Children detected no real distinctions between the various denominations be they Catholic or Protestant or even Jewish for that matter. Children were able to go beyond the underlying differences in favor of the universal human race. Creed subscription only exacerbated the problem. A person's character, not the creed he or she subscribed to should be the ultimate test of endorsement. God wasn't interested in whether we were Baptist or Episcopalians. We could learn from the children as they were experiencing something better than their pedantic, Sunday differences. The children recognized a God of all things whose mercy similarly extended to all regardless of the minute variations in the creeds they subscribed to. Opening his religiosity up to the entire world Crapsey noted that God

> loved the Sanscrit when he worshipped Veruna in the stars. He loved the Greek when he worshipped Athena in the air; He loved the Hebrew when he worshipped Jehovah on Mount Zion. He loves the Christian who sees in Jesus the indwelling of His presence. He loves the Catholic who beholds His tenderness in the face of the Virgin. Whenever there is a soul devout and honest, there is the spirit of the Father. And it is this religion that we are teaching our children in the public schools.[47]

As times changed and the world progressed Crapsey noted how the Jew was no longer despised just because he was a Jew but he could now be judged by how he behaved. He mentioned how Rabbi Dr. Landsberg recently lectured from a Presbyterian pulpit. He declared that in America anti-Semitism had been abolished. Crapsey looked to the church of the state as the one thing that was needed in society. Crapsey broadened the meaning of the state to encompass religious terms and envelop the sacred. He considered the mayor and the health officer as "ministers of religion," who were working for the public's "common salvation." He portrayed the mayor as selflessly devoted to the well being of the people. Likewise he depicted the public health officer as saintly in character because hundreds of children's lives were saved through his efforts. The previous average of children's deaths resulting from cholera in the month of August was at least five. However, in the past several years not one had occurred. Science had accomplished something truly positive in the realm of

[47] Ibid.

children's health. This justified Crapsey's belief that "scientific religion is the salvation of the people."[48]

Crapsey called for political reform with religious enthusiasm. It was time to preach the gospel to the poor. What was the use of building cathedrals if our cities still suffered from slums and sweatshops? Why should we send out missionaries if we despise the teachings of Christ? Why ask people to come to church if the church accepted corrupt commercialism treading on the people they employ? He called for a reformation passionately declaring that the "abomination of the desolation was in the holy place."[49]

To conclude his lecture series, Crapsey left his audience once again with the voice of the prophet. This time however, it took the form of challenge and confrontation. He would both warn the people and define their mission. Crapsey cried out to the common folk who were put off by all the useless expressions like "trinities and incarnations" and were sick of the "Greek dialectic" used by the denominational leaders. Prior to Rauschenbusch's landmark social gospel statement in *Christianity and the Social Crisis,* Crapsey declared a radical social gospel of his own by declaring that the responsibility of the Christian was not so much in attaining an otherworldly heaven as leaving behind heaven on earth. After his generation was gone he wanted their legacy to be one of social commitment, their principal work being the establishment of the "great church state of America." For Crapsey, that meant a complete and total relationship between politics and religion. He did not want to leave behind a nation of moral corruption, social disorder and religious discord. The heritage of the people demanded it. Their legacy would be written in a matrix of political and religious cooperation through empirical science, social democracy and institutional innovation.[50]

---

[48] Ibid.

[49] Ibid.

[50] Ibid.

CHAPTER SIXTEEN

"Now the Works of the Flesh are Manifest"

After the last lecture, Mrs. Crapsey provided a dinner party. Amongst their guests were Crapsey's walking tour companion, Judge John Warrant Castleman, as well as Howard Mosher and Judge Sutherland of the Supreme Court. During the conversation about the astonishing lecture they had just heard, Sutherland mentioned how they needed to stand behind Crapsey just in case any problems surfaced. Crapsey stated that with those words, he realized the possibility of a major difficulty for the first time. However, he certainly welcomed the publicity and provided written texts to the press for publication. He obviously intended to create a stir.[1]

The published lectures were forwarded throughout the country and the United Kingdom. The lectures were so widely disseminated that he received mail concerning them from as far away as India. One correspondent wrote,

> I have just read an extract from your lecture in which you have dealt upon the subject of inerrancy of the Bible and the manhood of Jesus, the son of Joseph, 'born as we are born, dying as we die.' I am glad to know that the churchmen in Europe and America do now come forward to speak their hearts with such a liberty. Have you got any lectures of yours published? If so, I shall be obliged to you if you can send me a copy of it by post. Under a separate cover, I send you an interesting literature and shall be glad to send you more on hearing from you.[2]

The lectures created a commotion in the local Christian community. Conservative churchmen of all denominations came forward to defend the traditional faith. Local pastors published their opinions about the Crapsey sermon, and others responded during their Sunday morning messages. In one sermon, Rev. S. Frazer Langford of the Parsells Avenue Baptist Church, in Rochester, regretted how supposed ministers of Christ with the

---

[1] Crapsey, *Heretics,* p. 252.

[2] Letter from Mahammad Sadig, dated July 4, 1905, Qadian District, Gurdaspur, India. Reproduced in A.S. Crapsey, *Heretics,* p. 253.

support of their denomination could attack the historic tenets of the faith, step outside of the creed of their church and get away with it all. If he didn't believe the historic dogma of the church then he should leave the church. Moreover Langford wondered sarcastically what it meant that the churches were unscientific in their means? How could one measure the true extent of love, could you dissect these kinds of principles, could one weigh out the amount of holiness a person contained or define individual value on a scale somehow? Certainly the beauty and the lovely fragrance escaped when the flower was subjected to an analysis under the scalpel of the scientist's laboratory. One could never analyze these kinds of things under a microscope. Langford quoted learned men of science like British scientist Sir Oliver Lodge. He agreed it was necessarily true that faith was not scientific. Pure science held no faith, and one could not expect to discover an absolute and infinite God through finite experimentation. It was impossible. Thankfully, that was the opposite of faith.[3]

Langford scoffed at Crapsey's assertion that an educated man could no longer maintain traditional beliefs. Langford assured his listeners, if anyone thought the scriptures were incapable of providing the revelation of God or somehow distorted in their ethical ability they were simply wrong. Langford listed several Anglican scholars with similar views to his own including Brooke Foss Wescott, Fenton John Anthony Hart, Canon W.J. Edmonds, Stalker, Fairbanks and Dean Farrar.[4]

Rev. Evan H. Martin of St. Thomas Episcopal Church, in Rochester noted that science and Christian faith were not necessarily hostile to one another. Nevertheless, one was obviously mistaken if he believed that the limited ability of human research or science could account for all knowledge and truth. Concerning the miraculous birth of Christ and its rejection as unscientific, Martin stated, "people like Crapsey were unable to believe it because of the inability of science to explain the mystery of it."[5]

Pastor Milton M. Livingston of the Advent Christian Church, in Rochester stated that the foundational doctrine that all the rest were based upon was the divinity of Christ. Livingston noted, it follows if man had evolved to his present state of morality through natural processes he would eventually be capable of redeeming himself. Livingston mused; "obviously we had no need for a savior then. Under that scenario, the

[3] Column reported in the *Rochester Democrat & Chronicle* Mon., Feb. 27, 1905 p. 11.

[4] Ibid. p. 11.

[5] Ibid. p. 11.

entire plan of salvation was superfluous. Mankind rejects the scriptural account and flatters himself by becoming his own deliverer."[6]

Similarly, Livingston noted that if a man contradicted the faith, by not believing in Christ's deity or the inspiration of the Bible, he should leave the church so as not to confuse himself with others who came under the sanctity of the church. He should therefore attack Christianity openly, not disingenuously from within the walls and protection of the church but from the outside where he belonged. Satan had adapted to contemporary forms of conducting his business. He doesn't simply deny the faith from an atheistic standpoint like before, he now attacks from the inside insidiously through the sacred offices of the church under the guise and guile of posing as a minister of the gospel to confuse the parishioners in their comfortable pews.[7]

Rev. John Nicum D.D. of St. John's Evangelical Lutheran Church, in Rochester looked at the question of Crapsey's divergence from a historical perspective. If one went back to the time after the Revolutionary War one would realize the prevalence of French atheism, English deism and German rationalism in the nation. Nicum noted, "Bishop Meade of Virginia concluded that it was nearly impossible to find any sophisticated person who believed in the historic Christian faith." But in light of the cultural defeat of the rationalists in the past, Nicum maintained, as a nation, "they were not willing to succumb to this latest attack on Christianity or admit that they needed a new gospel or a new savior."[8]

At St. Paul's Episcopal Church in Rochester the Rev. Murray Bartlett, in a sermon entitled, "Is Science Enough?" stated that science was indeed beneficial to humanity but of all of its discoveries and benefits none were able to truly explain the origin of man. Scientists had even failed in their attempt to discern the essential ingredients of matter, motion or energy. The Bible alone was authoritative in its avowal of the absolute by stating, "'In the beginning was God.' God was the Alpha and the Omega and it was shameful to believe that science was adequate for understanding the vast expanses of the universe"[9]

In the same local newspaper a full-page editorial appeared, written by Rev. John S. Littell, the rector of St. Luke's Church, in Brockport, New York. Another of Crapsey's Episcopal brethren, Littell headed the Rochester and Vicinity Clerical Association. Littell wrote that the

[6] Ibid. p. 11.
[7] Ibid. p. 11.
[8] Ibid. p. 11.
[9] Ibid. p. 11.

Episcopal clergy's reluctance to come forward should not be construed to mean compliance with Crapsey's views. Then, hinting at the ominous clouds on the horizon, he stated that the bishop presided over these kinds of specific matters. Littell outlined the various objections that clergymen might have regarding Crapsey's views. Crapsey's ordination vows headed the list. Littell noted that when he was made a deacon of the church he was asked if sincerely believed the Canonical scriptures. His answer undoubtedly was, yes. Littell mentioned sarcastically "perhaps Crapsey had forgotten his pledge considering the length of time that had passed." Littell alleged hypocrisy in the performance of Crapsey's official duties in the church. As a priest Crapsey declared his unqualified belief in the traditional faith and the scriptures daily. He repeated the doxology, his morning and evening prayers, the litany and all the other official declarations concerning the miraculous and Christ's deity over and over again. "Those official utterances declared a miraculous Christ, born of a Virgin, conceived by the Holy Ghost, one who rose from the dead, the bearer of our sins, the redeemer of the world, His ascension, His position in the heavenlies and His physical return." Littell demanded to know where Crapsey truly stood on these matters.[10]

Littell listed a series of confusing utterances in Crapsey's lectures. He desired clarity demanding he identify his beliefs whether they be what he says to the public through the lectures and the press or what he leads his congregation in during his service. If Crapsey had appealed to the public's opinion then "he should go to the public. Did not the public recognize the hypocrisy between what he was saying and doing? How could Crapsey be taken seriously under such contradictory circumstances? Even if there were no heresy charges leveled against him the public's opinion of him was assuredly secured by the statements he had made."[11]

Littell conferred Crapsey's charges of clerical aloofness back on Crapsey by stating "the accusations pertained to him and not to his fellow clergy." He condescendingly accused Crapsey of "needing to rest his mind after his many years of extremely hard work." Moreover, he attacked Crapsey's popular novel finding it "untenable that such high levels of morality would come from such a fictional premise."[12]

---

[10] Column in editorial section entitled, "Current Topics Discussed by Correspondents of the Democrat and Chronicle." in the *Rochester Democrat & Chronicle* Mon., Feb. 27, 1905. p. 7.

[11] Ibid.

[12] Ibid.

Littell described the contents of a pastoral report from the House of Bishops concerning how a group of students in Cambridge, Massachusetts had recently applied for ordination while claiming the freedom to deny Virgin Birth. The bishops had decreed the Virgin Birth as an essential element of the Episcopal faith. Littell remembered part of the letter written by the bishops stating that the essence of the Apostle's and the Nicene creeds were exact and contained immutable meaning, "at all times to all people." Therefore the bishops decreed that the creeds could not mean anything other than what they "appeared to mean."[13]

Littell echoed the others. It was much better for one to simply resign, forsake the faith and join the opposition then to continue in dishonesty in the ministry. Littell concluded his discourse by appealing to the principle of consistency in the character and honor of men. It was a simple quandary to him. For the first time, an opinion had surfaced from the official head of a clerical association suggesting Crapsey's removal. Littell concluded, "If this is a surgical case, let it be done quickly, and God give us charity to supply anaesthetics as well as antiseptics."[14]

By the time that Littell's editorial appeared in the local news, Bishop Walker was making his last minute arrangements before his wedding on March 4, 1905. Walker intended to marry Bertha B. Bach, reportedly a disarmingly beautiful woman, of 44 East Eightieth St. New York City. They planned their wedding at the Church of the Heavenly Rest, in New York City with the Right Rev. Henry Codman Potter officiating. After the wedding Walker planned to take a trip out west and then possibly to Cuba before returning to the diocese. He was also in the process of having a new home constructed by the time he and his new bride returned. Walker was indeed a busy man. As he planned for the happiest day of his personal life he looked ominously at the storm brewing on the ecclesiastic horizon.[15]

Regardless of Walker's personal plans, the Crapsey lectures were the principal concern on his professional agenda. On Saturday, February 25, less than a week after the last of the lectures, Walker stopped in Rochester on church business. Probably under pressure from some of the local clergy and laity, he called a conference of the Episcopal rectors of the Rochester vicinity. It was to be held at the home of Rev. Edward P. Hart of St. Mark's Church. The meeting was scheduled for Tuesday, February 28,

[13] Ibid.

[14] Ibid. p. 7.

[15] Column in the *Rochester Democrat & Chronicle* Tues., Feb. 28, 1905 p. 12.

just hours prior to his departure for New York City. The bishop's wedding would be held only five days later.[16]

Rumors surfaced that some of the clergy desired formally to request that Crapsey step down, abandon his post as rector of St. Andrew's and quietly leave the denomination. However, others felt that presentment would be the only answer. When one anonymous rector was asked if the others would request Dr. Crapsey to leave the denomination his reply was, that was an irregular way of doing things. The normal way of proceeding was through presentment. Walker had ascertained the overall demeanor of Rochester's Episcopal clergy concerning Crapsey's statements. As ecclesiastical administrator of a huge diocese whose clergy might complain to the House of Bishops, Walker's responsibility was overwhelming and he was forced to get involved.[17]

The informal luncheon held in Hart's home at 118 Troup St., an upscale neighborhood in the Corn Hill district, included virtually all of the rectors of Rochester except Crapsey and one or two others. Those present cautiously agreed that whatever happened next would depend on Crapsey. As one of them stated, they were not questioning Crapsey's earnestness noting that Crapsey retained the natural ability to alter his beliefs if he deemed necessary. Court proceedings in the Episcopal Church were rare except for occurrences of immoral behavior. The clergy wished to downplay any obvious differences over doctrine. Moreover, no clear direction of their deportment concerning any statement of charges against Crapsey was forthcoming. It was further stated that "there wasn't any probability of such as far as one of the rectors was concerned."[18]

The mention of presentment publicly, rippled through the press and was obviously calculated to intimidate Crapsey so he would change his behavior. However, the bishop and clergy of the diocese clearly hoped the whole matter would simply end. They anticipated that Crapsey would stop his utterances, realize the indiscretion of his statements and change his course. The qualification that the interviewed clergyman suggested was that Crapsey should amend his ideas to conform to the standards of the church. As Walker headed off for his nuptial bliss, Crapsey remained to brood over the criticisms of the clergy. Nevertheless, the press realized the public's interest in Crapsey's case and promptly attempted to resuscitate the dozing giant that the bishop and the rectors had tried to put to sleep. Letters published in support of Crapsey called for church reforms

---

[16] Ibid., p. 10.
[17] Ibid.
[18] Column in the *Rochester Democrat & Chronicle* Wed., March 1, 1905 p. 10.

considered long overdue. One individual agreed with Crapsey that the church needed reform and the best place to begin was with society's politics, but he had such a terrible time articulating his words that it nearly obscured his thought that Crapsey should be applauded for his attempt to secure the reforms so desparartely needed in the church.[19]

On Friday night March 3, the Church Club of Rochester, composed of members of the area's Episcopal Churches, gathered to hear addresses on topics given by leading members of the local clergy. Responding to those pressing for reform, three speakers tackled the subject of "Church Work," splitting the topic into three distinct sub-headings. Each speaker addressed one of the sub- topics. Rev. Andrew Graham spoke on "Spiritual Work," Rev. Murray Bartlett on "Social Work," and Rev. Edward Parrott on "Institutional Work." All three dealt with general issues that Crapsey had brought up during his lecture series. Each speaker shared concerns about the church and political action. Parrott cited two churches known for their institutional work. One, on the Tavana River in Alaska, was known for its hospital of thirty beds. The other, Grace Church, New York City, boasted over fifty clubs and societies, at least one of which Crapsey was instrumental in beginning many years previously.[20]

At this point, Rochester's Protestant Episcopal clergy far from shunned their illustrious brother. They hoped instead to shift the public's focus to reform. St. Luke's Church invited Crapsey to speak at Lenten Services in downtown Rochester. These Lenten services were becoming a traditional event in Rochester. Several of the speakers arrived from outside the area. Due to the recent attention placed upon broadening horizons the Episcopal Churches decided to open the event to Christians regardless of denomination. Crapsey was asked to begin the lectures by providing messages on the first two days of Lent. Each speaker received two consecutive days with twenty minutes set aside at the noon hour to deliver his messages. This way, businessmen and others could hear the speakers during lunch. The first speaker's position was an honor that the Episcopal clergy perhaps hoped would bring the renegade rector back to his senses. Crapsey's subjects commenced on March 8th and 9th entitled, "God a Presence," and "God a Power." [21]

While the Protestant Episcopal Church encouraged Crapsey to downplay his extreme views, others outside of the denomination pressed for clarification while commenting on Crapsey's lectures. Dr. William R.

---

[19] Editorial in *Rochester Democrat & Chronicle* Thurs., March 2, 1905 p. 7.

[20] *Rochester Democrat & Chronicle* Sat., March 4, 1905 p. 17.

[21] *Rochester Democrat & Chronicle.* Mon., March 6, 1905 p. 9.

Taylor from the Brick Presbyterian Church close to Crapsey's parish, found some serious errors in the lectures. Taylor's sermon on IITimothy 2: 19, spoke out against "vain babblings." In the text, the Apostle Paul warned young Timothy about two men who were to be avoided because of their disturbing utterances about the resurrection. Taylor warned that Crapsey's teaching would capsize the faith of some, and it would eventually eat into the church like a disease. Although Crapsey's messages contained some heavy facts, terrible mistakes were made. As such, Taylor saw fit to warn his Episcopal cousins like Paul warned Timothy of "the consequences of vain and deliberate errors."[22]

Taylor's warnings proved prophetic. Just two days later Crapsey delivered one of his twenty-minute lectures on the "Presence of God." As the Right Reverend Walker honeymooned with his wife, Crapsey found occasion to speak about the dearth of God's presence in nature, society and in the hearts of men. Crapsey's demeanor became stern and filled with admonition and rebuke. Crapsey's twenty-minute warning to the people was, as always, controversially thought provoking. He was, in his own mind, becoming the prophet crying out in the wilderness. He denied the presence of God in men's hearts, in the government, the Christian church, even in the clergy. He spoke of how Abraham found God in nature, how Moses established God in civil polity, and how Jesus found God in the heart of men. But now, he stated,

> We ask ourselves, 'where do we find God?' 'Where is He now?' In some country beyond the sea, in some books written long ago, in men that are dead? And until we can once more have the desire for the presence of God, which animated Abraham, Moses and Jesus we shall find this world void of any presence that can delight us, guide us and comfort us. Let it be then our Lenten work, to seek after God that our souls may live.[23]

Jesus held the key to religious enlightenment for Crapsey because Jesus understood the potential of God in men. Just as Jesus became an inspiring example of attaining oneness with God, as a modern prophet Crapsey would try to elevate men's understanding to a place of divinity. Crapsey's God was the God of truth in nature, proven by science. The scriptural accounts recorded ancient renditions of people seeking God throughout the ages. But they were not conclusive. Only God was. The scriptures were important because they led humankind progressively

---

[22] *Rochester Democrat & Chronicle* Mon. March 6, 1905, p. 10.

[23] *Rochester Democrat & Chronicle* Thurs. March 9, 1905, p. 12.

towards God. For Crapsey however, the scriptures were neither inerrant nor absolute truth.

Crapsey continued with his quest to reform the church in his own way. Shortly after his Lenten lectures, he invited Herbert Symonds, a leader of Christian Unity in Canada and the Anglican Vicar of Christ Church Cathedral Montreal, to St. Andrew's to deliver a series of addresses.[24] Symonds' final lecture on "The Future of Christianity," gained widespread coverage in the press. In it he mentioned in clear social evolutionary terms how the church's organization developed "by adaptation to its environment." He then classified and ordered the events to clarify how the system evolved. The system of creeds, formularies and worship with all their organizational capacities came after the spirit of Christ. Symonds saw the creeds as developing over time and space. They were not received as whole and perfect. Of the differing manners of worship and the continual doctrinal differences, Symonds noted were important considerations. But, the diversity and sheer amount of disagreement on these issues precluded both the possibility and the utility of present day heresy.[25]

The religion of the future for Symonds would be pure. It would be completely spiritual, "a religion of the spirit," and it would be embodied by endeavors and accomplishments. One might call it a religion of works righteousness. Therefore, adaptation to the environment was the key. Things changed and developed over time, only inanimate objects or dead things never changed. The answer would be found in progressive adaptation both for the organism as well as for the organization.[26] Without adaptation the organism would die and the organization was destined to fail. In the future less and less focus would be placed on creeds or forms of worship. As formalities would decrease, spirituality would increase. The religion of the future would establish correct relationships between men and would be loving and altruistic. It would at long last end the antagonism between science and theology with theology finally capitulating to the fact that science had sought hard after the truth and after all, every truth was of God. For Symonds, science based on empirical truth was supportive of religion, not against it.[27]

---

[24] Personal communication with Luc Lepage, archivist at Synod's office for the Anglican Diocese of Montreal and Terry Thompson archivist of the General Synod (National archives), in Toronto.

[25] *Rochester Democrat & Chronicle* Mon., April 13, 1905.

[26] Ibid.

[27] Ibid.

Men like Crapsey and Symonds broke the ranks. Symonds declared that worship would no longer consist of the,

> groveling of men before a deity who longs for flattery nor an attempt to bribe a deity with forms and ceremonies. It would be the going out of the infinite part of ourselves in adoration and love to the infinite source of all things.[28]

Likewise, doctrine would be relative to the teacher and the student. It would be received if there were agreement between the two. Certainly Symonds stopped far short of Crapsey's proposed definition of the new religion. However, his avowal of free thought in the church was exactly what Crapsey desired to present to his congregation and diocese. Symonds' support of his views constituted an international perspective underscoring the unity principles Crapsey emphasized. It was also an offensive act considering the language Symonds used about the groveling that the clergy now engaged in. Finally, it was a defensive act considering Crapsey's need for high status churchmen to come to his support, especially as Bishop Walker would soon be apprized of Crapsey's continuing remarks and visibility. Meanwhile, Walker was in the process of traveling from church to church in the Rochester area confirming classes of young men and women into the Protestant Episcopal Church.[29]

Crapsey's refusal to retreat from his positions, coupled with his continuing utterances and political maneuvering to support his positions, caused several Episcopal clergymen to send a communiqué to the Diocese of Western New York. Ten of Crapsey's ecclesiastic brethren signed the letter, addressed to the Standing Committee. They asked for an investigation of Crapsey's public statements. They also recorded the alleged heretical statements Crapsey made during the Religion and Politics lectures noting that Crapsey furnished them to the press. The letter declared that Crapsey had violated his ordination vows. Moreover, he was openly teaching doctrines contrary to the Episcopal Church. Under the Canons of the General Church these alleged offenses constituted the basis for a trial. Crapsey additionally contravened the rules by declaring that he had the liberty to preach whatever he was motivated to since he was ultimately answerable to his own conscience. The opinion of the ten clergymen was that any action taken should be a collective one

[28] *Rochester Democrat & Chronicle* Mon. April 13, 1905

[29] *Rochester Democrat & Chronicle* Dated, April 4, 1905.

representative of the diocese as a whole.[30] The letter concluded with the recommendation that,

> We the undersigned, hereby respectfully petition you that you investigate the matters which we have now to your notice and that, if you find them to be as above set forth, you thereupon make presentment against the Rev. Algernon S. Crapsey, D.D. as provided in Ordinances for the Ecclesiastical Court of this Diocese.[31]

The same day the letter was brought before the Standing Committee another special committee was appointed for the purpose of nominating ten clergymen to the council of the Ecclesiastical Court. Although an Ecclesiastical Court already existed, several irregularities were involved. One member was retired and one was also a member of the Standing Committee responsible for recommending presentment, others had sat on the court for years. The petition called for disqualification of the Standing Committee members due to a conflict of interest. Crapsey would later allege that the diocese provided a kangaroo court, to try him, but the charges were baseless. On May 5, 1905, the Standing Committee met again and the special committee on nominations made their report. At the meeting Bishop Walker asked for the Standing Committee's advice concerning Crapsey's alleged heretical statements. The Standing Committee adopted a resolution that read in part:

> Resolved, That the Standing Committee advises the Bishop to appoint a Committee of Investigation as provided in Sections III and IV of the Ordinances for the Ecclesiastical Court, pursuant to the provisions of Canon 2, Title III, of the Canons of the Diocese of Western New York. Provided, public denial or repudiation of the alleged utterances by Dr. Crapsey shall not have been made on or before June 1, 1905.[32]

On the same day, *Outlook,* a progressive New York magazine, ran a three-page article entitled, "The Living Church." Declaring that nothing would be decided by the trial of Dr. Crapsey short of the stance of those who constituted the court and the bishop. The author warned the church to consider the times. The concept of the church was changing from a

---

[30] Letter sent to Standing Committee of the Diocese of Western New York, recorded in the minutes taken from the records of the Standing Committee dated May 2, 1905, in Burrows, *Diocese,* p. 120-1.

[31] Ibid., p. 121.

[32] Ibid. p. 122.

philosophical idea or a body of doctrine to a living entity continuously growing, changing and adapting to its environment and new challenges. Christianity was not a dogmatic corpus or some philosophic system or an organization of the clergy, it was the spiritually revealed, living "body of Christ." The secret of the life of the body was not found in the formularies or the creeds but in the life of the spirit.[33]

The author observed a similarity between the strict interpretation of the constitution and the creeds and dogma of the historical church. He contended that humanity was a long way from attaining the truth." He wrote:

> Those who are demanding an infallible authority and a final statement of faith, complete in its expression, mathematically exact in definition, to be accepted by all men of all times and races in precisely the same sense, are demanding a complete and finished world, a society in its final forms, a race that has come to the end of its life, touched all points of experience, sounded all depths, climbed all heights, and reached the goal. This is not the divine idea of the world. The very nature of men makes this rigid and literal definiteness impossible.[34]

According to the *Outlook* article, liberals perceived a need for progressive understanding, not rigid formularies defining the extent of the truth about God. New concepts about God's nature and man's understanding needed to be explored. The future Church would be broadly based. People with a variety of interpretations would be allowed to worship regardless of their style or perspective. Similar to the ability to embrace the most radical of Republicans, Democrats, prohibitionists or Socialists this political broadness of the nation could apply to the church as well. It proved that the charge of heresy was obsolete. The article concluded, the reality of a truly broad church makes the accusation of heresy impossible. Completely ignoring the tradition of the Episcopal form of ecclesiastic government the editor of *Outlook* felt that the decision of whether Crapsey remained should be left to Crapsey and his congregation.[35]

Rev. Andrew J. Graham of Christ Church, Rochester, Crapsey's adversary and the chief respondent to his public statements utilized the Jubilee Celebration at his church to answer Crapsey's political alliances

---

[33] Article entitled "The Living Church" In, *Outlook* vol. 83, May 5, 1905 pp. 13-15.

[34] Ibid.

[35] Ibid.

with liberal colleagues. Graham used the occasion of the fiftieth anniversary of the founding of Christ Church to bring in a missioner of his own. It is no great coincidence that one speaker, Dr. Walton W. Battershall took as his topic, "The Church Today." Battershall spoke about how Christianity had changed in the past century in America.[36]

Battershall's understanding of the contemporary church differed dramatically from Crapsey and his supporters. Battershall exhorted the members of Christ Church to continue the work that God had ordained in Rochester. He encouraged them to become more involved with their service in the church, while warning them to beware of the vagaries of the day. The society was gradually spiraling downward. "Therefore recognize the voices that warn you, discern the reality of the times and hold close to the church of Christ."[37]

Batershall stated, "Christ was alive today in the church more powerfully than when he actually walked the streets of Jerusalem." The proof was demonstrated in the lives of Christians. Battershall questioned whether the traditional concept of the need for Christ was outmoded. "Could the world ever progress beyond the essential need for Christ? Would mankind withdraw from the reception of His sure rescue? And what of the church, was it really outmoded and unnecessary? No, the need remains" he argued.[38]

By the middle of May the lines were beginning to be drawn between those that either supported or opposed presentment. Rev. Murray Bartlett of St. Paul's Episcopal Church stepped forward as one of the first members of the local Episcopal clergy to publicly come out against a heresy trial. Knowing that the Ecclesiastical Court would meet on Tuesday the sixteenth of May, Bartlett was quoted concerning his views on the heresy trial on Monday the fifteenth. The headlines of the column reporting Bartlett's opinions read "Is Opposed to Heresy Trials," and beneath it appeared the words, "Spirit Wrong Says Rev. Murray Bartlett."[39]

The press took up the issue, rousing public opinion prior to the trial. An editorial on the same day that the Diocesan Council met to elect members to the Ecclesiastical Court in Corning, NY ran the headline, "From Heresy Trials Good Lord Deliver Us!"[40] Quoting Bartlett, the

---

[36] *Rochester Democrat & Chronicle* May 8, 1905.
[37] Ibid.
[38] Ibid.
[39] *Rochester Democrat & Chronicle,* Mon., May 15, 1905.
[40] Editorial opinion in *Rochester Democrat & Chronicle* Tues., May 16, 1905.

editor related how nothing was certain when it came to heresy. Bartlett was further cited as saying that the Apostle Paul was considered a heretic for his views and that "the heresy of today may be the truth of tomorrow." Moreover Bartlett redefined the gospel in light of these changing issues, arguing that "virtuous Christian living including the fruits of the spirit of love and peace and kindness and so forth were immutable."[41]

Bartlett's expression of a new gospel of toleration, peace, love and works righteousness was indicative of how far some of the clergy of the church had moved away from the subscription to the creeds.[42] When reporting on the meeting of the Diocesan Council to nominate the Ecclesiastical Court the *Democrat and Chronicle* speculated that Rev. Littell would present the charges to the Bishop and that Rev. Graham of Christ Church would second him. Meanwhile, Crapsey was quoted as stating, "he would not leave the church unless compelled to do so."[43]

Nevertheless, the Episcopal Church administration remained focused on the matter at hand. Ten names were placed in nomination before the Diocesan Council of which five were chosen. The court was duly appointed. At the advice of the Standing Committee, Bishop Walker also eventually appointed a five man Committee of Investigation to scrutinize the question of the breach in the ordination vows and the public statements of the Rev. Crapsey, prior to bringing the matter before the Ecclesiastical Court. The action by the bishop sought to insure the fairness of the procedure and take the personality conflicts and public disagreements out of the equation.[44]

The Annual Council of the Episcopal Diocese of Western New York opened in Corning, New York on May 17, 1905. Bishop Walker delivered his annual address to the members attending. Most of the clergy of the diocese had not had the pleasure of meeting the new wife of the bishop. The delegates were joyfully engaged at the subsequent reception for Bishop and Mrs. Walker at the home of Senator W.J. Tully. The press used the occasion to exploit the sentiment of the readership concerning the heresy trial. Crapsey attended the meetings and was reported as "very warmly received." The newspaper once again chose to quote the amiable Rev. Bartlett. He portrayed the meetings as full of grace and peace. A feeling of fondness pervaded the council meeting. Moreover, Bartlett denied there was any contemplation for convening a heresy trial at all

[41] Ibid.
[42] *Rochester Democrat & Chronicle* Mon., May 15, 1905.
[43] *Rochester Democrat & Chronicle* Wed. May 17, 1905.
[44] Burrows, *Diocese,* p. 122.

except from some relatively young and inconsequential theologians. Bartlett used the occasion to further express his hope that the Crapsey matter would just dissipate and die.

> Nothing was said in the council about a heresy trial, but from my talks with prominent and influential delegates from all parts of the council I have come to the conclusion that there will be no trial.[45]

As the press continued to exploit rumors surrounding the Crapsey situation, instead of receiving their information directly from the diocese, they sought out Rev. Graham of Christ Church for his opinion on the case. They assumed that he would either make formal charges against Crapsey or second the same from Littell or someone else. As a member of the Diocesan Council, Graham already knew that Crapsey would be under the scrutiny of the investigating committee, relieving the personal pressure from him, Littell and the ten men who had asked for an investigation. Graham subsequently released a statement to the press asserting,

> The statement made in the daily papers of Corning, Rochester and New York, that the Rev. Andrew J. Graham of Rochester, is to join with Rev. John S. Littell, rector of St. Luke's Church, Brockport, in presenting Rev. Algernon S. Crapsey, rector of St. Andrew's parish, Rochester, for trial for denial of Christian doctrine, is absolutely and unqualifiedly without any foundation in fact.[46]

Graham had stated from the inception of the controversy that no Rochesterian should take the lead in prosecuting Crapsey, for a number of reasons. The paper stressed that his denial of the rumor in no way invalidated the what he considered as the seriousness of Crapsey's transgression The article continued,

> In common with fully 90 per cent of all the clergy of the diocese of Western New York, he feels that the rector of St. Andrew's has made statements in lectures and public print which have wounded the most sacred experiences and hopes of many people and caused profound sorrow among his brethren.

[45] *Rochester Democrat & Chronicle* Thurs., May 18, 1905.
[46] *Rochester Democrat & Chronicle* Fri., May 19, 1905.

Graham acknowledged that the situation was now in the hands of the bishop and Crapsey alone. He desired that the matter be settled justly without unnecessary conflict. [47]

[47] Ibid.

CHAPTER SEVENTEEN

"That No Prophecy of the Scripture is of Any Private Interpretation"

In June of 1905, *Outlook*, reported that there had been recent discussion in the Church of England concerning creed revision.[1] During the previous year a committee was appointed to contemplate the revision of the Athanasian Creed. A report at a meeting of the Canterbury Convocation affirmed that the creed provided a statement that was unqualified considering scriptural standards and inconsistent with the great teachers of the church. The Canterbury Convocation however, refused to simply omit the parts of the creed that were not necessary to the confession of faith.[2] Bishop Charles Gore moved that the bishops should be authorized to allow clergymen to dispense from reciting the Athanasian Creed if they so desired, but a final decision would have to wait for the Lambeth Conference of 1908, when the general opinion of the pan-Anglican Communion could be obtained.[3]

Such reports may have inspired Crapsey to push his issues to a conclusion. In a series of chess moves that would eventually bring him into checkmate, Crapsey attempted to attack the conservative citadel and force its hand. Receiving reports that the bishop of the diocese had attempted to contact members of the vestry of St. Andrew's Church, Crapsey assumed that he had done so to undermine his authority and create insurrection in his church. Crapsey responded by sending the bishop a terse letter stating that it was against ecclesiastic law for him to meet with any of the members of the body without first meeting with the head of that body.[4]

---

[1] Description of *"Outlook"* by Hugh M. Jansen Jr. in *American Religious Heretics* George H. Shriver ed. (New York, 1966) p. 201.

[2] *Outlook* June 17, Vol. 80, May- August 1905 p. 409.

[3] Ibid.

[4] Letter from A.S. Crapsey to Bishop Walker June 17, 1905. Recorded in A.S. Crapsey, *Proceedings Upon the Trial and Appeal of the Rev. Algernon Sidney Crapsey* New York: Thomas Whitakker, 1906 pp. 123-4.

The letter obviously provoked the bishop. He was not used to a rector of his diocese quoting technical legalities in an attempt to keep him from communicating with members of a parish that he was charged by God to oversee. The bishop responded despondently that due to Crapsey's letter he was forced to assign a Committee of Investigation.[5] The Committee of Investigation formally assembled on July 19, 1905.[6]

As with other voluntary organizations attended by busy professionals, getting things done in a timely fashion was impossible. After appointing the Committee of Investigation the members did not meet again until September as the Chancellor of the Diocese was in Europe. In his absence an attempt to settle upon procedural policy was made by Dr. Ashton who assumed the temporary position of chairman. The committee maintained correspondence between the members during the summer and the threat of an investigation dragged on.[7]

Once again, Crapsey took the initiative. He forced the issue of freedom of interpretation from his pulpit. In Crapsey's mind this would benefit all who dared to think independently beyond the constraints of the creeds. Moreover, by the end of the summer of 1905, Crapsey's book *Religion and Politics* was published. He claimed to have published the lectures later in order to clarify his views and be evaluated by the entire corpus of opinion rather than a select part of it. But Crapsey's objective was to stir up people inciting them to action, as well as to convey historical information. Crapsey figured that only a small portion of the series could be considered truly heretical and as such he appealed to the public to judge the entirety of the lectures.[8]

Crapsey's ostensive plan was to promote a detached investigation of religion from a historical perspective. He appealed to both the reason and the emotions of the community to vindicate him. The Virgin Birth was especially germane to his case. Crapsey hoped to demonstrate that the burden of proof for the birth narratives of Christ was, like in a court of law, incumbent upon those who claimed something completely contrary to nature. Arguing from a vantage point of the empirical and scientific, Crapsey reduced the matter to the natural, observable evidence testifying that a child must have both a mother and a father. He claimed that no testimony of eyewitnesses, written in the time of Christ could confirm that

---

[5] Ibid., p. 124.

[6] A.S. Crapsey *Appeal of the Rev'd. Algernon Sidney Crapsey STD to the Court of Review of the Protestant Episcopal Church*. New York: Thomas Whittaker, 1906.

[7] Burrows, *Diocese*, pp. 122- 3.

[8] A. S. Crapsey, *Religion,* See preface p. 1.

Jesus was born of a virgin. But, conversely, neither could anyone validate or disprove the claims of the scriptures through reliance on scientific evidence. Scientific methods could only corroborate the natural, not test the validity of the truth one held in faith. Therefore, validation by either side remained at an impasse.[9]

Crapsey's published lectures coupled with the heightened controversy created intense scrutiny. As reviewers regularly pointed out, his historical scholarship was meager. One noted how most lectures of the type Crapsey presented were usually inaccurate; Crapsey's was no exception. He detailed heinous errors: "James Deuse (John XXII) was incorrectly called Cardinal D'Eusa. (p.195). Prignano was misspelled three times on the same page. (p. 199). It may have been all right to call Peter Philargi, Peter Candia but when he considered him a 'Muscovite friar' instead of the Greek he really was, he demonstrated his ignorance of his subject matter since the pope obviously could not belong to the Russian Church. (p.204). Sigismund never went to Spain but to Perpignan, which was in France, but at the time, was in Rousillon. (p. 208). Gregory was cited as giving up the papacy for the office of the cardinal, but Gregory had actually been a cardinal in the past and what he in reality acquired was a 'good pension.'" (p.208).

The reviewer concluded that he could continue almost endlessly. Though these might seem like small matters, precision in details established the writer's credibility concerning his overall perspective. He concluded that Crapsey simply didn't possess the depth of knowledge necessary to give lectures on church history.[10]

Although Crapsey advocated detailed knowledge as fundamental for his proposed religiosity, his poor scholarship and inadequate education betrayed his ability to bring it to pass. The declaration of how he stood for dispassionate judgment through historical scholarship in light of his own research was obviously farcical and impudent. But Crapsey's work was not about accuracy in scholarship. The publication demonstrated to the clergy and laity of the Diocese of Western New York that Crapsey was determined to press the matter to either full adjudication or complete dismissal. He would be the martyr he intended to be. Moreover, his temerity solidified the resolve of the diocesan committees. Something had to be done, as Crapsey was simply not going to let this matter fade away. Considering the length of time between the appointment of the Committee

---

[9] Ibid., preface, pp. 1-8.

[10] Book review in *London Quarterly Review* London: Charles Kelley, Vol. CV Fourth series, Vol. III Jan – April 1906 pp. 175-6.

of Investigation and any type of official response about the Crapsey case, it is instructive that the diocese did not act at all until after Crapsey published his lectures. Crapsey later related that having his lectures written down rather than delivering them extemporaneously, as was his usual manner of preaching, demonstrated the error of his ways, as the press took his notes and published his major points. Thus, he was somehow trapped by the press reports published about his lectures. But even if that was true, Crapsey obviously knew that by publishing his lectures in book form he was forcing the hand of the diocese. The diocese had been extraordinarily patient and reservedly silent on the matter. His act boldly presented written proof before the public. The book demanded a response.

Crapsey continued to press the matter. On September 2, 1905, *Outlook* magazine ran a five-page article written by Crapsey entitled "Honor Among Clergymen." He sought to clarify his thoughts and give voice to his underlying concerns. Crapsey cited the pastoral letter from the bishops at the General Convention of the previous year that in effect stated, if one suddenly discovered that they held views in variance with one's ordination vows and the foundational truths of the faith "they should maintain their integrity either by keeping it to themselves or by leaving the church."[11]

Crapsey took issue with the statement as it did not identify exactly what the fundamental verities of the Christian religion were. Crapsey defined them as the truths contained in the two great commandments of the law mentioned in the Lord's Prayer and the five ordinances of righteousness from in the Lord's Sermon on the Mount. (Matthew v. 21-48). Crapsey appealed to the highest court in the matter, considering Jesus the ultimate authority on the subject.[12] Cleverly applying the verities he defined rather than citing the traditional doctrines of the church that the pastoral letter alluded to, Crapsey stated,

> We are ready to admit that if a man cannot from his heart say the Lord's Prayer, if the two great commandments of the law have no validity with him, and if he look upon the five laws of righteousness as impractical, then that man has no right to remain in the ministry of the Church of Jesus, for he differs fundamentally from the whole conception of Jesus concerning religion and life. And those who think with the present writer hold that no ecclesiastical organization, however venerable its history, which is not

[11] A.S. Crapsey *Outlook*, 2 Sept., 1905 pp. 25- 9.
[12] Ibid.

based upon the foundation laid by Jesus himself has any right to call itself the Church of Jesus.[13]

Crapsey perceived no problem with the pastoral letter as long as he could have the freedom to interpret the truths of the faith as he defined them. But Crapsey knew better than that. He understood the meaning of the fundamental verities described in the pastoral letter completely. He acknowledged that deviation from the verities would be considered dishonest. After establishing his definition of the fundamental verities Crapsey set forth the traditional definition. However he considered the traditional verities as historical and philosophical ideas and theological designations found in the creeds of the Protestant and Catholic Churches.[14]

Crapsey differentiated between the way the bishops at the General Convention perceived fundamental verities and the way he did. He stripped away the façade of philosophical conception and theological definition from the fundamentally pure teachings of Jesus. He noted that if one did not accept the traditional conception of the fundamental verities, then they were not considered worthy to remain in the church.[15]

But Crapsey knew he was hardly the first to discover the faults that he wrote about. He disingenuously presented what he was in the process of doing. What Crapsey really wanted was to have his understanding of the verities of the faith accepted. In fact, the fundamental verities that Crapsey subscribed to were not solely what he proposed to the readers of *Outlook,* they were denials of the traditional interpretations in favor of the new, rational, scientifically formulated ones. Whether Crapsey realized it or not, his ideas were antithetical to the traditional ones, not just something that one could just add in the name of toleration. Adaptation of his definition by the diocese would render the traditional formularies meaningless.

Nevertheless, Crapsey complained that he had been deprived the right to express his beliefs. Realizing the weakness of this argument he qualified it by how he had actually lost that right when he became a clergyman of the church. Nevertheless, many a Unitarian with views almost identical to Crapsey's had somehow retained their right to be clergymen. Conservatives made it clear that in this free country one was as free to leave the church, as they had been to come. But for Crapsey, this

---

[13] Ibid.
[14] Ibid.
[15] Ibid.

was an issue of human rights. Crapsey made it clear that there would be no problem with this kind of condition if the church could verify the dogmas they presented as truth. Crapsey felt they should prove their case historically and scientifically. If they were established it would be a joy to proclaim the historic doctrines of the church. But Crapsey knew that faith, not reason was the underlying premise of all religion.[16]

To the conservatives, Crapsey's statements, lectures and written treatises were not merely the expressions of a man who had changed his mind. They were the utterances of one who was in the process of leading others to their eternal damnation. To the conservative, faith was not verified by scientific investigation.

But Crapsey had always downplayed the ascendancy of faith in the Christian life. As an Anglo-Catholic, he was consistently Pelagian. Crapsey now sought to "verify the verities." Obviously, he knew that validating faith through natural means was untenable. But he chose to wrestle for the sake of the truth, as he defined it. He stated that the creeds were without historical validation. He contended that later generations had turned earlier legends into hard fact by insisting on their acceptance as evidence of one's orthodoxy. If all of that were obvious to the trained intelligence was it honest to accept everything while one's reason protested? Should the unlearned clergy be the ones who defined for society what the nature of the universe was?[17]

At the peak of his rhetoric Crapsey contended that the hierarchy of the church says to remain silent or leave. If you investigate these matters and find them wanting for the sake of honor remain silent or depart. But where was the honor in that?[18]

Crapsey contended that those who protested the loudest betrayed their real feelings of doubt. As such they were the most pitiful of all men. Others simply concealed their doubts. These men were cautious about being frank. Unconscionably, they had one set of doctrines for themselves and another for the people they ministered to. But such an exercise in deceit was fraught with danger to the withholder of his convictions. For Crapsey those who placed their trust in the traditional faith didn't understand what they believed in. They carefully skated around their concealed doubts because they were dangerous. It was easier to hold back than to embrace the truth and fall into adversity. Many pitiful ministers

---

[16] Ibid.

[17] A.S. Crapsey *Outlook.* 2 Sept., 1905 pp. 25- 9.

[18] Ibid.

thus quietly hid the creeds in their closets like skeletons. He warned that they were hypocritically involved in a historic suppression of the truth.[19]

Two alternatives remained for Crapsey. He could express his convictions and endure the inevitable explosion or withdraw. But for Crapsey, dishonor only accompanied withdrawal from one's convictions. Besides, for Crapsey like other clergymen, the church was his spiritual habitat. He had lived in it virtually for his entire life and he loved it dearly. Outside its walls things were uncertain. Although there was much amiss on the inside the problems merely provoked him to stay to deal with them. Crapsey believed the result would be a better church.[20]

For Crapsey, one could endure no greater catastrophe than to be separated from his past and his lifelong relations. Perhaps he envisioned himself, his wife and children as being suddenly ostracized and estranged from the people they had known and helped to comfort for so many years. To Crapsey and his family, that would be disastrous, to be considered only as a last resort. The result would bring a hopeless state of mind and a great sense of loss.[21]

It distressed Crapsey that they might be forced to leave their home and church. As a family they had brought life and love to the people of St. Andrew's parish. Moreover, Crapsey still had children to send off to college. He wondered about their living quarters, amply provided for them for so many years. Crapsey had much to lose. Although he believed he should stay put as long as possible, he saw the situation before him as "fighting the good fight," He felt that God had placed him there and it was his duty to stay and fight until he was removed.[22]

Crapsey maintained that the salvation of his denomination might actually hinge upon the series of events unfolding before him. Crapsey related the history of the church during the Anglo- Catholic controversy. He noted how Pusey suffered through a great deal of anguish after Newman left the church. Many including William Palmer believed the Anglican Church was on the verge of destruction. Many felt that a moral catastrophe had occurred.[23] Comparing his situation to what Pusey faced Crapsey quoted Palmer who believed that Pusey's resolve ultimately provided deliverance for the Church of England. With the separation of

---

[19] Ibid.
[20] Ibid.
[21] Ibid.
[22] Ibid.
[23] William Palmer's *"Narrative of Events,"* quoted by A.S. Crapsey in *Outlook*, 2 Sept., 1905.

Newman into the Roman Catholic Church, Pusey was exposed to the wrath of the others who blamed him for the schism. Palmer, who had forcefully opposed the Oxford Movement later concluded that he owed a debt of gratitude to Pusey for his strength of character by remaining.[24]

Instead of abdicating like Newman, Pusey stayed firm in his determination. By implication Crapsey's exoneration would also come in time. He would eventually receive a debt of gratitude for holding the communion together. Visions of his grandfather's martyrdom at the hands of those too conservative to recognize reality flooded the depths of his mind. Turning to the opposite side of the Church of England he noted how Dr Temple accomplished as much for his faction of the church as Pusey did on the opposite side. After the publication of *"Essays and Reviews"* Temple and others were considered traitors to Anglicanism and Christianity alike. Some were actually presented on charges of heresy, but the result broadened the liberties of those in the church. Ultimately, Temple became the Archbishop of Canterbury. To Crapsey, that was the ultimate exoneration indeed. Crapsey mentioned how those events demonstrated how great leaders maintained their convictions, Pusey, Marriott and Keble on the right and Temple, Colenso, Stanley and others on the left. Their convictions in total, though disparate and antithetical, eventually saved the church.[25]

For Crapsey then, to run away would be a heinous crime. Like Pusey and Temple, his convictions must be received and implemented by the church. Anything less would be unacceptable. His duty was to bring the church into the twentieth century. He denied the authority of the episcopate when church doctrine came in conflict with the progressive nature of scientific research. Simultaneously he declared his authority as given by God was above the church's. He exclaimed that the church needed to be enlightened and true knowledge needed to be declared where it was most unknown. The church's organization alone had no real teaching ability. It was the prophets and those anointed by God who truly edified the church.[26]

Crapsey saw himself as a modern-day prophet. Speaking of himself and like the prophets before him, he stated boldly, he received his charge directly from God. It was the prophets who remained as the fonts of truth to the church. The church then takes the words of the prophets and summarizes them for the edification of the people. Crapsey viewed the

---

[24] A.S. Crapsey in *Outlook* 2 Sept., 1905 p. 28.
[25] Ibid.
[26] Ibid.

church and its inhabitants as merely deficient and incomplete and as needing to be reeducated by the voices of the prophets. The application of the creeds disallowed the efficacy of the living prophetic voice to the people of God.[27]

It was all conveniently relative to time and place for Crapsey. God's word must be continuously re-interpreted to fit the needs of the present-day circumstances of life. Otherwise, the church was dead and without any hope of life. Their authority resided in the interpretations of the past. Crapsey brought it into contemporary terms by declaring that modern-day prophets brought forth a modern-day message in the vernacular and cultural setting of the time.[28]

It was all about power. Martyrdom was the ultimate power. It was irresistible to Crapsey. Just as Jesus died at the hands of His people, Crapsey would endure his lumps for the sake of the truth. The only way for an effective prophet to be recognized was for him to prophesy against the present-day evils in the church and society as a whole. A prophet must stand fast and speak the truth, and never withdraw as a traitor would. Prophets were not popular as evidenced by so many dying at the hands of the authorities of the time. Crapsey noted that unless one was ready to pay the price that the prophets had traditionally paid one should not presume to take on the office of a prophet. Crapsey summed up his defense of himself and the prophetic office by noting that the prophet was not to depose himself or take his own life. That was the work of others. His job was to simply communicate the Word. In an obvious aside to Luther's advice, Crapsey noted that "the Word would do the necessary work."[29] Moreover, in another reference to Gamaliel's council to the Sanhedrin concerning the persecution of the apostles, Crapsey said, if the Word was not of God it would "come to naught."[30] Truly God was in control.[31]

On Monday, September 4, the local newspaper ran a synopsis of Crapsey's article in a nearly full-page column. It also carried the editorial comments from the *Outlook*.[32] Crapsey's article claimed he was responsible to do the honorable thing. His calling was sanctioned beyond that of the bishops. His authority came directly from God. He spoke as

---

[27] Ibid.
[28] Ibid.
[29] Roland H. Bainton *Here I Stand A Life Of Martin Luther* New York: A Mentor Book , 1950.
[30] Acts 5: 34-38.
[31] Crapsey, , In, *Outlook* 2 Sept. 1905 p. 28
[32] *Rochester Democrat & Chronicle* Mon., Sept. 4, 1905.

God gave him utterance. No one could claim authority over his writing, teaching, preaching or speaking.[33]

In the same edition of *Outlook* however, an editor wrote a column speaking to the points that Crapsey made in his submission. The editor agreed it was Crapsey's duty to speak the truth as he understood it. The same applied to Christ, Paul, Luther and Wesley in times past. It was the only alternative for the wise and honest teacher in the true church to take. Others must determine whether they could countenance his fellowship and calling as a teacher.[34]

But the writer disagreed with Crapsey's assumed responsibility within the Church and his interpretation of the fundamental verities of Christianity. The editor believed the distinguishing characteristic of Christianity was not the law but the gospel. The message of Christianity was found more in the story of the prodigal son than in the all books of the Torah. The true message reflected God's blessing upon mankind rather than His unbending legislation of righteousness. The editor also pointed out that theological errors often contained some semblance of the truth, attesting to their ultimate acceptance. After presenting several examples the editor concluded the value of the creeds laid in their exposure of error. Therefore, they should be insulated from attack.[35]

The editor also disagreed with Crapsey's rash indiscretion by noting how reform should never be mistaken with iconoclasm. He derided Crapsey's lack of depth by pointing out how Crapsey failed to look beyond the mere verbiage of the ancient creeds to the spiritual truths they were essentially protecting. The author called for Crapsey to restate the creeds in the modern vernacular to bring clarity to the modern mind and conscience rather than simply reject them.

The *Outlook* editor believed that Crapsey's statements needed interpretive control. Of all the things one could learn from the Japanese, hara-kari should not be one of them. It profited no one to commit suicide as officials caught in dishonor in Japan did. Submission to execution was one thing but suicide was not the way of a Christian minister.[36]

But for Crapsey silence constituted acquiescence and he would never compromise. His was an absolute affirmation of the relative truth. He would never shirk from his impending commitment to martyrdom. It was

---

[33] Ibid.

[34] "Is Hari- Kari Ever a Minister's Duty?" In *Outlook* Sept. 2, 1905 pp. 14- 15.

[35] Ibid.

[36] Ibid.

his legacy carried in his name and passed down through the generations as part of his heritage.[37]

After Crapsey's article appeared in *Outlook* Dr. Ashton, the chairman of the Committee of Investigation, upon his own initiative, requested that Mr. Hoffman the Secretary of the committee, extend an invitation for Crapsey to meet with the Committee in Buffalo on September 5. Crapsey's reply was instructive,

> I shall be very glad to meet and confer with the Committee of which you are a member, but at that conference I would like to have two or three of my friends among the Clergy who believe and feel as I do in the matter in hand...I agree with your Committee, hoping that a settlement may be reached which will, at the same time, secure the rights of the Clergy and the peace of the Church.[38]

Crapsey's request met with some approval. But overall, the members of the Committee of Investigation felt that Crapsey's desire to be accompanied by his friends would add onto the committee beyond the acceptable limit. They were to be selected by Crapsey and the committee had no authority to allow such an action. The committee felt this course was obviously unacceptable. Moreover, they realized that granting his request would imply that they were incapable of attending to the business committed to them. It would also imply that the committee was biased against Crapsey and his interests needed protection. Moreover, it could pack the court in Crapsey's favor. Finally the committee did not wish to turn the meeting into a theological debate about doctrine. The sole function of the committee was to ascertain facts concerning the case.[39]

The Committee of Investigation convened on September 26, 1905. They met first in the Iroquois Hotel and later reconvened in the parish house of St. Paul's Church in Buffalo. They released no statements other than that the session was preliminary.[40] The committee considered the statements signed by the ten presbyters, the book *Religion and Politics* and the article written for *Outlook*. After much discussion they decided that a sub-committee should meet with Crapsey to answer some of the questions brought up at the meeting. The sub-committee met with Crapsey

---

[37] Ibid.

[38] Letter by A.S. Crapsey to Mr. Hoffman Secretary of the Committee of Investigation, Episcopal Diocese of Western New York, reported in Burrows, *Diocese*, p. 123.

[39] Burrows, *Diocese*, p. 123.

[40] Reported in the *Rochester Democrat & Chronicle* Wed. Sept. 17, 1905.

at St. Andrew's on the very next day. Mrs. Crapsey, wearied by the ordeal, simply could not entertain the men. However, Adelaide, home from Europe, graciously received the men into their home at St. Andrew's.

Crapsey answered all of their queries voluntarily. Two members of the sub- committee, Amos Skeele, and Philip Mosher discussed the problem as diplomatically as possible. Hoping for a positive resolution, Mosher asked Crapsey, "Dr. Crapsey, we know that different persons put different interpretations upon various texts of Holy Scriptures; one man will give to a passage this meaning, and another man that. Now taking this fact of various interpretations into consideration, do you believe that the Holy Scriptures are the Word of God?" To which Crapsey replied, "Certainly if I may, as I must, apply this principle of interpretation, I hold and preach that in the Bible is to be found divine revelation." Realizing an affirmative chord, Mosher continued, "Applying this same principle of interpretation to the Creed, do you hold that the Apostle's Creed is the true Creed of the Church and contains the essentials of salvation?" Crapsey had been handed a plum and responded accordingly, "Certainly, if I may, as we must, interpret the Apostle's Creed in the light of history, I hold and teach that it declares the true faith, and so I preach."[41]

Recognizing a common ground from which to address the problem the three proceeded to fellowship together. They were entertained by Adelaide, and served refreshments before embarking on their journey back to report to the committee. Perhaps seeking poetic justice in the matter, Adelaide served the men tea spiked with rum. By the time the men left the rectory their countenances had changed considerably from when they had arrived.[42] The two asked Crapsey to record his responses for the other members of the committee on paper. Crapsey agreed if they were posed in the exact same manner as he received them from Mosher and Skeele. As he left Dr. Skeele turned to Crapsey and said, "There will be no trial."[43]

Shortly afterwards on October 3, Crapsey traveled to Niagara Falls to meet with two members of the sub-committee. They encouraged Crapsey to write his answers to the questions to provide a visual record of his position. Opinions differ as to the events that followed. The diocese records that Crapsey took the questions home to Rochester with him. After considering the questions he returned his written answers to the

---

[41] A.S. Crapsey, *Heretics*, p. 255.

[42] Event reported in Alkalay- Gut, *Alone*, pp. 152-3.

[43] Crapsey again may have misremembered the situation as he stated that afterwards Mrs. Crapsey served refreshments. He prefaced his remarks with "If I remember correctly." Crapsey, *Heretics*, p. 255.

committee.[44] Crapsey however, stated that while in Niagara Falls they worked on a document together to bring before the bishop. Crapsey and Mosher continued in the vein that they had begun at St. Andrew's, developing a series of questions and answers granting the greatest latitude to the principle of interpretation. Crapsey later wrote ungratefully,

> If this had been submitted to the bishop and at the same time published to the world, it would have been impossible for the bishop to have rejected it, because the whole world would at once have approved of this solution of the difficulty and both the clergy and the laity would have been released from slavish obedience to the letter of both Creed and Scripture.[45]

Crapsey subsequently wrote that the document was never submitted. He accused the committee of burying the paper allowing the bishop to press the matter and interfere with the committee's autonomy. But it was actually Crapsey who pressed the matter. He maintained a high profile by first publishing his opinions and then his rebuttals of those who came out against him.[46]

On September 30, *Outlook* magazine ran an article written by Dr. Edward Abbott, of St. James Episcopal Church, Cambridge, Massachusetts.[47] He further considered Crapsey's article entitled "Honor Among Clergymen." Abbott developed his article in the form of twenty questions to examine the validity of Crapsey's argument. He inquired whether Crapsey really believed that the fundamental verities of the Christian faith consisted solely of the "two commandments of the law, the Lord's Prayer, and the five laws of righteousness as are found in the Sermon on the Mount?" Abbott also wanted to know if Crapsey found the teachings of Jesus untrue in any way. Had he read Crapsey's book he would have known the answer. He questioned rhetorically whether as clergymen of the Protestant Episcopal Church they were not voluntarily constrained by the church's regulations and compelled by their responsibility to remain within the confines of their policies? Like Christ, their individual rights were mitigated by their service to the greater body.[48]

---

[44] Burrows, *Diocese,* p. 123.
[45] Crapsey, *Heretics,* p. 256.
[46] Ibid. p. 256.
[47] Abbott id. personal communication with Sandra Sudak, Archivist of Episcopal Diocese of Massachusetts.
[48] Editorial letter by Dr. Edward Abbottwritten in *Outlook* Sept. 30, 1905 pp. 284-5.

Episcopal Church ordination vows declared a belief in the canonical scriptures of the Old and New Testament. If Crapsey changed his mind would that not impair the validity of his ordination? Abbott questioned whether Crapsey rendered obedience to the church governing over him by his actions. Had both not promised to "minister the Doctrine and Sacraments and the Discipline of Christ…. as the Church had received the same." Would that not negate this promise if they now taught according to convictions gained through their own newer and clearer light? Did any clergyman have the right to substitute his own private interpretation contrary to the doctrine, sacrament, or discipline of the Church? Would it not be more honorable to simply leave the ministry if he could no longer fulfill his duties in good conscience? Indeed, the clergy considered their ministerial duties a sacred trust.[49]

Abbott asked rhetorically if Dr. Frederick Temple, the Archbishop of Canterbury, identified the fundamental verities the same as Crapsey had? Had Temple ever repudiated the Nicene or Apostle's creeds or openly questioned the great spiritual truths of the faith? Was there not a teaching power given to the church through the great commission of the Lord? Who was superior, the church or the clergyman? Did Crapsey make a distinction between a prophet and a clergyman? Weren't the rights and obligations of a clergyman prescribed whereas those of a prophet were not? What prevented an ex-clergyman from remaining as a prophet? If one truly could no longer fulfill his clerical vows, why not withdraw and truly fulfill the office of a prophet with all its liberties.[50]

Arguing he had been given a lack of space, Crapsey answered Abbott briefly. He refused to submit to the questions Abbott had posed, but rather answered Abbott and his other critics as he defined the argument. He wrote a vague response concerning organisms and life. Life was in the soul of the individual because that was where truth was found. Abbott and Crapsey's critics represented the organisms and Crapsey represented life.[51]

To Crapsey, the church was made up of men and man was the special force by which it received life and power. Men differed from one another in their function. For Crapsey his manhood came before his ministry. He would never surrender his indispensable rights because of the ministry. Therefore, Crapsey appealed to men to decide between them. The church owed as much to men as men did to the church. The church should respect the man who had devoted his life to the body and it actually sinned against

[49] Ibid.
[50] Ibid.
[51] Crapsey's reply to Edward Abbott in *Outlook* Sept. 30, 1905 pp. 285- 6.

a man if it deprived one of his basic right to teach what his conscience declared as truth.[52]

To Crapsey, the church held its ministers back from developing intellectually. He asked, "should a man have the same mind at eighty as he did at eighteen? Nor should a man of the twentieth century believe as a man of the fourth century did. How could a creed of ancient times be worthwhile if it was maintained until the present without developing intellectually?"[53]

To Crapsey the church had no authority other than to demonstrate the life of God on the earth. The church must apply the same standards to test the validity of the historic Christian doctrines that it uses to judge other faiths. The churches of his day were dying because they could not incorporate the life of the soul with the dynamics of progressive thinking. Crapsey wrote of a leader in his field who talked an aspiring young man out of a career in the ministry in favor of pursuing the vocation of scientific economics. He related the man's intentions as "joyfully diverting the young man from an exhausted vocation to a useful one." In the end, Crapsey posed the question, "Will we continue to support the creeds at the cost of losing the young and the talented?" He rested his case on the inquiry of "Where did real significance lie upon the man or upon the creed?"[54]

Outlook also presented an editorial opinion to the public. The editor submitted that scores of clergymen from various denominations had changed their beliefs since they had grown up. They didn't want to leave nor did they want to stay where they were not wanted. They simply kept quiet about doctrine. Thus, many were diverted from the embarrassment of the ministry. The creeds were unable to communicate real spiritual truth due to the unscientific ineptitude of their language.[55]

On October 7, a review of Crapsey's book, *Religion and Politics* was published in *The Literary Digest.* The author stated how Crapsey enthusiastically criticized the various churches of Christendom in *Religion and Politics.* For those prone to read the reviews instead of the book, the review brought out Crapsey's criticisms of the modern church. Most importantly, there was no mention of the controversy or the heretical

---

[52] Ibid.

[53] Ibid.

[54] Ibid.

[55] Editorial in *Outlook* Sept. 30, 1905 pp. 253- 4.

passages, only Crapsey's disposition towards science, socialism and evolution as the new great religion that would unify the world.[56]

[56] Taken from review entitled "Aloofness of the Churches from the Modern Spirit" In "*The Literary Digest* Vol. XXXI., [No. 15], October 7, 1905 p. 491.

CHAPTER EIGHTEEN

"With Such An One, No, Not To Eat"

Liberals continued to raise the modernist standard in support of Crapsey. Professor George M. Forbes of the University of Rochester lectured in local churches willing to open their doors to him. He couldn't understand how a man who had accepted all the spiritual wisdom of the Hebrew people could be excluded from his church because of the method he used to arrive at his concept of the truth. He wondered how essential the methodology was in light of the greater knowledge gained. Without mentioning Crapsey's name he pondered why he was being made to feel as if he were an atheist when he should be granted the same fellowship as those who maintained conventional positions.[1]

Liberal churchmen welcomed the assumed supremacy of the new scientific viewpoint. The future was clear. What began with Darwin would continue as greater insight emerged. The biblical narratives would be rationally deciphered. As the world moved forward through the scientific corroboration of the evolutionary facts, Professor Forbes believed that the traditionalists' views were things of the past The modern outlook was unfolding with great momentum and nothing could stop its acceptance. The responsibility of the church was to stop condemning the obvious and find a way to adapt to it immediately as none of the truths taught by Christianity's Founder were necessarily in contradiction with the truths of modern science.[2]

Others also questioned the reasoning behind silencing men like Crapsey. In light of all the technological progress, advances in medicine and the growth of the academy, they wondered why they should not consider finding ways to make traditional and modern views correspond with one another? After all, spiritual truth was being preserved.

---

[1] Lecture series given by Professor George M. Forbes of the Univ. of Rochester, at Park Avenue Baptist Church, Rochester, NY reported in the *Rochester Democrat & Chronicle,* Mon. Oct. 16, 1905.

[2] Ibid.

On the other hand, conservatives shored up their resolve by reiterating their faith in the traditional scriptural way. While realizing that the momentum of modern society was working against them, they maintained their convictions. They emphasized the miraculous nature of their faith, especially in the deity of Christ more than ever. One local rector stated how comforted he was that even in the face of all the liberal criticism he could rely on the testimony of Paul, Matthew, Luke, John and Peter and the rest who actually experienced the presence of the incarnate God in Christ Jesus.[3]

On October 24th, the sub-committee met to inquire about the evidence the ten presbyters possessed regarding their allegations of Crapsey's heresy. Only one presbyter offered an affidavit concerning a conversation he had had with Crapsey. Another declared that he could submit one also but declined to do so until he was fully apprized about the proceedings of the committee. He wanted a complete understanding about all the evidence before submitting anything against Crapsey.[4]

Either this rector was willing to come onboard only if he felt there was enough evidence to convict Crapsey, or he was friendly to Crapsey. One member of the committee had stated that some of the ten may have signed the request for investigation because they were sympathetic to Crapsey and wanted the investigation to thoroughly exonerate him.[5] Eventually the affidavit was signed and delivered to the committee. Nevertheless, the other eight presbyters had nothing either personal or legal to add other than their opinions about the book, *Religion and Politics.*

Meanwhile the diocese received severe criticism for the length of time it took investigating the matter. *The Church Standard* considered that both justice for Crapsey and church harmony demanded a swift determination of the affair.[6] Seizing the opportunity to capitalize on the opinions expressed by the church papers, Crapsey wrote two separate letters to the diocese stating that the delays were causing undue injury to both the church and himself.[7] Meanwhile, the case was being argued subjectively

---

[3] Sermon by the Rev. E.M. Martin of St. Thomas Church reported in the *Rochester Democrat & Chronicle* Mon. Oct. 23, 1905.

[4] Burrows, *Diocese,* p. 123.

[5] Words of Rev. Edward Macomb Duff of St. Thomas' Episcopal Church, Buffalo, NY. Reported in the *Rochester Democrat & Chronicle* Thurs. Sept. 28, 1905.

[6] Burrows, *Diocese,* p. 124. Also reported in *The Church Standard,* Oct. 7, and Oct 14, 1905.

[7] Letters by Crapsey to the Diocese of W. N.Y. dated, Oct. 27, 1905 and Nov. 16, 1905, in Burrows, *Diocese,* p. 124.

in the church papers. *The Church Standard* under the editor Dr. John Fulton and *The Living Church* under the Anglo-Catholic Morehouse, were in agreement with the prosecution while the *New York Churchman* and the *Pacific Churchman* expressed clear sympathy for Crapsey.[8]

The Pacific Churchman summarized Crapsey's reply to Edward Abbott in mid October. The editorial reiterated Crapsey's argument. It explored all the possibilities of maintaining his changing beliefs without leaving the church. Obviously, the argument depended on this point. By mutual opinion Crapsey's only acceptable course of action was to remain in his church. Furthermore, the *Pacific Churchman* wrote of Abbott, "He is a strict constructionist."[9]

Crapsey later wrote that the *Pacific Churchman* affirmed the implausibility of accepting the creeds in their rudimentary form. The concept of a compartmentalized universe containing the elements of heaven, hell and the earth was simply impossible for modern, educated mankind to embrace. The same issue of the *Pacific Churchman* also reviewed Crapsey's book, *Religion and Politics*. Contrary to Crapsey's earlier secular detractors, the new reviewer found it a "very able book" and "infinitely refreshing" that a man of Crapsey's moral character and passion would write on such central issues concerning the church and state. Though there was much to disagree with Crapsey about, this reviewer felt he had presented his argument so earnestly that one could pass over the far-reaching mistakes and inaccuracies in favor of his visionary objective.[10]

In other words, the liberal churchmen were willing to excuse the accuracy of what Crapsey said because of the clever way in which he said it. The press enjoyed Crapsey's rhetorical ability. They also appreciated his lack of discretion and brusque observations about the church's failures coupled with the corruption of the state that contributed to the contemporary condition of America's brazen society. The press concentrated on Crapsey's proposed reforms at the expense of his historical accuracy. In short, he was a good story!

Shortly afterwards, Crapsey's book *Religion and Politics* was placed on the Roman Catholic Church's *Index* and was condemned by some Protestants as well. Under pressure from the official organs of the church, Thomas Whittaker Inc., withdrew the book from the market. Crapsey

---

[8] Ibid. These are the opinions of G. Sherman Burrows, not of this author. p. 124.

[9] Editorial article of the *Pacific Churchman* October 15, 1905. Also in Crapsey, *Heretics,* p. 257.

[10] *Pacific Churchman* Oct. 15, 1905.

subsequently offered it elsewhere but in a day when controversy did not necessarily command profit it was refused. Crapsey attempted to supply some of the demand by himself but was unable to continue for long.[11]

The Committee of Investigation completed their inquiry by early November. Perhaps sensing some wavering by the members, Bishop Walker expressed some strong words at the laying of the cornerstone at St. James' Church in Rochester. Amongst the other addresses made by Drs. Converse and Graham, Bishop Walker stated,

> I am here in this city to stand up for the faith of the Catholic Church as it is taught in the Gospel, as it is taught in the Creed. I cannot sympathize with the man who teaches anything contrary to that which he has promised to teach. God be thanked that there is a Church still, and that the faith still abides. I have been observing your present rector. He is walking in the footsteps of his predecessor. This church stands for work. Here is preached the Church's doctrine as it is embodied in the Creed.[12]

The Committee of Investigation analyzed both the passages in the book, *Religion and Politics* and the articles Crapsey wrote in *Outlook.* This included not only the first article entitled "Honor Among Clergymen," but also his subsequent reply to Rev. Edward Abbott. In rendering their decision to Bishop Walker the committee noted the writings that were obviously offensive to the faith. Moreover, they felt obliged to render their uncomplimentary opinions of Crapsey's "intellectual vagaries," while applauding his ability to defend them.[13]

The committee wrote that Crapsey had been obsessed with the extreme opinions and spiritual interpretations of the rationalistic school of theology. His affirmation of the creeds of the church was not as they were originally received, in their historical sense. In that, the committee was undivided in its denunciation of Crapsey's position. They explained, his ordination as a priest of the Episcopal Church was contingent upon his avowal to both administer the sacraments and maintain the doctrines of the church as they were received. They noted that Crapsey swore an oath to do so with the help of God.[14]

The committee agreed that he had deliberately substituted his own message and subverted the church's dogma and polity by declaring the right to teach his understanding of the truth in place of that which the

---

[11] Crapsey *Heretics,* p. 259.

[12] Speech by Bishop Walker at the laying of the cornerstone at St. James' Church, Rochester, NY, in *The Living Church* Nov. 4, 1905 Vol. XXXIV, No. 1.

[13] Burrows, *Diocese,* pp. 124- 5.

[14] Ibid.

church had historically received. He brought out theories from his pulpit that were deeply controversial and categorically disagreed upon by the scholars of the church. The result was grievous to many of his clerical brethren.[15]

The committee sought after considerable corroborating evidence when they contacted all of the petitioners. However, they obtained only the affidavits signed by the two willing presbyters who testified of the conversations they had had with Crapsey. According to their signed affidavits, Crapsey questioned the integrity of the gospel narratives and forsook the "Articles of the Christian Faith." When examined closely it was learned that one of these conversations took place about a year and the other nearly a year and a half prior to their coming forward. The other petitioners had nothing substantive to offer except the published writings that were already public knowledge.[16]

After carefully considering the affidavits the committee decided that they could be entered as corroborative verification although they thought it injudicious to prefer heresy charges without something more than two private conversations without witnesses as evidence. The committee also disagreed about the significance that Crapsey's book, *Religion and Politics* held as evidence.[17]

Three members of the committee were unable to conclude that the book contained adequate confirmation to obtain a conviction of heresy. They felt the book was not a doctrinal statement of any consequence but merely a poor attempt to present a historical interpretation through the lens of a certain critical school of thought. Therefore, they disagreed whether the evidence was enough to reveal that the book was the author's belief or simply his means of presenting a historical account and forwarding opinions that others held. The members argued that the book was rhetorically confusing and much hung on the interpretive value of certain words or wording. The three members felt that conclusions about Crapsey's beliefs were construed by implication rather than by clear unambiguous speech. Therefore, they refused to present him to the Ecclesiastical court.[18]

The report surfaced publicly only two days after Crapsey sent his second appeal to the diocese asking for expedience in the matter. One local newspaper ran a column with the headlines stating glaringly, *"Will*

---

[15] Ibid.
[16] Ibid.
[17] Ibid.
[18] Ibid.

Be No Heresy Trial." The article reported on the findings of the committee and the recommendations made to Bishop Walker.[19] Another editorial expressed the hope that the decision of the committee would be final. Anyone daring to reopen the case, be they clergy or layman, would be foolish. The writer concluded that the decision reflected the general tenor of the public without a doubt.[20]

The majority recommending that the bishop decline to present Crapsey for trial consisted of Edwin S. Hoffman, Eugene J. Babcock and Philip W. Mosher. Only two members of the five on the Committee of Investigation, J. W. Ashton, and E. W. Duff, were able to find sufficient grounds in the book *Religion and Politics to* advise the bishop to present Crapsey for a trial for heresy. Ashton had assumed the chairmanship of the committee, and Duff had been fairly accessible to the press about the Crapsey situation. Both agreed that there were ample grounds for the presentment. Moreover, coupled with the corroborative testimonies of the two affidavits they believed they were sufficient not only as grounds for presentment but to obtain a conviction as well. The statements Crapsey made could be construed as nothing less than a denial of the Apostle's Creed, the doctrine of the Virgin Birth and the resurrection on the third day. In the opinion of the two dissenters, Crapsey's language was clear and his writings could mean nothing less than what he was accused of.[21]

Needless to say, Crapsey continued to actively participate in liberal functions. On the 13th of November the sixth annual New York State Conference of Religion was held in Rochester. The conference was dedicated to the principle of "less theology and more religion." In their assault against the traditional dogma of the church the attendees felt theology divided while religion united people. All questions concerning the creeds were intentionally ignored. Their motto was "Religions are Many, Religion is One." The purpose of the conference was to bring men together from diverse theological backgrounds. Several luminaries were present at the conference. Washington Gladden, Josiah Strong, Paul Moore Strayer, Rush Rhees, president of the University of Rochester, Augustus Strong, Max Landsberg, Professor George M. Forbes, Joseph T. Alling and Andrew V.V. Raymond president of Union University all attended. The dais included a multiplicity of eminent churchmen, university presidents, and Jewish rabbis.[22]

---

[19] *Rochester Democrat & Chronicle* Fri. Nov. 17, 1905.
[20] Editorial in the *Rochester Democrat & Chronicle* Sat. Nov. 18, 1905.
[21] Ibid. See also Burrows, *Diocese,* p. 126.
[22] *Rochester Democrat & Chronicle* Fri. Nov. 10, 1905.

The festivities began on Monday evening, November 13, at the Brick Presbyterian Church. Crapsey opened the discussion on Tuesday evening, November 14, at Temple Berith Kodesh, on the "The University and Social Leadership." The move to lecture at a Jewish temple about the importance of the secular university in the cultivation of social leadership could not have endeared Crapsey to the hierarchy of the diocese or his conservative clerical brethren.[23]

Meanwhile, after rendering their report to the bishop, the committee waited to reap the whirlwind. One member wrote to another that he was trying his best to keep calm.[24] In their expectations, they were not disappointed with the barrage that followed. *The Living Church* ran an article entitled, "Is there no Evidence against Dr. Crapsey?" The editorial stated in part,

> This failure on the part of the Committee to return a presentment is one that cannot be too vigorously condemned, since it is clearly contrary to the evidence. But the committee had no right to weigh the evidence and determine whether the accused was guilty or not guilty. Their duty was merely to discover whether there was a *prima facie case* against him, and then leave the Court to conduct the trial.[25]

The matter had turned into a disaster for the diocese. Not only had the committee disagreed that there was ample evidence to present Crapsey for trial, they had also exceeded their charge and responsibility by pronouncing judgment on Crapsey's teachings. *The Living Church* continued,

> The committee have usurped the functions of an Ecclesiastical Court.... Instead of presenting him they have condemned him.... It does seem as though one might be forced to the conclusion that Clergymen as such, are not qualified to pass upon questions of evidence.[26]

The paper concluded it was absurd to accept their report as final. *The Church Standard* echoed the views of *The Living Church.* The paper stated that the report of the Committee of Inquiry caused more scandal

---

[23] Ibid. See also column of *Rochester Democrat & Chronicle* Mon. Nov. 13, 1905.
[24] Burrows, *Diocese*, pp. 126- 7.
[25] Ibid. p. 128. Also reported in *The Living Church* Nov. 18, 1905.
[26] Ibid.

than there was before.[27] Speaking of the denunciation of Crapsey the editorial writer noted that the function of the committee was not to censure or judge or condemn anyone. The committee's statements about Crapsey were both "gratuitous and impertinent." Moreover the committee surpassed the function of the ecclesiastical court by rejecting the admissibility of the affidavits submitted by the two presbyters. The committee had committed grievous, audacious and judgmental errors.[28]

Those presuming to speak as the official voice of the church condemned the committee as wrong in every way. Crapsey needed his day in court to either convict or exonerate him. The question of whether he should be presented however, was obvious. In their job as a grand jury style proceeding, they had failed in the simplest of tasks, to bring Crapsey before the court.

Others however, were decidedly in favor of the committee's recommendations. The Bishop of Tennessee, Dr. Thomas F. Gailor, wrote that he had read the report of the committee and disagreed with those calling it "a fiasco." He believed their failure to return a presentment should not be condemned. Instead, Gailor felt the committee should be complimented for saving the church and the country from a shameless, yellow journalism style, spectacle.[29] Likewise, Crapsey's old friend George Foster Peabody wrote a letter to one of the members of the committee praising the majority for keeping the church from the devastation of conducting a heresy trial.[30]

After the bombardment in the conservative church papers, one of the members of the majority opinion wrote a letter to the editor in response. In it he condemned *The Living Church* as excessively prejudiced and without critical discernment in consideration of the facts. He assured the editor that though they had been labeled as incompetent, the committee had come to their conclusion after much painstaking investigation.[31]

By the end of November the signs of change were everywhere. Dr. Langford C. Stewardson, the new president of Hobart College addressed

---

[27] Article entitled, *The Rochester Scandal"* In *The Church Standard* Nov. 25, 1905. Also in Burrows, *Diocese*, pp. 127- 8.
[28] Ibid.
[29] Open letter from Bishop Thomas F. Gailor to the editor of *The Living Church* Nov. 25, 1905. Also recorded in Burrows, *Diocese,* p. 128.
[30] Letter from George Foster Peabody to member of the Committee of Investigation dated Jan. 4, 1906. In Burrows, *Diocese,* p.128.
[31] Letter to the editor written by Edwin S. Hoffman reported in *The Living Church* Nov. 25, 1905. Vol. XXXIV No. 4, pp. 132-3.

the exclusive Genesee Valley Club on the importance of humanism in college life. Many of the local Episcopal clergy attended the banquet. The headlines the next day read, "Head of Hobart is a Humanist."[32]

From a legal perspective Crapsey felt that he was exonerated and as such he could push for the reforms he had identified in his lectures. Therefore, Crapsey continued to press the issue. Yet it was clear, Crapsey was either not satisfied that the matter had resolutely passed from him or he was conscientiously attempting to force the diocese to try him on heresy charges. As he continued with his "intellectual vagaries" from the pulpit of St. Andrew's, the conservative element of the church became more and more disturbed with the situation there. The *Church Standard* and *The Living Church* agreed that if Crapsey remained without recourse "the church would be divested of all teaching authority." The Roman Catholics declared that Crapsey's situation demonstrated how Protestantism's principle of private interpretation clearly led to natural conceptualization individually and rationalism over all.[33]

The press exacerbated the problem by granting Crapsey a high profile. The press reported every heterodox statement that Crapsey made. And made them he did. Moreover, the editorial warfare in the religious papers was showing no signs of abatement. J. Lewis Parks wrote the editor of *The Churchman* asking Crapsey to clarify his views seeing that he had nothing to worry about now in terms of prosecution. He figured Crapsey could stop skirting the issue and explain his views in simple, straightforward language as to whether he believed in the basic tenets of the historic Christian faith like the conception by the Holy Ghost, the Virgin Birth, and the bodily resurrection of Christ. Or, he wondered rhetorically, was it Crapsey's desire to keep his views sheltered and ambiguous to keep himself from the criticism and condemnation that would surely result if he spoke clearly and answered these questions frankly?[34]

Crapsey's patience was wearing thin towards those scrutinizing him. He would not be bullied into confessing anything detrimental to his ministry. Conservatives saw his vagueness as compromising and masking the truth. Crapsey underscored his impatience with the continuing inquiry by writing that he had already suffered the most searching of all investigations. Nothing, Crapsey replied, had been uncovered to warrant

---

[32] News Column in the *Rochester Democrat & Chronicle* Sat. Nov. 25, 1905.

[33] Hugh M. Jansen Jr., "Algernon Sidney Crapsey: Heresy at Rochester." In, George H. Shriver ed. *American Religious Heretics* (New York, 1966). Quote taken from *Current Literature* XXXIX (Nov. 1905), pp. 523-4.

[34] *The Churchman* Nov. 25, 1905, p. 849. Also in Alkalay- Gut, *Alone* pp. 155- 6.

any further inspection of his doctrines or his life. From Crapsey's point of view he had already endured more examination than any clergyman he could think of. He wondered caustically whether Parks' questions concerning his personal convictions were motivated by individual curiosity or by a desire to see the proceedings for presentment resuscitated.[35]

At the beginning of December Crapsey once again utilized the Sunday evening venue at St. Andrew's to lecture on the Second Advent. Crapsey proposed that a deeper meaning for the return of the Messiah was that of the kingdom of righteousness would fill the hearts of men. With the right conditions that vision would be realized. Had he stopped there he might have been left alone. But Crapsey pushed the issue by further stating he believed Christ was wrong in His prophesying about when the Second Advent would happen. Crapsey figured that Jesus changed His prediction of how things would unfold due to the reaction He received. Crapsey noted that in the beginning of His ministry Jesus believed that the reception of His great truths would change things. After His temptation He taught what Crapsey termed as supreme truths. However, the religious leadership was poised against Him and the majority of the people were unable to grasp the great meaning He conveyed. Therefore, Jesus concluded that a great catastrophe must take place before the Messianic Kingdom could occur.[36]

In conclusion, Crapsey argued that the literal return would never be realized. Jesus was wrong about the physical Second Advent. He was only right in applying the coming of the Kingdom to the hearts of men. He contended that Jesus' vision had not and would not ever be physically realized. It would be realized only in the spiritual sense and that, to Crapsey, was the greater sense. The belief in the physical return did function in a positive way by providing early Christians with a hope however irrational, that their Messiah would return. It encouraged the young church through the hardships of the early centuries. The belief helped the institution of Christianity to survive throughout its early years, regardless of whether it was realized physically or not. But the greater kingdom established in the hearts of men through righteousness and social commitment was being realized and would progress with each succeeding generation.[37]

---

[35] Ibid.

[36] *Rochester Democrat & Chronicle* Mon. Dec. 4, 1905.

[37] Ibid. Parenthesis and contents mine.

The headlines, "To Be No Second Coming of Jesus," followed by "An Oriental Conception Says Dr. Crapsey," further by "Never Will Be Realized," and finally, "In Deeper Sense Messiah Will Come Says the Rector of St. Andrew's Church, in Speaking of Christ's Conception of Final Judgment" caused deep concern with the conservatives.[38] They no longer pretended that this matter would somehow go away and they determined to resolve it. Once again, Littell attacked Crapsey stating, "to be an honest Episcopalian one had to believe in the second coming of Jesus in an outward physical sense."[39] But Crapsey reasoned that the belief in the Second Coming provided a mystical element of ecstasy to the believer's soul that afforded a willingness to renounce the world and disparage the state of one's present affairs. From that perspective, the belief in the Second Coming had been more influential in the life of Christians than virtually any other doctrine. As far as Crapsey was concerned,

> This doctrine surpassed in significance the doctrine of the resurrection. It was the conviction of the first generation that Jesus would return during that generation. However, it was a matter of history that Jesus did not return and that He had not returned since then.[40]

Therefore, the doctrine had to be understood spiritually, as the kingdom that would reside in men's hearts. Crapsey finally summed up his answer to his critics with a call for "spiritual interpretation." He quoted the passage "'The spirit is that which giveth life, the flesh profiteth nothing; the words I speak to you they are spirit, and they are life,'" and, "'The letter killeth, the spirit giveth life.'" Crapsey figured he was in good company with Jesus and the Apostle Paul who, he concluded, interpreted the law freely in prayer, scripture and doctrine. But, if men must accuse him, he would appeal to the judgment of God and not to men.[41]

Some supported Crapsey's spiritual interpretation of scripture, while others derided his compulsion to sow doubt. Littell believed that in the case of the indispensable doctrines, the acceptable understanding had to be literal. He quoted scholars who agreed with the traditional interpretation

---

[38] Ibid.

[39] This was Crapsey's rendition of what Littell said. Taken from letter to the editor from A.S. Crapsey dated Dec. 11, 1905, reported in *Rochester Democrat & Chronicle* Dec. 12, 1905.

[40] Ibid.

[41] Ibid. Biblical quotes from John 6:63 and 2Corinthians 3:6.

of scripture. He challenged Crapsey to "make their agreement complete." He listed the recitations of the Christmas season pertaining to the basic doctrines of the faith. He reiterated what these great truths meant in terms of how they applied to life. He spoke of the great martyrs Ignatius Bishop of Antioch and Justin Martyr, and how they had suffered for the cause of holding a literal understanding of the scriptures.[42]

Others also presented arguments against Crapsey's spiritual interpretation of the Second Coming. One individual cited the book of Acts, where the men who observed the ascension were informed that, "This Jesus which was received up from you into heaven, shall so come in like manner as ye beheld Him going into heaven." Obviously this passage could not be construed to agree with Crapsey's spiritual interpretation. Of those substituting spiritual interpretations for the literal, the author wrote, the traditional ultimate authority of Protestantism, the Bible, was being deliberately destroyed. The author noted how "higher criticism" had secured doubt in the minds of all of society while Crapsey's spiritual interpretation was completing the devastating process. The writer related with wonder, if Christ was nothing more than a good and moral individual then why did the liberals continue to ascribe their "heavenly interpretations" to Him. The modernists were more dogmatic than the "dour Puritan" had ever been. While boasting of freedom and liberality they actually led men into wildernesses of speculation and doubt relying on their moral selves rather than the power of God through the truth of the gospel to transform lives.[43]

Bishop Walker was already instructing the Standing Committee to meet to consider the new public rumors concerning Crapsey. Controversy was certainly nothing new to the denomination but in their socially portentous manner it was supposed as bad form and not the Episcopalian way. Things had progressed too far. Crapsey was becoming a thorn in the flesh of the diocese. On December 23, a special meeting of the Standing Committee was held to consider the public rumors.[44]

---

[42] Letter written in editorial column by Rev. John S. Littell, dated Dec. 13, 1905, in the *Rochester Democrat & Chronicle* Thurs. Dec. 14, 1905.

[43] Letter to the editor from C.B. Stoddard dated Dec. 22, 1905, in the *Rochester Democrat & Chronicle* Sat. Dec. 23, 1905. The author concluded, "I sincerely hope that a man of such superior ability as he possesses will not spoil it all and end his usefulness by entering this merely speculative field; it grows only one crop-doubts, and the Christian cannot live on that fruit." Biblical quote from Acts 1:11.

[44] Burrows, *Diocese,* p. 129.

The controversy even showed up in some of the Christmas submissions that clergymen contributed to the local newspaper. The submissions underscored the polarity between the liberal and conservative opinions. One article by Andrew Graham was entitled, "Denial of Incarnation Is to Deny the Gospels." Another submitted by a noted Unitarian W.C. Gannett read, "A God- Man is Born on Every Human Birthday."[45] Although the ambiguity of public opinion remained, the opinion of the Episcopal clergy had taken a decided turn away from the renegade rector. As preparations reached the final stages at Christ Church for its official fifty-year jubilee celebration, Bishop Walker arrived to consecrate the church and celebrate its new freedom from debt. Clergy and laymen throughout the diocese were invited to attend the festivities.[46]

All of the Rochester clergy attended, as did most of the clergy from Buffalo. Clerics from virtually every county in the diocese were present. Crapsey was given only the smallest part in the affair. Most of the clergy were seated in the chancel and the sanctuary, while Crapsey sat in the congregation. It appeared to some as an intentional slight by the presiding clergy.[47]

After praising the work of the previous rector of nearly a quarter of a century, William D'Orville Doty and the present rector Andrew J. Graham, the consecration message was delivered by Bishop Walker. The bishop then "gave counsel" to those present. After consecrating the church where many present had worshipped for fifty years, Walker turned to the question of "What is the Church?," Walker stated that it wasn't a building as such but a human expression of a divinely consecrated organization. He quoted Article XIX of the Articles of Religion explaining that

> the visible Church of Christ is a congregation of *faithful* men in which the pure Word of God is preached and the Sacraments be duly administered according to Christ's ordinance, in all those things that of necessity are requisite to the same.48

Walker stressed the government of the church and the responsibilities of its officers under its Constitution. He underscored the need for order and discipline in the institution. He spoke of the office of the priest as a

---

[45] *Rochester Democrat & Chronicle* Sun. Dec. 24, 1905.

[46] *Rochester Democrat & Chronicle* Sat. Dec. 30, 1905.

[47] *Rochester Herald* Sat. Dec. 30, 1905.

[48] Address of Bishop Walker at the consecration of Christ Church, Rochester, NY reported in *The Living Church* Jan. 6, 1906, Vol. XXXIV No. 10, pp. 358-9.

solemn trust to whom were given the responsibility of securing the timeless doctrines deposited in the church. Walker noted how the priests received the sacred charges of the organization by taking a solemn oath in the sight of God from the moment they were ordained. Their responsibility was to maintain and teach the doctrines *"as this Church hath received the same."* It was not forced upon them. Walker noted somberly, that conscious deviation from their vows was an unadulterated definition of perjury.[49]

Crapsey must have squirmed not a little in his seat with the congregation. Virtually everyone in the building realized what the bishop was speaking about. The situation had been reported and debated and reiterated in the pages of the press, in the sermons of every denomination and in the conversations of the laity and clergy alike for the past year. Crapsey had continued with his statements knowing full well that the bishop was under significant pressure to address the matter. Walker was simply not willing to allow this to continue any further without consequences, at least without the effect of Crapsey hearing his expressed opinion in the matter. He was incensed that the ordination vows of one of the clergy had been so publicly and rudely broken. Their oaths were not temporary or open to revision or discardable. The conditions of one's dedication to the ministry were like the character of God Himself, immutable.[50]

In Walker's eyes Crapsey had committed ecclesiastic treason. Clerical pledges were final. Denial of the vows in their entirety or even of certain parts were tantamount to betrayal, and that was worthy of the forfeiture of one's rights and one's part in that sacred organization just as if they had betrayed their country by renouncing one's loyalty to it. Therefore, that individual should leave.[51]

The key to continuing in clear conscience was to remain consistent with the church's teachings. These teachings were plainly expressed through the Nicene and Apostle's Creeds. Walker forcibly reiterated their historic purpose and the position of the church in maintaining their principles. The creeds were unambiguous, lucid and inflexible. They were "uncontestable facts and historical truths." And they have been acknowledged as the doctrines of the body of Christ since the church began. As such, they must be considered seriously. Walker maintained,

---

[49] Ibid.
[50] Ibid.
[51] Ibid.

> We in ordination, solemnly affirm that we believe it all- Nicene or Apostles' Symbol, as the case may be. We promise to teach it. We dare not deny any part of it, or ordaining hands would never have been laid upon our heads, or the commission to administer the Holy Sacraments and to preach Christ's Gospel, been given.[52]

Walker attacked the validity of personal interpretation at the expense of the traditional formularies of the church. He stressed that if any claimed the right to maintain mental reservations and hold to personal interpretation, then one was being "disingenuous, and dishonorable." Even the pagans refused to tolerate disingenuous behavior. How much more the church must revile against it and regard it with contempt.[53]

For Walker, the state of affairs was crystal clear. He would no longer vacillate. He spoke clearly yet caustically of integrity and honor to those present, emphasizing the precedence for subscription to the creeds. He noted,

> The Creeds have not changed, nor have their forms, either. Those gathered Articles of Belief are a group of quartz crystals, clear and pure as the limpid spring water, that wells forth from lofty mountain's heart. The utterances of Nicea and Constantinople are the utterances of all Christendom to- day. They bind us as they bound Athanasius, or Bede, or Cuthbert, or Wycliffe, or Cranmer, or Keble, or the saint who fell asleep in Jesus yesterday.[54]

Walker spoke of the entrusted verities of the Church Catholic. He likened them to a sacred trust deposited in the hands of one who had been confided in and entrusted into one's own family. He further spoke of the scorn that was rightly due when one betrayed that trust. He stated unequivocally, one had no "liberty of interpretation if one denied the facts, the truths, the dogmas, which the man solemnly vows to hold and to teach." Allegorically speaking, if one taught his own children to be disingenuous and disloyal, he was rightly considered a monster. Walker had passed the stage of subtlety. He was preparing to depose a traitor of the faith. The time to act had come. There was a wolf amongst the flock and the shepherd was responsible to distinguish himself from a hireling and rid the flock of the intruder. Spiritual interpretations were not terms or

---

[52] Ibid.

[53] Ibid.

[54] Ibid. See also Hugh M. Jansen Jr. "A.S. Crapsey, Heresy at Rochester" In George H. Shriver ed. *American Religious Heretics,* (New York, 1966) p. 199.

conditions suddenly open to redefinition by those breaking away from the historic faith. Walker continued to a climax asking,

...what shall be said of the men who play fast and loose with the Church's standards, by claiming a 'spiritual' interpretation of sacred truths, which attempts to explain away or discredit, or throw overboard simple Articles of the Faith of Christ? Is it spirituality to declare that facts are not facts? Is it a spiritual interpretation when we deny the truth of what we at the same time affirm in words? Is there 'a Pickwickian sense' in which the holy doctrines of the Saviour's Religion are to be received, and is this the spiritual explanation thereof? If so, then may heaven defend this poor world from the mockery of so transparent a falsehood! May God deliver the Church from the shameful dishonor of a ministry which would feed on the Church's bread and be recipients of the emoluments of her offices and yet stab her with poisoned stilettos, as by subtle indirection, or by guarded ambiguity, or by cloaked denials they seek 'to overthrow the faith of some!'[55]

If, in good conscience, one could no longer subscribe to the dogma of the church or continue in one's ordination vows, one should quietly leave. He cited the examples of men like John Henry Newman, Frederic Dan Huntington, Ward, Faber and Manning and of the others who were true enough to their own consciences to resign their posts and leave their fellowships believing it false to remain and continue in the old truths when they believed they had a new light to share.[56]

Comprehensiveness in the church, which Walker supported, did not include denials of its faith or disloyalty to its standards, and the Creeds were as technical and exact as any of the sciences. In fact

> they are the statement of that highest of all sciences- the Science of the Great God... It is to such a loyalty, such a faith, and such a Church of God, that this now consecrated building gives its adhesion and its sworn fealty to- day.[57]

A luncheon at the posh Genesee Valley Club followed. Toasts were given to the bishop and to his new bride. Bishop Walker good-naturedly related how he was happy to be relegated a secondary status to his wife as

---

[55] Ibid.
[56] Ibid.
[57] Ibid.

the toast had been made to his wife first and then to the bishop. He related how after the March 4th wedding he called upon the president, as he had known him as the Bishop of North Dakota when Roosevelt was a rancher there. The president had received him and told him how happy he was to see him again but he was even more pleased to meet his wife. The bishop noted how the president turned and talked to his wife for most of the time they had together. Nevertheless, he was content to "play second fiddle."[58]

At the luncheon it was noted that Crapsey sat by himself. His wife chose not accompany him to the consecration nor attend the luncheon. She undoubtedly felt the hostility and decided not to subject herself to it. There was a noticeable lack of warmth and geniality displayed toward the priest that to many appeared obvious. Crapsey partook in only a single course before leaving the clubhouse, causing some to gossip about what was going on beneath the surface. One of the rectors admitted that those present may have lacked some affability or cordiality towards Crapsey. The overall feeling might have materialized instinctively after such a stirring message. Nevertheless, it was concluded there was no intentional slight. Crapsey had excused himself under the pretext that his Sunday school was putting on a Christmas festival. It was also noted that others had similarly left the luncheon before its completion for various reasons. The Episcopal clergy obviously wanted to downplay the incident but one newspaper stated "Dr. Crapsey Met Cold Reception From Clergy."[59]

The gossip may have precipitated the situation in some people's minds, but the antagonism that Crapsey experienced was real. He knew the time had come to meet his accusers. Unbeknownst to Crapsey on the day prior to the jubilee celebration for Christ Church, the Standing Committee had appointed a special committee to arrange the presentment against Crapsey. There would be no getting around this one.[60] Crapsey's brethren had publicly shunned him demonstrating a hard biblical principle prescribed by the Apostle Paul to the troubled church at Corinth, that

---

[58] *Rochester Democrat & Chronicle* Sat. Dec. 30, 1905.
[59] *Rochester Herald* Sat. Dec. 30, 1905.
[60] Burrows, *Diocese,* p. 129.

when such a transgressor was present and amongst them, "with such an one, no, not to eat."[61]

[61] 1Cor. 5: 11.

CHAPTER NINETEEN

"Holding the Mystery of the Faith in a Pure Conscience"

Anglo-Catholics were incensed that the Committee of Investigation had been so pathetically double-minded in their inability to bring Crapsey before an ecclesiastical court. They noted incredulously that even though the committee recognized that Crapsey was wrong in his beliefs they could not tell whether he really believed them. Moreover, they condemned Crapsey for teaching his own idealized form of religiosity instead of keeping his vows but, then again, they were not really sure that he had actually done that. Conservatives wondered how the committee could witness one thing and then not follow through with what they were observing. *The Living Church* stated that the Committee of Investigation had accomplished nothing because it was highly unlikely that Crapsey would suddenly silence himself on matters of doctrine and dogma.[1]

Crapsey didn't. He continued to promote his newly developed dogmatic. Over the Christmas season, Rev. Dr. Van Allen declared the outlook of the Anglo- Catholic faction of the church by stating there was a unique character to their liturgies in the Collect through the way they presented the Blessed Virgin. Van Allen repeated the liturgies in print avowing unequivocally that if Crapsey continued to minister them at Christmastime without truly believing the spoken words he would be committing a great sacrilege.[2]

Crapsey could not let the charges leveled by Van Allen pass without commenting. He argued that he had been acquitted and it was bad form for a spectator to accost the acquitted at the end of the trial and goad him to admit his guilt after all. Van Allen stated that Crapsey had impugned the honor of the church and of both the Mother and Son of God. Crapsey retorted sarcastically, "this whole affair added something new into the

---

[1] Quotes taken from editorial in *The Living Church* Nov. 18, 1905. Vol. XXXIV No. 4, pp. 78- 9.

[2] Ibid. p. 342. Reported in *The Churchman* Dec. 24, 1905.

equation because until then he hadn't realized that God actually had a mother."[3]

Recognizing the impending danger to Crapsey's position, his friends disseminated a reprinted editorial from the sympathetic *Pacific Churchman,* along with the supportive review of his book, *Religion and Politics*. George Foster Peabody circulated the packets to various churches to garner support for Crapsey. The packets bore the request, that "if one agreed with the information enclosed to pass it on to the principal officers of the church."[4]

Peabody lobbied hard for Crapsey. He sent whatever information he could obtain to the local newspapers to demonstrate ecclesiastic support for Crapsey. Peabody also submitted the opinions of significant clergymen to the local newspapers. One message stated that contrary to what the *Church Standard* had been publishing about Crapsey, especially as expressed by Dr. Fulton's article, it should be understood that "Crapsey maintained a considerable amount of support for his custom of communicating freely."[5]

The support Peabody alluded to came from the Bishop of Arkansas, William Montgomery Brown. Considering his position in the church, it was significant indeed. Brown wrote how gratified he was to be in agreement with both Peabody and the editors of the *Pacific Churchman* concerning Crapsey's attitude. Brown noted how one needed to express the historical doctrines of the church in one's own terms lest one were to become "a mere phonograph." In Brown's estimation, that kind of preacher was not capable of providing much insight to his congregation.[6]

Brown's backing coupled with Bishop Gailor's of Tennessee, constituted formidable assistance for Crapsey's cause. Others also surfaced to voice their support. Meanwhile, the discourse was becoming more and more hostile on both sides of the fence. Walker realized that if Crapsey was presented and exonerated it would mean a tremendous loss of power.

Others tried to convince the rector to repent and rejoin his brethren. The archdeacon of the district wrote that the general hope of the diocese was that Crapsey might change his mind, re-embrace the truth once more and re-enter back into his duties. Many maintained that hope despite the

---

[3] A.S. Crapsey letter to the editor of *The Churchman* Jan. 6, 1906 p. 13.
[4] *The Living Church* Jan. 6, 1906 Vol. XXXIV No. 10 p. 342.
[5] Letter from Bishop Brown of Arkansas to George Foster Peabody recorded in the *Rochester Democrat & Chronicle,* Jan. 11, 1906 p. 12.
[6] Ibid. p. 12.

grief and misunderstanding caused by the Committee of Investigation. Moreover, the archdeacon noted that Crapsey himself had misinterpreted the report of the committee. He noted with astonishment how Crapsey continued to state enigmatically that he had been acquitted.[7]

Indeed Crapsey had not been. Washburn understood the sum of the ecclesiastical problem at hand. He realized how unprofitable ecclesiastical courts had historically been. The only ones who truly benefited by such affairs according to Washburn were "the dialecticians." Little would be accomplished of any substance except the pronouncement of moral judgment or the declaration of formal penalties. But he maintained that the real question before them as an ecclesiastic body was one of preserving a "common conscience." His hope was that what was unfolding would be instructive. Indeed, when one found himself transgressing from that common conscience one might muster the courage necessary to bring himself back in line, to an acceptable place where he could honorably continue his charge before God.[8]

But Crapsey's very being was unconventional in the deepest sense. He freely admitted that he had "ceased to be orthodox."[9] He visualized his task as a revolutionary might. He now also had the support of men like Seth Low and George Foster Peabody who lobbied hard for the renegade rector along with the two liberal bishops. His support had grown both in and outside of the diocese and in the press as well.

The first indication that a showdown was near was the resignation of Crapsey's assistant. Frederick J. K. Alexander had been with Crapsey since July of 1904. He was disturbed by statements Crapsey continued to make and may have intended to help with the prosecution of Crapsey by taking notes at his evening lectures. By the first of the year, Alexander was rejecting his duties at St. Andrew's. He refused to conduct services and proceeded to write his resignation on the fifth of January. He was reported to have said, that he was unwilling to be associated with one whose heterodox opinions had caused so much grief to his clerical brethren.[10]

In the confusion surrounding the resignation of Alexander it was reported that Crapsey had requested Alexander's resignation. Apparently he realized that Alexander was hostile to him after his refusal to conduct

---

[7] Louis C. Washburn's letter to the editor *Rochester Democrat & Chronicle* Tues. Jan. 11, 1906 p. 7.
[8] Ibid. p. 7.
[9] Ibid. p. 7.
[10] *The Living Church* Jan. 27, 1906 Vol. XXXIV No. 13 p. 456.

services and he stated disingenuously that the finances did not justify keeping him under the conditions they had agreed upon. Nevertheless, in a show of condescending, and perhaps feigned affection for his assistant, Crapsey implored Alexander to remain until he received another position. In reality, Crapsey needed to both save face in the diocese concerning how he dealt with his assistant and he needed Alexander to conduct the business of the church while he went to Cambridge, Massachusetts. Crapsey was en route to the Episcopal Theological School to procure the assistance of one of the most respected historians of the Episcopal Church, the later biographer of Phillips Brooks, Alexander Viets Griswold Allen. Meanwhile, Alexander immediately secured a position at St. Luke's, Rochester, under the direction of Dr. Rob Roy Converse. Alexander had to wait until the 20th of January to assume his duties with Converse as Crapsey was in Boston until then.[11]

Allen agreed to assist Crapsey even though he was not sympathetic with Crapsey's position on the creeds of the church. Allen simply considered it a question of personal freedom. He eventually prepared a brief for the forthcoming defense concerning the question of "freedom in the church." The brief later expanded into a book resulting from the Crapsey case. Crapsey figured by bringing in noted, sympathetic theologians he could establish that his teachings were accepted in the upper echelons of education within the church. Nevertheless, Allen was not sympathetic to his theology.[12]

The appointment of Alexander by Dr. Converse by no means indicated that Converse was unsympathetic to Crapsey's situation. The action merely portrayed his pressing need for an assistant. Converse's church membership exceeded one thousand people.[13] Converse had been relieved from his duties on the Standing Committee the previous May, and was replaced by Rev. Andrew J. Graham, Crapsey's arch adversary, through election by the diocesan council.[14] There may have been a sense of estrangement with Converse over his liberal leanings. Perhaps the bishop and others sensed Converse's disenchantment with the direction of the proceedings. Perhaps Converse asked to be replaced. Converse had been

---

[11] For further confusion as to dates and times of Rev. Alexander's resignation, see Crapsey, *Proceedings,* pp.53-69.

[12] Hugh M. Jansen Jr. "Algernon Sidney Crapsey: Heresy at Rochester." In, *American Religious Heretics* edited by George H. Shriver New York: Abingdon Press, 1966 p. 207.

[13] *Rochester Democrat & Chronicle* Fri. Jan. 19, 1906.

[14] Burrows, *Diocese,* p. 120.

personally available for Crapsey during his trying times, officiating at his children's funerals.

By early February, Converse was one of the four clergymen in the diocese who signed the *Declaration on New Testament Criticism.* The document originated in Great Britain and was signed by seventeen hundred clergymen of the Church of England. It contained five sections. The first article acknowledged the need for a combined faith in the guidance of the Holy Spirit in an effort to resolve the problems involved with critical discussions on religious issues. The second article desired those in positions of power to welcome the "progressive criticism" of the New Testament as they had with the Old Testament. The third article expressed fear that the desire for ordination might be stifled in those advocating historical methods and many highly qualified men might therefore be lost to the ministry. The fourth article stated,

> Our conviction that it is not without grave responsibility and peril that any of us should build the faith of souls primarily upon details of New Testament narrative, the historical validity of which must ultimately be determined in the court of trained research- although many of us, until such final decision takes shape, may cling devotedly to the traditional details in question: [15]

The fifth article avowed the confidence in the continuity of the faith that without risk would testify of the efficacy of the creeds and the historical experience, which was the spiritual foundation of the church. The American signers changed only a few of the words in the body of the document including those referring to how they needed the general consent of rulers and other sections describing authoritative corroboration that were inapplicable to the American church's conditions.[16]

Interestingly, Crapsey did not sign the document. Perhaps he could not agree with the fourth and fifth articles as his mind was already made up. The language implied an assent to the narrative and the creeds until proven differently. Nevertheless, the document must have given Crapsey great encouragement. It advocated determining the validity of the New Testament narrative and creeds through progressively determined

---

[15] Column entitled "Declaration on New Testament Criticism and other subjects." Document reproduced in *The Living Church* Feb. 3, 1906, Vol. XXXIV No. 14, p. 486.

[16] Ibid.

scholarly means. Moreover, it acknowledged support for historical criticism.

By the end of January reports surfaced that the Standing Committee would consider presentment.[17] Crapsey had not given up his war in the public forum. He utilized the press by releasing statements about his place in the church. During a Sunday service obviously referring to the renewed controversy Crapsey stated how he would remain in the church as a "presbyter in good standing," who desired to accomplish a new work. He would lead his people to a higher calling and continue with his involvement in the movement towards acceptance of historical criticism and spiritual understanding of the creeds. Crapsey counseled his people that they would be judged by their entire history of service not just by the controversial aspects of late. He wished he could return to the work he was called to do in the parish rather than existing in the center of all the controversy. Moreover, he was in agreement with his antagonists in their veneration of the past but where he differed from them was in his deference for the present and the future.[18]

It is hard to believe that Crapsey truly wished to end his role as the one in the midst of the controversy on whom all the attention was focused. Even if he did, the situation had developed far beyond his control. He had become a cause. Others were rushing forward to support him. Rev. Murray Bartlett provided the press with information supporting Crapsey in his ongoing fight with the diocese. Bartlett cited the consecration of the new Bishop of Michigan, Dr. Charles O. Williams, a liberal, broad churchman. The *Democrat & Chronicle* article stated;

> although they were unaware of any support given by the bishop to Crapsey's cause in particular, it was obvious that the bishop was in general agreement with Crapsey's position on researching the truth and he will evidently give license to those under him to utilize the methodology that Crapsey prescribes.[19]

Under these circumstances Bartlett declared again, there would not be a trial for Crapsey. However by the first week in February, it was reported there would be a "second trial for Crapsey." There had never been a first

---

[17] Reported by *The Churchman,* Sat. Feb. 3, 1906, of a report made in *The Church Standard,* week of Jan. 27, 1906.
[18] Crapsey sermon Sunday Jan. 28, 1906 delivered at St. Andrew's Episcopal Church, in *Rochester Democrat & Chronicle* Mon. Jan. 29, 1906 p. 15.
[19] *Rochester Democrat & Chronicle* Wed. Jan. 31, 1906.

trial but the rhetoric was helpful as it lent support for Crapsey's cause. One moderate editorial related how the author though not in agreement with Crapsey's positions, could not sympathize with a diocese that was in relentless pursuit against the rector after the original committee had refused to present him. He noted how the diocese seemed to be hounding Crapsey until they found a committee that was willing to convict him. They considered that kind of pursuit repugnant in a civilized state and especially unfeasible for the church. Under the "Anglo-Saxon concept of jurisprudence, a man might not be tried for the same offense more than once."[20]

The rhetoric was effective albeit misleading. The Standing Committee had every right at the discretion of the bishop to investigate a clergyman whom they considered in error. Moreover, Crapsey had not been tried for anything yet. He had merely been investigated for a problem that continued to grow. The conservatives felt the publicity Crapsey's supporters circulated, including the *"Declaration of New Testament Criticism,"* clouded the issue at hand. The issue remained, was Crapsey guilty of heresy? It was not about whether the New Testament was open to interpretation or whether there was any efficacy in using historical criticism, but whether Crapsey was a heretic.

Ultimately this brought up the question what is a heretic? The liberals sought an open forum for redefinition, but only if it allowed for the widest interpretation possible. One correspondent stated that if certain church presses were right in asserting that no one, as long as they believed what they said, could be considered a heretic then what about the centuries of church history? What about the extrication of Simon, Cerinthus, Arius, Nestrorius, Eutyches or Pelagius and all the others? Were they now forced to draw the conclusion that heresy never really existed since we cannot conclude that the aforementioned were truly heretics? Nevertheless, they were excluded from the communion of the church for reason of heresy.[21]

In the midst of the polygamy controversy concerning the Mormon Church the same correspondent asked, wouldn't it be suitable for a man to have two or more wives if they truly believed it was acceptable to do so? Wouldn't it be all right for them to teach others that it was an acceptable practice?[22] The mere avowal of one's sincerity did not exonerate a man for his deliberate perversion of the truth held in the doctrine and practice

---

The Churchman Sat. Feb. 3, 1906, Vol. XCIII No. 5.

[21] Letter to the editor written by John Williams of Omaha, Nebraska, in *The Churchman* Sat. Feb. 3, 1906, Vol. XCIII No. 5, p. 181.

[22] Ibid.

of the historic Christian Church. Heresy was the sinful exhibition of one's own will contrary to the known faith, or moral practice of the church. A historical precedence remained. Crapsey needed to discover the truth and recover his honor. If Crapsey could not remain true to his vows he should leave the church and free his soul and in doing so retain some semblance of honor.[23]

Such was the passionate concern of the conservative church. Crapsey's push for the issues was not to be confused with the matter at hand. Honor demanded his removal lest the church become complicit in the heresy. Morgan Dix, one of the best respected of all the Anglo- Catholics, emerged to clarify the matter at hand. Dix had mentored Crapsey and obviously carried a great burden with him about the upcoming proceedings. Dix preached a sermon from St. Agnes's Chapel, New York, entitled, "The Creed. A Full and Sufficient Statement of the Christian Faith," Dix was not willing to allow his personal feelings for an old friend to get in the way of his calling. He noted how the creeds of the church were elevated beyond the level of mere intellectual ascent. They carried with them not the stiffness of the intellect but the essence of faith through history and continuous pious practice.[24]

On the contrary, others came forth stating there were things that were definitely worse than the dead orthodoxy of the creeds, including live heresy." One spoke of the "dwellers in glass houses," and all that that metaphor portended to.[25] Nevertheless, it was the unanimous decision of the Standing Committee on February 23, 1906, to present Crapsey for heresy. The members of the Standing Committee were the Rev. Dr. J.A. Register, Rev. Dr. Walter North, Rev. Dr. Charles H. Smith, Rev. Dr. Andrew J. Graham, Dr. Henry R. Hopkins, Henry Hathaway, and the Honorable Seldon S. Brown. Nathaniel Rochester, a layman from Buffalo, was sick and could not attend. The bishop received the recommendation of the Standing Committee on the 26th. The news media speculated as to the disposition of the bishop now that a formal request from a diocesan committee had been received. Because of the passionate and heated sermons he had preached regarding the Crapsey case, they had assumed that he would "order a trial."[26]

The offense was described under section I of Canon 23, of the Canons of the Protestant Episcopal Church. The only other man in recent history

---

[23] Ibid.

[24] Sermon of Dr. Morgan Dix reported in *The Churchman* Feb. 17, 1906, p. 257.

[25] Letter to the editor, *The Churchman* Sat. Feb. 24, 1906.

[26] *Rochester Democrat & Chronicle*, Feb. 25, 1906.

charged for the same offense and tried was the Rev. Howard MacQueary, from a small town in Ohio. At the tender age of twenty-four, MacQueary had written a book entitled, *The Evolution of Man and Christianity.* He was tried and found guilty by an Ecclesiastical Court in Cleveland in 1891. However, the bishop of the diocese had overstepped his authority during the process. MacQueary obtained an injunction against the imposition of the verdict. He soon wearied of the controversy however and left the church to become a Universalist clergyman.[27]

Because the members of the court were from various towns outside the Rochester and Buffalo area, it was rumored that the diocese was planning to hold the trial in a small town accessible to the members of the court. [28] But amidst all the speculation, by the end of February the bishop had not yet delivered the presentment to Judge Seldon Brown the chancellor of the diocese. Walker met with Judge Brown in his chambers on the 27th, causing the newspapers to contemplate that the document as it was drawn contained weaknesses needing resolution.[29] Rumors abounded in the press including the conjecture that others might be mentioned in the presentment as well. They speculated that certain younger members of the diocese might be investigated, especially those affected adversely by the teachings of Crapsey.[30]

During this time, Bishop Walker attempted to convince Crapsey that he should take some time off and reconsider his position. The bishop hoped that after some well-needed rest coupled with thoughtful reflection Crapsey might see things from the proper perspective. But although there seemed a point when Crapsey might acquiesce to the counsel of the bishop, the time passed without success, and the circumstances continued to escalate. Crapsey had gone too far to back down by that point. His will allowed for nothing less than either total exoneration and full acceptance of his cause or martyrdom.[31]

On the third of March, Walker finally delivered the presentment against Crapsey to the chancellor of the diocese. Judge Brown delivered it to Crapsey that same evening. The Ecclesiastical Court already elected the previous May, consisted of Rev. Morton Sills and Rev. Charles W. Hayes of Geneva; Rev. W.C. Roberts of Corning, Rev. Charles H. Boynton, of Geneseo, and Rev. William F. Faber. Rev. Francis S. Dunham of Albion

---

[27] *Rochester Democrat & Chronicle* Mon. March 4, 1906.

[28] *Rochester Democrat & Chronicle* Mon. Feb. 27, 1906.

[29] *Rochester Democrat & Chronicle* Feb. 18, 1906.

[30] *Rochester Democrat & Chronicle* Fri. March 2, 1906.

[31] Quotes taken from Burrows, *Diocese,* p. 129.

was nominated by Walker and subsequently elected by the Standing Committee to take the place of Rev. William F. Faber who had left the diocese during that year. It was to be an "open trial," Brown declared, and it was to commence on the Tuesday after Easter. The diocese provided both sides with forty-five days to ready themselves for the trial after the announcement of the presentment.[32] By canon law a trial was not to be held for at least thirty-five days after presentment. The diocese intentionally gave Crapsey an extra ten days to prepare although Brown could have legally held on to the presentment for those ten days before delivering it to Crapsey.[33]

Crapsey was presented on two charges. The first was a violation of sub-section *(b)* of section I of Canon 23. The charge alleged that: "A bishop, priests or deacon of this Church shall be liable to presentment and trial for the following offenses, viz.: *(b)* Holding and teaching publicly or privately and advisedly any doctrine contrary to that held by this Church."[34]

Canon 23 had been adopted at the General Convention of 1904, and became canon law on January 1, 1905.[35] The first charge carried two specifications with it.

The first specification stated that,

> At divers times during the years 1904 and 1905 the said presbyter did openly and privately utter, avow, and declare and teach doctrines contrary to those held and received by the Protestant Episcopal Church of the United States of America *by the delivery of sermons* thereafter published in said book *'Religion and Politics'* and among other statements *in said sermons* in particular *by the use therein* of the following languages, words and terms" – there being "then quoted fifteen passages- it being *intended* by said language, words and terms to express the presbyter's disbelief in and to impugn and deny.[36]
> (1) The doctrine that our Lord Jesus Christ is God, the Savior of the world;
> (2) The doctrine that our Lord Jesus Christ was conceived by the Holy Ghost ;

---

[32] *Rochester Democrat & Chronicle* Sun. March 4, 1906.
[33] *Rochester Democrat & Chronicle* Fri. March 9, 1906.
[34] Edward M. Shepard, *Argument of Edward M. Shepard as Counsel for the Rev. Algernon Sidney Crapsey Before the Court of Review of the Protestant Episcopal Church Upon His Appeal from the Judgement of the Court of the Diocese of Western New York, October 19, 1906.* Report in Andover Theological Seminary Library, 1907.
[35] Ibid. Statement repeated in Shepard's argument.
[36] Ibid.

(3) The doctrine of the Virgin birth of our Lord Jesus Christ;
(4) The doctrine of the resurrection of our blessed Lord and Savior;
(5) The doctrine of the Blessed Trinity.[37]

The second specification under the first charge held that Crapsey "did on or about December 31, 1905, openly, publicly and privately declare and teach doctrines contrary to those held by the Church, "by the delivery of a sermon . . . in the course of which, among others, he made in substance the following distinct statements:

(1) Jesus was born of parents belonging to the middle class.
(2) He was born of a simple father and mother.
(3) He was the son of a carpenter.
(4) The fact that the early Christians predicated a miraculous birth of Jesus was to be regarded as one of the greatest misfortunes that had ever befallen mankind.

And that by such language Dr. Crapsey "intended" to express his disbelief in and impugn and deny the doctrines:

(1) That our Lord Jesus Christ is God, the Savior of the world;"
(2) That He 'was conceived by the Holy Ghost;'
(3) Of the 'Virgin birth;' and
(4) Of 'the Blessed Trinity.'"[38]

The second charge alleged Crapsey violated sub- division *(f)* of Sect. 1 of Canon 23. The charge read; "A bishop, priest or deacon . . . shall be liable to presentment and trial for . . . "*(f)* Any act which involves a violation of his ordination vows."[39]

The second charge also carried two specifications. The first stated that "by his utterances and conduct set forth in the first charge and its specifications- that is to say, by his *advisedly* and *intentionally* impugning and denying the doctrines of the Church, Dr. Crapsey did 'violate and break' his ordination vows:

(1) Of belief that the Holy Scriptures are the word of God and contain all things necessary to salvation, and that he would 'conform to the doctrine, discipline and worship' of the church.

---

[37] Ibid.
[38] Ibid.
[39] Ibid.

> (2) That he would give faithful diligence always so to minister doctrine, sacraments and discipline 'as the Lord hath commanded and as this Church hath received the same' and teach the people committed to his charge 'to keep and observe the same.'
> (3) That he would 'be ready with all faithful diligence to banish and drive away from the Church all erroneous and strange doctrines contrary to God's word.[40]

The second specification read:

> Upon many occasions during the years 1904 and 1905 the said presbyter did publicly use the liturgy of the Church . . . and did minister to many people the sacraments of the Church, and . . . that by his conduct in so doing taken in connection 'with his public utterances' quoted under the first charge he broke his further ordination vows-
> (4) To be 'diligent to frame and fashion himself and his family according to the doctrine of Christ,' and to make himself and them, as much as is in him lay 'wholesome examples and patterns to the flock of Christ.'"
> (5) To 'maintain and set forward . . . quietness, fear and love among all Christian people.'"[41]

Crapsey retained Congressman J. Breck Perkins as his primary counsel for the defense. Mr. E. M. Shepard, one of the best-known lawyers in the nation, a previous candidate for the mayor of New York City and one of the signatories of the *Declaration of New Testament Criticism* also volunteered his services for the defense. He was signed on as his secondary counsel. The prosecution named John Lord O'Brian of Buffalo as the Church Advocate. O'Brian was one of the finest attorneys in Western New York. Attorney Franklin D. Locke of Buffalo and Judge John H. Stiness of Rhode Island assisted him. Judge Stiness was a well-respected former Chief Justice of the Rhode Island Supreme Court. Almost twenty years before the "Scopes Trial" electrified the nation with its legal celebrities, Crapsey's trial included high profile attorneys on both sides of the legal fence. They were the courtroom heavyweights of the day.

Crapsey and the Broad Church faction intended to produce a redefinition of what was ecclesiastically acceptable through the official decisions of the court. The liberals demanded the trial be an exercise in the philosophical definition of truth with the freedom of expression as the

---

[40] Ibid.
[41] Ibid.

ultimate rationale for holding it. Seth Low, the onetime mayor of New York City and the contemporary President of Columbia University described "The Far- Reaching Implications of the Crapsey Trial," best from the liberal standpoint arguing that one could understand the dimensions of Christian truth from two standpoints. The one views the truth as a diamond perfect in its form and in how it is revealed to the world and in that way it is immutable and treasured and guarded for its invaluable nature. The other envisions the truth as a seed that must change and develop, grow and produce and as it does it takes on various characteristics and forms. These kinds of thinkers cannot see virtue in the crystallized truth as static. They must imagine it a vital thing. Low concluded that the Episcopal Church must be capable of providing a sanctuary for men of both opinions to qualify as a true church. Unfortunately, Low did not leave the argument there. His opinion was that Crapsey should be allowed to go wherever his scholarship might lead him. Low felt Crapsey was well within his rights as an Episcopal clergyman as long as he saw the creeds as significant, authoritative proclamations of the historic church full of "spiritual truth."[42]

Obviously the conservatives demurred. An editorial in an Anglo-Catholic publication expressed what it perceived as the basic purpose of the trial. The issue was one of fact, not one of determining the faith of the church. The paper predicted the motives of the Broad Church faction as they prepared for the trial. They realized that their plan must be to elaborate on their beliefs and to find a sympathetic ear in both the church as well as in the media. Moreover, they must be convincing enough to have open and free interpretation officially accepted by the church. The defense plan necessitated making the church correspond with the priest, rather than visa versa. Anticipating this plan of the defense, the writer reminded his readers, the church was not on trial, the priest was.[43]

Other respondents also wrote about Seth Low's statement concerning Crapsey's right to "pursue his scholarship wherever it may lead him." One wrote that he had "seldom read a vaguer phrase than this latter one." After further elaboration the author wrote how Low's rhetoric was beautiful like that of an apple on the outside but when you bit into it, it was empty, tasteless and even filthy inside.[44] Furthermore the author wrote that the principles that Low and others advocated would add to the schismatic

---

[42] Letter to the editor by Seth Low in ***The Churchman*** April 7, 1906, (15), p. 523.

[43] Editorial in *The Living Church* March 17, 1906 Vol. XXXIV No. 20.

[44] Letter to the editor written by Alexander Mackay- Smith in *The Churchman* April 21, 1906 (15), p. 611.

problems that have historically torn Christianity apart. Though the church would be relieved of a problem "In such a crisis, the Unitarian body would gain the real advantage.[45]

Others in the more moderate faction perceived that Crapsey was deceived by teaching that was in open contradiction to his profession of the faith. One could consider Crapsey ignorant or perhaps intellectually confused but not necessarily guilty. As such, what indeed was the church's responsibility to those many clergymen who were in a similar state? Their answer was to inform, not expel those who were seeking the truth.[46] But the question remained, inform them about what, if the truth was not really comprehensive or perhaps even discernible?

The Churchman's moderate editors pursued a via media of their own. Another editorial read that it was manifestly clear that a priest who denied the dogma of the church should not remain at its altar. Heresy and treason were intolerable and indefensible. They were enemies of the truth held in righteousness. The question that the church needed to answer was how to confront and prevail over these enemies.[47] The editors found no value in dragging this matter into the public forum just to expel the renegade rector. But their recommendation for resolution of the problem was even more vague than Seth Low's recommendations of letting Crapsey follow his scholarship. *The Churchman's* recommended, "the positive and effective exposure of error whether in life or thought by establishing the truth in the Spirit of Christ."[48]

The editors opined that after the truth had been established in the public forum, this action would compel the transgressor to vacate his post or it would necessitate the church to pull back from an untenable position. The point was, the truth had to be intellectually and culturally established. The one who held views contrary to the truth would then ideally withdraw. For the editors of *The Churchman* the truth was on trial and could only be arrived at by consensus. This was perhaps the most repulsive of all the opinions to the conservative churchmen.

So the discussion went back and forth generating public contention between the factions of the Protestant Episcopal Church. But the controversy went far beyond the boundaries of the Protestant Episcopal Church. It affected people who wondered how a churchman of good character and service to his church for over a quarter of a century could

---

[45] Ibid.
[46] Editorial article in *The Churchman* March 17, 1906, (8), p. 408.
[47] Editorial article in *The Churchman* Sat. April 28, 1906.
[48] Ibid.

suddenly be tried for heresy! How could a man once enlightened by the truth of God, suddenly deny the basic tenets of the historic Christian faith? Why was the church not able to find a place for him considering his quality, character and the length of service? Was there not room for all opinions in the church? The presentment raised a plethora of questions as basic as the character and fairness of the case and as universal as how we as a culture define the truth. Was our definition of the truth a result of our faith, or, was the definition of our faith the result of our understanding of the truth? The forth-coming trial anticipated all of these questions and more.

Perhaps even more interesting were the opinions in the secular papers concerning the Crapsey case. Some were sympathetic to Crapsey and his cause. The *Auburn Citizen* of Auburn, NY stated, this trial was central to the issue of whether the church would constrain its membership to those who thought the same, "like a medieval sect" or whether it would be broad and open to those who sought new understanding and "new truth."[49] *Outlook* magazine's editors remained perhaps the most consistent in their support for Crapsey declaring, "Heresy trials have always brought to the front the most offensive and unchristian elements in the Church."[50]

But the bulk of the secular newspapers saw the issue from a distinctly positive perspective concerning the church's stance on basic historical creeds. They ironically refused to confuse the issue of how the church might bow to intellectual developments that the secular realm was rapidly embracing. *The Standard Union* of Brooklyn wrote of Crapsey, the "manly, correct and beneficial thing for both Crapsey and the unorthodox churches that agree with him would be to resign from the church he doesn't hold similar beliefs with and take up with those he does."[51] *The Washington Post* wrote, "given the vast variety of churches, as well as the freedom of choice in this nation Crapsey could relocate himself as often as he desired."[52] A *New York Times* editorial declared "there was no sense of persecution involved here, nor was this a question of the freedom of speech. Anyone who voluntarily joined an organization remitted at least some of his freedom of speech by agreeing to the assertions of the

[49] *The Churchman* May 12, 1906.
[50] *The Churchman* May 12, 1906 p. 729.
[51] Quote from *The Standard Union* of Brooklyn, NY, in *The Living Church* May 5, 1906. XXXV No.1 pg. 12.
[52] Quote from *The Post* (Washington, DC), in *The Living Church* May 5, 1906, XXXV No. 1, p. 12.

group."[53] The *Minneapolis Journal* stated, "Crapsey could bypass the problems involved if he would simply realize his duty and resign rather than causing the church to try him."[54]

Other papers submitted opinions of a similar attitude. An editor from the *Springfield Republican* asked, "What does the Prayer Book mean?" The editor asked what did the ancient ceremony mean that Crapsey conducted every Sunday if not exactly what it bespeaks of and not the opposite as Crapsey says in his "certainly excellent sermons?"[55] The Knoxville, *Journal and Tribune* editor wrote bluntly "if a man changes his mind from the doctrines by which he is granted the right to teach he should quit the church."[56] The editor from the Chicago *Inter- Ocean* wondered caustically how "those who defend Crapsey might consider the secular repercussions of allowing one who denies the truth as defined by the church's profession of faith to continue practicing its liturgy each week."[57] The *Providence Journal* forwarded the opinion that "even though Crapsey might be exceptionally bright, accomplished and loved locally that didn't necessarily mean he was being victimized. Nor did those facts mean what was happening was particularly scandalous to the Protestant Episcopal Church. What it meant was that his position was deeply regrettable."[58] Finally, *Harper's Weekly* stated amusingly, "the creeds of that church 'endorse' among other things 'the doctrine of the Immaculate Conception,' in which Dr. Crapsey is said to have proclaimed his disbelief," confusing the Immaculate Conception with the Virgin Birth.[59]

Various denominational Church papers forwarded their opinions of the case. Outside of the Episcopalian communion there seemed little regard for Crapsey's position. The *Lutheran Observer* stated, "Whatever Dr. Crapsey's message may be, ... It is not the message of Christ and His apostles. It may be a religious message, but it is not Christianity." *The Baptist Examiner* wrote, that Crapsey's statements were, "a curious example of what an intelligent man can do in the way of muddling a very

---

[53] Ibid.

[54] Quote taken from an editorial in the *Journal* of Minneapolis, Minnesota. Recorded in *The Living Church* May 5, 1906, XXXV No. 1 pg. 12.

[55] In *The Living Church* April 7, 1906. XXXIV No. 22, p. 789.

[56] Ibid.

[57] *The Living Church* April 21, 1906 XXXIV No. 25, p. 861.

[58] *The Living Church* April 28, 1906 XXXIV No. 26, p. 892.

[59] Statement regarding quote from *Harper's Weekly* April 7, 1906 issue, in *The Churchman* April 14, 1906, (11) p. 563.

plain subject.... The real point is, does he believe what his Church requires him to believe as a 'priest' of her communion?" The *Pittsburg Christian Advocate* wrote, "it would be a wholesome thing if the Episcopal Church should have the nerve to convict such a man. If he is really guilty." *The Congregationalist* stated, that if Crapsey were allowed to remain in his office the inaction of the authorities would amount to "a repudiation by the Church of the belief in the Virgin Birth and the physical resurrection of Jesus Christ as essential elements of the Christian faith."[60]

Even Unitarians found reasons to criticize the Crapsey case. *The Unitarian Register* declared, "the question in the trial is not whether the standards of the Episcopal Church represent the truth, but whether Dr. Crapsey is true to the standards." The *New Unitarian* wrote, "if Dr. Crapsey cannot say the words of the creed in their natural sense, he should leave the Church and spare it the scandal of tolerating an ecclesiastical conscience which would not be respectable in Wall street or (say) before an insurance investigation committee."[61]

Some Roman Catholics offered their opinions as well. One Protestant clergyman described a poignant discussion he had with a Roman Catholic on a train ride from Graniteville back to St. Louis, Missouri. "Well!" said the man after indulging in some of the free Champagne provided at a party. "You are a Protestant clergyman and I am a Roman Catholic. The only difference, as far as I can see, is that you Protestants open the stoppers of your bottles, and away go your doctrines in volatile gases; whereas, we Roman Catholics never open our bottles; we label them 'mysteries,' and put them away on the back shelf where they are not to be opened, and there they stand for all time.

"'Yes,' he concluded, 'it's a mistake to open a bottle that contains a mystery.'

---

[60] All quotes taken from *The Churchman* May 12, 1906 pp. 728- 9.

[61] Ibid.

"Here is the point of the present case:" wrote the clergyman about the Crapsey proceedings, "Is it, or is it not, a mistake to open the mysteries?"[62]

Crapsey had indeed opened the bottles. Perhaps the church might cork them up in time. But like any bottle that had been once opened, its gasses would continue to escape, slowly yet perceivably from that time forward.

[62] Letter to the editor by William Wilberforce Newton in *The Living Church* March 17, 1906, XXXIV No. 20, p. 701.

CHAPTER TWENTY

'Doth Not the Ear Try Words?'

By early April, Crapsey's defense team challenged two members of the Ecclesiastical Court. The court as it was first constituted by election through the diocesan council were, Rev. W.C. Roberts of Corning, New York, Rev. Charles H. Boynton, of Geneseo, New York, Rev. Francis S. Dunham of Albion, New York, Rev. C. Morton Sills, and the Rev. Charles W. Hayes, both of Geneva, New York. The two Genevans, Sills and Hayes, were challenged due to their outspoken opinions in the pulpit and the press.[1] Walker nominated two other men who were both subsequently elected by the Standing Committee to the Ecclesiastical Court. They were, Rev. G. Sherman Burrows, of Tonawanda and Rev. Nathan W. Stanton rector of St. Mark's Church, Buffalo.[2] The defense then challenged Stanton and Rev. John M. Gilbert of Phelps, New York was nominated and elected in his stead.[3] Gilbert's career paralleled Crapsey's. He attended St. Stephen's College at Annandale on the Hudson and graduated from General Theological Seminary. Gilbert also ministered in New York City. At thirty-seven, he was younger than the rest of the court and Crapsey might have considered him both friendly and impressionable.[4]

Shortly after the presentment, Walker received a letter signed by fifteen prominent members of the diocese, seven lay and eight clergy urging him to postpone the trial until after the election of the new diocesan council in May. The situation looked dreadful for the diocese. The diocesan council elected members both to the Standing Committee who had presented Crapsey and to the ecclesiastical court who were to try him. Members of the diocese, many of whom were unsympathetic to Crapsey, signed the statement urging the bishop to wait until after the diocesan elections to assure an evenhanded perception of the trial and dispel any untoward criticism.[5]

---

[1] Crapsey, *Heretics*, p. 262.
[2] *Rochester Democrat & Chronicle* Sun. April 8, 1906.
[3] Burrows, *Diocese,* p.129 for procedure if court members were challenged .
[4] *Rochester Democrat & Chronicle*, April 18, 1906.
[5] Burrows, *Diocese,* p. 130.

Bartlett and other supporters of Crapsey signed the letter. They also undoubtedly leaked the contents of the letter to the press. Although the local press questioned the validity of the trial and the constitution of the court, one dismayed churchman wrote to the editor that the defense had already produced enough changes to the court. Moreover, had the defense left the court alone without challenging it most of the court would already have been elected by the council.[6]

The bishop forwarded the petition to the Ecclesiastical Court deferring the decision concerning the proposed adjournment. As the one correspondent noted, if Crapsey had left the court as originally constituted it would have been a completely elected body. Therefore, they reasoned that the present court was preferable for the defense. Putting the trial off would only cost the diocese additional expenses by bringing witnesses and experts back again to testify. In their estimation the constitution of the court was impartial. The two replacements, Burrows and Gilbert were initially quite sympathetic to Crapsey. Realizing that criticism would follow regardless, they decided to proceed.[7]

The trial of the Algernon Sidney Crapsey was scheduled to begin on Tuesday the 17th of April at the Parish House of St. James in Batavia, a small town approximately half-way between Rochester and Buffalo in western New York. Those sympathetic to Crapsey speculated about why the trial was held in Batavia. They presumed support was so great for Crapsey in Rochester that the diocese would experience intense pressure to acquit the defendant there. Indeed many of the local clergy became increasingly vocal in their opposition to the trial. The designation of a neutral site accomplished two things; a withdrawal from the tensions involved with the locality of the trial and it made the site more accessible to all the members of the court, most of whom were from small towns outside of the Rochester and Buffalo areas. Converse figured that had the proceedings been held in Rochester there would have been "an ecclesiastical volcano."[8]

The first day began quietly as Crapsey disembarked from the train and walked unaccosted to the parish house of St. James' Church, Batavia. Perkins and Crapsey's daughter Adelaide, recently home from Rome, where she had studied language, literature, sculpture and archaeology at

[6] Letter written by Rev. William H. Goss, rector of St. John's Church Honeoye Falls, NY dated April 17, 1906, to the editor of the *Rochester Democrat & Chronicle* Wed. April 18, 1906.

[7] Burrows, *Diocese,* pp. 130- 1.

[8] *Rochester Democrat & Chronicle* April 26, 1906.

the School of Classical Studies, accompanied Crapsey. She supported her father whose love and affinity she clearly held. Given his wife's previous inability to tolerate the criticism of her husband, Adelaide, her namesake, was an obvious comfort.[9]

The small town had yet to take on the festive atmosphere it would later.[10] At least fifteen newspapermen, several dignitaries of the Protestant Episcopal Church and twenty or more spectators attended the trial. The facilities were inadequate for so many interested parties. Reverend Francis J. Hall the professor of dogmatic theology at Western Theological Seminary assisted the prosecution with questions of theology, while Elwood Worcester of Emmanuel Church in Boston, Crapsey's old disciple, and Samuel McCombs assisted the defense. Other churchmen arrived, curious about the event they felt might shape the destiny of the modern church.[11]

The procedures of the court started abruptly with the motion by Mr. John Lord O'Brian, "In the name of the Standing Committee of the Diocese of Western New York, I move that the trial of the Rev. Dr. Algernon Sidney Crapsey, on the charges preferred in the committee's presentment proceed."[12] The presiding officer of the court, Rev. Mr. Walter C. Roberts, who wore his divinity school graduation robes to portray the office of the presiding judge, was clearly taken back, unprepared for the assertiveness of the high-powered attorneys. He asked demurely if anyone seconded the motion. As the matter was followed by a chortle of laughter, Mr. O'Brian advised the court that no seconding of any motion was necessary. Crapsey would later relate acerbically that the court was comprised of country clergymen, none of whom had any judicial experience.[13]

Had Crapsey's defense team left the court unchallenged they would have had at least one man on it from one of the largest city churches in the diocese. They would also have had two other very well educated and

---

[9] Alkalay- Gut, *Alone*, 1988 p. 160.

[10]Crapsey, *Heretics*, Crapsey later portrayed the proceedings as a farcical and carnival- like for the purpose of undermining its legitimacy. pp. 260-8.

[11] *Rochester Democrat & Chronicle* April 18, 1906 p. 13.

[12] Ibid.

[13] Crapsey must have misremembered the exact context of the "seconding incident," he later thought it took place when it was asked if the court would reconvene at the Genesee County courthouse. Crapsey, *Heretics*, p. 263. The press put the incident at the opening of the trial. Compare with *Democrat & Chronicle* April 18, 1906 p. 13.

sophisticated churchmen present. Moreover, Francis H. Dunham was a Ph.D. Fortunately, the Hon. Safford E. North the former County Surrogate and a well-respected attorney from Batavia assumed the role of the Assessor to the Ecclesiastical Court. Under Judge North's guidance the courtroom assumed an atmosphere of decorum and respectability.[14]

Crapsey's lawyer the Hon. James Breck Perkins unassumingly asked for instructions as to how they should proceed with the filing of the formal reply of the defendant to the charges. He suggested that it would be better if they were to file, if and when an adjournment was granted. Mr. O'Brian, the church advocate, objected to the adjournment desiring a speedy trial in the matter. The court ordered the defendant to file an answer to the charges made by Standing Committee. Unable to receive an adjournment through subtle suggestion, the defense formally petitioned the court for an adjournment. With Perkins' busy legislative agenda in Washington, Shepard's full schedule of court dates in New York and the scope of the case before them, the defense needed more time to prepare. The defense also argued that it was unfair to require Crapsey to be prepared then. He had just finished the Lenten season and was obviously busy with church business.[15]

Crapsey's lawyer explained that they had petitioned to have the trial adjourned for the specific reason of fairness. The letter written by members of the diocese favoring an adjournment to assure a fair trial was read by the defense in the courtroom. Perkins asked that the court be adjourned until June. Immediately Mr. O'Brian objected again to the adjournment noting that the defense had already been granted sufficient time, in fact, ten days more than necessary under the canon law. He stated it was patently absurd to petition a court to adjourn beyond the constituted life of the court.[16] He also resented the inference that the court was not fair in the way it was composed. O'Brian characterized the petition as presumptuous in its allegations of judicial prejudice.[17] He further mentioned the court's responsibility considering the expenditures involved to the diocese in the matter of bringing people back at a later date. The court was there to courageously and steadfastly bring about justice.[18]

[14] Editorial in *The Living Church* May 5, 1906 XXXV No. 1, pp. 9-11.

[15] *Rochester Democrat & Chronicle* April 18, 1906.

[16] Ibid.

[17] Full account of the trial in *The Living Church* May 5, 1906, XXXV No. 1 pp. 9-11.

[18] Quotes of Mr. John Lord O'Brian, *Rochester Democrat & Chronicle* April 18, 1906.

The prosecution came prepared. O'Brian's confident expertise and courtroom assertiveness were obvious throughout the proceedings. As the church's advocate O'Brian's adversarial role was extremely effective. One of the facts established throughout the trial was the prevailing competence of both O'Brian and Stiness as the church advocates. In contrast, Perkins and Shepard appeared somewhat reticent, figuring that they would be able, without too much difficulty, to deal with the "country clergymen" in their unfamiliar role of an Ecclesiastical Court. Shepard was not even present for the first day of the trial. Moreover, they assumed they could simply demand an adjournment and due to their important and busy schedules one would be granted to them. The defense appeared pathetically unprepared, not only with their inability to proceed with the trial, but also by not respecting the noteworthy abilities of O'Brian and Stiness.

The court ordered that Crapsey's formal reply to the charges be filed on the opening day, April 17. The reply stated that he, "was a presbyter of the Protestant Episcopal Church and the rector of St. Andrew's Church in the Diocese of Western New York, for twenty-seven years," that during that period he, "used the liturgy of the church and ministered to the people the sacraments thereof. " He admitted to the publication of the book *Religion and Politics,* and that "the passages quoted in the presentment were contained in the said book." He also admitted, "that the lectures contained in said book were delivered at St. Andrew's Church."[19]

Concerning his ordination vows Crapsey stated," he was ordained as a presbyter of the Protestant Episcopal Church on or about the 1st day of September 1873, by Horatio Potter, bishop of the diocese of New York in said church; and at said ordination he answered in the affirmative to all the questions contained in the ordinal in the book of common prayer."[20]

Crapsey acknowledged that he was "determined out of the said scriptures to instruct the people committed to his charge and to teach nothing, as necessary to eternal salvation, but that which he should be persuaded may be concluded and proved by the Scriptures." Moreover, "he would be diligent in prayers and in reading the Holy Scriptures, and in such studies as help to the knowledge of the same."[21]

---

[19] Ibid. Crapsey also asked for a forum to further explain the contents of his book. The complete corpus of the letter, the "Formal Reply to Charges of Presentment," was published in the local newspaper.

[20] Ibid.

[21] Quotes taken from Edward M. Shepard, *Argument of Edward M. Shepard Before the Court of Review, Oct. 19, 1906,* photocopy provided by the Andover Theological Seminary Library.

Crapsey denied specification two of the presentment. He submitted, "And the said respondent further answering charge one and charge two of the said presentment, denies the same and each and every part thereof; except so far as he has admitted the statement contained in specification one of charge one as herein before answered unto."[22]

For the record, Crapsey asserted that the Committee of Investigation had already investigated his situation and found he was not guilty of any charge worthy of either presentment or trial. The defense maintained that because the bishop and the Standing Committee accepted their findings, the matter should have been concluded. The reply noted that presentment by the diocese could not be sustained as it was "contrary to the ordinances and canons of the Diocese of Western New York and of the Protestant Episcopal Church of America."[23]

The defense additionally protested that the presentment "involved questions of doctrine faith and worship" of the church that have "not yet been established by the general convention of such church, and that the court of the Diocese of Western New York cannot lawfully or properly entertain or consider the charges made in the said presentment for the reason that they involve questions of doctrine, faith and worship." In conclusion the reply stated, "Wherefore he prays that the said presentment and the said charges against him may be dismissed." Crapsey, Perkins and Shepard signed the document.[24]

After an adjournment the court reconvened in the afternoon rendering their decision against the petition for adjournment by a vote of four to one. "Mr. Dunham," it was announced by the president of the court, to the obvious embarrassment of Dunham, had "dissented from the majority's view." One correspondent wrote that Rev. Dunham who was a rather "rotund individual" and "possessed of the amiability that one might expect of rotundity, looked placidly about him, as if he had taken the attitude that the heavens should fall."[25]

Obviously the president of the court was clearly outside of his element. Mr. Perkins continued to plead his case for an adjournment stating he had to be in Washington at seven o'clock that evening. The defense threatened to withdraw their client and declare a default judgment. When the church advocate Mr. O'Brian suggested that they be granted another week, even

---

[22] *Rochester Democrat & Chronicle* April 18, 1906.
[23] Ibid.
[24] Ibid.
[25] Ibid.

though the prosecution was prepared, Perkins argued for two. The court finally gave the defense until Wednesday, April 25th.[26]

The busy Congressman was visibly upset with the decisions of the court after the first day. Things were obviously not going as planned. When asked by a reporter if he expected the trial would take a long time Perkins stated, "There seems good prospect that the trial will be short." A reporter noted how the Congressman puffed uncharacteristically hard on his cigar afterwards. The case would be more difficult than he had anticipated.[27]

The trail reconvened on the 25th at the more accommodating Genesee County Courthouse in Batavia. The scene was quite different from the first day of the trial. The "quiet country town," Crapsey had come to eight days previously had changed visibly. Churchmen, lay people, newspapermen and other interested spectators swelled the population. The fathers of the Society of St. John the Evangelist arrived to support the "Catholic sect" of the church. Recalling their presence in Batavia one correspondent astutely observed that the fathers were "assuming a role similar to that of the Egyptian monks who trailed St. Cyril of Alexandria."[28]

The fathers had undoubtedly read Dr. Van Allen's opinion of Crapsey's occupation of the pulpit during Christmas as being a sacrilege against God. Van Allen also mentioned the "mother of God," in his statements. When Crapsey feigned "he had never known that God had a mother" a new controversy emerged that smacked of the church's legal precedent involving heresy. Most well informed churchmen knew about the Nestorian controversy adjudicated at the Council of Ephesus in the fifth century.[29] The controversy established the limits of Trinitarian orthodoxy. The council considered statements quite similar to those Crapsey uttered fifteen centuries later. The Cowley fathers of St. John the Evangelist felt their presence emphasized the significance of the church's history.

Dr. Van Allen of the Church of the Advent, in Boston, arrived to advocate for the diocese. Van Allen and Rev. Elwood Worcester, rectors from two very different churches from the same city, were both accompanied by large delegations. Each sat on "opposite sides of the

---

[26]Ibid.

[27] Ibid.

[28] George E. DeMille *The Episcopal Church Since 1900: A Brief History* New York: Morehouse- Gorham Co., 1955 p. 98.

[29] John S. Delaney *Dictionary of Saints* New York: Doubleday, 1980, p. 169.

courtroom and glowered at each other."[30] A correspondent noted how the "Broads were on the right" side of the bench and the "orthodox on the left;" The Catholic writer noted, that the seating arrangements were "a reversal of the position of the sheep and the goats."[31]

Crapsey's entourage included the Rev. Wilfred Lawrence Hoopes, of Cambridge, Mass., Rev. Alexis W. Stein, the newly elected Chaplain of Columbia University, Rev. John Wallace Suter, rector of Epiphany Church, Winchester, Mass., Rev. Edwin S. Hoffman, the former member of the Committee of Investigation of Christ Church, Hornellsville, New York, Rev. George Clark Cox, rector of Calvary Church, Cincinnati, Ohio, and Rev. Elwood Worcester rector of Emmanuel Church, Boston. All came to confirm that what Crapsey taught was contemporarily consistent with the institutions of the Protestant Episcopal Church.[32]

Crapsey met several of the eminent churchmen at the Powers Hotel in Rochester, prior to the reconvening of the trial on the 25th.. Crapsey had asked a number of other experts on theology to testify for the defense as well. Some were unable to attend. Crapsey had hoped for the testimony of Roland Cotton Smith, rector of St. John's, Washington, DC, Percy S. Grant, rector of the Church of the Ascension, New York City, Dr. Sylvester Nash professor of New Testament Exegesis, Cambridge Theological School, and Frank S. Nelson of Christ Church, Cincinnati.[33]

The proceedings started with arguments over submissions to the court. The defense argued again for an adjournment. Shepard, who finally arrived from New York City, made the motion. The defense also appealed to amend their formal reply made on the opening day. The amendment emphasized their view that the court was unfair to the defendant restating that the recommendations of the Committee of Investigation that Crapsey not be tried, be upheld. They argued that the court should therefore proceed no further. Both O'Brian and Perkins argued the matter before the court. Once again O'Brian's logic prevailed, the Standing Committee's function was only that of a grand jury. It never assumed guilt or innocence in the case. It merely affirmed the warrant for bringing the action before the court. O'Brian noted,

---

[30] Crapsey, *Heretics*, p. 263.

[31] *The Living Church* May 5, 1906. XXXV No. 1, p. 10.

[32] Hugh M. Jansen Jr. "Algernon S. Crapsey :Heresy at Rochester," In, *American Religious Heretics* edited by George H. Shriver New York: Abingdon Press, 1966 pp. 208-9.

[33] *Rochester Democrat & Chronicle* April 25, 1906.

> To say that the court is not properly constituted because the Bishop and the Standing Committee have passed upon it is an ugly charge and one which has no basis. The defendant has exercised his right of challenge. The court is properly constituted for the reason that it was organized long ago, before these charges were ever brought before it. This system of ecclesiastical courts came into existence in 1883, and we have had such courts since that time. We cannot change the whole policy of church government because one man, charged with an offense, objects.[34]

At this point the actual trial began. Judge North deemed the reading of the charges against Crapsey unnecessary. After further argument with the defense, the prosecution placed passages of Crapsey's book, *Religion and Politics,* as evidence. The church advocates then cited passages in both the constitutions and canons of the church. Finally, O'Brian cited lengthy passages from the *Book of Common Prayer* as evidence for the prosecution.[35]

After lunch, the court argued over the admissibility of Crapsey's book in its entirety. Eventually, the prosecution limited itself to certain unorthodox passages, and finally called a witness. Crapsey's former assistant, Frederick James Kerr Alexander was first. Alexander established that Crapsey had made statements during his sermon on December 31, 1905, that "he believed were contrary to the doctrine of the church as witnessed by Scripture, Creeds, and confirmed by the *Book of Common Prayer.*" Alexander testified that Crapsey had declared, "Jesus was born of parents belonging to the middle class," and that "He was born of a simple father and mother." Alexander noted "the climax of his sermon came when he said, 'The fact that the early Christians predicated the miraculous birth of Jesus was to be regarded as one of the greatest misfortunes that had ever befallen mankind.'"[36]

Alexander endured a vigorous cross-examination by the defense. He admitted that he took notes during the sermon. The defense tried to establish that Alexander had asked for a raise within the past year when the Crapsey crisis was at an uncertain point. The request had been denied. The implications were clear. Nevertheless, Alexander was defensive and feisty on the stand. He refused to succumb to the leading of the defense, calculating his answers carefully. The defense succeeded at one point to confuse him. But Alexander recovered noting that he was not sure of the

---

34 *Rochester Democrat & Chronicle* April 26, 1906.

35 Ibid.

36 Testimony of Rev. F.J.K. Alexander recorded in *The Living Church* May 5, 1906. XXXV No. 1, p. 10.

time when he actually received the letter from Crapsey asking for his resignation. However, the letter was in his hotel room and he would provide it for the record the next day, which he did.[37]

The defense hoped to nullify Alexander's credibility due to his disloyalty and his ulterior motives concerning his employment at St. Andrew's. They tried unsuccessfully to prove that Alexander had applied to the vestry for Crapsey's job if he were to leave. O'Brian however, reestablished that Alexander had spoken to Crapsey about his problem with Crapsey's heterodoxy prior to his resignation. He noted how it bothered Alexander that the controversy created dissension throughout the denomination. The defense contended that Alexander's note taking revealed his intentions to use Crapsey's sermon against him. But the prosecution established that Crapsey made the alleged utterances and they were corroborated by eye-witness testimony and first-hand documentation.[38]

Shepard later said:

> it would be a sad day for the influence of the church in this community, if a man with the standards of life of Dr. Crapsey must be thrown out, and a man with the standards of life of Mr. Alexander shall stay in.[39]

However, others reported that Alexander admitted that he had indeed taken notes. Nevertheless, although he was under intense pressure by the defense brought on by the cross-examination as well as his temperamental way of dealing with it all, his testimony was not discredited.[40]

The next day began with Alexander's submission of the letter requesting his resignation from St. Andrew's. The letter was dated January 5, 1906. Crapsey apparently received it one day later. When interviewed afterwards Alexander stated that the defense had done "an injustice to him in not permitting him in further direct examination to place a more favorable construction on his conduct while curate at St. Andrew's Church."[41]

After submitting more of the *Book of Common Prayer* as evidence, the prosecution called Rev. Francis Woodward, the rector of St. James Church, Rochester. Woodward's testimony was challenged by the defense. The defense argued the precedent of an English church trial of a

---

[37] *Rochester Democrat & Chronicle* April 26, 1906. Also in Crapsey, *Proceedings.*

[38] Ibid.

[39] Ibid.

[40] *The Living Church* May 5, 1906 XXXV No. 1, p. 10.

[41] *Rochester Democrat & Chronicle* April 27, 1906.

Dr. Williams where testimony was denied because evidence was extraneous to the presentment. The prosecution denied that Woodward had been called to corroborate Alexander's testimony, or that it was anything other than first-hand information. Rather, they planned to prove intent through Woodward's conversations with Crapsey in February of 1906 that Crapsey habitually referred to Jesus as the Son of Joseph. The objection was overruled and the testimony denied.[42] The prosecution had also planned to call Rev. Francis S. Lippitt, the rector of the Church of the Ascension who had been the curate at St. Andrew's Church for six years. He had left St. Andrew's two years prior to the trial. Lippitt was summoned to Batavia and in attendance but was not called. O'Brian probably figured Perkins would counter with the same objection. O'Brian had also planned to cross-examine Crapsey's organist, Mr. Cash. However, he never showed up, even though Crapsey had offered to pay for his trip. At this point, he prosecution rested its case.[43]

After a short recess the court resumed. The defense called Rev. J.A. Leighton Ph.D., professor of philosophy and the Chaplain of Hobart College. Perkins submitted several books into evidence of "distinguished men," corroborating Crapsey's opinions. Among the books were the *Encyclopedia Biblica,* edited by Cheney and Black, *Virgin Birth of Christ,* by Paul Lobenstein, *Christ*, by Rev. S.T. McConnell, *Bible and Modern Life"* by Canon Hensley Henson, *Studies in Theologic Definition* by Frederick Parker, letters written by the Dean of Westminster to the Archbishop of Canterbury, works by Rev. W.R. Inge, and Dr. Charles A. Briggs and many others. Leighton was asked if he was familiar with the books. He stated that he was and that the men were all priests of recognized standing in the Church of England. As Perkins mentioned that the works were representative of what might be determined as "the faith of the Church," an undercurrent of disdainful laughter from the left side of the court ensued.[44]

O'Brian humorously congratulated Perkins for his knowledge of theology. A short recess followed while Leighton read the presentment. "I now ask you," Perkins continued,

> whether in your opinion there is anything in the statements contained in the specifications of the presentment that are in your opinion contrary to

---

[42] *The Living Church* May 5, 1906 XXXV No. 1 p. 10.
[43] *Rochester Democrat & Chronicle* April 27, 1906.
[44] *The Living Church* May 5, 1906 XXXV No. 1, p. 10.

> the doctrine of Christ as the Lord has commanded and the church has received the same?[45]

"I object to the question," said O'Brian.

> I do not consider that the witness is impersonating an ecumenical council, or the Protestant Episcopal Church. He may be a learned man, and I do not doubt that he is, but he has no authority to interpret the doctrines of the Protestant Episcopal Church. The Protestant Episcopal Church is an organization having its doctrines and its laws. This question calls upon the witness to say what are the fundamental bases of the Protestant Episcopal Church. That church is not a Lutheran body, its doctrines are not determined by consensus of opinion.[46]

O'Brian argued,

> It would be of no weight if all the clergymen in good standing in the country came here and gave their individual conceptions of the doctrines of the Protestant Episcopal Church. The church has laid down its doctrines, and this book, the prayer book, is the embodiment of those doctrines. For any person or set of persons other than a regularly constituted council of the church to say what the church holds is manifest absurdity. The Apostle's and the Nicene Creed, contained in this book, fortunately contain the facts as to the belief of the church, stated in comparatively simple language.[47]

O'Brian realized that Episcopalians highly esteemed the *Book of Common Prayer*. The prayer book uniquely distinguished the church and documented its accepted orthodoxy, liturgical practices and traditional Episcopalian authority. O'Brian declared,

> For any man to presume to say offhand whether certain words accord with the statements of these creeds is nothing less than impertinence. What the church does believe is laid down in these creeds in as exact language as could be used, with the precise purpose of excluding from the church erroneous doctrines. No man can exercise the privilege of determining what that doctrine is. The law is stated. It is a question of the law of the church, not a question of fact. There is nothing in it in which the services of a witness will be required. If the testimony of this character is admitted, we shall have to go into everything- or may be called upon to go into

---

[45] *Rochester Democrat & Chronicle* April 27, 1906.
[46] Ibid.
[47] Ibid.

> everything that any clergyman of the Church of England or of the Protestant Episcopal Church has written.[48]

"If the court please," interjected Perkins;

> It is charged that Dr. Crapsey has violated obligations as a clergyman of the Episcopal Church, in that he has advanced doctrines contrary to the doctrines of Christ, 'as the Lord hath commanded and as this church hath received the same.' What is the church? The church is composed of the clergy and laity of its membership. We desire to know what representatives of the clergy hold is the obligation of the church put upon them. Our friend says that, supposing all were heretics, it would make no difference with the standards of the church. Then according to him, perhaps all might be heretics but the Standing Committee.[49]

"And its counsel," interrupted O'Brian.[50] "Its counsel," said Perkins, adding facetiously "and I doubt about him." Perkins surmised that if books written by men, like the prayer book, and the *Thirty- Nine Articles,* were accepted as evidence he saw "no reason why the spoken opinions of men standing should not be taken."[51]

Finally Judge Stiness entered into the fray. As a retired State Supreme Court Justice and an expert on ecclesiastic law, he deciphered the subtle legal issues. He was not willing to allow the proceedings to digress beyond the purpose of the trial. He declared that …

> the court was constituted to pass upon questions raised by the presentment; namely whether Dr. Crapsey had uttered certain words in his teaching and, in the second place, whether those words were contrary to the doctrines of the church as determined in its creeds. In determination of that no expert testimony was needed.

According to Judge Stiness,

> These positions were self- evident. If in every diocese the church were permitted to decide by the employment of experts what the church held, endless confusion would result. The church would have different standards in each diocese.[52]

---

[48] Ibid.

[49] Ibid.

[50] *The Living Church* May 5, 1906 XXXV No.1, p. 10.

[51] *Rochester Democrat & Chronicle* April 27, 1906.

bid.

As Stiness sat Shepard rose. Shepard illustrated the differences between the acceptance of the Athanasian Creed by two different Anglican bodies. The English Church incorporated it into its prayer book, while the American Church did not. However brilliant Shepard might have been as a trial lawyer in the secular courts, he was as much out of his element, in an ecclesiastic trial as Roberts was in presiding over an ecclesiastical court. Shepard related how Athanasius conferred the Athanasian Creed. He attempted to show how the acceptance by the church of an individual's interpretation in the past should allow for the same acceptance in the present. He felt this demonstrated the competence of submitting modern scholarship as evidence. But O'Brian jumped on the fact that though the creed was called the Athanasian, it had been demonstrated without doubt that there was no relationship between the man, Athanasius, and the creed. O'Brian stated, "He had not so connected Athanasius with the creed." There was a noticeable outburst of laughter from the prosecution's side of the courtroom. Shepard tried to regain his composure by arguing his original point that various interpretations were acceptable in the greater Anglican communion. But his ineptitude in the eyes of the clergymen seated on the court had been established. His clumsy mistake demonstrated to the court exactly the opposite of what he was arguing. As Stiness had assured, open interpretation, even by well-informed and intelligent people, if allowed would lead to error and confusion.[53]

The court took a recess to consider the arguments. The question before them held the destiny of the trial. During the recess, most of the visitors at the Richmond Hotel agreed that if the trial was opened to expert theological testimony that there would be no end to the opinions concerning the question before the court. The liberal side obviously welcomed that end, whereas the conservatives saw confusion and division resulting from such a reception.[54]

After due consideration Judge North announced the decision of the court. "Gentlemen," he started, "I am constrained to believe this evidence is plainly incompetent." The court must have been abuzz with onlookers considering the ramifications of Judge North's statements. North continued,

> The witness is asked to substitute his opinion for the judgment of the court. These five men, the members of this court, are here to decide these

[53] Ibid.

[54] Ibid.

> questions. In ordinary procedure the defense could call six men, or even twelve men, to offer expert testimony, and in equal justice the other side could call as many more. But gentlemen, would this tribunal be edified by such testimony?

North had stifled the defense by disallowing expert testimony. Had it been received, their argument would have caused considerable damage to the church's position concerning the authority of the historic documents of the church. North concluded,

> The witness is asked to testify as to his opinion of a book that has been written. It is analogous to putting a witness on the stand to testify as to the constitutionality of the statutes. It is purely and solely a law question. This testimony must be excluded. The objection is sustained.[55]

Finding no relief from the court, Perkins called each and every witness to the stand, to have them state their credentials and publications to demonstrate the support of learned men for Crapsey's cause. Perkins called Wilfred L. Hoopes of Cambridge, Massachusetts, Alexis W. Stein of Columbia University, John W. Suter of Winchester, Massachusetts, Edwin S. Hoffman of Hornellsville, NY, George Clarke Cox of Cincinnati, Ohio, John P. Peters of New York City, John Howard Melish of Brooklyn, NY, Charles Henry Babcock of New York City, Frank H. Nelson of Cincinnati, Ohio, and Elwood Worcester of Boston, Massachusetts.[56]

Meanwhile, O'Brian objected and objected and objected again and had each testimony excluded. The prosecution prevailed. The defense could not articulate their case before the court. As Stiness had so aptly stated, the case was not about determining the legitimacy of expert opinions within the church. The trial's purpose must be adhered to. Shepard attempted to recover by charging that the Committee of Investigation had failed to discover anything in either Crapsey's statements or his spoken words that justified the charge of heresy. After objection by the prosecution the report of the Committee of Investigation was allowed in the record.[57]

Shepard tried another tactic. He declared the utterances of Crapsey were not delivered at a regular service of the church but at a later, special service. Perkins insisted "that the hour for evening prayer at St. Andrew's

---

[55] Ibid.

[56] *The Living Church* May 5, 1906 XXXV No. 1, p. 10-11.

[57] *Rochester Democrat & Chronicle* April 27, 1906.

was 4:30 o'clock and that the brief service of prayer which preceded the special service at which the sermon was preached, was a special service of prayer." O'Brian wondered as to the stipulations, and why they wanted them recorded as such. At that point, Mr. Locke, another prominent Buffalo attorney assisting the prosecution stated dryly, "Could it be, that things that were heterodox before six o'clock became orthodox after?" His statement produced an audible laugh from Crapsey breaking the tension of the trial. Crapsey realized that the defense was struggling. Their only means of combating the charges were to undermine the traditional doctrinal authority of the church. He figured his case was to no avail, so the proceedings became a farce to him. Further arguments concerning the summing up procedure, now a reality, were heard. It was assured that all would be heard, and the defense would be last. The court was adjourned. No one thought that the trial would be over so quickly.[58]

The trial reconvened for its concluding arguments on Friday, April 27, 1906. Mr. Locke began with the summarizing statements for the prosecution. He related,

> All we hear of this defendant is most lovely and Christ like, but that makes his crime all the greater. He, an officer of his Church, in his official capacity, denies the fundamental doctrines of his Church; in his pulpit he denies the Creed. For this offense, we demand from this court a verdict of guilty with the consequences that follow.[59]

Locke noted, that the Apostle's Creed was "part of the faith and doctrine of the Protestant Episcopal Church as it has been received." He continued,

> It is admitted here that the respondent denied these concrete statements of the creed. This Protestant Episcopal Church is then, not for him- let him go to the Unitarian Church or to the synagogue. We do not deny him the right to believe in those places other doctrines than those of the Episcopal Church.

Locke wondered,

[58] Ibid.

[59] Crapsey perhaps again misremembered the order and content of the statements made by Mr. Locke placing them at the beginning rather than the end of the trial. Crapsey, *Heretics,* p. 264.

> How can a church remain a church unless it demands that its standards shall be obeyed? I want to say this, that everything I hear about this respondent as to his daily life, his love for humanity, his service to his fellows, is of the highest; but I say that that magnifies his offense.[60]

As Locke's statement concluded, Congressman Perkins stepped up for the defense. Perkins added a statement of Crapsey's faith hoping to defuse the controversy surrounding his orthodoxy. In it, Crapsey defined his faith in the best possible light to prove his agreement with scripture, even though it conflicted with the creeds and the prayer book. Crapsey declared that the church needed the creeds only at the point when it became a huge institution that was politically significant. They needed discipline and set directives for catechism and baptism. But to Crapsey, the creed was not the means by which God's word was offered to the people. The creed simply provided details about God and was not a comprehensive presentation of the gospel of Jesus Christ. Moreover, the creeds were remiss about Christ's moral nature, practice or teachings. Considering all these problems Crapsey noted the creeds needed to be interpreted. Crapsey believed they had to be interpreted in their historical context and in light of the factors that surrounded them. The creed alone could not be considered as the singular declaration that must be subscribed to for Christian fellowship to result.[61] Crapsey stated,

> Believe me, I say from my heart, day by day and hour by hour: I believe in God the Father Almighty maker of heaven and earth; and in Jesus Christ, his only Son, our Lord who was conceived by the Holy Ghost, born of the Virgin Mary, suffered under Pontius Pilate, was crucified, dead and buried; he descended into hell; the third day he rose again from the dead; he ascended into heaven and sitteth on the right hand of God, the Father Almighty. From thence shall he come to judge the quick and the dead. I believe in the Holy Ghost, the Holy Catholic Church, the Communion of Saints, the forgiveness of sins, the resurrection of the body, and the life everlasting, Amen.[62]

Crapsey asserted his belief in scripture as authoritative, but open to interpretation. He argued that even if he did not give the same elucidation

---

[60] *Rochester Democrat & Chronicle* April 28, 1906.
[61] Ibid.
[62] Ibid.

of the creeds as others did his interpretation was consonant with the scriptures and the character of God. [63]

Had Crapsey stopped there he might have gained some sympathy with the court but he arrogantly reasserted his concept of the humanity of Christ:

> It has been asserted that I have denied the incarnation of Jesus Christ, our Lord. Nay, I have not denied; I have asserted the Incarnation. If the Word was made flesh and dwelt among us in Jesus Christ our Lord, then that flesh was human flesh and human blood, and the flesh in which the Word dwelt had its origin in the seed of man's flesh from which it is generated by a process so marvelous that it is an everlasting and constant miracle, and, therefore, instead of denying, I assert positively the incarnation of the Word of God in Jesus Christ my Lord.[64]

Crapsey continued by declaring his belief in the Trinity. He perceived in the Trinity "the unfolding of the one, not the addition of the three, to make one." He wrote,

> I see in Jesus the very substance of God the Father. He is of the same substance not of like substance. I see in Him a perfect union with the Father. I have in the Holy Ghost proceeding from the Father and coming to me the very substance of the Father Himself.

Then, suddenly Crapsey's tone became combative,

> I care not by what words these great spiritual facts are described, nor am I compelled by my ordination vows, or any other vows, to think in terms of Greek philosophy or in terms of the schoolmen. I have the right to think, and my generation has the right to think, in terms most apt to make these great truths real to our souls. To me God is not a definition; He is a living Being and no definition can confine or fully describe His nature or my relation to Him. It is heart against heart, my heart in the heart of God.[65]

Crapsey also expressed his formal belief in Jesus. He felt it specific enough that no one could question his ambiguity. His belief in Jesus included the manifestation of human life coupled with divine revelation. Jesus was worthy of worship and adoration because he saw in Jesus the

---

[63] Ibid.
[64] Ibid.
[65] Ibid.

consummate perfection of man's nature, coupled with the "fullness of the Godhead bodily." He continued,

> Jesus manifests the Father to me. He has brought me to the Father. He has taught me in all of my trials and tribulations, in my hours of joy and sorrow, to kneel down with the full assurance of faith and say: 'Our Father who art in heaven.' So that in Jesus, the human and the divine become one. He is in the Father and the Father is in Him, and whosoever hath seen Him hath seen the Father, because for all the purpose of revelation to the human spirit, Jesus is all- sufficient as the revelation of God to man. And so when I say that I believe in Jesus, that is my faith.[66]

But without stating that Jesus Christ was God the Son, and understood by him in a way that affirmed the literal nature of the historic creeds, as the ones who wrote them intended and in the way the church originally received them, Crapsey was in their eyes, incompatible with the true church. His attempt to make his confession of the person of Jesus conform to the church's doctrine had fallen short. It was too little, too late and too Unitarian. His definition of salvation was a perfect example of his vagueness. Crapsey stated, "God is our Father. What more can we say of Him? Jesus has saved us by showing us the way of salvation. We will follow him in the way."[67]

He ended his statement with the puzzling testimonial:

> And we believe in the persistence of personality, and especially in the persistence of the personality of Christ. We believe that Jesus, the great person, has fathered to himself all that we have ever felt and thought concerning their god. As an article of our faith we believe that he is the virgin- born, we believe that his personality embodies for us all that is pure, all that is holy, all that we must aspire after, and we believe that the full person Christ is with us to-day, not simply in the sacraments of His church, where his body is broken and his blood poured out, but in and of us as it is written: Christ shall dwell in our hearts by faith that we, being rooted and grounded in love may apprehend with all saints and know the love of God, which passeth knowledge.[68]

After reading the statement in full, Perkins immediately asked,

---

[66] Ibid.
[67] Ibid.
[68] Ibid.

> Who believes that the world was created in six days, that the sun goes around the earth, and that at the word of a man the sun stood still? If the position of counsel for the prosecution is correct, any person who deviates in the least from any printed words from the literal signification of any phrase in the *Book of Common Prayer* must be expelled from the Church. There is not one person in our Church, there is not one person in the court, who believes the Apostle's Creed as it was believed by the men who framed it.[69]

The submission of Crapsey's statement of faith and Perkins' presumptions about the faith of the court was a huge blunder by the defense. It simply affirmed that Crapsey fashioned the doctrines of the historic church to conform to his own beliefs. The statement of his faith could only have been a last ditch, desperation tactic. Nonetheless, the defense was so plainly misinformed and ignorant of the mindset of those sitting in judgment over them that it was almost pathetic.

The theological experts McComb and Worcester spoke for the defense and Hall for the prosecution. Worcester told the legendary story of how Crapsey had given his coat to a stranger who had need in the dead of winter. He walked home and came down with pneumonia and almost died from the experience. Crapsey later admitted it was the first he had heard about the supposed situation. He subsequently wrote about how the counselor was evidently manipulating the sentiment of the court.[70]

Shortly afterwards Hall intended to destroy the defense's argument about the English Judicial Committee and the Privy Council by demonstrating how Crapsey impugned the foundational dogma of the Episcopal Church. During Hall's lengthy discourse Crapsey fell asleep. His embarrassed daughter summarily awakened him, but Crapsey had definitely lost interest. He had already surmised the verdict of the court. Nevertheless, Hall responded carefully to Worcester's point about the ultimate authority of scripture in contrast to the authority of the creeds or the prayer book. Hall stated that scripture corroborated that which the church instructed about the "controversies of the faith" and those were the doctrines that resulted from the teachings of the church. In essence the church interpreted the scriptures by their doctrines. He also defended Bishop Walker's quartz crystals metaphor about the creeds. They were clear and hard as rocks. They declared timeless and unchangeable truths

---

[69] *NY Times* April 28, 1906.

[70] Crapsey, *Heretics,* p. 266. Crapsey wrote, "I had never heard this story until then and I smiled with incredulity. In my heart I accused my reverend council of playing to the gallery."

that had become the legal credentials of the church and as such they did not grow or modify in their character.[71]

Rev. McComb's occasion to close for the defense started ignobly, by an outburst from the gallery. As he declared in a deep brogue, "If it plase the court, we are in the prisence of three alternatives." Someone yelled out, "He's an Irishman!" Everyone in the courtroom laughed and the tension was broken once again.[72] But the comic relief did not quell the seriousness of his tone or the significance of his message. McComb intended to demonstrate that Hall's view of the church was of "a narrow, obscurantist, and intolerant sect" of the church. He argued that it was not God's will that church remained rigid in its interpretation that the prosecution claimed was defined by the creeds. McComb referred to Frederick Denison Maurice's trial for heresy by the Church of England. The precedent established through his case contained the questions that needed addressing. Like Maurice, was Crapsey indeed dedicated to the underlying truths that the church rested on? Did the positive aspects of his life and teachings outweigh the negative and affirm the need to retain him for the body of Christ? McComb declared,

> You can then say to him: 'We may not be able to agree with this or that point of your teaching, we cannot sympathize with your way of putting things; still we believe you to be a true Christian and a devoted son of the Church and as such you are innocent at this bar.'[73]

Because of the length of the summations and to save in trial related expenses, the court reconvened on Saturday. Consequently, Shepard realized that his religious acumen would benefit from an expert. He addressed the court with a brief prepared by AVG Allen. Shepard shifted the focus to the freedom of clergy to express themselves in the church. The question remained whether the church would be broad and Catholic or narrow and legalistic in spirit. The Reformation had proved the interpretive power of the individual in the church. Shepard spoke of "honoring the creed in letter, yet not in spirit." He continued, "there were those who would make of the church a thing no doubt precious but small, no doubt sacred but unfruitful, no doubt exalted but without infinite career or growth."[74]

---

[71] Jansen, "Heresy " In. Shriver, ed. *American* pp. 210 -211.
[72] Crapsey, *Heretics,* p. 267.
[73] Jansen, "Heresy" In Shriver ed., *American,* pp. 212- 13.
[74] Ibid.

Shepard's statements were idealistic but they hardly met the pragmatic replies of the prosecution. The prosecution considered the remarks of the defense superfluous. Stiness, appreciated the elocution of the defense but disparaged them for their inability to relate their case to the vital question before the court. O'Brian surprised the court with the extent of his knowledge concerning the authority of the church. The prosecution had come prepared exhibiting great expertise in the matter at bar. The court was instructed as to,

> the hard task of their responsibility before God. The question before them had a simple answer, guilty as charged. There was no alternative lest the church be accused of double-mindedness and worse yet, spinelessness. Truth could be discerned by contrasting the statements rendered by Crapsey with the statements of faith contained in the creeds, and the prayer book.

O'Brian constrained the members of the court again "to do their duty," and that "the church must be in all things the Church of Truth." O'Brian's concentrated and impervious countenance betrayed of the intensity of his convictions. He had come to win and would not allow the defense to obscure the focus and intention of proceedings. The court was given until the 15th of May to come to a verdict.[75]

---

[75] Ibid., Also in Crapsey, *Proceedings,* pp. 247 and 257.

CHAPTER TWENTY-ONE

'I was Constrained to Appeal Unto Caesar'

Crapsey wasted no time continuing his controversial role. He spoke the very next day on two occasions at Cornell University. The trial seemed to spur him on to more provocative utterances. Crapsey stated in his morning sermon,

> ... If we wait for some far-off Saviour, if we wait for a curtain of blue to open and for some mighty being to come and achieve our salvation, we wait forever. The day will never come. It is not necessary. It is a degrading idea that perfection exists the like of which we cannot attain, albeit it be predicated on one hanging on a cross.
>
> Jesus mighty man of old, call Him what you please, divine, yet He was one of us and needs us almost as much as we need Him. We help saints and prophets of old to achieve perfection by our kind words, our noble deeds, and our tender thoughts. You cannot put on the righteousness of like a garment over our own unrighteousness. The cross is a small price to pay to attain perfection, even as our Father is perfect...[1]

Crapsey's statements were derived from the text on Hebrews 11: 39-40. He attributed the book to someone unknown to history, perhaps a woman. In the afternoon, Crapsey pointed out the variances in the different gospel accounts between Matthew, Mark, Luke and John concerning the resurrection. He attributed the differences to developments occurring during the establishment of tradition. He further described the condition that precipitated Peter's ability to feel the existence of the crucified Christ as psychological in nature. Crapsey distinguished the term narrative from history. He noted how the narratives of the resurrection were derived from the soul, but they were not history as we contemporarily define it. Crapsey noted that in Paul's description of the resurrection there was absolutely no detailed concept of the physical form of the risen Christ, no reference to the bodily resurrection at all.[2]

---

[1] *NY Times* April 30, 1906.

[2] Ibid.

The members of the Ecclesiastical Court met in Batavia at St. James' Parish House where they had started, on May 9, 1906 to confer with one another and to render a decision in the case. The court remained in session until 4:30 in the afternoon, with Judge North being present one hour before the final adjournment. North rewrote the findings into the proper legal form. They were signed on the evening of the session and forwarded to Bishop Walker. While the court deliberated, a clever newspaperman had hidden himself in the basement of the building with some sort of a listening contraption or what Crapsey later referred to as having a Dictaphone machine set up. He cleverly stationed an assistant outside the window to whom he relayed written notes to while the court discussed the key issues of the trial. He was the first to scoop the Crapsey story before it was even announced. Astonished, Roberts asserted there was "absolutely no truth in any statement that may have been printed saying the ecclesiastical court in the case of Dr. Crapsey, or any member of it, to my knowledge or in my belief, has announced what the verdict is. All that has been given out is the simple statement that a verdict has been reached." The findings of the court were supposed to be delivered first to the bishop and then to the public through an open announcement. But due to the clever scheming of the reporter, the New York City newspapers consequently received the verdict before the local papers did. The *NY Times* ran an article on the next day stating "Crapsey Verdict Reached," It continued, "No Statement as to Findings- Report has Him Guilty 4 to 1."[3]

The decision stated:

> Dr. Crapsey impugned, if he did not deny, the doctrine of the divinity of our Lord and the doctrine of the blessed Trinity: that he impugned and denied the doctrines of conception by the Holy Ghost, the birth of the Virgin Mary and the resurrection from the tomb; that he did by his utterances contained in his book, *Religion and Politics,* and his sermons violate and break certain of his ordination vows.[4]

In the rendering of their decision the court recommended,

> that sentence when pronounced, should suspend the defendant from exercising the functions of a minister of this Church until such time as he shall satisfy Ecclesiastical Authority of the Diocese that his belief and

---

[3] *NY Times* May 10, 1906.

[4] Burrows, *Diocese,* p. 133.

> teaching conform to the doctrines of the Apostle's Creed and the Nicene Creed as this Church hath received the same.[5]

The court further,

> expressed their hope and desire that the respondent might see his way clear, within thirty days, which under the canons must intervene before sentence may be pronounced to fully satisfy the Ecclesiastical Authority of such conformity on his part.[6]

The court did not reach a unanimous verdict. Burrows, Boynton, Gilbert and Roberts were convinced of the prosecution's case while the "amiable Rev. Dunham, Ph.D." rendered a minority opinion of his own. As Dunham, the eldest member of the court, considered how the divinity and the deity of Christ might be construed differently, Mr. Gilbert the youngest member of the court answered Dunham's ruminations derisively. While staring out of a window he motioned towards the road, stating, "There is no more divinity in Crapsey's Christ than there is in that telegraph pole."[7]

The decision would have been more conclusive had Dunham not dissented. But Dunham was a long-time acquaintance of Crapsey's. He had been Crapsey's sponsor at his baptism at Christ Church in New York City. He was obviously sympathetic to Crapsey. Crapsey's acute Catholic comprehension of the sacrament of baptism led him to envision himself in the eyes of Dunham as his "spiritual child." The feeling was obviously mutual.[8] Dunham felt Crapsey erred solely in a presumptuous manner of attempting to define the doctrines that God had never fully revealed. Crapsey had done so in a "way not generally received by the church." Although, according to Dunham, he had merely interpreted them in another way, not rejected their truth or their authority. Dunham simply refused to recognize the divergent, contrary nature of Crapsey's interpretations.[9]

On May 15, 1906 Judge Seldon S. Brown, Chancellor of the Diocese of Western New York delivered the verdict to Crapsey. All the major newspapers carried the story. Shepard later accused the diocese of appointing a packed court. Shepard complained that the prosecution had

---

[5] Ibid.
[6] Ibid.
[7] Crapsey, *Heretics*, p. 268
[8] Ibid.
[9] Burrows, *Diocese,* p. 133.

seated the court and as such it was unfair and a desecration of the convention of our common law. Shepard stated dismally that from the onset he had considered Crapsey's case as virtually predetermined due to the nature of the court and the majority's obvious resolve to convict him. Unfortunately, Shepard felt the trial was merely an arduous procedure they had to go through with. He declined consideration of an appeal without speaking to Perkins or Crapsey.[10]

Though Shepard believed all was unfair in the case, the bishop of Shepard's diocese, Bishop Burgess concluded that those who attempt to overthrow the church's authority necessitated the trial. Such individuals must be judged and convicted. A *NY Times* editor concurred stating the bishop was obviously correct. The editor concluded that,

> And all the talk about 'persecution' and 'heresy hunting' in such a case is equally silly and unjust, whether the talker happens to sympathize or not to sympathize with the intellectual attitude of the writer whom the Episcopal Church had under its laws simply no choice but to suspend from his clerical duties.[11]

The trial may have been over, but the case was far from closed. Everyone had an opinion about the case and they were more than willing to share it. Perhaps the immense interest developed from the implications concerning the state of the church and society that the trial engendered. But perhaps even more so, the question boiled down in some people's minds to the nature of a man's freedom and the nature of the truth. The result of the trial had certainly not quelled the contention that the church itself was on trial. Like it or not, as Crapsey would eventually capitalize upon, it was indeed.

On the Sunday after Crapsey's trial another Episcopal Churchman preached a controversial sermon in Cincinnati. Dr. George Clark Cox had been invited to the Crapsey trial and was obviously upset that his testimony had been ruled incompetent. He was not as subtle as Crapsey when it came to his denial of cardinal doctrines of the faith. He stated boldly that he did not believe in the virgin birth or the bodily resurrection of Jesus Christ. He had often preached that the doctrine of atonement was questionable both from a scriptural perspective as well as a rational one. Moreover, Cox stated that he entirely disassociated himself from the doctrine of original sin and many times attempted to refute it. Cox

[10] *NY Times* May 16, 1906.
[11] Editorial opinion, *NY Times* May 17, 1906.

strongly supported Crapsey and wanted the world to know that other parish priests did not follow the prayer book without qualification.[12]

There was a less than pervasive opinion amongst the broad church that the trial had been unfair. However, many that Crapsey called to support him viewed the case with frustration. Rev. Percy Grant called the decision "stupid, not to say idiotic." Rev. J.W. Suter declared the verdict was "ridiculous, weak, and a compromise."[13] Dr. Elwood Worcester would later write in his autobiography that the entire trial and the way it was conducted was a sham. Worcester declared condescendingly that five men appointed by the bishop decided Crapsey's fate. Three of the men were young, inexperienced and fresh out of seminary. He figured they were unlearned and uninterested as well and he was ashamed to converse with them about the Bible and modern theology.

Worcester also characterized John Lord O'Brian, whose brilliant legal abilities subsequently led him to become the Assistant Attorney General of the United States in the Hoover administration, as a "clever sharp man," mentioning that his Irish colleague Dr. McComb described him as a "pettyfogging scoundrel." Worcester also stated that Crapsey "was convicted of several heresies," and that "Dr. Crapsey was convicted by a vote of three to two."[14]

G. Sherman Burrows, one of the judges and a later historian of the diocese, responded that the statements of those sympathetic to the defense were simply false. He asserted that it was the chief legal counselors on either side who controlled the conduct of the trial. Furthermore, the decision was nearly unanimous at four to one not three to two. Burrows commented with incredulity on Worcester's autobiography published many years later. He noted that the youngest man on the court had been ordained fourteen years prior to his appointment on the court. None were young, or inexperienced, nor were they disinterested in the greater issues of the case. After Worcester published the misinformation, the Bishop of

---

[12] *NY Times* Aug. 11, 1906.

[13] Opinions of the trial by Crapsey's supporters recorded in *The Churchman* May 26, 1906 p. 817.

[14] Excerpts from Elwood Worcester's autobiography *Life's Adventure* were quoted as footnotes in Burrows, *Diocese,* p. 134. Burrows further asserted in his footnotes, "It will be perceived by those at all acquainted with the character and churchmanship of each of the signers of the original inquiry, by which investigation was precipitated, that they were fair and liberal minded men; and that the trial was not brought about by narrow and bigoted complainants, as has sometimes been charged."

the Diocese- the Rt. Rev. Cameron J. Davis wrote Worcester a critical letter apprising him of the obvious inaccuracies and misrepresentations found in his autobiography. The bishop suggested that Worcester make a retraction or correction of some sort publicly.[15]

Every faction held an opinion of the Batavia verdict. The defense refused to drop the issue that the case was really all about human freedom and the nature of the truth. For the conservatives it was a simple matter. The argument at bar was whether an office of the church instituted for the purpose of protecting and propagating doctrine could be filled and used by one for the opposite reason, to attack and overwhelm those historical doctrines. The contention that Crapsey's trial was an attempt to repress science and criticism was superfluous as well.[16] The moderates questioned the wisdom of the trial as usual. One editorial stated that the verdict was not necessarily the error of the trial. The damage was done when the case went to trial to begin with. That was where the real error occurred.[17]

Other opinions were not so kind. One editorial writer mentioned that, "the Church cannot afford to coquette with apostasy." The author viewed Crapsey as "representative of a time of open rebellion from modernist priests and one-sided theologians who are making shipwreck of the hope of innumerable souls." He noted incredulously how priests in the church of God were its worst traitors. "But they have violated their vows and foresworn their allegiance and-

> "With traitorous kiss, their Saviour stung,
> "Denying Him with unholy tongue." [18]

The question of the clergy saying one thing while meaning another had been brought to bear by the press on all sides of the issue. It had become increasingly apparent that the public had been utterly moved by this question of ministerial sincerity. One writer underscored the moderate position, differentiating between the literal and spiritual and the individual and corporate conceptions of the faith. Each generation would have to

---

[15] Ibid.
[16] *The Living Church* XXXV No. 3, May 19, 1906 p. 77.
[17] *The Churchman* Sat. May 19, 1906.
[18] Letter to the editor from John M. Peacocke, MD *The Living Church* May 19, 1906 XXXV No. 3, p. 95.

reexamine the veracity of the creeds for themselves and what seems authentic for one generation may be totally unreal for another.[19]

Another editorial railed against the former author's instability of dogma in the church declaring sarcastically,

> how beautifully simple a cure for heresy, just say all the right words such as, this is the creed as the church has received the same and then one can put any spiritualization or interpretation they like on any statement. This would surely be the comprehensive method for including the entire world.[20]

The moderates noted the difficulty for both sides to define the issue. Moreover they discerned a real problem concerning the terminology employed because the two factions could not effectively communicate one with the other. The moderates added disconsolately that they didn't even appear to speak the same language as they mean different things by the words, 'real,' 'material,' 'spiritual,' and so on. Their patterns of thought were extensively different from one another demonstrating the same antagonism that has been a part of the church's dilemma from the beginning.[21] The moderates' suggested inconsequentially that they would all do well to simply recognize the sincerity and integrity of one another.

But Dr. Van Allen wondered if the secular papers could virtually unanimously recognize the double-mindedness of churchmen who affirmed and denied sacred concepts while simultaneously attempting to harmonize them. So why couldn't the church? The *Brooklyn Standard Union* agreed declaring, "'Dr. Crapsey convicted himself,' and made his conviction doubly sure by his sermons on the Sunday following his trial. 'He has not made himself a martyr. He has only made himself an object lesson to other clergymen.'" The *NY Times* forwarded a similar opinion that, "A Church is not an arena nor a forum, but an organization established to attain definite and valuable ends by stipulated means." The *New York World* believed that "from the standpoint of the church the verdict was just," but, it demonstrated no "reflection upon Dr. Crapsey's character or conduct," and that "No obloquy attaches itself in these days to the term 'heretic.'" The *New York Evening Post* implied its support in an oblique way. The "Post" stated that the judgment of the court was,

---

[19] Letter to the editor by Rev. Dr. John P. Peters, *The Churchman* May 19, 1906 p. 769.

[20] Unknown author *The Churchman* May 19, 1906 p. 769.

[21] Ibid.

> not so severe a blow to Dr. Crapsey as it is to those Episcopal clergymen who think as he does, yet who have not the courage to speak out as he did, and who will presumably continue to remain silent and in good standing and contempt.[22]

Others concurred that the Crapsey trial was virtually a drop in the bucket considering the breadth of clerical transgression from the faith. One letter to the editor of the conservative magazine *The Living Church* asked if they were yet unaware at the amount of clergymen who were invalidating the scriptures by their statements and were complicit in the same crime Crapsey was convicted of? Nevertheless the author continued, you continue to work side by side at the altars with those who are subverting the doctrines you declare.[23]

The issue was an important one for all those who dared to look closely at the clerical state of affairs in the Protestant Episcopal Church. It was confusing to the laity. The author wondered how they were going to return to the faith of the past by deposing one man when the ranks of both the clergy and laity are filled with similar subversives? Any celebration for the casting out of a single enemy would be misguided since other more devious collaborators know how to conceal themselves within the affirmation of the creed.[24]

Crapsey now had time away from the limelight to consider what the verdict would mean personally, to his family, his friends and his pastorate at St. Andrew's. There was an overwhelming sense of loss concerning all that could possibly be taken away if his appeal were not entertained. The first step was to file with the president of the Court of Review who had jurisdiction over New York and New Jersey. The defense needed to file within thirty days before the sentence was carried out so Crapsey could remain in his ministry at St. Andrew's. The President of the Court of Review was John Scarborough, the Bishop of New Jersey. The appellate court consisted of Dr. William R. Huntington Rector of Grace Church, New York City, Rev. Arthur B. Baker D.D. rector of Trinity Church, Princeton, New Jersey, the Very Reverend John Robert Moses, Dean of the Cathedral, Garden City Long Island, the Honorable Charles Andrews, Chief Justice of the New York State Appellate Court, the Honorable

---

[22] Compilation of secular newspaper accounts reported in *The Churchman* May 26, 1906 p. 817.

[23] Letter to the editor from F. Washburn, of Newburgh, NY, to the editor of *The Living Church* May 19, 1906. XXXV No. 3 pp. 96- 7.

[24] Ibid.

Frederick Adams, Judge of the Circuit Court of New Jersey, and the Honorable James Parker of Perth Amboy, New Jersey.[25]

The appeal dated May 29, was filed on June 6, 1906. It stated eleven reasons that the defense considered as grounds for an appeal. The first noted that the court was illegally and unjustly structured. While the Standing Committee and the bishop brought the charges against Crapsey they also selected all the members of the court. The second reason considered that the court wrongly disallowed the defense enough time to prepare for the trial. The third reason accused the court of making the mistake of refusing to adjourn the trial until after May 15, 1906 for the purpose of allowing the court to be reconstituted by fair selection at the convention of the Diocese of Western New York. The fourth article of exception stated ironically that the court had by its decision presumed to "determine questions of doctrine, faith and worship." The fifth article stated, that the court erred in not allowing evidence of the common practice and the doctrinal understanding of the clergy of the church that demonstrated that Crapsey was within his rights in making whatever statements he made.[26]

The sixth premise asserted that the prosecution had obtained inadequate and unreliable evidence concerning the sermon he preached on December 31, 1905. The seventh stated the court had found incorrectly that he had "impugned doctrines of this Church." The eighth declared that the court found erroneously that he had expressed his denial or negated the doctrine of the church. The ninth stated that he had not broken his ordination vows. The tenth exception stated the court's decision was wrong for other reasons as well that appeared "upon the face of the said decision and in the record of the proceedings of the court upon the trial of the presentment." The final reason for the defense's grounds for appeal was that it was erroneously decided that for punishment Crapsey would not be able to minister again until he satisfied those in authority over him as to his conformation with the Apostle's and Nicene Creeds "as the church had received the same."[27]

The controversy over the Crapsey trial provided new insights for the broad faction to consider when dealing with the question of heresy. One seminarian asked a faculty member what the minimum requirement of belief was for those who entered the ministry? The faculty member replied, "The Apostles' and the Nicene Creeds in their integrity." The

---

[25] Crapsey, *Heretics,* pp. 269-270.

[26] "Dr. Crapsey's Appeal" in *The Churchman* June 16, 1906 (11) p. 963.

[27] Ibid.

difference in comprehension was now discerned through the terminology employed to explain the subscription to the creeds. The distinction concerned the term integrity. The way the broad churchmen understood it, integrity meant, "such a holding of the language of the Creeds as is consonant with spiritual facts and historic events upon which they are based."[28]

The Court of Review organized in 1903, convened in New York City at the Diocesan House on Lafayette Street. It met for the first time since its inception on Wednesday September 5, 1906. Crapsey brought his wife to court for the first time. O'Brian, asked the court to consider the canon law stating that the defendant should have but one counsel and that counsel should be a communicant of the church. Apparently these remarks were aimed at Congressman Perkins. After some delay O'Brian chose to drop the issue. Though Shepard had prepared for the appeal since June he noted he had not been provided a copy of the record of the Batavia trial until just three days before the opening of the appellate court. Even then it had to be copied at the expense of a layman. The one that had been previously given to him had been full of errors and Shepard needed time to examine the new document.[29]

Judge Andrews asked the defense if "they agreed that the question of doctrine could be brought before the court." Perkins hesitated for some time and finally denied that it should be brought before the Court of Review. Andrews explained that he was concerned over the jurisdiction as it related to the length of time granted for the postponement that Shepard was seeking. The court then took an adjournment until after eight P.M., at which time Dr. Huntington mentioned that there would be an adjournment granted until October 19. This provided Shepard with the time he had requested of approximately six weeks.

When the court reconvened on October 19, Shepard's argument for the defense lasted for over three hours and it was so captivating that the court remained in session rather than adjourning at its regularly scheduled time.[30] Crapsey called Shepard's appeal "powerful and brilliant." He noted how Shepard entered into a discussion about the principle of interpretation as it applied to all historical documents including the Constitution. Between the trials, Shepard had done his homework studying the history of the creeds and he paid close attention to the English court decisions

---

[28] Quote from a letter from William A. Guerry to the editor of *The Churchman* June 23, 1906 (18) p. 1010.

[29] *NY Times* Sept. 5, 1906 16: 4.

[30] Jansen, "Heresy at Rochester" in, Shriver ed., *American,* p. 216.

involving them. Still thinking politically, rather than practically, the defense had its argument printed including Crapsey's statement that was read before the original court in Batavia, as well as at the Court of Review to help publicize their cause. The defense continued to have their case tried in the public forum. Crapsey considered Shepard's speech a classic that should adorn law libraries throughout the nation.[31]

However, the defense's publication was long and tedious. It was hardly a paper that the average laymen might consider essential reading material. The pamphlet included several opinions of those who had hoped to be heard in Batavia. It also provided the famous cases of Bishop Colenso of South Africa, Dr. Temple of the Rugby School, Worcester on Christ's resurrection, S.T. Coleridge on English Church Divines, Dr. H.S. Nash, professor of New Testament Interpretation at the Episcopal Theological School on the subject of the Virgin Birth and the minority opinion before the original court.[32]

John Lord O' Brian completed the arguments before the Court of Review. He continued to hammer home the same points he had made at the trial, keeping focused on the standard of the church's right to hold their interpretation of the creeds in the way they have received them. Crapsey considered his argument later by analogy;

> if a man is a member of a club or association and sees defects in its constitution and by-laws, he must not disturb the peace of the club by moving any amendments within the club itself, but go out on the sidewalk and throw stones through the club windows.[33]

But the Protestant Episcopal Church was not a club. It was supposed to be an organism and as such a part of the body of Christ. If it was an organization as well then it was supposed to be a consecrated one dedicated to the sacred trust described in the scriptures and interpreted by the church over centuries of disputation. The doctrines were distinguished in the creeds and the prayer book. They became a compilation of the dogma that the Protestant Episcopal Church felt one must subscribe to to remain orthodox.

The Court of Review adjourned to consider the merits of the matter before it. Shepard had exonerated himself after his former public embarrassment and his inability to be ready for the original trial. The court

---

[31] Crapsey *Heretics* p. 270-1.

[32] Shepard, *Argument.* Also in Jansen, "Heresy," in *American* Shriver ed., p. 217.

[33] Crapsey, *Heretics,* p. 271.

adjourned until November 3, at which time the court announced that it was considering further evidence and adjourned for two more weeks. Bishop Scarborough stated that the decision was not to be rendered public by the Court of Review until the court could send it first to Bishop Walker.[34] Crapsey however had already succumbed to defeatism. He realized that the higher court would not overturn the lower court decision. He mentioned that he heard Judge Adams prior to the argument made by Mr. Shepard state that "We cannot permit a clergyman to use the pulpit of the church to defame the Creed of the Church." These words, written some eighteen years later when the tensions had cooled down, memories faded and the effects had taken their course were, if true, an indictment of the impropriety of the court.[35]

The adjournment was accompanied by a revival of interest causing the old controversies to resurface in the press. The public had not lost interest. The Bishop of the Diocese in New York City who had ordained Crapsey to the priesthood expressed an especially significant opinion. At the Convention of the Diocese Bishop Potter repeated part of the pastoral letter addressed by the House of Bishops to the General Convention in 1904. He declared that if one in the ministry loses his belief in the underlying truths then for the sake of honor and common integrity let him either silence or remove himself. He further noted that it was a man's consecrated duty to withdraw until he solves the problems contributing to his doubts.[36]

Potter believed if a man were ordained to the priesthood but didn't agree with the definitive statements of the faith as described by the creeds, he had no place in the church. Moreover, if the same man felt it was his calling to free the church from such ancient superstitions he would have to accomplish that from outside and not inside the church. Potter hoped to bring a sense of decorum back to a church now divided by the Crapsey situation. Crapsey's personal honesty revealed the irony of the case as exceptions taken to his clerical impertinence were expressed in like manner. Potter concluded,

> For it is impossible in the minds of the people who hold fast to the principles of common honesty to respect either the consistency or the integrity of one who eats the church's bread, accepts the church's

[34] *NY Times* Nov. 3, 1906 7:3.
[35] A more complete synopsis of the proceedings of the appellate court summarized in the *NY Times* Oct 21, 1906 6:4. Also in Alkalay Gut, *Alone,* pp. 175-6.
[36] *NY Times* Thurs. Nov. 15, 1906. 4:1.

> dignities, enjoys the church's honors, and impugns the church's faith. If he must assail her beliefs, then the dictates of the of ordinary righteousness would plainly seem to be that he must, first of all, withdraw from the fellowship to whose fundamental beliefs he cannot readily assent.[37]

Crapsey wrote that within ten days the appellate court rendered its decision confirming the Batavia court decision.[38] In reality the court considered the appeal from October 19, through to the sixteenth of November. It was the twentieth of November before the decision was announced. The clerk of the Court of Review, Henry Anstice, delivered the decision to Bishop Walker as prescribed by the protocol of the church. Accompanying the decision was a letter from the Bishop of New Jersey and the president of the court, John Scarborough. It stated,

> New York, Nov. 16.
> The Right Rev. William D. Walker, Bishop of Western New York:
> Pursuant to the general canon, you are hereby notified that the Court of Review of the Second Judicial Department has determined the appeal in the matter of the presentment of the Rev. Dr. Algernon S. Crapsey by unanimously affirming the judgment of the ecclesiastical court of Western New York. [39]

Walker subsequently released a statement declaring that the Court of Review decision was final and there would be no appeal. Walker stated that after full consideration of their responsibility and the questions presented them, the Court of Review unanimously voted that the decision of the Batavia Trial Court must stand affirmed.[40]

The Court of Review provided a twenty-four-page summary of their decision. It was delivered in seven parts. The *First* part affirmed, "The ecclesiastical court of the Diocese of Western New York had jurisdiction to try the accused for the offense charged in the presentment." The *Second* agreed, "The trial court was legally authorized in conformity with the canon and ordinances of the Diocese of Western New York." The *Third* part declared that "The finding of the court is that the accused in making statements charged and admitted to have been made by him violated and broke certain declarations made by him at the time of his ordination

---

[37] Ibid.
[38] Crapsey, *Heretics,* p. 272.
[39] Letter recorded in the *NY Times* Nov. 20. 1906. 6:2.
[40] Ibid.

involving the finding of what was the doctrine of the Church on the subjects to which the declarations related."[41]

The *Fourth* part noted "The point that the charge does not allege the publication of the book as an offense is not, we think, well taken." The *Fifth* part of the findings of the Court of Review stated, "The Court of Review sustains the trial court in refusing a further adjournment of the case on April 27, 1906." The *Sixth* part affirmed, "The Court of Review sustains the trial court in the matter of deciding on the credibility of witnesses." The *Seventh* part asserted, "The Court of Review sustains the trial court in refusing to receive evidence offered in behalf of the defendant."[42]

At least one member of the Court of Review, Dr. William Reed Huntington, was considered a leader of the broad faction within the Protestant Episcopal Church. Sincerely concerned about his judicial balance he consulted with other churchmen of diverse opinions without discussing the particulars of the case. One churchman known for his high church views that Huntington held a high regard for was Dr. William Thomas Manning, then assistant to Dr. Morgan Dix, later the rector of Trinity Parish, Crapsey's old parish, and eventually the Bishop of New York in 1921. He shared letters with Manning written to him about the questions engendered in the minds of some of his parishioners and other young churchmen by the Crapsey case. Huntington had previously written, "My convictions on this point are expressed to a dot in the article on "Clerical Veracity" which appeared last week in the *Post*... Sedgwick's opinion here quoted, wherein he draws the distinction between interpreting articles of the Creed and denying them, seems to me absolutely accurate; and I marvel that this distinction should have played so small a part in the discussions at Batavia. To my mind, it is the key to the whole situation."[43]

There was no question of impropriety in Huntington's rather sketchily formulated opinions about the Crapsey case prior to its review. In the end Huntington broke with Crapsey regardless of how he felt about broad-church issues. Both Manning and Huntington agreed that a specific discrepancy existed in the veracity of Crapsey's responses that could not

---

[41] Summary of the findings of the Court of Review recorded in *NY Times* Nov. 20, 1906. 6:2.

[42] Ibid.

[43] Letter from Huntington to Miss Meredith, reprinted from John Wallace Suter *Life and Letters of William Reed Huntington: A Champion of Unity* (New York and London, 1925) pp. 447-448.

be rectified by clever maneuvering. They agreed, "Interpretation of the articles of the Christian Faith, as contained in the Apostles' and the Nicene Creeds, shall *not* mean the denial of the eternal verities contained therein."[44]

Crapsey received the decision from the clerk of the court, Rev. Dr. Anstice, on the same day.[45] He realized the gravity of the decision, and pondered even that he might still be able to maintain his administration of the parish temporarily through the visitation of the members. But Crapsey would never consider allowing others to preach in his stead and take over the spiritual duties of his parish. As Anstice departed from the rectory Crapsey entered into St. Andrew's Church. He walked up and down the aisle pondering his past experiences of twenty-seven years in the ministry, all that he had accomplished over the years, mourning his present circumstances, the loss of his ministry, and considering his future. The church he had virtually built by his own works would soon be deprived to him. It finally hit him. His wife came into the church and kissed him. She perhaps had the hardest part in the entire affair. She had tried to continue with all the ministrations and the needs of the family, without knowing what might happen next. Now she too realized, it had finally come to this. Where would they go and what would they do? There was so much to consider. And of course there was the emotional attachment to the place they had been at home with for over a quarter of a century, the friends they had made and the people who had supported them. It was all so terribly distressing. But the fight was over. Encouragement came from many places. People tried to sympathize but no one could truly understand the personal tragedy that had befallen the Crapsey family. One letter came from a group of students at the Union Theological Seminary. The thirteen students who signed the letter wrote,

> Dear Dr. Crapsey:
>
> We should be false to our highest ideals if we failed to show you the hearty sympathy with which we have watched you fight your good fight. We sympathize with you because you exalt truth above ecclesiastical authority. We admire you because you dare to express unequivocally the truth you exalt. We see in you a spirit quite akin to Jesus of Nazareth, who dared to differ with the traditional religious dogmas of the Jews. We

---

[44] Hughes, W. Dudley F. "Agreement on Fundamentals, Correspondence between Dr. Huntington and Dr. Manning on the Crapsey Case, 1906." In *Historical Magazine of the Protestant Episcopal Church* 25:3 (Sept. 1956): 263.

[45] Crapsey, *Heretics*,p. 273.

> theological students of several denominations wish you to know our sympathy and admiration.[46]

Members of the St. Andrew's choir also drafted a letter to their rector mentioning how much they sympathized with and appreciated him. They admired his devotion, his unselfishness and his kind demeanor towards all. They noted his "common sense" approach to Christianity and how even the most unlearned could understand Crapsey's sermons and apply them to their lives. They considered it a mistake to interfere with his work when true Christianity was portrayed in the attributes of an all-loving all-mighty God as well as through the example of Jesus Christ that was pure and perfect in whom they would attempt to emulate with their lives.[47]

All the members of the choir probably signed the letter. Including Crapsey's son Arthur, there were twenty-four signatures. Judging from the rather crudely constructed sentences they were presumably quite young. Arthur, Crapsey's youngest would have been only about ten at the time. They obviously desired to show their affection to the man who had done so much to help them achieve their utmost. Crapsey was similarly fond of the vested choir. There would be a noticeable emptiness in his heart with the absence of the young boys.

On the other side of the theological fence, Bishop Niles from the Protestant Episcopal Diocese of New Hampshire wrote,

> I pity the man who can bring himself to go on destroying his innocent followers faith in their Bible, which he has solemnly declared to be 'the Word of God.' But if he can do that dreadful work, can the church allow her to do it as her officer? Can she consent to do it through him? A thousand times no! Be the trouble, the difficulties, the pain of an ecclesiastical trial what they may be, the Church has no option. She must keep the faith and protect her children from being robbed of theirs.[48]

The expenses incurred from the Crapsey trial amounted to close to two thousand dollars to the Diocese of Western New York. The Financial Board of the Diocese was ordered to pay the costs on two separate occasions. In May of 1906, after the Batavia trial verdict was reached the Financial Board paid out $1342.32. After the appeal, the Diocese ordered

---

[46] Ibid. pp. 272-3.
[47] Letter in the A.H. Crapsey Jr. Collection.
[48] *NY Times* Nov. 26, 1906. 11:3.

another $600.00 paid in 1907. The amount represented a considerable cost to the diocese.[49]

Crapsey was always a hard worker, and at the age of 58, he had barely slowed down. In fact he was always busy. The thought of losing his job of the past twenty-seven years was hardly something he looked forward to without great anxiety. His services were packed from that point on to the end. People came to hear the famous heretic before he was deposed. There was a sense that a piece of living history was passing on that was valuable whether one agreed with Crapsey or not.

In his third to the last sermon he preached on the text John 5: 17, concerning Jesus' words to his disciples, "My Father worketh hitherto, and I work." Crapsey noted that man has expanded great effort in understanding the connection between God and work and God and the world because they appear so hostile one to the other. Crapsey associated his life with the working of God in history and related to his congregation that in the ever-changing world man must pay with great labor for the higher goals he attempts to achieve. One will recognize the bones of the martyrs all along the way.[50]

Crapsey had come to the point where he spoke of the God in nature and the nature in God. Crapsey's interpretation of scripture now demonstrated that not only was God necessary to man but man was necessary to God. He stated that like the parts of his body were not alone but a part of and dependent upon one another so was God and nature. Crapsey saw God's work in everyone who lives in the world, including women and children who were agents of his power. That, to Crapsey, was the message of Jesus of Nazareth.

Crapsey's understanding of the relationship between God and man was now free to be exposed for what it was. It was Unitarian to the core. "Jesus believed that God was in Him and He in God, " According to Crapsey, Jesus believed that He could get to God without ascending. Crapsey stated defiantly that Jesus' life added onto God. The church has recognized the divinity of Jesus but erred in that it had failed to recognize and deify everyone else who also works righteousness.[51] Crapsey declared:

> When God expresses Himself by any word or deed He becomes a greater God. He is not unchangeable. In a million eons the world will be much

[49] Burrows, *Diocese,* p. 102.
[50] *NY Times* Nov. 26, 1906 2: 7.
[51] Ibid.

> different from what it is to-day. God will change with the universe. Think no more of any eternal God sitting in judgment on the poor sons of men. There is no such God as that to make a nightmare of our lives. Every one of our failures is God's failure. He weeps when we fall because He falls with us.[52]

The God of traditional Christianity bore little resemblance to the god that Crapsey now preached. Crapsey fashioned him into the god that he would have him to be. He was the god of Crapsey.

It was rumored there would be a demonstration, hardly an Episcopalian way of expressing opinion, but the protest never materialized. Moreover, it was reported that several prominent members of the church would resign their positions in support of Crapsey. Neither did that happen.[53]

Crapsey could not accept the ruling of the court any more than he could accept the literal interpretation of the Bible or the creeds. He would never recant as for Crapsey it was his God given right to explain the things that were set before him to his people. His only recourse was to renounce the ministry of the Protestant Episcopal Church and request for the bishop to depose him. Crapsey finally drafted a letter to the bishop. Even in deposal Crapsey desired to be in control of his destiny. The letter read;

> "My Dear Bishop:
>
> Under existing conditions I deem it my duty to make a formal and final renunciation of the ministry of the Protestant Episcopal Church; and in consequence I ask that you will for reasons as to time already given, not earlier than the 3d, not later than the 6th of December, take order under Canon 31 of the General Canons of the Church to accomplish my deposition from the priesthood.
>
> I am certain that you will be glad to acknowledge that I am not compelled to take this action by anything that reflects upon my moral integrity or calls in question my faithfulness as a pastor. My sole difficulty lies in the fact that a long, careful, conscientious study of the Holy Scriptures has compelled me to come to certain conclusions concerning the pre-natal history of Jesus which are not in physical accord with the letter of the creeds, and hence have compelled me in order to hold the creeds to give to certain articles an interpretation that will harmonize them with the truth as I find that in the teaching of the Holy Scriptures. But recent judicial decisions have declared that any such harmonizing of the creed

[52] Ibid.

[53] Ibid.

with my own convictions of the truth is not permissible in the Protestant Episcopal Church.

In my own case I recognize the right of the constituted authorities of the Church to define the limits of interpretation, and in order to hold fast to the truth must let go of the creed as now interpreted by the courts. I am not now, and never have been, conscious of any insincerity in giving such interpretation of the various articles of the creed as are demanded by present conditions of thought and the present state of knowledge, any more than I am conscious of insincerity when I say the sun rises and sets, though, as a matter of fact, the sun does nothing of the kind.

If I am to hold the creed at all I must give to certain, if not all, of its articles a spiritual rather than a literally physical interpretation. When I say of Jesus that He ascended into heaven I do not mean that with His physical body of flesh, blood, and bones He floated into space and has for 2, 000 years been existing, somewhere in the sky, in that very physical body of flesh, blood and bones. Such an existence would seem to me not glorious, but horrible, and such a conception is to me not only unbelievable; it is unthinkable. What I do mean by this phrase is that Jesus having accomplished His work in the flesh, ascended into the higher life of the spirit. Also when I say of Jesus that He was conceived by the Holy Ghost and born of the Virgin Mary, I do not mean that the great and living God, in order to get into this world, had to violate His wonderful law of human generation, break into the sanctities of marriage, and cause a Son of Man to be born without a human father. Such a notion is most repugnant to my ideal of a wise and holy God.

I was not, therefore, alarmed, I was relieved when a careful study of the Holy Scriptures convinced me that this notion of the origin of Jesus was without foundation in history. Jesus was not lessened in my worship, He was ennobled by this discovery. When I reached the conclusion, as I did some years ago, that the infancy stories were not historical, I did not cease to believe in Jesus. I believed in Him all the more, and I gave to the words 'born of the Virgin Mary,' an interpretation that harmonized with my knowledge of the facts. He was a Child of the Holy seed, sanctified from his mother's womb. A Son of God all the more, in my estimation, because He was the Son of Man. Then I saw for the first time into the meaning of those words of John when he said; 'The Word was made flesh and dwelt amongst us and we beheld His glory as the glory of the only begotten of the Father full of grace and truth,' and I could understand how in the same chapter Philip could say of this incarnate Word, 'We found Him of whom Moses in the Law and prophets did write Jesus of Nazareth the Son of Joseph.'

Now this conception of Jesus, based upon a careful study of Holy Scriptures, is the very warp and woof of my intellectual and spiritual life, and it is not probable that it will ever change. I will carry it with me into the spiritual world where I will see Jesus face to face. But I am told by judicial decision that this conception is not permissible in the mind of a minister of the Protestant Episcopal Church. I bow to that decision. I cannot change my mind- I therefore leave the Church. I do not blame my judges, they acted according to their light- let them not blame me if I follow my light, which is lightening me to the everlasting day. But whether they blame or not I cannot do other than I do- I must obey God rather than men.

But while I thus feel that their decision is final for me, I am equally certain that it is not for the Church. I have reason to know that there are hundreds of clergymen and thousands of laymen in the Protestant Episcopal Church who have reached the same conclusion that I have, and, Sir, I beg to say to them in this letter to you, that their position in the Church is just as tenable as it ever was.

This judgment affects no person except myself. Let no man be dismayed. Let every man stand in his place- speak his mind boldly, and the truth will soon have such a multitude of witnesses that all in the Church must hear. So confident am I in the truth as it is in Jesus that I appeal from those in places of authority in the Church to the Church itself, to the great body of the people, secure in their wise, sane, serene possession of the truth. Again, I exhort my brethren of like belief to stay where they are.

I am about to carry our case to the high court of free intelligence and the enlightened conscience of the world, and if I win it there, I will win it for every church and every soul in Christendom. If I fall before that court, it will be because I am wrong in my conception of truth; and then I will be glad to fall, for my contention is not for my conception, but for the eternal truth of God. Let my brethren with the Church abide the issue of this trial. For when the Great Tribunal of Free Thought has decided this contention, the men who administer the Church on earth will conform to this decision. It is to this work of showing that God is in man and man is in God that I consecrate the rest of my life.

In asking my dismissal from the Church of my lifelong devotion, I do so with the deepest gratitude for the opportunities of worship, of preaching, and of service which have been the privileges of my office. To pray before the altar of my Church has been my daily habit. To preach the gospel of Jesus from the pulpit of my Church has been my weekly delight. But far dearer to my soul than all ministry within the walls of the Church has been the opportunity that has come to me as the glorious privilege of my pastoral office of being of daily service to my people in all the changes and chances of their mortal lives. If I seem to have unduly contended for my ministry, let my pardon be that I value the ministry, and deemed it due to others as well as myself, and above all to the Church itself, to have an authoritative and deliberate decision.

It is to me more than meat and drink to have the right to be with my people in every critical hour of their lives, to give them in the name of the living God courage to live and courage to die. My conviction is that we need no miracle to account for Jesus of Nazareth is confirmed by my daily contact with the lives of the people. In these men and women of my charge who go forth to their work and to their labor until the evening; who bear the world's burden without receiving the world's reward, many of whom endure sufferings unspeakable and privations that are often appalling, who, with all their faults, are yet heroic in their patience, whose daily toil is the support of the world; in these men and women, I say, I see not the cursed seed of any Adam, but the blood brothers and sisters of Jesus of Nazareth. To leave this daily ministry to such a people is to break my heart. But better a broken heart than a life made false and loathsome by cowardly retraction.

In leaving the organized Church, so far as its ministry is concerned, I feel that I can take with me the best that the Church has given me; the fasts and the feasts, the vigils and the fears of the Church have become mine by right of possession, and not all the courts and Bishops of the Church could take them away. I shall watch in Advent, be merry at Christmas, fast in Lent, weep on Good Friday, rejoice at Easter, even though the Church's servants shut its doors upon me. Yes, all the more because they have shut their doors upon me, driven me from the earthly tabernacle, I shall have to take refuge in that tabernacle not made with hands, which is the tabernacle where God dwells with all his saints and angels.

And if I seem to have lost my hold on some of the traditional and physical interpretations of the creed, let it not be thought that on account that I have lost my hold on the Gospel of Christ. Nay, rather because I have let go these temporary and unstable interpretations of the creed I find strength to hold more firmly than ever to the gospel. I believe as never before that to love the Lord my God with all my soul and all my mind and all my strength, and to love my neighbor as myself is not only more than the law and the prophets, but is also more than the creeds and the churches. I see more clearly than ever that the five negative laws of righteousness laid down by Jesus, which laws command us not to be angry, not to lust, not to take any oath or vow, not to resist evil, not to hate the stranger, though he be an enemy, I see, I say, more clearly than ever that these laws are the hedges of that straight and narrow way that leadeth unto life. To walk in that way has been and will be the constant labor of my soul.

Let no one think for a moment that I do not love the Lord Jesus Christ and would not have served Him to the last in this Church, which is to me the historic Church of the great English-speaking race, if only its men in authority had let me. All I asked of them was tolerance. But they have refused to extend tolerance to such as I, and I must with a grief which only my own heart knows accept my dismissal from the service of the Church. But though cast down, I do not despair. As I have been true to God, so I believe God will be true to me. I believe that He has work for me to do, and this is His way of calling me to that work. In His name, therefore, Right Reverend Sir, I beseech you to forgive me my offenses and let me go.

Assuring you that I go without the slightest animosity to any that I leave behind, and with love unspeakable to that host of men and women within the Church who have comforted me in my tribulation, and most of all, with a gratitude that will never die, to four men who have done for me what men can seldom do for another- to Seth Low and George Foster Peabody, to James Breck Perkins and Edward Morse Shepard- to these men I leave my undying gratitude, and with contrition to the Church for all the faults and failings of my ministry, I remain, Right Reverend and dear Sir,

Your servant in the Lord Jesus Christ,

Algernon S. Crapsey. [54]

[54] Entire body of the letter from A.S. Crapsey to Rt. Rev. Wm. D. Walker recorded in *NY Times* Mon. Nov. 26, 1906.

CHAPTER TWENTY-TWO

'If There Arise Among You a Prophet'

Though perhaps haphazard in his scholarship, Crapsey was highly intelligent and articulate. He was a man of moral integrity capable of expressing himself with eloquence in the public forum. Men of high standing in the Protestant Episcopal Church protested the actions of the bishop and the Diocese of Western New York. One warden of the church, deputy to the General Convention and trustee of the General Theological Seminary wrote that he protested the verdict rendered in Batavia. Though he realized that the adjudication was conclusive he would not accept it as the final articulation of the Protestant Episcopal Church concerning the Crapsey case. The writer appealed to those, especially the young men, who stood at the threshold of the church. He implored them not to acknowledge this verdict as the decisive, general opinion of the church.[1]

The hard feelings did not end there. Edward M. Shepard, Crapsey's attorney expressed his feelings that while the court denied the role of the bishop in the prosecution's case it was obvious that he was the main antagonist. He did not question his integrity. He considered him deceived. Rather, he expressed his vehemence for Bishop Potter, stating he could respect Walker's behavior more than the Bishop of New York's. Shepard noted how Potter had used his influence and position to manipulate the clergy appellate court by making untoward remarks about Crapsey's desire to remain in the ministry for economical reasons (without mentioning him by name), while the appeal was still in consideration. At a time when it behooved the senior bishop to be quiet in the matter at bar he displayed the utmost injustice through his irresponsible statements. Shepard continued virtually unabated in his counter-attack. He declared that the bishop's act was contemptuous and it would be his ignoble legacy along with the fact that he was even more heretical in his preaching than Crapsey.[2]

---

[1] Letter written by Spencer Trask of Saratoga Springs, NY to the editor of the *NY Times* Nov. 26, 1906.
[2] *NY Times* Tues. Nov. 27, 1906. 2:1.

These were serious charges against the senior Bishop of New York. For his part, Walker was sorry that Crapsey had decided not to take his advice to take some time off someplace where he could think and rest and meditate on the whole picture. He also regretted the loss of someone he had great respect for. Walker was quoted as stating,

> This is the most painful happening in my life. I have known and respected Dr. Crapsey for many years and have honored and respected him for his great abilities. I have great affection for him and have watched him as he grew up in Church work, so the matter of the present gives me great pain.[3]

Crapsey did Walker a favor by asking for his deposal by letter. By Crapsey sending Walker his resignation it relieved him of performing the painful duty of deposing him in person. That Crapsey wrote the letter of renunciation as a means of relieving Walker of the anguish associated is doubtful. He most assuredly did it as a means of representing the matter publicly from his perspective and keeping any dishonor away from himself, his wife and his family.

Crapsey's relief of his official duties did not bar him from being a communicant in the church. But his declaration that the decision would affect no one but himself did not correspond to the section in the decision of the Court of Review that stated,

> But the Church, as the guardian of the Christian faith as it has received and declared it, cannot, without betraying its trust, when called upon to act, permit doctrines which it holds essential and fundamental, to be impugned by those who minister at her altars, however pure their motives or sincere their convictions.[4]

Indeed the Court of Review had attempted to set a definite precedent if bishops of the dioceses cared enough to agree. Several however, had already strayed far from this ruling by allowing views that the court might similarly consider unorthodox. Some would attempt to be more discreet in the future. In reality however, the ruling had not set a precedent that could be seriously followed. The court could not usurp the tenor of the culture. The scholarship that the church placed such a high opinion upon was moving conspicuously away from a literal interpretation of the creeds.

---

[3] Ibid.

[4] "Judgment of the Court of Review," *Appeal by the Rev'd Algernon S. Crapsey to the Court of Review* New York: Thomas Whitakker, 1906. Recorded in *NY Times* Tues. Nov. 27, 1906 2:1.

Shepard counseled Crapsey to appeal his case to the civil court declaring that appellate court's ruling would be shattered there. Shepard cited the decision of the case of Supreme Court of New Jersey some years previous when they considered the deposition of Bishop Scarborough against the Rev. Mr. Jennings void.[5] Crapsey refused to consider it. Perhaps he thought of the scriptural precedents that admonished those in the church not to take their differences before the courts of the world.[6] Perhaps he had accomplished what he set out to by becoming a religious martyr. More likely he was just tired of the whole affair.

Bishop Potter eventually replied calling Shepard's remarks "gratuitous, and impertinent inference, without foundation in fact." He attempted to shrug them off, not allowing the issue to stick. Obviously, he was aware of his own impertinent comments, inferring that Crapsey was holding on to his job for the purpose of making a living for his family. Crapsey may have been many things, including a heretic, but he was not disingenuous about his beliefs, not a welcher, a loafer or a hypocrite.[7]

Meanwhile, it was reported in the press that was becoming friendlier with Crapsey every day, that he was penniless, and that he desired to develop his theory of the new dogmatic. He would speak, lecture and carry on proclaiming his concept of the new religion. He had already started writing a new book that he hoped would bring in the revenue he needed to support his family. He would submit to the review of the popular press.[8]

Life provided a full-page cartoon in its December issue portraying a man leaving a darkened monastery with his robes half off, his hands in the fresh air exalting in the rapture of the sunshine that he was previously deprived of. Behind him a monkish, hunched-over, clergyman closes the door and thereby shuts the light out as well. The caption reads, "Exit Dr. Crapsey." The message was clear. Crapsey had left the darkness of the traditional church behind and he could now be free to revel in the light.[9]

The same week of the reply to the bishop, the vestry called a meeting of the congregation of St. Andrew's to allow Crapsey the opportunity to

---

[5] *NY Times* Tues. Nov. 27, 1906. 2:1

[6] 1Cor. 6: 1- 11.

[7] *NY Times* Tues. Nov. 27, 1906. 2:1.

[8] Ibid.

[9] Cartoon in *Life* Dec. 20, 1906 Vol. XLVIII p. 779. *Life* was not at the time the photography publication it later became under Henry Robinson Luce's leadership. This *Life* magazine was published at 19 W31st St., New York, NY, J.A. Mitchell editor.

address them without all the sightseers. Crapsey wanted the opportunity to say farewell to "his people." The meeting was mid-week, on Wednesday, November 28, 1906 the day before Thanksgiving. Almost all of the members of the church were present. Crapsey spoke lovingly and appreciatively while criticizing the ones who had created the problem. He noted that his ecclesiastical superiors had not appreciated the intelligence of the members of St. Andrew's Church. He said that he tendered his resignation bringing an end to his pastoral relationship with them involuntary. It brought him the greatest sorrow he had ever known in acknowledging that he could no longer stand in the pulpit, preaching to his people or minister the sacred offices from the altar.[10]

But Crapsey encouraged the people not to forsake the church. He compelled them to continue the work that he was forced to leave behind. The bishop could not stop that. Moreover he was still a member of the Protestant Episcopal Church and no one "would dare excommunicate him," he said defiantly. He noted how absurd the situation was. The laity believed what the clergy was not permitted to believe. Therefore, he prophesied, that the office of the teacher would be lost to the clergy and found in the laity. The instability of the situation should compel them to stay and fight especially if they believed in the "scientific and historical" interpretation of Jesus. Those who did must dutifully remain because after all, it was not the province of the church but that of science to determine the physical origin of Jesus. According to Crapsey, when the scientific facts were finally established the church would receive them. The duty of the church was one of practicum instructing the laity to live lives like Jesus and teach the lessons that He taught. Only if the church completely surrendered its responsibility would it be their duty to leave it.[11]

Crapsey also praised the dedication of his wife stating that hers had been the best part of their ministry. She had been the guiding inspiration producing great works for the church and though it was relatively a small thing for a man to leave his home for her it was the tearing asunder of her life.[12]

Crapsey concluded his farewell statement with,

> But what must we think of that evil which calls for so cruel a remedy? Surely, nothing but a conviction that the very foundations of the universe

[10] Farewell address of A.S. Crapsey recorded in part in *NY Times*, Thurs. Nov. 29, 1906. 6:1.

[11] Ibid.

[12] Ibid.

were in danger could lead men thus to separate a mother from the home her lifelong love. But let that pass. And let all anguish, and regret, and animosity pass with it. It is only another sacrifice in the cause of truth and righteousness; and in the cause of truth and righteousness no sacrifice is too dear.[13]

Many of the parishioners wept openly, not trying to conceal the pain of loosing their pastor. To them he was simply a good man. He had done a good work regardless of his beliefs. Crapsey's wife and family were visibly affected by the ordeal. Most of the children like Philip and Adelaide and Paul and Rachel were old enough to understand the controversy. Young Arthur however, must have understood things from a ten-year old's perspective no matter how precocious he might have been. He knew that men of his profession were relieving his father from his duties. And he understood all to well that he was to leave the only home that he had ever known. His friends were members of the choir and his life was intrinsically intermeshed with the workings of St. Andrew's Church. All were more than simply upset by the dilemma; they were deeply traumatized by it.

The Thanksgiving message was on "Joy." The church was crowded again. The sermon was reportedly "beautiful." Again, Crapsey gave a parting message.[14] The final service came on December 2, 1906. A member of St. Andrew's Church who had been to the last of Crapsey's services stated:

I want to tell you about yesterday at St. Andrew's. It was a 'great' day and yet one of the saddest days in the history of Rochester and the church. A noble man and the father of many spiritual children was turned out of his home and his children are left sorrowing. The services began at 7:30 in the morning, and the church was filled with St. Andrew's communicants to receive the last sacrament from their loved pastor's hands. We have never had so large number out for an early Easter communion. As the people came back from the altar their faces were stained with tears, even the children. It must have been a trying ordeal for Dr. Crapsey and I was afraid he wouldn't be able to speak aloud at the 11 o'clock service, as he had no one to help him in the service. At 11 o'clock the church was simply packed; men and women stood during the whole time. Some even sat on the steps of the altar, in the transept and close up to the pulpit and reading desk, besides the crowd in the chapel. I believe that many were turned

[13] Ibid.

[14] Letter recorded in the *Catskill Examiner*. A.H. Crapsey Jr. Collection. Also in Crapsey, *Heretics*, pp. 284-5.

> away who couldn't get in at all. There was an unusual number of men in the church; rich and poor, high and low, all seemed anxious to show their sympathy and love for the rector.
>
> At the signing of the hymn 'Blest be the tie that binds,' there was deep emotion shown and people could not sing for weeping. Then the sermon followed which was very strong and inspiring. I am sure we all felt that what was true of Jesus was true of Dr. Crapsey; he certainly is following in the footsteps of the master, and his persecutors 'know not what they do.' Dr. Crapsey looked worn and as if he were endeavoring to suppress his emotion, but spoke in a strong, impressive way. The crowd was so silent and attentive you could almost hear the silence. The collection had been taken before the sermon, so immediately after Dr. Crapsey had stopped speaking the choir formed and he walked out of the church down the middle aisle in death-like stillness (there was no music), broken by the sobs of the people to whom he has ministered so long and faithfully. It was heartrending to us all. Everything was done so quietly and without any dramatic effect, but the deep and real sorrow was so evident. It is too soon to tell what the future of the church will be, but I feel sure that Dr. Crapsey's work for the cause of freedom is just begun, and that he and his brave wife will have the strength they need.[15]

Bishop Walker formally deposed Crapsey from the ministry on December 4, 1906 at St. John's Chapel, Buffalo in the presence of various clergymen.[16] Walker complied with Crapsey's wishes concerning how the trauma would end. The Crapsey case was an emotional shipwreck for the Protestant Episcopal Church. Bishop Walker hoped to pick up the pieces and encourage those who had ears to hear to continue on. For the Crapseys their new life had just begun, full as it was of uncertainty and sorrow. Crapsey considered that on the day of his departure from the priesthood he simultaneously entered into the work of a prophet. The vestry of St. Andrew's had graciously allowed the Crapseys to remain until they could find another place to live. Six of their children had been born in the rectory and two had died during their time there. Mrs. Crapsey had planted lovely flowers and trees and shrubs and watched them grow and mature like her children. She was devastated by the loss of her home and despaired that she would never have another like it. To Crapsey, the joys and sorrows of life had consecrated the rectory in making it their home. They could have decided to go virtually anywhere, but Rochester had become their home. For the Crapsey family the trauma had not ended.

---

[15] Ibid.

[16] Burrows, *Diocese,* p. 134.

Their mourning for the life they had once lived continued unabated like another death in the family. They were deeply affected.[17]

Crapsey endeavored to pull his family together through the Christmas season. Christmas of 1906 was unlike any they had previously experienced with children running in and out of the rectory and preparations being made for the various services and events. It must have been inconceivably harder for the family considering all the nostalgic associations with the Christmases of their past. That was the price Crapsey knew he had to pay as a modern martyr. His attitude was one of painful sorrow at the distress of his wife and children but personally he found martyrdom glorious. Speaking of his wife and children the deposed rector stated, that "they were suffering quietly and anonymously" from the result of that martyrdom.[18]

Crapsey later recalled how an act of compassion distinguished their last hours at the rectory. Two women, one with a bag of oranges and the other with a bag of cookies came to the door. Neither of them were from their parish and yet they were given to such a spirit of kindness and love in their selfless presentation of the gifts that the Crapseys were extremely grateful. It somehow made their departure a little less traumatic.[19]

Crapsey would not allow himself to remain idle. He found a house at 630 University Avenue. They left the rectory on January 15th, 1907. Crapsey's recurrent exposure had made him a celebrity of sorts. He soon received an invitation from Dr. Samuel McChord Crothers to speak at First Church in Cambridge, Massachusetts in the late winter and again at a Peace Conference in New York City in April.[20] Crapsey was obviously gratified that his reputation had preceded him. By the end of February, Adelaide's mother Harriet Gunn Trowbridge died.[21] A streetcar struck Adelaide's carriage just a few days later. While the horse and driver were severely injured Adelaide was only badly shaken.[22] Crapsey was so busy he barely had time to minister to her needs. Life must have been terribly difficult for Adelaide at that point. As Crapsey left to give his speech at

---

[17] Crapsey, *Heretics*, p. 286.

[18] Crapsey, *Heretics*, pp. 287-8.

[19] Crapsey, *Manuscript*, p. 396.

[20] Ibid. 360. First Church and First Church (Parish) split the former is Congregationalist the latter Unitarian. Crapsey spoke at the Unitarian body. Personal communication with Linda Baker, First Church, (Parish).

[21] Alkalay- Gut's *Alone*, p. 187.

[22] News clipping in A.H. Crapsey Jr. Collection, Also in Alkalay- Gut *Alone*, p. 187.

Harvard, and then New York, Adelaide must have despaired at her suddenly uncertain circumstances.

In Massachusetts, Crapsey impressed the "Dons of Harvard" with a sermon from Dr. Crothers' pulpit. President Charles W. Eliot was in the audience and later invited Crapsey to dine with him. Crapsey was delighted that he had impressed such a large intellectual assembly. After the sermon several influential men and women came forward to congratulate him. Amongst them was Mr. Edwin Ginn, a wealthy publisher and philanthropist who had followed his famous trial. He asked Crapsey whether he would consider a proposition to represent the American Peace Society at the upcoming conference at The Hague. Before long the arrangements were made for Crapsey to be a delegate from the organization that contained several wealthy and prominent members, including Andrew Carnegie.[23]

Shortly afterwards Crapsey spoke at the Peace Conference in New York. His speech was as usual, controversial. His unpredictability must have shocked and infuriated those present with the disclosure of his opposition to disarmament.[24] By April he was expounding on the pages of *Arena*, on the "Historical Aspects of the Virgin Birth." Amidst criticism concerning the deficiency of his research, Crapsey presented his case against the Virgin Birth of Christ. He traced the writings of Clement and St. Ignatius, considering their exclusion of any mention of the Virgin Birth as evidence for the early church not knowing about it.[25]

In May of 1907 Philip, their eldest, died of complications from a fever, probably malaria, which he had contracted while training during the Spanish-American War. Philip had started a business originally called the Standard Electric Construction Company. The business had grown and he had since added two partners. He eventually changed the name of the company to the Rochester Electric Contracting Company. Philip had been as energetic and enterprising as his father in his early life. After his time at the military academy at Manlius he took a job at Scrantom-Wetmore Company in Rochester and then went to Medina, New York to work as a clerk in a factory. He worked at his grandfather's newspaper in Catskill and then went into the military as the Spanish-American War began. He contracted what Crapsey termed "a fever" in Hawaii. Back home he went to work for the Adjutant General's office in Albany. He achieved the rank

---

[23] Crapsey, *Manuscript,* p. 360.

[24] Alkalay- Gut *Alone,* p. 188.

[25] A.S. Crapsey "The Historical Aspects of the Virgin Birth." In *Arena* April, 1907, Vol. 37 No. 209 p. 337.

of lieutenant and distinguished himself at a labor riot in Albany. His platoon had been cut off from the main body of troops and surrounded by violent demonstrators. Philip kept his poise and eventually brought the troops out of the situation without having to engage the rioters or firing into the crowd. Thanks to his coolness under pressure, the turbulent situation ended without casualties on either side. Back in Rochester, he worked for Stromberg-Carlson Company and became a master electrician. Eventually he went into business for himself.[26]

The effects of the malaria continued to hound Philip. It affected his heart. He finally succumbed to the disease after an unrelenting two-week bout with the symptoms. Crapsey returned from New York just before leaving for Europe and just in time for his son's passing. Obviously the Crapsey's were once again devastated. Crapsey's family of nine children was now down to six. Adelaide had been teaching in Connecticut, Rachel was married and living in New Jersey, Paul was in the army and young Algernon was pursuing studies in architecture. That left only Marie Louise and Arthur the baby of the family, at home with their mother. Dr. Converse again officiated at the funeral as he had at Ruth Elizabeth's and Emily Margaret's.[27]

The Silver Cross Society at St. Andrew's later placed a font cover in St. Andrew's Church in memory of Philip. In a letter to Mrs. Crapsey the president of the society, C.V. Evans later wrote, it was an act of kindness that was also in gratitude for the all of the Easter seasons they had enjoyed together [28]

While Crapsey was in New York at the Peace Conference, St. Andrew's Church finally called another rector. The new rector, J.B. Thomas, was reportedly both orthodox theologically and a competent community worker. The church vestry had recoiled from the recent downswing of events and opted for a conservative pastor. Thomas had an interesting background. Indians had murdered his father, also a clergyman, at a young age while negotiating a peace treaty with them. Thomas graduated from the Episcopal Theological School in Massachusetts. He later traveled to Germany where he studied economics and received a Ph.D. in 1901. He had worked at various churches as a curate. St. Andrew's was his first position as a rector.[29]

---

[26] A.H. Crapsey Jr. Collection

[27] Ibid.

[28] Letter from C.V. Evans to Adelaide Trowbridge Crapsey in A. H. Crapsey Jr. Collection.

[29] *Rochester Democrat & Chronicle* Sat. April 20, 1907.

Regardless of the circumstances, Crapsey refused to pass up the opportunity to go to Europe as a representative of the American Peace Society. He realized that if he simply dropped out of sight he would not be worth much on the lecture circuit or in print for long. He needed to maintain his visibility. With his wife emotionally in shambles, Crapsey decided only one week after the funeral to leave for The Hague. Mrs. Crapsey was not one for traveling overseas. Her experience coming back from Bermuda had dampened her enthusiasm for travel and solidified her resolve to remain on dry land. Crapsey chose instead to take his daughter Adelaide with him. Adelaide had been a tremendous support during the time of the trial. She suddenly had the opportunity to return to Europe where she was not a stranger, having previously studied in Rome.[30]

Crapsey and his daughter were intellectually similar. Crapsey was far closer in type to young Adelaide than he was with his wife. Crapsey needed Adelaide's companionship at this time. He must have felt encouraged that he once again had the opportunity to enhance his daughter's intellectual horizon with the trip to The Hague.

On June 1st, 1907 they embarked for Antwerp from New York City on a Red Star Steamer. Mrs. Crapsey must have taken her cue from her husband to continue on. The trip would take three months and Mrs. Crapsey undoubtedly received the emotional support that she so desperately needed from the ladies in her sewing guild.

The conference was a gnarled mass of commissions and sub-committees with meetings and sessions designed to overcome the incivility of war. The program was vague and lent itself to argumentation over nebulous topics. Agreements were rare. Moreover, the language of the conference and news reports concerning it was in French. Fortunately, Adelaide was fluent in the language. [31]

Ultimately Crapsey despaired of the ineffectiveness of the conference and became extremely cynical. He wrote:

> But as far as any usefulness that he accomplished, Dr. Crapsey might as well have stayed at home. The Man of Peace was not present at that Conference, nor could his representative get any kind of a hearing. The utter futility of that meeting impressed itself at once upon the observer. The membership was composed of the diplomats of the nations; they were mostly old men, doddering with age; they had no thought whatever of bringing about the permanent peace of the world; that meant the loss of

[30] Alkalay- Gut, *Alone,* pp. 137- 144 and, 190- 202.

[31] Alkalay- Gut, *Alone,* p. 194.

> their jobs. I saw them only when they were going about the streets and they seemed to me hardly alive, and I despaired of the peace of the world if the making of that permanent peace were in the hands of these ghosts of the past. The sessions of the Conference were secret. From time to time some information would leak out and we learned that every proposition toward the limitation of armaments was vetoed by Germany, and the whole conference seemed to stand in awe of that Imperial Power. Germany then and there served notice on the World that it meant in due time to conquer the World; then and there was the time when the Nations of the World should have combined against Germany and outlawed it, establishing a boycott against all German goods. That was my thought at the time and I so expressed it.[32]

Crapsey soon saw the demise of the peace initiative. He left The Hague and traveled to Paris. He accepted an invitation from Dr. Reginald Campbell to travel with Adelaide to Penmayenwayr, North Wales and speak at the Summer School of the New Theology. Crapsey called the place, "a college of English liberals." Crapsey spent a week there attacking traditional doctrines of the church, especially the sinfulness of man and the sovereignty of God. Asked at one point to fill in for an Oxford lecturer who could not make it to the school, Crapsey delivered a speech on "The Christian Conception of God with Implications as to Divine Immanence," before men he considered the most intellectual and knowledgeable in the world. Without much more than a few moments of preparation he went out onto the speaker's platform and before university professors and writers and other famous British liberal thinkers he gave a rousing extemporaneous speech that surprised even himself with the reception it received.[33]

Crapsey maintained enough self-confidence that he was able to speak without difficulty. Nonetheless, he merely spoke on the subject that he had been living with. In reality, Crapsey had been preparing for this speech and others like it since the onset of his problems with the church. He was accustomed to speaking before large audiences without much preparation. Besides, preparation had caused Crapsey problems in the past. His style made for delightfully lively lectures, but when transferred to paper and subjected to critical scrutiny his remarks were often considered trite. Judicious and analytical attention was not characteristic of Crapsey.

He began the lecture by going back to Augustine and what Crapsey considered as the origination of the notion of a personal God. He

[32] Crapsey, *Manuscript* pp. 361- 2.
[33] Ibid. p. 363.

continued with Clement's contribution historically by distinguishing God as an all-pervading influence. He attacked the old dogmatic system that was always at the forefront of his mind. Crapsey stated sardonically that if one took sin out of the equation Christian priests and pastors would have little left, as preaching about sin was their specialty. Underscoring his new concept of religion Crapsey considered that God worked through our own intelligence and our social institutions and that was the only God necessary to depend upon. In conclusion Crapsey stated unabashedly, "we have to be for the time being gods unto ourselves." Crapsey had shaken off any vestiges of theological caution.[34]

When Crapsey finished the audience gave him an enthusiastic reception. Campbell rose and addressed the assembly, stating how the speech was miraculous intellectually in that Crapsey had presented a highly organized body of thought on such an important subject without virtually any time for preparation. He was awe-struck at the feat and duly impressed. Several British papers carried the story of Crapsey's remarkable discourse. The *New York Herald* was later apprised of Crapsey's accomplishment and published a column about it as well.[35]

Crapsey proceeded to Scotland where he had been invited to stay with Andrew Carnegie. Carnegie had contributed to the fund that allowed Crapsey and his daughter to go to the Hague. Carnegie had established a home at Skibo Castle in the land of his ancient heritage. Crapsey was invited to dinner at the castle. Many other guests attended the dinner party and all were entertained by Carnegie's cuisine, wit and later his imported music. After dinner he was given a room and awakened early by a Highlander playing the bagpipes. The next day Carnegie provided Crapsey with a couple of hours to converse. They talked about politics and religion as Carnegie had been interested in his heresy trial. Crapsey mentioned that in matters of religion Carnegie was a Universalist and an agnostic.[36]

After his extended stay in Great Britain, Crapsey and his daughter returned to the United States in late August. His family spent together what remained of the summer, first at a cottage in Forest Lawn, Onondaga County, New York and then back in Rochester. Things were looking up. Crapsey was offered and accepted another invitation to lecture some thirty times beginning in October at the Lyceum theater for the "People's Sunday Evening Hour."[37]

---

[34] Crapsey, *Manuscript,* p. 363- 4. Also in Alkalay- Gut, *Alone,* p. 196.

[35] Crapsey, *Manuscript,* p. 364.

[36] Ibid. p. 369.

[37] Alkaly- Gut, *Alone,* p. 196.

Amidst the tranquil languor of September in the Finger Lakes region of Upstate New York, news came to Crapsey that another wealthy individual was interested in providing assistance to the Crapseys. The Vice President of Mechanics Savings Bank, William Rossiter Seward of Rochester who had admired Crapsey and followed his endeavors, donated an old cornfield on Averill Avenue to the Crapseys for the building of their home. The materials and labor would be provided as well. Seward established an understanding with Crapsey that the work that he had begun would continue at this house. Subsequently, Crapsey named it the Brotherhood House.[38]

---

[38] Crapsey, *Heretics*, pp. 288- 90.

CHAPTER TWENTY-THREE

'There is a Way That Seemeth Right Unto a Man'

"A Wet Sunday"
The clouds are Dark
The rain comes down
The trees all bless the sparrows
The grass looks up and so must I
For rain is good and spring is nigh.[1]

"*A Wet Sunday,*" complete with music stanzas was written by young Arthur illustrating the optimism the family felt as their tide of bad fortune seemed to be turning. Crapsey went right back to what he had always done. The only difference was, this time he was doing it without the covering of the church. Drawing upon his unique ability to organize men and women into fraternal societies he reestablished the brotherhood of St. Andrew's. Termed simply as, the Brotherhood, Crapsey drew upon people that were previously attracted to the church. Humanism was religion to Crapsey now portrayed by the fact that he taught Sunday school and considered himself the pastor of the Brotherhood.[2]

Crapsey made a point of stating publicly how he wanted his people to remain in the church whether at St. Andrew's, or wherever. Privately however, Crapsey admitted that the Brotherhood resulted from his organization of people reacting to his deposal from the church. He worked tirelessly to further the agenda of the new religion while undermining the old dogmatic of the church. The list of the directors of the Brotherhood was distinguished. Three were members of the Board of Education, including the president of the board, five were faculty members of the University of Rochester. One was a former pastor of one of the leading Presbyterian Churches of the city, and both the president and vice

---

[1] Song entitled *"A Wet Sunday."* By Arthur H. Crapsey Sr. dated Oct. 20, 1907. Scrapbooks A.H. Crapsey Jr. Collection.
[2] Crapsey, *Manuscript,* p. 387-8

president of the Chamber of Commerce were members. There was his ex-counsel and Republican Congressman, James Breck Perkins, as well as the chairman of the Democratic County organization, prominent members of the Rochester bar and other distinguished men and women of various vocations. Both Jews and Gentiles alike were members of the Brotherhood.[3]

The purpose of the Brotherhood was,

> to give expression in a simple way to the Brotherhood of Man which follows necessarily from the Fatherhood of God. If God is the Father of all men, then all men are the brothers of one another. The Brotherhood knows no difference of race, nationality, class or creed. It declares that all men are one in that Divine Humanity which is the birthright of everyone who is born of a woman. The purpose of the Brotherhood is to unify the race of mankind in God and in one another. By being at one with each other we shall also be at one with God.[4]

By the time of the first annual meeting Crapsey had organized the Brotherhood into two departments. One was a continuation of the sewing guild that had been started at St. Andrew's by the ladies of the church. It was classified as the Department of Social Betterment. He expanded it to include the sewing and receiving of clothing, the visitation of the sick as well as the provision of Thanksgiving and Christmas dinners for those in need. By 1909, the department was putting out over twelve hundred garments a year, forty-nine packages of medical and toilet supplies and over seventeen hundred articles of foodstuff like jellies, fruit, cocoa, and other groceries.[5]

Crapsey also reestablished what he termed "maternity work." He noted how on a Valentine's Day they re-instituted their maternity work. Many of the old workers from St. Andrew's joined them again keeping the spirit of the work alive and fresh once more.[6] The Brotherhood also dispatched a woman who was engaged in continuous visitation. Maud Jerome Guilford worked as an unpaid nurse who patiently ministered to babies and invalids and others in need of her services in their own homes.[7]

---

[3] Ibid. p. 385.

[4] Pamphlet, *"First Annual Report of the Brotherhood."* In A.H. Crapsey Jr. Collection.

[5] Ibid.

[6] Crapsey, *Manuscript,* p. 396.

[7] Ibid. p. 396.

Crapsey also established a Lecture Department. By 1909, there were over forty meetings. Lectures were given almost twice a month promoting both the new religiosity and other humanitarian ideas. Ten lectures were held in the Unitarian Church where on an average evening approximately four hundred people attended. A bigger facility was soon found in the Lyceum Theater.[8]

Crapsey figured he was walking in St. Paul's footsteps because when Paul was unable to preach at the synagogues he went to the theatres and elsewhere to make the word known. Crapsey felt at liberty at the Lyceum to preach the way he wanted to unconstrained by the creedal bonds he was forced to endure for the last years of his ministry. He felt that the freedom he enjoyed added onto the power, clarity and inspiration that were so evidently recognizable there.[9]

Crapsey reported thirty-three meetings at the Lyceum Theatre with an average attendance of six hundred and fifty people. Crapsey estimated that the total number of people that year attending the lectures was over twenty-five thousand. Some of the lectures in addition to Crapsey's were by Rabbi Stephen S. Wise, Nathaniel Schmidt, the Honorable Seth Low, Professor Edward A. Ross, Professor Charles Zueblin, Mrs. Anna Garlin Spencer and Miss Katherine Davis.[10]

The Crapsey's rented home at 630 University Avenue was close to the University of Rochester. While there he maintained contact with several professors. He also utilized the library. Crapsey worked on several writings there including a book that he had started while still at St. Andrew's. He had vowed to continue the work in printed form that he had begun with the lecture series. The book that resulted was entitled, *The Rebirth of Religion.*

He was now free to express his mind without qualification. Like *Religion and Politics,* his current book was derived from lectures. Crapsey had established himself as a good draw for people to come and hear. He attempted to insulate his endeavor from criticism by declaring that the lectures were informal rather than academically succinct. He targeted the churches of western civilization's old dogmatic system. Crapsey contended the system was aged, feeble and weak and doomed to pass away even though many were hanging onto the prospect of renewal rather

---

[8] Pamphlet of the *"First Annual Report of the Brotherhood."* In A.H. Crapsey Jr. Collection.

[9] Crapsey, *Manuscript,* p. 388.

[10] Pamphlet of the *"First Annual Report of the Brotherhood,"* A.H. Crapsey Jr. Collection.

than succumbing to its inevitable demise. The purpose for Crapsey was not to simply document the dying, old system. Instead, Crapsey proposed something productive by also chronicling the rebirth of religion.[11]

The book was an attempt to provide through his perspective, the history of the Christian dogmatic system. Crapsey's growing Marxist outlook was now brought to bear upon a organization in the world in which Christianity was the chief facilitator. Poverty, slavery, exploitation of various heathen people, and the establishment of social class structures were the result of this organization. Crapsey dealt in generalities about the relationship between Christianity and the social, political, and economic systems of the world. In the process, he insulted the intelligence of indigenous peoples who, according to Crapsey, couldn't distinguish between the religious and other aspects of the encroaching westerners' civilization. In places like Japan however, Christianity, was rejected through judicious counsel. According to Crapsey, the wise men of Japan advised the emperor that though Christianity was exported with great enthusiasm it was a failure in its own lands.[12]

In the regions where Christianity was once vigorous it was now subjugating indigenous peoples. Concerning the Russians, Crapsey remarked how they hated the Orthodox Church as it was purveying the same bureaucratic system that was exploiting the people. He prophesized that both church and state would eventually fall with a vengeance to the wrath of the Russian people. Crapsey used the example of both the Russians and the Japanese as they had both been in the current news. Social Darwinians pondered how it was possible that a non-western society like Japan was able to defeat a great European power. Crapsey inferred that the reason was not only because of the Russians' abject bondage to dogmatic and corrupt Christianity but also owing to the rejection of the same by the Japanese. Old, corrupt, dogmatic Christianity was the problem.[13]

Similar to the fundamentalist end of the intellectual spectrum, Crapsey saw the intellectual experience in adversarial terms. Statements like "the University is the enemy of the Church and the Church is the deadly foe of the University," were characteristic of him.[14] Crapsey attempted to again reconcile Christianity with the scientific and philosophic. He attempted to show how thought developed in the Christian traditions, evolving from

---

[11] A.S. Crapsey *The Rebirth of Religion* New York: John Lane Co., 1907 pp. 9-11.
[12] Ibid. pp. 14-22.
[13] Ibid. pp. 22-3.
[14] Ibid. p. 25.

several sources such as Hebrew literature concerned with the poetic and ethical, Greek philosophical influences and Western rationalistic traditions. He tried to show how the concept of a triune God developed and how the need to explain anomalies in the scriptures led to the development of the creeds. They were an attempt to make some sort of association between the infinite and the finite, between God and man. But Crapsey did not stop there, he scrutinized the entire realm of Christian doctrine from the concepts of sin to soteriology, hell to heaven, God to mankind.[15]

Crapsey presented his new dogmatic once more, including his notion of how humans, in correspondence with their progress, brought forth a succession of new gods at each new level of development. In his attempt to describe the evolution of human thinking concerning deity, Crapsey came down to the position that love, justice and peace would inevitably reign in the kingdom of righteousness. He reduced the great doctrines of Christendom to the statement that, "it will be a great day for religion when the friend God of Abraham becomes the friend God of every man." In like fashion, Crapsey proposed his definition of the path to salvation. Crapsey prescribed the method that Jesus proposed. The way to salvation was not so much through the relationship to a personal God as through social activism. For Crapsey, the Christ of the gospels was a Christ of social concerns. Crapsey dismissed the three methods of salvation expressed through the old dogmatic: "salvation by submission, salvation by definition, and salvation by substitution." Crapsey considered the vicarious atonement as degrading to mankind turning men into beggars for undeserved favors. There was a way however, that made sense to him from the beginning. The plan he termed as the new dogmatic was salvation through social commitment. Crapsey had come to believe that men did not become saved by evading one's society but in association, together with them. For Crapsey, salvation was "all or none."[16]

Though some academics accepted Crapsey's new literary endeavor because of his dedication to the cause of an ethical society, others were unable to countenance his poor scholarship. One reviewer noted frankly,

> It is hardly expected that Dr. Crapsey's experience would lead him to take a well- balanced view of the situation. And it is an ungracious task to criticize with severity the work of a man whose personal character is so high, whose labor for men has been so disinterested, and who has passed

[15] Ibid. Each theme received a chapter in Crapsey's book.
[16] Ibid. pp.261- 293.

> through such a trying experience. But if the truth be spoken, the book is utterly devoid of any scholarship and of theological insight. It is hardly more than a combination of the commonplace and the untrue.[17]

Moreover, in a way very similar to how other reviewers had received his previous attempts at historical scholarship the reviewer concluded,

> The book abounds in inaccuracies and misstatements. They show loose thinking, lack of scholarship, and carelessness of expression. The volume would attract no attention and would not be worthy of serious notice were it not for the prominence in which circumstances have placed its author.[18]

Nevertheless, Crapsey's life was beginning to look up. He had come to consider that a deposed churchman could get along quite well without the church after all. His new world was a much grander place than the world he had previously inhabited inside the church. There was now liberty and a panoramic view of life as the authority of the church faded away.[19]

Crapsey was invited by Mr. Samuel Burns Weston to speak at the Ethical Society in Philadelphia in 1907. He continued the practice approximately five times a year until late in his life. Crapsey lectured at the Academy of Music and the Broad Street Theatre, and was the guest of prominent business people including several Quakers, while in town. He established friendships with numerous people while lecturing in Philadelphia. He also lectured often in Chicago, usually at Lincoln Center. Crapsey may have lost some of the intimacy of the parish pastor's duties but his work with the Brotherhood compelled him to write, "I could almost say with Wesley, 'My parish is the world.'"[20]

On one trip Crapsey debated an atheist at Orchestra Hall about the historicity of Jesus. Crapsey reckoned that the size of the gathering signified the times he lived in. Crapsey's fame derived from his deposition from the ministry of the Protestant Episcopal Church. The public wanted to see the eloquent, caped, little preacher in all his candor. The atheist acerbically asked for a "saying of Jesus that actually came out of his mouth." It was as if the question had been custom made for Crapsey. Not surprisingly, he quoted the story of the rich young ruler who came to Jesus and asked, "'Good Master, What shall I do to inherit eternal life?' Jesus said, 'Why callest thou me good? There is but one good, that is God.'"

---

[17] *NY Times Book Review* Nov. 23, 1907 746: 2. No author of the review recorded.
[18] Ibid.
[19] Crapsey, *Rebirth,* pp. 297-8.
[20] Crapsey, *Manuscript,* p. 401.

Crapsey used the scripture not only to contend with the atheist but to establish the greater point of his disputation with the church, that from the mouth of Jesus Himself, He had declared that He was not on a par with God. Ironically this time, Crapsey chose the literal rather than the spiritual interpretation to establish his argument.[21]

Christmas of 1907 was difficult for the Crapseys. For the first time they celebrated the holiday away from their precious rectory home. But the Crapseys also received gracious expressions of sympathy from certain people that tempered the pain of their separation. That Christmas in particular, Crapsey remembered one experience. His wife who loved Christmas more than any other day was feeling blue. But there was a ring at the doorbell. Dr. Hanna, the Catholic priest who would later go on to be the Archbishop of San Francisco, came to the house and extended his hand and with tears in his eyes to each of them he merely exclaimed, "God bless you." That simple act of kindness provided the Crapseys with the thought that they were somehow still remembered.[22]

Meanwhile, Crapsey's work with the Brotherhood took on further dimensions. Their operational efforts were expanding as more works were proposed for the various departments. On the last day of the year 1907, he endeavored to present a benefit show for the old folks, children of various orphanages and other institutions in the city. A play called *"Circus Man,"* had previously failed, and they had left behind their scenery. Crapsey decided to make good use of it, and present a show of his own for the disadvantaged of the city.[23]

Crapsey arranged to have 1,900 needy people brought to the Lyceum Theatre in railway cars and automobiles donated for the occasion. Reportedly the show was packed to the brim with the disadvantaged of Rochester. Old people from the Church Home were allowed to sit in the front row. The rest of the audience was made up of inmates of the Rochester Orphan Asylum, the Jewish Orphan Asylum, and the Deaf Mute's Institute. Crapsey started the performance as the Ringmaster with a whip and told stories and jokes throughout the performance. A local

---

[21] "Did Jesus Really Live? A Debate Held in Orchestra Hall, Chicago, January 21st, 1908." *Debate Series* Vol. 1. Stemway Hall, Chicago: Original Research Society, 1908.

[22] Crapsey, *Manuscript,* pp. 441-2.

[23] News clipping entitled "Santa Claus at Lyceum Circus. Children from Institutions made Happy by Brotherhood. Happiness Reigns Supreme. New Circus Man Full of Merriment at Charity Performance under Dr. Crapsey's Direction. A.S. Crapsey Ringmaster." In A.H. Crapsey Jr. Collection.

newspaper reported that Crapsey kept the spectators laughing all through the show. Brotherhood members dressed up like a Lion, a Teddy Bear and an Elephant and an individual named Jack Moore dressed up like a clown and did a wonderfully amusing pantomime act. The children enjoyed all the characters especially when the Teddy Bear danced with the Lion. Even Crapsey's introverted daughter, Marie Louise, played one of the peanut girls.[24]

In the next act Crapsey dressed up as Santa Claus and brought the audience into the play by telling the children that he couldn't find the chimney into the tenement house. As the children in the audience gave Santa suggestions about what to do, Crapsey found an elevator and was able to distribute the presents throughout the house. One wise guy called out that the people were just fake sleeping. A young immigrant child thoroughly entranced in the play replied "No, he no maka da fake, they maka da sleep all right." At the end of the play all of the characters in the performance went down into audience delighting the children by distributing candy.[25]

By the onset of his lecture series the house at 678 Averill Avenue was in process of being raised on the cornfield donated by William Rossiter Seward. Algernon Jr. developed the plans with help from Claude Bragdon an eccentric friend of the family's. The house reflected the openness of the Brotherhood with ample space for the functions of the ministry. There would be room for the large family and others. There would also be room for gardens like those Mrs. Crapsey had planted at St. Andrew's and for more practical gardening needs as well. The building project moved rapidly and by January of 1908 they were in their new home. On March 3, 1908, Crapsey had a reception for all the people who had donated their time and energy to making the home at 678 Averill Avenue a reality. Many dignitaries including the mayor of Rochester attended. But the gathering was primarily for the workingmen and women who had labored to build the house that the Crapseys had always wanted. Crapsey remarked that one never got tired of the place. Mrs. Crapsey had been careful to preserve the charm and the integrity of the design. The walls were not filled with unnecessary decorations nor were there clumsy ornaments cluttering every empty space. Mrs. Crapsey tastefully decorated with a simple vase and solitary picture on the wall.[26]

---

[24] Ibid.
[25] Ibid.
[26] Crapsey, *Manuscript,* p. 384a.

Crapsey used the occasion to read a humorous, lyrical poem he had composed about the builders of the house. In it Crapsey paid tribute to everyone involved in the project from Seward down to the first inhabitant, a mouse. He also documented his talented son's architectural skill. He delighted his workmen guests by naming each and every one in the body of the poem. He expressed his gratitude with a sense of humor in his rendition of the building process. Crapsey's ability to delight his friends with his graciousness and wit was evident in the final sentences of the poem. He concluded his history in rime, with the lines,

And now our house stands fair to view,
A house of love and light,
Its cry, 'To every man his due,
To every girl her right.'

Its front door opens to the east,
Its back door to the west;
To eye it is a daily feast,
To the weary soul a rest.

Here may it stand from age to age,
Its simple tale to tell,
How workmen wrought for honest wage,
And did their work so well.[27]

William Crawford Barry of Ellwanger and Barry nurseries helped Mrs. Crapsey plant the garden that she had always dreamed of. The nursery furnished plants, trees and professional guidance. Henry Brooks Ellwanger of the same firm had assisted Mrs. Crapsey at the rectory at St. Andrew's with her garden close to thirty years before. They remained friends of the Crapseys throughout the years.[28]

Seward had not only given Crapsey a new home on a lovely lot at the edge of the city, he also sent periodic checks to Mrs. Crapsey for support. One such letter stated,

"My dear sister Adelaide,
The endorsed check is not intended for "The Brotherhood" or for the Sunday-school nor for the sewing guild- but for your personal and family use.

---

[27] Pamphlet entitled, *The Builders of the House, A History in Rime.* Read at the reception given to the makers of the Home by Mr. and Mrs. Algernon S. Crapsey. Tuesday evening March 3, 1908. In the A.H. Crapsey Jr. Collection.
[28] Crapsey, *Manuscript* pp. 384a-384b.

Your (unable to decipher),
W.R. Seward.[29]

Crapsey intended to bless others as others had blessed him with the house. His new duties with the Brotherhood were pastoral as well as delivering lectures. He ministered in this new capacity as he had in the past. However, he added a new component to his ministry that went well beyond the mere visitation of the sick. In his zeal to go further than previous efforts and achieve his social and economic reforms, he brought tuberculosis patients into his home and the homes of other members of the Brotherhood willing to care for them.[30] In attempting to do "that which seemed right to a man," he exposed his family to a dreadful disease.[31]

Adelaide came home during the winter of 1908–1909 before going back to Rome and the School of Classical Studies with her friend from England, Alice Pritchard. Adelaide was, like her father, diminutive. Unlike him however, she was delicate in constitution. She had been afflicted with other illnesses that year and when she came home to stay with her family before her departure to Europe, she was suffering the effects of exhaustion caused by the long trip and her busy life. Adelaide had been afflicted with chronic fatigue at least since the death of her sister and loving companion, Emily Margaret.[32] All of these factors put together and the sudden exposure to tuberculosis may have caused Adelaide to contract the disease that would eventually kill her. From that point on Adelaide was continually weak, to the point of hospitalization after her arrival in Rome. She was either unable to receive the proper diagnosis or the language barrier caused her to not grasp the problem. But that is doubtful considering her ability with languages, including Italian. She would however, continue undiagnosed for at least three more years.[33]

During this time Crapsey's socialistic agenda matured. The YMCA had moved from its conservative evangelical moorings during the progressive era, becoming more receptive of liberal social programs. Two liberal theater programs were allowed to participate at the Rochester

---

[29] Letter from W.R. Seward to Adelaide Trowbridge Crapsey dated, Oct. 28, 1908 A.H. Crapsey Jr. Collection.

[30] Crapsey, *Manuscript,* p. 388.

[31] Crapsey wrote, "During the past winter the Brotherhood has taken as a special department of its work, the care of the sick, especially tuberculosis patients in their own homes." Pamphlet of *"First Annual Report of the Brotherhood, (1909)"* A.H. Crapsey Jr. Collection.

[32] Personal communication with Karen Alkalay- Gut.

[33] Alkalay- Gut *Alone,* See pp. 205 & 263.

YMCA. While reformers like Rauschenbusch and Paul Moore Strayer provided programs geared toward the social gospel, Crapsey brought a more radical format to his theater series. Eventually the evangelical spirit returned infusing the social consciousness of the liberals with the traditional YMCA program. Crapsey's radicalism undoubtedly had much to do with the return of a more conservative agenda to the Rochester YMCA.[34]

As the Brotherhood developed, other dimensions were added to the work. Crapsey, his son Paul and another man, W. Trueman, set up the Vacant Lot Gardening Commission. It was an ingenious attempt to get unemployed, disabled and others considered unproductive to produce food. By the end of the summer in 1909, Crapsey announced that the commission was bringing in 1,500 bushels of potatoes, 5,000 head of cabbage and other vegetables enough in fact to feed as many as 80 families over the course of a winter. The vegetables had been raised on vacant lots in the city of Rochester.[35]

On October 17, 1909 he detailed the work of his Vacant Lot Gardening Association at the Rochester City Club at a time when the club was still known as the City Lunch Club. Crapsey had been instrumental in establishing liberal clubs in Rochester such as the Rochester City Club. He promoted the club along with Walter Rauschenbusch, Joseph T. Alling and Rev. Paul Moore Strayer. At a club that would eventually feature such speakers as Franklin Delano Roosevelt, Samuel Gompers, Margaret Sanger, Emma Goldman, and many others of national recognition and renown, Crapsey was its first speaker.[36]

The Brotherhood was deeply involved in changing the conditions of life in the local region. Even the mayor had utilized the resources of the Brotherhood as he turned to the organization for relief after another great fire afflicted the city.[37] Crapsey's thoughts as to the role of the Brotherhood were instructive. He thought the Brotherhood could grow to a point where it would abolish poverty and set society on an equal footing. He did not believe it would be accomplished in his lifetime. But, they hoped to establish the process that would grow and eventually rival primitive Christianity in its effectiveness. Therefore, Crapsey preached the

---

[34] Blake McKelvey "The YMCA's First Century in Rochester." In *Rochester History* Vol. XVI Jan. 1954 No.1, p. 17.

[35] Column entitled "20 years ago today." In A.H. Crapsey Jr. Collection.

[36] Blake McKelvey "A History of the Rochester City Club." In *Rochester History* Vol. IX Oct. 1947 No. 4.

[37] Crapsey, *Manuscript,* p. 389. Handwritten as p. 390.

concepts of equalization and the abolition of poverty and the public sustained their aspirations with their favor.[38]

Crapsey believed that the abolition of poverty would come through the intrinsic right to use the land and the proper education of men to attend to their needs. The avarice of private property ownership cut off access to usable vacant lands that could be put into production for the good of the community. He believed that with the free use of lands and the proper training made available, the abolition of poverty would result.[39]

Even if one did not agree with Crapsey's presumptions about religion and politics, he was the author of so much beneficial social work that it was sincerely hard to despise him. The heresy trial had ironically conferred upon Crapsey a kind of public persona that was the stuff that local legends were made of. By the time of his autobiography Crapsey obviously began to believe his own press and the tales of greatness created about him.

In his elder years it was his wife and William Rossiter Seward's benevolence however, who actually picked up the economic slack for the family. Seward not only sent periodic checks for the personal use of the family, but he eventually gave them substantial interests in Kodak stocks which helped Mrs. Crapsey with the resources necessary to get her clothing company started. It also helped to keep their daughter Adelaide in pursuit of her academic interests in Europe.[40]

With their nuclear family dwindling, the Brotherhood became the extended family for the Crapsey's. Paul worked as an unofficial officer in the department of Social Betterment, and eventually as the secretary for the sewing guild that had grown steadily until it became an entity onto itself. The guild was eventually renamed, The Adelaide T. Crapsey Company.[41]

The A.T. Crapsey Co. began humbly as the sewing guild in 1881 at St. Andrew's Church and continued at 678 Averill Avenue, and by 1912 had moved into its third home at 34 Priem Street. The factory specialized, as one advertisement read, in making "Dainty Smocks and Frocks," for young girls. The work was originally designed to aid children of the poor. Smocks and frocks were sent to places such as hospital fairs where they were displayed and gained the attention of women for their excellent quality. Crapsey boasted that his wife was an artist who sought perfection

[38] Ibid., p. 388.
[39] Ibid., p. 388.
[40] Quote from Alkalay- Gut *Alone,* p. 238.
[41] Scrapbooks, A.H. Crapsey Jr. Collection.

from her associates. The fact that the work was originally offered freely to the needy or the sick inspired the workers. They produced a quality garment that surpassed those on the shelves of the best stores. As the commercial demand increased, inexperience in business ultimately showed up as a loss due to charging for only labor and material but not any overhead.[42]

The situation was soon rectified and by 1912 the company that had started out by making offerings to the poor girls of the area was now selling its goods to one of the finest upscale department stores in Rochester, the B. Foreman Company. One advertisement read, "Handmade Brotherhood Outfits- For Babies and Children, B. Foreman Co." From that point on the factory grew and had to remove itself to bigger and more industrious quarters almost every year. They moved to their fourth home in 1915 at 214 South Avenue. The fifth home was on Court Street. By 1917 they required yet another location at 11 Atlas Street. By 1917, the Adelaide T. Crapsey Company was making 100 frocks a day.[43]

Crapsey basked in his wife's success. He boasted that she had turned her laborers into a factory family where there were no economic divisions between the employee and the employer. As such, it gained the attention of economists as an example of an industrial experiment that was working. With employer and employees working together in a common enterprise, Crapsey postulated that this was the solution to the problem of economic exploitation. In reality W.R. Seward paid the bills providing the Brotherhood with an economic cushion to operate and giving the Crapsey's room to experiment.[44]

Nevertheless, it was a factory like no one had ever experienced before. It was bright and airy with hardwood floors, the walls were a soft buff color and the pillars of the room were ivory white.[45] There were rocking chairs for the ladies to sit in while doing the finishing sewing and embroidery. The great room had a large piano gracing it.[46] There was also a Vitrola to listen to, and ferns that hung from the ceiling and walls, while goldfish adorned the room to give one a sense of comfort and ease. Moreover there were gas plates to heat tea on for the ladies. The rest room

---

[42] Ibid.

[43] Ibid.

[44] Ibid.

[45] Column written for the *Christian Statesman* (Pittsburgh) reproduced in Crapsey, *Manuscript,* pp. 392-6.

[46] Ibid. p. 395.

was equipped well enough to serve as a temporary hospital in case of sickness or an accident. The light in the hallway was adorned with a red shade to give one a sense of warmth and serenity. There was a housekeeper who took care of the fish and the plants and the place was unusually clean to meet the highest standards of sanitation. Later, a dining room was added with an attendant to prepare and serve the food. This factory was a pleasure to work in indeed, and the Crapseys endeavored to create truly a family atmosphere. Moreover, those who described the factory stated it was more than a place where smocks for young children were made. The atmosphere was one of a joyful sewing bee with the gentle laughter, the soft creaking of the rocking chairs and the availability of refreshments.[47]

Crapsey was referred to as the "father of the factory." He encouraged the women and sustained close personal friendships with many of them. Paul Bontecu Crapsey eventually became the general manager maintaining the family integrity while at the same time its familial uniqueness and the quality of its products. They referred to themselves as the factory family and never as the employers or employees of the Adelaide T. Crapsey Co.[48]

Several of the women were physically disabled or handicapped in one way or another. Crapsey and his wife gave economic hope to these women. Sadie Halloran a crippled woman, bid Mrs. Crapsey goodnight one evening and went home and passed away two hours later. Others like Irishwomen Nan Connors were considered socially crippled in some way. Nan ran the dining room. Crapsey composed another of his lyrical poems about her.[49]

Crapsey's work in the other departments was flourishing as well. By 1912, Crapsey was lecturing in New York, Chicago, Philadelphia, and Erie, Pennsylvania as well as in closer areas like Batavia and Lyons, New York. Over the course of the year 1912, Crapsey gave twenty-three lectures dealing with politics and economic problems from a moral and spiritual context. Crapsey also taught a Wednesday evening class except when he was absent from the city, at which time professors from the University of Rochester usually stood in for him. In his pastoral capacity he celebrated the weddings of ten couples and officiated at the burial of

---

[47] Quotes from *Rochester Herald* April 8, 1919. Column in scrapbook in A.H. Crapsey Jr. Collection.

[48] Quote in the *Christian Statesman* reproduced in Crapsey, *Manuscript,* p. 395.

[49] Poem in scrapbook dated April 6, 1921, in Arthur H. Crapsey Jr. Collection.

twelve others. In his ministerial capacity he visited the sick and the needy and was available in his office for counseling.[50]

By 1912, the Brotherhood's total expenditures and receipts of income balanced out at $10,433. 82. By this time the Brotherhood had incorporated and under Crapsey's direction was becoming more radical in outlook. Crapsey wrote that the object of their labors was to promote the "prosperity, peace, health and wealth of all men." Crapsey set forth a global perspective, willing to arbitrate disagreements amongst nations in the interest of international peace. Concerning prosperity, Crapsey noted they would advocate for laws that would govern the means of production to enhance the overall quality of life. To promote health the Brotherhood sought ways to serve the well-being of both the individual and the community. In the interest of wealth they actively promoted the equal distribution of resources to abolish poverty.[51]

The Vacant Lot Gardening was now termed the Gardeners Club. They publicized that with expenditures of $550 they received returns of two to three thousand dollars. One hundred families now cultivated gardens under the direction of the commission. The effort was maintained through the labor of working men and women.[52]

Crapsey's audience was growing steadily averaging between 700 to 1500 people. He estimated that 27,000 people heard him speak in 1912. The theatre at the Lyceum was inadequate for the growing audiences so the Brotherhood changed their lecture location to the larger Victoria theatre. The speakers who accompanied Crapsey were internationally recognized lecturers. They included Professor Nathaniel Schmidt of Cornell University, Rabbi Stephen S. Wise of New York City, Reginald John Campbell of City Temple, London, Cecil De Lisle Bums of Cambridge University, England, and Stanton Coit of the Ethical Society, London.[53]

In only the fifth year of the Brotherhood they were free from debt. The Brotherhood now transacted its affairs in a more efficient, more business-like manner. By 1912, there was no report of the taking in of tuberculosis patients. Perhaps they had realized the inherent danger involved. The Brotherhood now put out a brochure that advertised its mission and extolled the results. On the back it stated,

---

[50] Pamphlet, *Annual report of the Brotherhood* (1912). A.H. Crapsey Jr. Collection.
[51] Ibid.
[52] Ibid.
[53] Ibid.

> Opportunities opened to the mentally and physically incapable, the aged and other needy and unemployed persons to improve their condition morally, mentally and physically without pauperizing them.
>
> Increased industry, thrift, self- confidence, sobriety and honesty. Waste places turned into beautiful gardens. [54]

In the meantime, Adelaide had returned from Europe and was offered a job at Smith College. She eventually became so ill that she collapsed and was hospitalized at Pittsfield, Massachusetts. It wasn't until 1912 that she finally received a proper diagnosis. The doctor believed she had been suffering from an aggravated form of tuberculosis for three or four years. The aggressive symptoms progressed in a relatively short period of time. She was forced to leave her position and enter a sanatorium at Saranac Lake, New York. Adelaide was told that Robert Louis Stevenson had been cured there in 1887, under the direction of the brilliant founder, Dr. Trudeau. Trudeau believed that the cold mountain air killed germs, and the germ free environment contributed to the recovery of the patients.[55]

By the time that Adelaide arrived another doctor, Edward Baldwin had taken over at Saranac Lake. She was immediately sent to a cottage for the more severely afflicted patients. The accommodations were psychologically trying. There was virtually no one else housed in her cottage except briefly and outside her bedroom window there was, as if in prophetic invitation, a graveyard. Her writing and other activities were restricted while at the cottage sanatorium. Various treatments including pneumothrax where the lung was collapsed to give it total inactivity and respite and tuberculin, or the injection of the live germ into the patient, subsequently failed. Dr. Baldwin consequently noted that Adelaide was much too delicate physically and too sensitive emotionally to bear such a debilitating disease. Crapsey immediately came to meet with Baldwin and discuss the possibility of having his daughter return home. Her brother Paul finally met her at the end of August, 1914 in Utica and brought her back home. She had intended to find another sanatorium closer to her family or possibly near Rachel in New Jersey, but the symptoms worsened with the effects of the humidity in the region.[56]

She had grown steadily worse during her stay at Saranac Lake, but she wrote some of her finest poetry at that time. The continuous coughing,

---

[54] Ibid.
[55] Alkalay-Gut *Alone* pp. 266-7.
[56] Ibid., pp.267-293.

elevated temperature, sweats and the general strain of her invalidity distressed everyone at the house. Her friends arrived to comfort her but without much success as her strength declined daily. At the beginning of October her illness suddenly worsened. Ferne Hincher her nurse, cradled her over her shoulder in her strong but gentle arms so she could breathe.[57]

Ferne later married Adelaide's youngest brother. From their union her son Arthur Jr. maintained the family records allowing both Adelaide and her father's stories eventually to be told in detail. Adelaide fought to continue on. On Tuesday she lingered through the night as her nurse tried to comfort her in any way possible. Mercifully she remained unconscious for much of the time. She died the next day at three o'clock, October 8, 1914, after a time of terrible suffering. Both lungs had collapsed. Her best friend Jean Webster and her colleague and friend at Smith College, Ester Lowenthal, presented her parents with a volume of verse she had written entitled simply Verse. She had kept the poetry from her parents to shelter them from the knowledge of the physical and emotional trauma associated with her suffering. She was cremated, her ashes placed in an urn donated by her classmates at Vassar. Her ashes were interred at the family plot at Mt. Hope Cemetery. Her father spoke at her funeral. Rather than losing himself in the emotion of the moment he chose to express the beliefs of his new religion concerning death. He stated death was simply an element in the overall plan of things. It was as natural as birth and it couldn't be evil because as Goethe said, it was universally experienced. For Crapsey,

> To die is to change one's state; to go, 'either to the country of the blessed God, or else to enter into that great unconsciousness which is the source of all unconsciousness, to enter into that sleep out of which comes all awakening.' What is to come to pass after our death does not disturb us any more that what came to pass before our birth. Before we were born we existed in the thought of God, and after we die we shall have our place in that Infinite Intelligence.[58]

Crapsey had perhaps tired of trying to figure out why now four of his beloved children had passed on before him. But for the time being, he simply resigned himself that death was a natural process, not to be despised or coveted but merely to be accepted. He struggled to find

---

[57] Ibid., p. 299.

[58] Sister Mary Edwardine O'Connor, *"Adelaide Crapsey: A Biographical Study"* (Master's Thesis, Notre Dame, 1931) p. 37. Also in Alkalay-Gut, *Alone,* p. 303.

58 Poem by Adelaide Crapsey recorded in Karen Alkalay- Gut *Alone in the Dawn* (Athens, 1988) p. 303.

comfort in his new revelation of life and death. But Adelaide was especially precious to him. She was so much like him in so many ways and he loved her dearly.

One similarity was demonstrated by the fact that Adelaide chose to write her own epitaph. One poem in particular spoke to her and her father's shared belief that what one did in one's life would be one's memorial.

The Immortal Residue
Inscription for my verse
Wouldst thou find my ashes? Look
In the pages of my book;
And as these thy hand doth turn,
Know here is my funeral urn.[59]

---

[59] Adelaide Crapsey, poem recorded in Karen Alkalay-Gut *Alone in the Dawn* (Athens, Ga, 1988) p.303.

CHAPTER TWENTY-FOUR

"Neither Shall They Learn War Any More"

On December 3, 1911, Crapsey spoke at the Free Synagogue, in Carnegie Hall, about the "Social War in the Modern World." The speech addressed the subject now dearest to Crapsey's heart, socialism. Crapsey believed that the confession of the McNamara brothers to a political bombing in Los Angeles was the worst blow to organized labor in its history. Crapsey added incredulously that the so-called friends of the cause committed it. The anarchists' bombing was the most serious situation that America had experienced since the time of John Brown's exploits.[1]

The analogy did not go without notice by those who had supported Crapsey in his cause to bring about a more ethical society. Describing the terrorism of the McNamara brothers as comparable to the events preceding the Civil War was to declare its legitimacy. At that point Crapsey's wealthy backers began to reassess their support. Crapsey was advocating something that was dangerous to them personally. Crapsey told the crowd at Carnegie Hall that there was a struggle before them in the starkest of terms. The conflict between the forces of capital and that of labor would mean the ultimate destruction of the commonwealth. Innocent bystanders would suffer, as they would be naively brought into the affair. As the same precipitous struggle was going on everywhere at all times, it was in fact happening just then.[2]

Crapsey blamed the capitalistic system for perpetuating the crisis. He believed the incident was caused by the exploitation of the capitalists over labor. If it continued more disasters were sure to follow. As the situation progressed there would be more capital in fewer hands, the result would be that the masses would loose their purchasing power and eventually the whole system would be useless. Crapsey's ideology was rapidly becoming a liability to his wealthy backers.[3]

---

[1] *NY Times* Dec. 4, 1911. 3: 1-3.
[2] Ibid.
[3] Ibid.

The next spring Crapsey returned to New York. He marched in the May Day, suffragettes' parade.[4] Crapsey had championed women's causes since his evangelistic days of ministering to prostitutes. Some men opposed suffrage due to the high visibility of women in the temperance movement and their affiliation in organizational issues. They assumed that if women received the vote, they could politically take their alcohol away from them. Crapsey however, had no such inhibitions. Women's suffrage was simply a matter of the democratization of society.

By 1912, Crapsey was sixty-five years old. Yet he rarely slowed down. He remained extremely active and became more and more accessible as a speaker for radical causes. Crapsey loved to walk and even at his age he would walk for days. His conversion to "the doctrine of human redemption by human effort" motivated his wanderings. In his enthusiasm he was filled with an evangelical zeal for the message he needed to express. He had fled from the shores of capitalism and had arrived at the shore of socialism like so many other pilgrims on their journey through life. He became the consummate itinerate preacher on the highways and the byways, in the open fields or in the dankest cities. Although he experienced no real results from his efforts he believed that they would come eventually. He was merely the sower of the seeds, another would reap the harvest in due time.[5]

Crapsey loved to walk. He hated what man had done by killing the birds and cutting down the trees and yet, mankind still could never really destroy the charming beauty of nature. He felt a tinge of nostalgia thinking back to the medieval days when men made true pilgrimages. Those were the times when people would walk from village to village actually communicating with each other along the way. Crapsey disparaged how they now traveled in little boxes and no one actually walks any more. Travel was synonymous now with weariness and fatigue as there was no effort or exercise involved nor did anyone talk to anyone else. He considered that the day of the itinerant preacher had passed. No one was even interested enough to stop and listen anymore as they could read whatever tickled their fancy in the press.[6]

Crapsey's penchant for walking made people uncomfortable especially when he refused rides from well-meaning strangers. Police officers often mistook him for a vagabond without any means of transportation. Crapsey pointed to their crass attitudes in not allowing for the freedom of one that

---

[4] Alkalay-Gut *Alone*. p. 255.
[5] Crapsey, *Manuscript*. p. 416.
[6] Ibid., p. 422.

preferred to walk. However, he exacerbated their uneasiness by refusing to answer questions, often telling officers to mind their own business. He endured their profanity and indecent allegations. One time he was threatened with a club and dragged through the streets by his collar. When brought into the station Crapsey told the sergeant he was "a free citizen of the United States" and later that he was "a socialist lecturer." That obviously didn't help his immediate situation. When told by the sergeant he must "walk down to the railway station and set until his train came," Crapsey replied that "he would take no orders from him, and that he would sit or walk at his own will and pleasure."[7]

In October 1912, while Crapsey walked through Sullivan County preaching the gospel of socialism, he became apprised of a strike at Little Falls. The authorities were clamping down and had prohibited either public assembly or public speaking.[8] Crapsey went to the park adjoining the mill around noon and began talking to a crowd about the Sermon on the Mount.[9] But his sermon on the mount had dire political implications. He was pulled off the park bench by a police officer and taken brusquely to jail. All the way to the station a crowd accompanied them both cheering him on and jeering at the officer.[10] The press reported sympathetically that he was led off with a Bible in his hand.[11]

Crapsey was one of several socialist agitators including Mayor George Lunn of Schenectady taken into custody. All were charged with felonies, including Lunn. Judge Collins took a conciliatory stance reducing the charges to misdemeanors. The Chief of Police of Little Falls knew Crapsey and appealed to him, "Dr. Crapsey won't you please go home and stop making trouble here and we won't bring any charge against you." Crapsey retorted, "I can't go home I'm under arrest." The Judge agreed that Crapsey should leave town. Crapsey demanded to know the charges against him. The Chief wrote the words disorderly conduct against his name on a paper. The Judge then went into the courtroom and called Crapsey in. He read the charge against him and asked him how he plead. Crapsey replied, "not guilty." Judge said, "You are discharged," subsequently waving him away. Crapsey figured that was the first time he had ever heard of a defendant acquitted through his own unsupported testimony. The socialist candidate for Governor, Charles Edward Russell

---

[7] Ibid., pp. 426-7.
[8] Ibid., p. 428.
[9] *Philadelphia Press*, Oct. 20, 1912.
[10] Crapsey, *Manuscript,* p. 428.
[11] *Phila. Press,* Oct. 20, 1912.

was expected to speak in the same park. Crapsey stayed until the strike was finished before leaving town.[12]

Crapsey's high visibility provided a fortunate end to the highly volatile political situation. Others were not so lucky. Robert A, Bakeman a former clergyman from Schenectady was arrested prior to Crapsey for similarly addressing a crowd, charged with violating a city ordinance and sentenced to fifty dollars or fifty days. Bakeman took the fifty days. Though the socialist leaders complained that they were not able to speak in public, in reality the city had provided a place at Main and Second Streets for them to speak as they pleased.[13]

Crapsey's conversion to socialism was now complete. But his public espousal of socialistic causes created a rift in his following. An exodus of prominent backers from his lecture series occurred. Crapsey experienced snubbing by individuals he had socialized with for years. He was a member of several clubs in Rochester. One was a group of sixteen elite men who initiated him after his notoriety had made him a national celebrity. The "Fortnightly Club" met every other week from October through April. The club included the President of the University of Rochester, Rush Rhees. It also included physicians and members of the legal profession. There were wealthy businessmen like Joseph T. Alling of Alling and Cory paper manufacturers, and highly visible men in the religious community like Father Edward J. Hanna, professor at St. Bernard's Roman Catholic Seminary.[14]

Crapsey dined often with the men. Afterwards they shared papers, held round table discussions and debated subjects of current interest such as scientific developments, politics, religion or other topics. But when Crapsey became an apologist for socialism in a group inhabited primarily by elite capitalists, he soon realized the tentativeness of his colleagues. Crapsey presented one paper on David Lloyd George's speech before the House of Lords in April of 1909, and another on the "Program of the English Labor Party." This time the bellicosity of the group reached a crescendo. One member, Mr. Mathews, a hardware merchant and disciple of Herbert Spencer, shook his finger in Crapsey's face extolling the virtues of the capitalistic system. Other controversies surfaced as well,

---

[12] Crapsey, *Manuscript,* p. 428.
[13] *Phila. Press*, Oct 20, 1912.
[14] Crapsey, *Manuscript, pp. 437-9.*

between himself and Father Edward J. Hanna, which inevitably ended in a subdued manner.[15] He eventually left the club.[16]

By the end of the year he applied for the newly created position of parole officer at the State Farm at Industry, New York. At age sixty- five, Crapsey wanted to increase his workload. He also felt responsible for supporting his family as things were changing at the Brotherhood especially concerning his marketability on the lecture circuit.

Crapsey was not beyond using whatever means necessary to get the job. He used his Civil War experience as a means of obtaining the employment.[17] He conceived of the job from an idealistic, humanitarian perspective. He believed that if you treated people right, regardless of what they had done, they would reciprocate. Moreover, he believed that the exposure of the delinquents to his civility would make a positive difference towards their subsequent rehabilitation.[18]

Crapsey continued to write as well. He was included in a short publication on the Socialization of Money, published by the Girard publishing group. Girard, Kansas was the home of J.A. Wayland who had established what was then considered the most widely distributed weekly socialistic newspaper in the world entitled Appeal to Reason, and the Coming Nation. Wayland published a variety of Little Blue Books, with contributions as perplexing as George Bernard Shaw's Socialism for Millionaires. Crapsey added to a short series written by Daniel De Leon, H.G. Wells, Margaret Sanger and George R. Kirkpatrick. His contribution taken from his most recent book The Rise of the Working Class, was entitled, "The Curse of Poverty." In it Crapsey declared nature was not cruel to the poor but it was man's economic system that excluded some from partaking in a decent lifestyle.[19]

Crapsey was eventually hired as a parole officer. He considered his experiences very valuable. After the Board of Directors at both Elmira Reformatory and Industry balked at his appointment he finally received a field position. He was responsible for visiting parolees and bringing back

---

[15] Blake McKelvey "Origins of the Rochester Public Library: Rochester's Literary and Book Clubs." Ruth Rosenberg Naparsteck ed. In *Rochester History* Vol. XLVIII Jan. and April 1986, Nos. 1 & 2.

[16] Crapsey, *Manuscript,* p. 441.

[17] Letter from A.S. Crapsey to Superintendent of the State Farm at Industry Nov. 9, 1912. In A.H. Crapsey Jr. Collection.

[18] Crapsey, *Manuscript,* pp. 429-436.

[19] A.S. Crapsey "The Curse of Poverty," in Daniel De Leon's *The Socialization of Money* Girard, Kansas, People's Pocket Series, 1921.

parole violators. The State Agricultural and Industrial School of New York at Industry later employed him. The school was a penal institution for male juvenile delinquents under the age of sixteen committed by the courts until the age of twenty-one. Crapsey's area of jurisdiction was the Albany district, extending from Montauk Point on Long Island to the St. Lawrence River, encompassing the Adirondack and the Catskill Mountains.[20]

Crapsey heard dreadful stories about the ferocity of the boys and was told to put them in irons and fetters until he returned them to the State School. He wrote about one experience entitled Holy Terror. He related how he went to the police station in the boy's hometown to try to locate him. The officers were physically huge, like giants. All were over six feet tall and weighed over two hundred pounds. They laughed that Crapsey would never retrieve this boy as he had previously jumped through a window breaking all the glass as he fled from his pursuers. He was truly a holy terror. Crapsey nervously went to the violator's home wondering what he would find there. What he found was a short, skinny redheaded Irish kid weighing about 80 pounds and not taller than four foot three. He trembled in his nightshirt and as he watched him sleep in the seat before him, on the way back to Industry. Crapsey wondered who was the real holy terror, the boy or the six-foot, two hundred pound policeman with the club.[21]

Another time Crapsey told of an overgrown Italian-American boy with a blind eye whom he had taken from a jail. He promised to go all the way back to the school at Industry with Crapsey. Crapsey demonstrated his trust by not handcuffing him and allowing him the liberty of staying alone in a hotel while Crapsey ran an errand. He felt his trust was rewarded when he was still there when Crapsey came back. They arrived in Rochester at an hour when they couldn't go on to Industry, still about thirteen miles south of the city. So Crapsey put the boy up for the night in the Salvation Army lodging house. When he returned for him in the morning the boy was gone. Crapsey feared for his job. Fortunately, he worked for a kind man, Mr. David Bruce. A year later the police wired Crapsey that they had apprehended the boy. Crapsey asked if there were any new charges against him. The police responded there were not.

---

[20] A.S. Crapsey, "Experiences of a Parole Officer." In *Standard* Nov. 1917 Vol. IV. No. 2, p. 49.

[21] Story related in Crapsey, A.S. "Experiences of a Parole Officer- The Runaway," in *Standard* Jan. 1918, Vol. IV, No. 4, p. 106. Also in Crapsey, *Manuscript*, pp. 431-2.

Crapsey told them to release the boy. The last Crapsey had heard about the boy, he was a political leader in the Republican Party in Westchester County.[22]

Crapsey believed that the time he had spent with the young man had helped to rehabilitate him. The boy was really good after all and now he could prove it. Time had exonerated him. Crapsey also told of a boy who had been required to stay after school and had refused to do what the teacher asked of him. When the teacher came at him with a ruler to beat him, the child pulled his jack-knife on her. Crapsey realized that such a serious charge would be a grave handicap for the rest of the boy's life. The boy was so remorseful about his wrongdoing that he burned his jack-knife. Crapsey declared that burning one's jack-knife was a sign of real repentance for a young boy. Consequently, Crapsey went to all the parties involved in the dispute. He found that the school was a fire and poisonous gas trap. The unventilated classroom subjected the children to the breathing of carbonic gas. Crapsey petitioned the court to have the boy released if the school agreed to take him back. He appealed to the teacher and the principal about the boy and to the Board of Education about the school. The boy was subsequently released and the school board members agreed to build a new schoolhouse. Crapsey acknowledged that because of his assistance the boy considered Crapsey a god.[23]

Crapsey used his position as a parole officer to sell his radical humanitarian agenda. He wrote to the press about the terrible psychological cost of carrying out the death penalty. He stated that the warden of Sing Sing, Thomas Mott Osborne, was a man who suffered greatly inside. He noted how the dreadful act of executing people at Sing Sing had "seared his soul." If he continued in that capacity it would surely mean the death of him. A bill pending before the assembly of the State of New York called for the abolition of capitol punishment. Crapsey attended a legislative meeting in March of 1915, in which Osborne spoke on behalf of the legislation. Three men had just been put to death the week before. Crapsey spoke about the effects of personal guilt on Osborne and the general inhumanity of the death penalty.[24]

Crapsey worked for six years as a parole officer. He considered his work significant because of his unique perspective on property and personal ethics. And yet, he decried the fact that the state had never even

---

[22] Ibid.

[23] A.S. Crapsey, "Experiences of a Parole Officer- The Desperado, " in *Standard* 4 (1917/1918) 190.

[24] *NY Times* Mar. 4, 1915 7:2.

asked him to share his experiences in order to help others with similar problems. He finally gave up, as with his advanced age and his radical outlook he could no longer countenance all that was wrong with the system. One incident in particular persuaded Crapsey that he had had enough. As he brought yet another unfortunate boy to Industry on the charges of truancy, Crapsey realized that this child was not the kind to sit in a classroom. He was an extremely active boy. Crapsey usually dealt with the boys by not shackling them. He felt if he demonstrated trust in them, he could expect it back from them. On the train to Rochester however, Crapsey fell asleep in the seat facing the child. The boy silently stole off into the bathroom, locked the doors, forced open the window and jumped from the train at forty miles per hour. Crapsey expected to hear about how his mangled body was found and his life had been wasted over such a trivial charge. However, the boy was never heard of again. It bothered Crapsey that this child desired his freedom so much that he would subject himself to the possibility of death to achieve it. For Crapsey, the system was corrupt and he had become a part of it.[25]

Crapsey stated cynically that from his perspective as a parole officer the State of New York should be congratulated for their role in developing a near perfect system for the continuation of crime. Crapsey viewed crime as of two types, one against person and the other against property. Crimes against property outnumbered those against persons ten to one. Crapsey believed that over fifty per cent of the population of the state was disinterested in the preservation of property rights because they didn't own anything. From Crapsey's perspective poverty caused crime. Moreover, the system perpetuated itself, often keeping an individual in the system for life.[26]

Crapsey turned to a completely radical agenda teaching the sociology of both Marx and Morgan. Crapsey commended Morgan in particular. His famous treatise on Ancient Society inspired Crapsey. Morgan explained that the effects of property ownership, management and diversification had become an unmanageable power. The time would come nevertheless, when humanity would rise up in its intelligence and gain the advantage over the direction of the state in relation to how it protects property. The interests of society were more important than those of the individual and the two must be brought together into a harmonious relationship. The amassing of property should not be the goal or the conclusive end of

[25] Crapsey, *Manuscript*, pp. 233-4.
[26] Ibid. p. 435.

human progress. That would end in self-destruction. Man would evolve to a higher level. For Morgan that meant,

> Democracy in government, brotherhood in society, equality in rights and privileges and universal education foreshadow the next higher plane of society to which experience, intelligence and knowledge are steadily tending. It will be a revival in a higher form of the liberty, equality and fraternity of the ancient gentes.[27]

After reading Morgan's book Crapsey declared that he would devote the rest of his life to achieving the kind of future that Morgan anticipated.[28] Crapsey also related to Morgan in his own way. Morgan's humanistic ethos affirmed a moral didacticism that was to Crapsey essentially religious. He considered Morgan "a modern prophet." Crapsey wrote that all the sacred institutions once considered as guarded by divine jealousy were the outcome of social processes. Just as the contemporary human mind and body were the result of evolution so were the social institutions that existed.[29]

Like Morgan, Crapsey's evolutionary perspectives were mutually concerted. But Crapsey went beyond intellectual agreement with Morgan; he revered him. At a joint meeting of the Rochester Historical Society and the Rochester Academy of Science, commemorating the ninety-seventh anniversary of the birth of Lewis Henry Morgan, Crapsey stated,

> Morgan has all the characteristics of a saint; his simplicity, his gentleness, his ardor for justice, mercy and truth all place him in the ranks of those rare spirits whose mission it has been to not only to make men wise but more to make men good. No one can come into contact with the spirit of Morgan without having toward that man the feeling of adoration which the Catholic has for the saint. One is inspired with the desire to erect some memorial that will spread abroad the knowledge of his sacred presence in our midst.[30]

Crapsey's religion was now socialism and humanism. He found that his lecture audiences began to change dramatically from the upper classes

---

[27] Quoted from L.H. Morgan *Ancient Society* Tucson: Univ. of Arizona Press, 1985 p. 552.
[28] Crapsey *Manuscript*, p. 414.
[29] A.S. Crapsey *Lewis Henry Morgan, Scientist, Philosopher, Humanist* Rochester: Rochester Historical Society, 1923.
[30] Ibid. p. 25.

to workingmen and women. The proletariat as Crapsey now termed them, started to actively support his role in the community. A third book came from another series of lectures on social issues entitled The Rise of the Working Class. Crapsey wrote that it was favorably received and widely commented on. He pointed to several reviews on the publication. One stated that Crapsey was advanced beyond other scholarship on the subject. Two chapters "The Downfall of the Father" and "The Responsibility of the Mother" evaluated how the modern family was disintegrating due to modern industrialization problems. He also wrote a chapter on prostitution entitled, "The Out-Family Woman." The reviewer stated that the book made people face the facts. It was unsettling and required deep thinking about important subjects.[31]

Crapsey reveled in the fact that he received so many favorable responses to his book and stated, "he did not recall a single drastic criticism."[32] Nevertheless, they were available had Crapsey looked. One rather harsh critic stated,

> The book is uncritical, excessively hortatory, and fundamentally narrow. It is a shallow stream of thought, and one strikes constantly against the rocks- or shall we call them pebbles- of an almost catholic unacquaintance with economic science.[33]

Released at the onset of the First World War Crapsey believed by the time of his autobiography that it had yet to be fully recognized. But Crapsey's radicalism was simply no longer in vogue after the war. Nor did his influence on popular culture through his encouragement of ethical thinking carry through to the academia that he held in such high esteem.[34] He wrote with pride how the book was subsequently "martyred" along with many others that were burned by the Loyal Legion in Seattle, Washington.[35]

---

[31] Article from the *Milwaukee Journal* recorded in Crapsey, *Manuscript,* pp. 412-13.

[32] Ibid. *Manuscript,* p. 412.

[33] Weyl, W.E. Review of A.S. Crapsey's *Rise of the Working Class* In *American Economic Review* 5: 1/ 2(1915) 379.

[34] Crapsey wrote several articles in the journal *Standard* stating on its cover that it was "Published to Promote Ethical Thinking & to Encourage Better Ways of Living." It was issued by the American Ethical Union, 2 West 64th St. NYC. He also spoke at many of their lecture platforms.

[35] Crapsey, *Manuscript,* pp. 414-15.

Crapsey continued to write and speak but his income was irregular and proceeds often went to the Brotherhood to promote charitable causes. Before long, the Brotherhood itself eventually became a casualty of his radicalism. By 1914, his public lecture series had utterly failed.[36] As Crapsey went out on the road with his socialistic message his wealthy benefactors deserted him. His itinerant preaching of socialism failed to bring in enough income making it necessary to rely upon his employment as a parole officer. However, Crapsey was nearing seventy years old of age and could no longer effectively chase youths all over New York State. Fortunately, the Adelaide T. Crapsey dress factory was producing income. Paul, the general manager diligently worked to keep his parents' vision alive.[37]

Crapsey initially tried to keep America out of the First World War by appealing to the nation's values. He wrote that three positions of the national government were contrary to the teachings of Jesus. The use of physical force, the idea of human enmity and the idea of preparedness were contrary to the teachings of Christ. He used the scriptures to support his argument. But he also saw a moral hypocrisy in the church's support of the nation's militarism. Considering the double standards he observed Crapsey stated that the people must either desert their religious system or use their religion to return to a social condition prior to the development of structured Christianity. The choice was between the real Christianity or the tyranny of the state.[38]

However, when the war came the Crapseys supported the effort. They helped with a funding effort for the Red Cross and with donations to the American Fund for the French Wounded. Crapsey remained a patriotic supporter of his country during wartime. He still believed in the concept of a just war. Arthur, now in his twenties, entered the military like two of his brothers before him.[39] Crapsey split with other socialistic, Christian leaders. He stood against Rauschenbusch's pacifism as the nation entered the war.[40]

Crapsey later published a pamphlet reprinting General Pershing's Thanksgiving Address to the American Expeditionary Forces. It was

---

[36] *NY Times* Dec. 4, 1916 13:3.

[37] Ibid.

[38] A. S. Crapsey, "Militarism and the Church" in *American Academy of Political and Social Science, Annals* 66(1916: July) 247-9.

[39] A.H. Crapsey Jr. Collection,. Scrapbooks.

[40] Dores Robinson Sharpe *Walter Rauschenbusch* New York: The MacMillan Company, 1942.

published in the Rochester Democrat & Chronicle on December 1, 1918 and again in brochure form. It was signed Algernon Sidney and Adelaide Trowbridge Crapsey. The back held the inscription:

> With Reverence for the Dead, with Gratitude to the Living, who on the field of battle have won a lasting peace for the world, this immortal address of General Pershing is republished as a memorial of their historic sacrifice.[41]

The First World War tempered the optimism of the humanists. Nevertheless, Crapsey continued to explain the world through his elaborate but contrived dogmatic. He believed that society could only advance by instituting and protecting a system of morality based upon reason. Ethical culture could be achieved through the rationale of men who could order human relations like an electrical circuit or any other technological development. The science of ethics would establish and teach true morality through the study of human relations. Ethical societies were presently being established for just that purpose. He described Felix Adler as the leader in the movement and considered his understanding of human knowledge was equivalent to Isaiah and Jesus.[42]

Crapsey identified a divergence between morality and religion. The future progress of humanity depended on the resolution of that conflict. Again, Crapsey identified the old dogmatic as the culprit, trying to have mastery over the hearts and minds of society. Billy Sunday's revival had just begun in New York City. Crapsey was disgusted with both the substance and the method of his message. He declared that Sunday needed to be contended with. He was an evil force in Crapsey's estimation threatening the welfare of society. Crapsey saw his success as merely a worldly accomplishment. He condemned his grassroots, homespun approach to Bible teaching noting that over 20,000 people listened to his message. Crapsey was appalled at his success. The people were not there to listen to the exquisite language of a Cardinal Newman or the poetic expressions of the great orators in Christendom, but to the common jargon of the saloon, the baseball field or the brothel. The response so outraged Crapsey that he was filled with horror at those who would sit under the

---

[41] Pamphlet in A.H. Crapsey Jr. Collection.

[42] A.S. Crapsey, "Revivalism, The Old, and the New Ethics." In *Standard* 3(1916/1917) 199.

man's "vile, filthy teaching" rather than subscribe to all that Crapsey held as true and decent.[43]

Crapsey recoiled with horror from contemporary revivalism. His understanding of religion was that which was "pure and undefiled." It was "To visit the fatherless and widows in their affliction and to keep himself unspotted from the world."[44] Sunday's preaching was the antithesis of all that. His ministry was a threat to all that Crapsey tried to establish through the past decades. He fumed that his ability to reach the unreachable was one of the most unfortunate facts confronting civilization. It demonstrated the spiritual, moral and intellectual degradation of society. He seethed, the evangelical church, which provided the bulwark of his support, demonstrated their blatant moral and spiritual impoverishment publicly.[45]

Sunday represented something deeply detestable in the innermost regions of Crapsey's psyche. He was the same sort of crude preacher that had made his mother faint when he consigned his dead brother to hell. Crapsey considered him "a preacher of hatred" who had nothing decent to say about man's goodness and the achievements of humanity. He was impertinent and crude, as well as ignorant. Crapsey finally found someone that was so unappealing to him that he could not restrain from personally attacking him. It was entirely unlike Crapsey to initiate such an aggressive assault. The high visibility of the evangelical functions completely nauseated him. Crapsey wrote that Sunday spoke with an unappealing voice and jumped around with foolish tricks acting like a baboon on stage. If all the high jinks were what was necessary to revive evangelical Christianity then all was lost, there was no use.[46]

Crapsey attacked the evangelical churches, holding them responsible for what their beloved evangelist was preaching. He wondered,

> do they reject the Copernican theory of the stellar universe? Do they reject the modern science of geology? Do they reject in toto the modern science of biology? If they do, then let them say so to their people, that their people may not be led astray by these errors. Do these clergy believe that all the people outside their churches are subject to the eternal tormenting wrath of their God? If they do, then let them say so; let them not hide behind the grotesque figure of this, their chosen minister.[47]

---

[43] Ibid.

[44] James 1: 27.

[45] A.S. Crapsey "Revivalism, The Old and the New Ethics." In, *Standard* 3(1916/1917), 199.

[46] Ibid.

[47] Ibid.

Crapsey stated that the Sunday's message was morally objectionable in the judgment of humanity. For Crapsey, the battle between the moral, rational man and the religious was now being decided. He spoke of warfare curiously akin to the biblical declarations of the enmity between the spirit and the world. Crapsey saw the metaphor of Christian warfare in stark, physical form personified by Sunday and the evangelical church. This was their last great resurgence.[48]

Crapsey knew about inciting human passions. He reasoned that the excitement experienced by the revivals were similar to one's deep, subconscious emotions. They were like sexual power that could be destructive. They were paralyzing and victimizing to the individual will as they deposed one's reason and left them at the mercy to their irrational inclinations.[49]

Just what exactly was the source of Crapsey's abhorrence was debatable, but not to Crapsey and certainly not to the evangelicals. They had experienced the vehemence of the world's repugnance before. Their detestation of all that Crapsey stood for had already been demonstrated albeit not without a great deal of soul-searching about the grace of God and the character of the church. Someone indeed however in this universe of polar opposites, was sincerely deceived about the truth of Christianity.

[48] Ibid.

[49] Ibid.

CHAPTER TWENTY-FIVE

"The Chariot of Israel, and the Horsemen Thereof"

Night Winds
The Old,
Old winds that blew,
When Chaos was, what do
They tell the clattered trees that I
Should weep? [1]

At the age of seventy Crapsey continued to labor with great energy. As an ex- clergyman with an interest in the ways of the gods and the ways of men, Crapsey decided to write once more about the historic development of religion in the world. His fourth book was a study of the history of various gods, including the idols of the Christians. Crapsey noted how the cults of the saints and the worship of the gods had changed through time and place. The cult of Joseph had even obscured the veneration of the Virgin in France. Crapsey wondered whether it was the fickleness of man in retrospect that they change even the veneration of those gods like we change our clothes or was there something deeper to it all? Were gods and men really creatures of fate after all?[2]

The Ways of the Gods was a Marxist interpretation of the religiosity of mankind throughout he ages. Crapsey wrote,

> I found, - or, at least, I think I found,- a necessary relation between the life of a god and the life of his people. The god of a given people is the embodiment of the economic conditions of that people, and the economic conditions determine the social and political institutions of a people. Hence it is that under certain economic conditions, with their attendant social and political institutions, a given god has sway over the religious life of a people. When these economic conditions change, this god disappears, and a new god takes his place. This principle is most perfectly

[1] *Night Winds* Poem by Adelaide Crapsey.
[2] A.S. Crapsey *The Ways of the Gods* New York: The International Press, 1921.

> illustrated in the religious history of the Western world, where the gods have followed one another in an orderly succession: their going and coming determined by the industrial development of the people and the consequent changes in social and political organization.[3]

Crapsey's purpose was to discern the natural causes behind the development of man's gods. He sought the reasons behind the different cults of saints. St. Joseph's changing status in the contemporary world inspired Crapsey to dig deeper into the processes and changes ocurring in religious life. He studied the gods of Morgan's evolutionary periods of savagery and early barbarism. Crapsey examined the gods of the Romans and the Greeks dating their ancestral origins back to the gods of the early Aryan peoples. He analyzed the decline of the Greek gods by the incursion of the gods of the Syrians and the east, and finally their overthrow by the God of the Jews. He then hypothesized that there was a transformation that took place from the Hebrew God of the Old Testament through the influence of the Greek dialectic, which eventually became the Triune God of the New Testament. He eventually brought the study back to the modern-day cults of the Virgin and the saints.[4]

The book was the culmination of Crapsey's work since his moorings were loosed from the church. It was the culmination of his new teaching through his later life. It was the dogma of socialism, evolutionary theory and scientific rationalism culminating in his concept of the new religion.

Once again however, Crapsey felt that his book experienced a similar fate. He submitted it to the publishers in the midst of the First World War. Because of their wartime commitments they were not able to consider its distribution. He then submitted the book to the Neal Publishing Company who in turn defaulted on their payments. He finally made arrangements with the International Press, and by 1921 the book was re-released. Despite the circumstances, Crapsey noted that the book's sales and positive response were satisfying. He mentioned that several reviewers had bestowed praise with their enthusiastic scrutiny upon the book. Crapsey was most pleased with his chapter on "The Degradation of the Gods." In it he described how the lust, shame and unclean faith of the Orient flourishing in Rome allowed for the reception of the Christian gospel with enthusiasm. Crapsey wrote that if one read nothing else in the

[3] Ibid.

[4] Ibid.

book except that particular chapter, it held enough value for the rest of the manuscript.[5]

One reviewer wrote the book was an astonishing study of collective psychology and how theology developed. The reviewer noted how Crapsey deduced several important suppositions through his historical evolutionary study. The reviewer wrote that Crapsey believed that the gods of mankind moved through stages until they are used up and then new ones arise and men worship them. He believed that Christianity as a true force in civilization ended at the start of the First World War.[6]
Others were less charitable. Another reviewer wrote,

> The book is a rationalistic attempt to explain the religion of Israel and the Christianity which was its successor. The attempt to explain the appearance of Jesus to Peter after His resurrection as a case of 'physic projection' is really too absurd. 'In times of cerebral excitement, when the objective mind is in abeyance, the psychic force projects the images of the subjective mind on the lenses of the eye, and the man sees what he thinks.' Rationalism is evidently more credulous than faith, and, judging from this book, has less to commend it to men of reason and insight.[7]

Crapsey's penchant for certain absurdities relegated him to a status of a kind of respectable eccentric in the religious press. At the age of seventy-five Crapsey embarked upon the most important work of his life, his autobiography. It was self-serving no doubt, and some have mentioned self-aggrandizing, in a kindly affectionate way, especially concerning his presumed significance in church history.[8] And yet, it was also an important book. It provided a personal perspective on the tremendous changes over three-quarters of a century in the American church's most unsettling period of history. Crapsey related how one man responded to the challenges of modernity amidst the erratic changes brought about by intellectual confrontations with traditional religious life.

Crapsey retired from public life after an illness in Peoria while attempting to keep up the pace of his reestablished lecture tour. He was taken to the hospital and ran a fever of 103. The next evening Crapsey

---

[5] Crapsey, *Manuscript,* p. 444.
[6] "J.C.R." *Medical World of Philadelphia* (April, 1921?). Quoted in Crapsey, *Manuscript,* pp. 445-6.
[7] *London Quarterly Review* London: The Epworth Press, 1921 Jan./ Apr. Vol. 185 5th Series 121.
[8] This was the opinion of his grandson who related the view of his family members again, in an affectionate manner.

spoke to an audience at the Universalist Church for more than an hour. Finally Crapsey's friends banded together to keep him in Rochester for the winter. He was too old to remain on the lecture circuit with the constant traveling involved. Rabbi Horace Joseph Wolf of Temple Berith Kodesh looked after Crapsey's welfare like a son might. Crapsey believed his liberal perspective and his work in the community had done much to heal the schism between Jew and Gentile. He believed that the liberal Christian and the liberal Jew had more in common than they did with the orthodox of either religion. As Rabbi Wolf called Crapsey into his office he was surprised to find his old friend, William R. Corris the manager of the Lyceum theatre there. They asked Crapsey to conduct a round table discussion and provide pastoral care for certain extreme cases that they would send to him. They offered him fifteen hundred dollars a year. Crapsey was not deceived. He realized this was their way of providing him with an income to meet his expenses and to complete his recovery. It also helped him to complete his autobiography.[9]

The round table discussions were held at the factory and at their home on Averill Avenue. One of the most memorable involved a discussion on race prejudice initiated by the Reverend James E. Rose, pastor of the Baptist Church known at the time as the colored Baptist Church. He made an impassioned plea for the intellectual education of the black man not just in the vocational arts. Two African-American physicians supported him in his entreaty, Dr. Charles T. Lunsford and Dr. V.T. Levy.[10]

Crapsey also taught a course at the Labor College on "The History of Labor." He had great fun and was encouraged about the prospects for the labor movement in the nation. Crapsey believed the movement was no longer like "blind Sampson (sic) shaking the pillars of the temple of Industry." It had grown to be led by knowledgeable, men with a sophisticated sense of history and direction for their future.[11]

When George Oppenheimer of Alfred A. Knopf Inc. finally decided to publish his autobiography the company circulated a full- page promotional story to eighteen hundred newspapers in the United States and seven hundred of their largest dealers.[12] The promotional story was entitled "Life Story of the Last of the Heretics: Dramatic Splitting of the Modern Church by Dr. Crapsey Follows Work of Famous Heretics of

---

[9] Crapsey, *Manuscript,* pp. 449-451.
[10] Ibid. pp. 451-2.
[11] Ibid. p. 452.
[12] Letter from Oppenheimer to Crapsey dated Nov. 1, 1924. In A.H. Crapsey Jr. Collection

History." In the promotion Crapsey was billed as "the first Modernist." He was elevated to a status in church history equivalent to John Hus, Martin Luther and John Calvin. He was compared with Joan of Arc considered not only a heretic but a martyr as well. The promotional story advertised what Crapsey had accomplished. It mentioned how heretics had suffered for their faith and how some had been exonerated through time. It concluded how Crapsey would also be vindicated eventually.[13]

Times would change indeed and the minds of men would move progressively on beyond the present intellectual currents, through time and space to the point of Crapsey's absolution. But in that, his ultimate prophecy, he would only be partially correct. Even in the title of his autobiography his lack of prophetic precision continued to be displayed publicly. Ironically, the church was embroiled in yet another controversy concerning heresy.

With the publication of his autobiography, Crapsey finally found real acceptance of his life and work. One reviewer wrote:

> It is Algernon Sidney Crapsey himself who invites us to analyze his career as 'the last of the heretics.' To be declared a heretic, as he was in 1906, may have caused him pain, but the sorrow of losing his office as rector of St. Andrew's, Rochester, has now become a fascinating reminiscence, of which Dr. Crapsey is no more ashamed than was Newman when he changed churches and was created a Cardinal. In fact, we have here Dr. Crapsey's 'apologia pro vita sua,' a spiritual autobiography, readable, amicably egotistic, utterly human and, like the author, humanly loveable. Dr. Crapsey has passed the allotted span of three score years and ten. His are the privileges of old age, and he writes too well to abuse them.[14]

Writers often counsel each other that to write well one must write about one's greatest passions. Crapsey had finally crafted something worthy of note because it was about his greatest passion, himself. But it was also a valuable historical account even if the old man still reveled in his excesses. His extreme behavior was somehow excusable now because of his age. But the question of significance remained. Just where did Crapsey's experience fall in the great classificatory scheme of human history? The reviewer believed that even though Crapsey considered himself as a present-day Martin Luther the passing of time has not clouded or obscured society's vision in this matter. It has allowed us to recognize what the case meant in its true proportions. The author, though

[13] Advertising promotion of Alfred A. Knopf Inc. In A.H. Crapsey Jr. Collection.
[14] *NY Times* Book Review July 13, 1924. III, 10:1.

appreciative of Crapsey's life story was hardly willing to ascribe to him the same status as a Martin Luther or even a Cardinal Newman.[15]

His life story culminated with the heresy trial. Alfred A. Knopf Inc. cut out large portions of his later years and much of his earlier ones as well. Knopf assumed that his historical significance peaked at the trial in Batavia. By the time of his autobiography Crapsey spent little time speaking of religion and the occupation of his life for over a quarter of a century. He wrote, "When I am asked in these days what my religion is, I hesitate and stumble, and men go away thinking that I have no religion." Interestingly chronicling just how far he had moved away from his earlier life of Anglo-Catholic orthodoxy Crapsey noted that he had a religion indeed. Crapsey acknowledged,

> But I have a religion and if asked to give it a name I should say I am a Pantheistic Humanist, and if one were to ask, 'What is a Pantheistic Humanist?' I should say one who believes in the divinity of a telegraph pole.[16]

This of course in reference to the remark made by Rev. John Mills Gilbert, the judge at his trial. Knopf gave Crapsey room to reply to his critics, of whom he now had an advantage over. In response to the personal criticism that Crapsey's Jesus did not have the divinity of a telegraph pole Crapsey responded displaying his special rhetorical gift:

> What is a telegraph pole? It is this tree of the forest, cut from its roots, stripped of its branches, planted firmly in the ground, with outstretched arms nailed to its trunk, and on these arms are placed the wires that carry messages of joy and sorrow, of gain and loss, from man to man all round the world.
>
> When I thought on these things I said if my Christ has in Him the divinity of a telegraph pole, then He is divine enough for me, and if I can share in that divinity I am content. Is not the telegraph pole the aptest symbol of my Master? Did He not begin as a human seed, invisible to the eye of a man? Did not that seed bury itself deep in the substance of humanity? Did it not by its own inherent strength break out from its hiding- place into the light and air of the earth? Did it not take of that light and air and change it into the flesh and blood and wisdom of a man? Did not that man become a man among men, with His relationships of son and brother, of friend and enemy? Did He not go out among His fellows speaking to them words of wisdom and comforting them in their sorrows? And when He was in the

[15] Ibid.

[16] Crapsey, *Heretics*, pp. 292-4.

> prime and glory of His manhood, was He not cut down by the ax of hate, stripped down to His nakedness and made, as it were, into a telegraph pole with outstretched arms to send out His messages of warning and encouragement, of love and peace, all around the world? And to this day is not the Cross the symbol of salvation to mankind?[17]

So Crapsey argued emphatically, to the end, that he was the "last of the heretics." He claimed that the church would not dare embark upon another such attack. Crapsey believed that society had finally learned from his case that heresy was a thing of the past. The church was a relic, a dinosaur in modern society. Crapsey noted that there were two trials with which he was tried, one in the church's court, the other in the court of the public's opinion. He argued that though the church condemned him, the public domain had exonerated him and granted him liberty. Moreover, because of the trial Episcopal priests were now free as well. The Episcopal Church would never dare to go through what they put Crapsey through again. There would never be another heresy trial in the Episcopal Church thanks to him.[18]

Crapsey cited the case of Bishop Manning of the New York Diocese against Dr. Percy Stickney Grant. Grant had preached what Crapsey had about the Virgin birth and the resurrection of Jesus but hid behind a cloud of ambiguity. When accused by the bishop of heresy he was unlike Crapsey able to discreetly find a way to maintain his covert heterodoxy. In the end, and not wanting to create a scene similar to the Crapsey debacle, the bishop simply gave Grant the benefit of the doubt. Crapsey saw himself as a "marker." He was the one who had been thrust between the old and the new. He was in his mind "the last of the heretics, the last man in any church who has been formally tried and condemned for heresy." In Crapsey's mind he had received the crown of victory and glory. He finally declared with the skill of a mature, political propagandist, that he had finally won.[19]

But Crapsey was wrong. One of Crapsey's old supporters, the ex-Bishop of Arkansas, William Montgomery Brown, was presented for heresy even after he was retired. Brown's case was similar to Crapsey's. He held Darwinian social and evolutionary views and was a Marxist like Crapsey. Brown was charged on twenty- three charges of heresy based upon quotations from his later book Communism and Christianism. The

---

[17] Ibid., pp. 292-4.
[18] *NY Times* Dec. 4, 1916 13:3.
[19] Crapsey, *Manuscript*, p. 456.

front cover of his book was adorned with a rising sun and the symbol of the Soviet Union, a hammer and sickle on it. The caption that encircled the picture read; "Banish gods from the skies and capitalists from earth."[20]

Crapsey described himself at the age of 77, as "a non-resistant communist." Crapsey believed that his communism was similar to that of the original church of the book of Acts. But Crapsey's comprehension of social order was obviously well removed from the church of Acts' way of thinking. Rather than embracing the separation of church and state that so many humanists considered the foundation of secular society, Crapsey believed that law and religion must be one. Crapsey noted how the Protestant Church was fragmented and literally crumbling all around them. The reason was simple, the conception of the universe and the teaching of the church were out of synchronism. Crapsey asked rhetorically,

> Why did the breakdown of 1914 come? It came because the world was organized on principles of competition instead of cooperation. Every nation, every man was striving to get the best of the next. In consequence it was inevitable that we went where we went and did what we did and that we are what we are. The world can only be saved as the primitive church saved it. There must, there will be a transformation without violence, by cooperation instead of competition, by the Government being the servant of the people and nothing else, by absolute liberty of thought and by pacifism, by which I mean non- resistance. State and Church must be one. State is the body, church is the soul, or, say, law is the body and religion is the soul. Law must be the religion of the future and religion the law. They must be one and indivisible.[21]

Crapsey could speak as he pleased at age seventy-seven. He did not worry about the agents of either the church or the government harassing him any more. He did however worry about his legacy. The appellation of the last of the heretics was one that he guarded with great rigor. Bishop Brown called for Crapsey via telegraph to come and testify at his trial.[22] Crapsey felt gratified to speak on behalf of the bishop who once spoke out in his defense. But what Crapsey truly wanted was proof through the exoneration of Brown that his was the last conviction for heresy. He desperately desired that legacy. It was poignant and ironic that the trial

---

[20] *NY Times* May 28, 1924 8:3.
[21] *NY Times* May 23, 1924 12:1.
[22] *NY Times* May 28, 1924. 8:3.

would happen at such an inopportune time for Crapsey, especially in light of the title of his latest book.

But Brown was convicted. He was pronounced a heretic, as Crapsey's book was still hot off the presses. Crapsey's autobiography came out in June of 1924, while Brown's conviction was in January of 1925. Fortunately Crapsey, forever given to interpretation, could do so with this situation as well. For Crapsey, all things were relative. Brown's conviction and Dr. Fosdick's calamity in the Presbyterian Church hardly produced the effect that his trial had. Therefore, in the relative romanticism of his own cosmology, he was still, the last of the heretics.

Crapsey reveled in his status. He used his notoriety to endorse those he felt would benefit the nation. Crapsey still got around, even stumping for Governor Alfred Smith's presidential nomination. He believed Smith's nomination was a breakthrough due to his Roman Catholicism. The nation had obviously turned from the old Protestant ethos that it had held so tightly from the beginning. The fact that the nation nominated a Catholic for president was evidence of a change in the social conventions. Crapsey was elated that Smith figured so prominently on the national scene. He noted how the majority of the voters in New York refused to recognize Smith's religion as a detriment. If they did they wouldn't have reelected him.[23]

At the age of 78, Crapsey wrote for *Standard* his last public utterances at the national level. He spoke of the "Depreciation of Theological Values" in terms that were both symptomatic of his advanced age and climactic of his many writings about the church. In his last statement on the religious life of his culture from his unique vantagepoint Crapsey depicted Christianity as a great dream. The Founder was "the Great Dreamer." Crapsey had sought to educate away the old dogmatic theology of the nation. He sought to disestablish it through education and rationality and establish the new in the same way. The dream metaphor was the final onslaught, relegating the old dogmatic to a status having no practical effect in Western society. Crapsey wrote; "it was empirically obvious that the rapid decline in theological values had proceeded for the past three centuries and would continue to until it would soon cease to engage the minds of rational thinkers "[24]

---

[23] Letter from A.S. Crapsey to A.E. Smith recorded in *NY Times* June 27, 1924. 6:2.

[24] Crapsey, A.S. "The Depreciation of Theological Values" In the *Standard* 11:6 (1925: Jan.) 158.

Crapsey believed that Jesus had declared Himself as the Son of God, and made that same declaration available to all men through His concept of adoption into the family of God, or the divine sonship of mankind. From Crapsey's vantagepoint that important principle was His attempt to destroy the social distinctions between the classes.

For Crapsey, Jesus was the great dreamer who became immortal through the content of His dream. The early church became the receptacle of the dream. He declared, the early church overcame through social activism while the world sold its theology. It wasn't the fear of God, but the love of the brethren that made it all work. The early social theology of the church held that belief in the Fatherhood of God and the Brotherhood of Men was what saved them and thus, they were saved.[25]

But, Crapsey demurred,

> the wide awake men of the wide- awake world rushed in, seized upon its offices, converted its riches to their own uses. These traitors to the dream of Jesus and his saints put an end to this communism and pacifism, brought back again all the evils of private property and public war; transformed Jesus into an implacable Judge, pictured by Michael Angelo (sic) as sitting at the right hand of the Father and with uplifted fist beating down sinners as they were rising from their graves. In the process of awakening, the dream of Jesus and the saints was changed into a nightmare.[26]

The world became rotten because of the selling out of the dream by covetous, religious pretenders. They cultivated the concept of hell for their own use to make merchandize of their theology. Crapsey looked at the religious history of the previous few centuries as psychologically inspired obedience through fear. Crapsey noted that they were at their theological best through the doctrinal teachings of damnation by Jonathan Edwards.[27]

Due to the new god of science, no one was doing business in the marketplace of theology any more. The gods were losing their value. It was all about the dream now, that great and altruistic notion that all men were created equal. Society must come together and free itself from all the known evils of war and prejudice of any kind, through the adherence to the great dream.[28]

He closed his treatise by writing that "men must dream the dream of Jesus, the prophets and the saints. They must envision a world where there

---

[25] Ibid.
[26] Ibid.
[27] Ibid.
[28] Ibid.

was complete equality no matter who you were or where you were from. If this dream were only shared by the churches and the synagogues theology might find a market again and the gods might revisit us once more." For Crapsey, the new social epistemology demanded it.[29]

Crapsey struggled with ill health on and off for the next several months. Nevertheless, his eightieth birthday was a happy occasion. His friends from every station and walk of life, every color and creed all came to wish him congratulations. Crapsey was quoted as saying that it was the "happiest day in his life." Hundreds either came to pay their respects or send a gift or a card to Crapsey. Ex-parishioners came, members of the Brotherhood of St. Andrew's, members of the factory, officials, friends, old acquaintances all came or got in touch with the old man.[30]

The house at 678 Averill Ave. was filled with flowers. Members of the immediate family served a great frosted cake and Crapsey's spirits were exceptionally high. His high energy level was restored and his health seemed generally good. Crapsey had become to Rochester a kind of offbeat, patron saint. The community knew him for his avuncular advice and selfless service. Crapsey spent the time at the party to reminisce about his life since the famous heresy trial. He spoke of his walking trip from New York to Rochester preaching the gospel of socialism along way. He laughed about experiences with the police in Dunkirk and Little Falls.[31]

Shortly before the end of 1927, the following statement was found in Crapsey's study concerning his belief about the death that he finally realized awaited him. He wrote,

> When I lay me down to die the angel of death shall lay on my bosom the comforting assurance that if this, my body, is to pass away, it will not pass away into nothingness; every particle of its blood and flesh and bones shall go to the building up and mayhap, the enrichment of some nobler form of life.
>
> Nor is it true that when I turn again to my earth that all my emotions cease to vibrate, and all my thoughts perish. Every pure feeling generated in and by the human soul, living or dying, joins with other drops to form the cloud that pours its cleansing water to refresh the weary earth and make the grass to grow upon the mountains and refresh the weary land.

---

[29] Ibid.
[30] News clipping in A.H. Crapsey Jr. Collection.
[31] Ibid.

> There can be no such thing as eternal death! There can only be changing forms and changing place in a changeless all in all."[32]

Perhaps Crapsey was concerned about the possibility of an eternal place of damnation after all. His thoughts betrayed the fact that he considered it. Yet, openly he rejected it. The universe, time, space, life and death were ever changing, progressive, relational and relative to Crapsey. He would not allow himself to go there mentally, at the expense of his life's work, his martyrdom and all he stood for.

Shortly before Christmas, Crapsey became suddenly ill. This time he seemed to be fading quickly. Algernon Jr. was called from New York City and Rachel now living in Sommerville, New Jersey came home as well. Adelaide worried desperately about his sinking health. After a short illness, Algernon Sidney Crapsey died at 7 A.M. at the age of 80, on the last day of the year of 1927.[33] Crapsey left his wife, two sisters, five children and six grandchildren. The Rev. Dr. Justin W. Nixon, the minister of the Brick Presbyterian Church, officiated at his funeral. It was a private affair. The pallbearers were members of the St. Andrew's Brotherhood.[34] He was cremated and his ashes placed in the family plot at Mt Hope Cemetery. There is evidence that Crapsey wanted to have Rabbi Stephen Wise of New York City officiate at his funeral. But as his name indicated, he refused to answer the requests realizing the exposure might not be good for Jews as they might be blamed for encouraging heretical beliefs.[35]

Crapsey was remembered in the press as being honest, tolerant and kind. The press noted that he fought for the truth, as he believed it. He was firm in his beliefs, yet understanding, never pushing them on anyone. He was a friend to all and a true Good Samaritan.

He was called a "practical Christian." Recalling his legendary status one account mentioned how he had taken coal and food to a needy family. It noted how he spent hours reading to blind workers, counseled prisoners and bereaved relatives and absorbed hoodlums into his night schools. The press chose to remember how he had worked tirelessly for a better city.[36]

He was remembered for establishing the first Kindergarten in Rochester and as a friend to so many notable people including George

---

[32] A.S. Crapsey in A.H. Crapsey Jr. Collection.
[33] *Rochester Times Union* Dec. 31, 1927.
[34] *NY Times* Jan. 1, 1928 19:1.
[35] A.H. Crapsey Jr. Collection.
[36] Unidentified column in A.H. Crapsey Jr. Collection.

Foster Peabody, and Seth Low of New York City, Samuel Fells of Philadelphia, John Haines Holmes, Professor Nathaniel Schmidt and William Rossiter Seward who had predeceased him. Crapsey dedicated his autobiography to Seward, writing, "My Father: My Father: The Chariots of Israel and the Horsemen Thereof."[37]

But it was his colleagues from the Ethical Society that would venerate him the most. He had been at home with them like no one else. In memory of their departed brother a memorial passage spoke of his kindly ways for which the world rewarded him by putting a star on his chest at his age and letting him run all over the countryside for truant children. He was simply, "the salt of the earth." Recalling his Napoleonic stature the writer noted when one asked if Crapsey was a small man he could only remember how he always seemed to have a "an aura of greatness" about him.[38]

One could spend years describing the ramifications of such a life. One might argue that Crapsey was only as important as his obscurity has made him out to be. Time has perhaps been less than gracious in remembrance of this extraordinary man. Crapsey desired time and the public mind to be his judge and prior to this less than perfect biography one might consider that it has been. The church of course, is still there with evangelicalism growing stronger while the liberal churches seem to decline proportionally. One must wonder who indeed was deceived through it all and yet, that begs us to both question and evaluate the life that few could hardly measure up to given the same time and circumstances. Let every man decide for himself the merit of such a man's life, his work and his values.

Crapsey's concerns at the end betrayed his thoughts of eternal consequences. Yet, he was a heretic without question. Perhaps his legacy like his life is simply that. But if we consider that to be the case we must look at the society that spawned him and consider whether the Episcopal Church and society itself for that matter has become subsequently heretical as well. We are certainly not the Christian nation we were in Crapsey's day. He was one of the conduits of progressive change that eventually led to an ever-greater societal transformation that by the end of the Scopes Trial almost twenty years later had become culturally pervasive. Nevertheless, at the onset of the new millennium, we now recognize a considerably factionalized society with the religious pendulum swinging back towards the old dogmatic. One has to wonder what

[37] Dedicatory to William Rossiter Seward A.S. Crapsey *Heretics.* Quoted from 2Kings 2:12.

[38] "News and Notes: The Late Dr. Algernon S. Crapsey; The Ethical Societies; List of Sunday Morning Addresses." In *Standard* 14:6 (Feb.: 1928) 191.

Crapsey would have thought. Perhaps his life like that old metaphoric telegraph pole, cut down and stripped of all his bark, beckons to us to recognize that he has purpose yet as well.

Crapsey's words closing his autobiography are sufficient here for the same purposes. I do not pretend to do it as well as he did, especially when it comes to writing about himself. He was a master at that. Like his daughter, let his work described by his words be the memorial of his life. After all is said and done, he would have wanted it that way:

> To speak in simple language, I am a heretic because I believe in the teaching of Jesus and do not believe in the doctrine of the Christ. I have long since lost all desire for the salvation by the blood of Christ, which the Church holds out to me. I do not want to be only a message; I want to be a pole that carries the message. Paul says that if in this life only we have hope, we are of all men most miserable. I do not think so; if I in this life can serve the purposes of the greater life, I am content. I have no desire for a heaven of robe and crown and harp and wine and song celebrating things accomplished. I do not know how it may be with others, but, as for me, I feel that I have had my full portion at the table of life. Every day for me the sun has come up and the sun has gone down. Every night for me the stars have come out into the sky and the moon in her seasons has silvered the earth. For me the snows have covered the ground in winter to keep it warm and the frost has prepared ice for me against the time of heat. For me the clouds have come with their cleansing waters and the winds with their cooling breath. Birds have nested in my garden and made my home vocal with their music. For me the flowers have bloomed, the trees fruited and the grapes have been purple in the cluster. I have known a father's companionship and a mother's love. I have grown up in the company of brothers and sisters; I have been enriched by the affection of wife and children; I have friends who have loved me beyond my deserving and enemies whom I have learned to love. I have been the heir of the ages. The wisdom of the wise has been mine and the song of the poet; my vision has been enlightened by the genius of the artist and my hearing attuned by the skill of the musician. It has been my lot to encourage the living and to comfort the dying. I have known the inspiration of joy and the discipline of sorrow.
>
> And besides all this, for nearly fourscore years it has been my high privilege to stand at the wayside of Life and see the Gods go by.
> It is enough.
> And now am I come to the uttermost marge of the shores of time: Standing on its sands, looking out over the ocean of Eternity, the waters of which are cold on my feet, I am watching the Sun go down; I am content.

> If, however, there is toil and care for me in the Great Beyond, I do not wish to shirk
> it.[39]

Crapsey's poem closed his autobiography and underscored his later beliefs:

Have I my work, out yonder
Where silence reigns supreme;
Have I my task, I wonder,
To pull against the stream?

Am I to do God's thinking,
With Him to work and plan;
From toil nor sorrow shrinking
As we build the soul of man?

Is my task in His vineyard
To dig and plant and prune;
To weigh upon His steelyard
His grapes in heat of noon?

Am I to fetch and carry
To workmen on His wall;
And will the task I marry
My energy enthrall?

Is there a God out yonder,
Sore troubled and beset;
In waters doth He flounder,
Is He faint, cold and wet?

Doth He cry to me for aid
Across the sea of doubt;
Must I Death's waters wade,
That I may help Him out?

Is there a God who needs me?
Then let Him tell me so,
When from this flesh Death frees me,
I'm His for weal and woe.

---

[39] A.S. Crapsey *Heretics* (New York, 1924) pp. 294- 7.

I care not for His heaven,
I do not fear His hell;
But if to me is given
His work, then all is well.

SELAH[40]

[40] Ibid.

WORKS CITED

Achtemeier, Paul J. ed. *Harper's Bible Dictionary* San Francisco: Harper & Row, 1985.

Ahlstrom, Sidney *A Religious History of the American People* New Haven: Yale University Press, 1972.

Albright, Raymond, W. *Focus on Infinity: The Life of Phillips Brooks* New York: The Macmillan Co., 1961.

Alkalay- Gut, Karen *Alone in the Dawn* Athens: University of Georgia Press, 1988.

"Another Open Letter, 'James A. Dormer of Buffalo Catholic Truth Society in Sympathy with Dr. Crapsey.'" Oct. 30, 1901. Publication unknown. Arthur H. Crapsey Collection, Rare Books Dept. Rush Rhees Library, Univ. of Rochester, Rochester, New York.

Armetrout, Don S. and Slocum, Robert Boak (eds). *Documents of Witness: A History of the Episcopal Church 1782- 1985.* New York: Church Hymnal Corp., 1994.

Bailey, William J. *St. Andrew's Brotherhood Organized by Dr. A.S. Crapsey, Origin and History from 1880-1930.* Rochester: St. Andrew's Brotherhood, 1930.

Birney, James Gillespie *The American Churches, The Bulwarks of American Slavery* Concord, New Hampshire: P. Pillsbury, 1885.

Book of Common Prayer and Administration of the Sacraments and Other Rites and Ceremonies of the Church According to the Use of the Protestant Episcopal Church in the United States of America. New York: Oxford University Press, 1928 reprinted from 1789 edition.

Brisbane, William Henry *An Eulogium of the Life and Character of the Late Hon. Thomas Morris* Cincinnati: L.-Hommedieu, 1845.

Brooks, Phillips "Essays and Addresses" In Raymond W. Albright *Focus on Infinity: The Life of Phillips Brooks* New York: The Macmillan Co., 1961.

Burrows, G. Sherman *The Diocese of Western New York 1897-1931* Buffalo: The Diocese of Western New York, 1935.

Butler, Diana Hochstedt *Standing Against the Whirlwind, Evangelical Episcopalians in Nineteenth Century America* New York: Oxford Univ. Press, 1995.

"The Cathedral Chimes" *Trinity Cathedral Parish* (Mar., 1893).

Chorley, E. Clowes *Men and Movements in the American Episcopal Church* New York: Charles Scribner's Sons, 1946.

Chronological Record Rochester: Calvary-St. Andrew's Church publication (no date).

The Churchman "In Memorium, June 23, 1898, Ruth Elizabeth Crapsey." In Arthur Crapsey Jr. Collection, Rush Rhees Library, Univ. of Rochester, Rochester, New York.

—. Column by Rev. Dr. Van Allen (Dec. 24, 1905).

—. Column, Standing Committee considering presentment against A.S. Crapsey (Feb. 3, 1906).

—. Column, compilation of quotes from various newspapers and magazines concerning the Crapsey case (May 12, 1906).

—. Column concerning opinions of the trial by Crapsey's supporters. (May 26, 1906).

—. Column, compilation of secular newspaper accounts of Crapsey verdict. (May 26, 1906).

—. Column, "Dr. Crapsey's Appeal." (June 16, 1906). (11).

—. Editorial concerning Crapsey Case (Feb. 24, 1906).

—. Editorial quote from *Harper's Weekly* April 7, 1906, (Apr. 14, 1906). (11).

—. Editorial concerning Crapsey verdict. (May 19, 1906).

—. Editorial (Apr. 28, 1906).

—. Letter to the editor by A.S. Crapsey (Jan. 6, 1906).

—. Letter to the editor by John Williams of Omaha, Nebraska Vol. XCIII No. 5, (Feb. 3, 1906).

—. Letter to the editor (Feb. 24, 1906).

—. Letter to the editor responding to Seth Low's letter to editor. (Mar. 17, 1906) (8).

—. Letter to the editor by Seth Low (Apr. 7, 1906). (15).

—. Letter to the editor by Alexander Mackay- Smith. (Apr. 21, 1906). (15).

—. Letter to the editor (author unknown) concerning Crapsey verdict. (May 19, 1906).

—. Letter to the editor from John P. Peters concerning the Crapsey verdict. (May 19, 1906).

—. Letter to the editor from William A. Guerry. (June 23, 1906). (18).

—. Open letter from J. Lewis Parks to A.S. Crapsey asking for clarification of his views. (Nov. 25, 1905).

—. Sermon of Dr. Morgan Dix (Feb. 17, 1906).

Church Standard Column, Standing Committee considering presentment against A.S. Crapsey (Jan. 27, 1906).

—. Editorial (Oct. 7,1905).

—. Editorial (Oct. 14, 1905).

—. Editorial concerning Crapsey Case XCIII No. 5 (Feb. 3, 1906).

"Coadjutor-Bishop of Diocese of Nebraska" Subtitled "Rev. Algernon S. Crapsey, Rector of St. Andrew's Church, May be Appointed to that Position by Episcopal Diocesan Council of Nebraska" Arthur H. Crapsey Jr. Collection, Scrapbooks, Rare Books Dept. Rush Rhees Library, Univ. of Rochester, Rochester, New York.

Courtney, Janet E. *Free Thinkers of the Nineteenth Century* Freeport, New York: Books for Libraries Press Inc., 1967.

Crapsey, Adelaide "The Open Road" Valedictory in *Kemper Hall Kodak* Vol. IV No. 9 Kenosha, Wisconsin: June, 1897.

—. "Immortal Residue" Poem in Karen Alkalay- Gut's *Alone in the Dawn* Athens: Univ. of Georgia, 1988.

—. *Night Winds* (Poem) In Arthur H. Crapsey Jr. Collection. Rare Books Dept. Rush Rhees Library, Univ. of Rochester, Rochester, New York.

Crapsey, Adelaide Trowbridge Letter to Dr. John Lowe. October 8, 1948. In Adelaide Crapsey Papers, Rochester Public Library, Rochester, New York.

Crapsey, Algernon Sidney *Adelaide T. Crapsey March 7, 1855-1892.* Poem in Arthur H. Crapsey Jr. Collection Rare Books Dept. Rush Rhees Library, Univ. of Rochester, Rochester, New York.

—. "Aloofness of the Churches from the Modern Spirit." Review of *Religion and Politics* In *Literary Digest* Review Vol. XXXI [No. 15], (Oct. 7, 1905).

—. *Annual Report of the Brotherhood* (1912). In Arthur H. Crapsey Jr. Collection. Rare Books Dept., Rush Rhees Library, Univ. of Rochester, Rochester, New York.

—. *Appeal of the Rev'd Algernon Sidney Crapsey STD to the Court of Review of the Protestant Episcopal Church* New York: Thomas Whittaker, 1906.

—. *Autobiographical Unpublished Manuscript* in Arthur H. Crapsey Jr. Collection, Rare Books Dept., Rush Rhees Library, University of Rochester, Rochester, New York.

—. *Builders of the House, A History in Rime.* (Pamphlet) Published by author (Mar. 3, 1908).

—. *Constitutional Defense of the Negro by A.S. Crapsey Delivered at a Mass Meeting of Citizens in the Metropolitan AME Church, Washington, DC, December 15th, 1901.* Rochester, New York: Published by the author.

—. "The Curse of Poverty" in *The Socialization of Money* Daniel De Leon ed. Girard, Kansas, People's Pocket Series, 1921.

—. *Das Mann frum Gross-heppach, by the Ghost of Hans Breitman* (Rochester, 1901).

—. "The Depreciation of Theological Values." In *Standard* 11: 6 (Jan. 1925).

—. *The Disappointment of Jesus Christ* Rochester, New York: 1902.

—. "The Experiences of a Parole Officer" In *Standard* Vol. IV No. 2 (Nov., 1917).

—. " The Experiences of a Parole Officer- The Runaway." In *Standard* Vol. IV No. 4 (Jan., 1918).

—. "The Experiences of a Parole Officer- The Desperado." In Standard 4(1917-18).

—. *First Annual Report of the Brotherhood* (1909). Pamphlet in Arthur H. Crapsey Jr. Collection. Rare Books Dept. Rush Rhees Library, Univ. of Rochester, Rochester, New York.

—. "Historical Aspects of the Virgin Birth." In *Arena* Vol. 37 No. 209 (Apr., 1907).

—. "Honor Among Clergymen" in *Outlook* September 2, 1905.

—. and Adelaide Trowbridge Crapsey *General Pershing's Thanksgiving Address to the American Expeditionary Forces* (Pamphlet) Dec. 1, 1918. In Arthur H. Crapsey Jr. Collection. Rare Books Dept. Rush Rhees Library, Univ. of Rochester, Rochester, New York.

—. *The Greater Love* New York: Abbey Press, 1902.

—. *The Last of the Heretics* New York: Alfred Knopf, 1924.

—. *Lewis Henry Morgan, Scientist, Philosopher Humanist* (Pamphlet) Rochester: Rochester Historical Society, 1923.

—. *The Life and Ministry of Sarah Wisner Thorne: The Story of a Simple Life* New York: Thomas Whittaker, 1900.

—. *Meditations on the Five Joyful Mysteries: Together with a Letter Dedicatory to Mother Superior of the Sisters of Saint Mary* New York: James A. Pott & Co.Publishers, 1888.

—. "Militarism and the Church." In *American Academy of Political and Social Science Annals* 66 (July, 1916).

—. *Nan Connors* (Poem) in Arthur H. Crapsey Jr. Collection, Rare Books Dept. Rush Rhees Library, Univ. of Rochester, Rochester, New York.

—. *Proceedings Upon the Trial and Appeal of the Rev. Algernon Sidney Crapsey* New York: Thomas Whittaker, 1906.

—. *The Rebirth of Religion* New York: John Lane Co., 1907.

—. *Religion and Politics* New York: Whittaker, 1905.

—."Revivalism, The Old, and The New Ethics" In *Standard* 3(1916/17).

—. *The Rise of the Working Class* New York: The Century Co., 1914.

—. *Voice in the Wilderness, Being a Plea for the Restoration of Primitive Christianity* New York: J. Potts & Co., 1897.

—. *The Ways of the Gods* New York: The International Press, 1921.

Crapsey, Arthur H. Sr. (Song). "A Wet Sunday" (Oct. 20, 19067). In Scrapbooks, Arthur H. Crapsey Jr. Collection Rare Books Dept. Rush Rhees Library, Univ. of Rochester, Rochester, New York.

Current Literature editorial XXXIX (Nov.1905).

"Death comes to J.H. Rochester." (Oct. 21, 1902). In Arthur H. Crapsey Jr. Collection, Rare Books Dept. Rush Rhees Library, Univ. of Rochester, Rochester, New York.

Debate Series Vol. 1. "Did Jesus Really Live?" A debate held in Orchestra Hall, Chicago. (Jan. 21, 1908). Stemway Hall, Chicago: Original Research Society, 1908.

Delaney, John S. *Dictionary of Saints* New York: Doubleday, 1980.

DeMille, George E. *The Episcopal Church since 1900: A Brief History* New York: Morehouse- Gorham Co., 1955.

Diocesan Journal Buffalo: The Diocese of Western New York, 1890.

Dix, Morgan *History of the Parish of Trinity Church in the City of New York Vols. I- IV.* New York: Putnam, 1898- 1950.

Dix, Morgan ed. *A History of the Parish of Trinity Church in the City of New York Vol. IV.* New York: G.P. Putnam's Sons, The Knickerbocker Press, 1906.

"Dr. Crapsey in Washington, Says the United States is Still Struggling with Slave Power." Scrapbook #7, in Arthur H. Crapsey Jr. Collection, Rare Books Dept. Rush Rhees Library, Univ. of Rochester, Rochester, New York.

"Dr. Crapsey's Protest" Oct. 20, 1901. In Arthur H. Crapsey Jr. Collection, Rare Books Dept. Rush Rhees Library, Univ. of Rochester, Rochester, New York.

Duffy, Mark A. ed. *The Episcopal Diocese of Massachusetts 1784-1984: A Mission to Remember, Proclaim, and Fulfill* Boston: The Episcopal Diocese of Massachusetts, 1984.

Echo (Hobart College Yearbook of 1902), Geneva, New York: Hobart College, 1902.

Eclectic (Boston: January, 1893).

"Emancipated Unity" Newspaper Article in Scrapbooks, Arthur H. Crapsey Jr. Collection, Rush Rhees Library, Univ. of Rochester, Rochester, New York.

"Episcopal Mission Begun" Subtitled, "Mr. Crapsey Draws a Lesson from the Burnt District." In Arthur H. Crapsey Jr. Collection Scrapbooks

Rare Books Dept. Rush Rhees Library, Univ. of Rochester, Rochester, New York.

Ewer, Ferdinand Cartwright *Four Conferences Touching the Operation of the Holy Spirit* Milwaukee: The Young Churchman, 1880.

Five Lectures Upon the Church Delivered at Trinity Church, New Haven, Connecticut, Before the Church Club of the Diocese of Connecticut. New Haven: The Tuttle, Morehouse and Taylor Press, 1897.

Foreman, Edward R. ed. *A Centennial History of Rochester, New York* Vol. III Rochester: Rochester Public Library, 1933.

Fox, William L. *William L. Sperry, The Quandaries of the Liberal Protestant Mind, 1914- 1939.* New York: Peter Lang, 1991.

Garraty, John A. and Carnes, Mark C. (eds.) *American National Biography* Oxford: Oxford Univ. Press, 1999.

"Gifts for the Beloved Rector of St. Andrew's Church." (newspaper column, no date) In Arthur H. Crapsey Jr. Collection, Rare Books Dept., Rush Rhees Library, Univ. of Rochester, Rochester, New York.

Greenleaf, Richard *Algernon Sidney Crapsey and the Beginnings of St. Andrew's Parish, Rochester, New York* Rochester: A Paper Read at the Annual Parish Meeting, November 28, 1966.

Guelzo, Alan C. *For the Union of Evangelical Christendom: The Irony of the Reformed Episcopalians* Union Park, Pennsylvania: Penn State Univ. Press, 1994.

Haselmayer, Louis August *Lambeth and Unity* New York: Morehouse-Gorham, 1948.

Hatch, Nathan O. *The Democratization of American Christianity* New Haven: Yale University Press, 1989.

Hayes, Charles Wells *The Diocese of Western New York: History and Recollections* Rochester, New York: Scrantom Wetmore & Co., 1904.

Hilary, Sister Mary CSM *Ten Decades of Praise: The Story of the Community of Saint Mary During its First Century: 1865 to 1965.* Racine, Wisconsin: DeKoven Foundation, 1965.

"His Anniversary. Dr. Crapsey Twenty-Five Years with St. Andrew's" (newspaper column, no date) In Arthur H. Crapsey Jr. Collection Rare Books Dept. Rush Rhees Library, Univ. of Rochester, Rochester, New York.

Historical Time Line Published by Calvary St. Andrew's Parish, Rochester, New York.

Hobart College Catalog (1998- 1999). Geneva, New York: Hobart and William Smith Colleges, 1998.

Hofstadter, Richard *The Age of Reform* New York: Vintage Books, 1955.

Hughes, W.D.F. "An Agreement on Fundamentals: The Huntington-Manning Correspondence on the Crapsey Case." In *Historical Magazine of the Protestant Episcopal Church* 25: 3 (September, 1956).

Huntington, William Reed *The Church Idea* New York: E.P. Dutton & Co., 1870.

—. *The Peace of the Church* New York: Scribner's Sons, 1893.

Jacob T. Crapsey Obituary. In Arthur H. Crapsey Jr. Collection, Rare Books Dept., Rush Rhees Library, University of Rochester, Rochester, New York.

Jansen, Hugh M. Jr. "Algernon S. Crapsey: Heresy at Rochester" in *American Religious Heretics* George M. Shriver ed. New York: Abingdon Press, 1966.

Kasler, Dirk *Max Weber, An Introduction to His Life and Work.* Chicago: Univ. of Chicago Press, 1988.

Keble, John "National Apostasy" In *Sermons, Academical and Occasional* Oxford: John Henry Parker, 1847.

"The Last of the Heretics." Advertising Promotion from Alfred Knopf Inc. In Arthur H. Crapsey Jr. Collection. Rare Books Dept. Rush Rhees Library, Univ. of Rochester, Rochester, New York.

Lewis, Leicester L. ed. *A History of the Parish of Trinity Church in the City of New York Vol. V.* New York: Compiled for Trinity Church by Columbia University Press, 1950.

Life Cartoon Vol. XLVIII (Dec. 20, 1906).

The Living Church Column, speech by Bishop Walker XXXIV No.1. (Nov. 4, 1905).

—. Column, "Is There No Evidence Against Dr. Crapsey?" Vol. XXXIV No. 4 (Nov. 18, 1905).

—. Column, "The Rochester Scandal." Vol. XXXIV No. 4 (Nov. 25, 1905).

—. Column, consecration of Christ Church Rochester, New York Address by Bishop Walker. Vol. XXXIV No. 10, (Jan. 6, 1906).

—. Column, the resignation of Rev. Alexander. Vol. XXXIV No. 13 (Jan. 27, 1906).

—. Column "Declaration on New Testament Criticism and Other Subjects." XXXIV No. 14 (Feb. 3, 1906).

—. Column, compilation of quotes from national newspapers concerning the Crapsey Case XXXIV No. 22 (Apr. 7, 1906).

—. Column, compilation of quotes from national newspapers concerning the Crapsey Case XXXIV No. 25 (Apr. 21, 1906).

—. Column, compilation of quotes from national newspapers concerning the Crapsey Case XXXIV No. 26 (Apr. 28, 1906).

—. Column, compilation of quotes from various newspapers concerning the Crapsey Case XXXV No. 1 (May 5, 1906).
—. Column, opinions about the Crapsey verdict. XXXV No. 3 (May 19, 1906).
—. Editorial concerning Crapsey Case. XXXIV No. 20. (Mar. 17, 1906).
—. Editorial concerning the heresy trial (summary). XXXV No.1 (May 5, 1906).
—. Letter to the editor from Rev. Edwin S. Hoffman (Nov. 25, 1905).
—. Letter to the editor from William Wilberforce Newton XXXIV No. 20, (Mar. 17, 1906).
—. Letter to the editor from F. Washburn of Newburgh, New York. XXXV No. 3 (May 19, 1906).
—. Letter to the editor from John M. Peacocke MD concerning the Crapsey verdict. XXXV No. 3 (May 19, 1906).
—. Open Letter from Bishop Gailor to editor (Nov. 25, 1905).
—. Open Letter from George Foster Peabody in support of A.S. Crapsey Vol. XXXIV No. 10 (Jan. 6, 1906).
"Looks Like Napoleon" Subtitled Dr. Crapsey Conducting a Mission at St. James, an Eloquent Preacher. In Arthur H. Crapsey Jr. Collection, Scrapbooks,, Rare Books Dept. Rush Rhees Library, Univ. of Rochester, Rochester, New York.
Letter from A.S. Crapsey to John Henry Houghton in Arthur H. Crapsey Jr. Collection, Scrapbooks, Rare Books Dept., Rush Rhees Library University of Rochester, Rochester, New York.
Letter from A.S. Crapsey to Superintendent of State Farm for Boys at Industry (Nov. 9, 1912). In Arthur H. Crapsey Jr. Collection Rare Books Dept. Rush Rhees Library, Univ. of Rochester, Rochester, New York.
Letter concerning Crapsey's farewell address at St. Andrew's Church from *Catskill Examiner* (no date) Arthur H. Crapsey Jr. Collection, Rare Books Dept. Rush Rhees Library, Univ. Of Rochester, Rochester, New York
Letter from C.V. Evans to Adelaide Trowbridge Crapsey in Arthur H. Crapsey Jr. Collection Rare Books Dept. Rush Rhees Library, Univ. of Rochester, Rochester, New York.
Letter from Mr. Oppenheimer to A.S. Crapsey (Nov. 1, 1924) In Arthur H. Crapsey Jr. Collection. Rare Books Dept. Rush Rhees Library, Univ. of Rochester, Rochester, New York.
Letter from W.R. Seward to Adelaide Trowbridge Crapsey (Oct. 28, 1908). In Arthur H. Crapsey Jr. Collection, Rare Books Dept. Rush Rhees Library, Univ. of Rochester, Rochester, New York.

Luther, Martin *Martin Luther: Selections from his own Writings.* John Dillenberger ed. New York: Anchor Books, 1951.

"Makes Every Word Tell, " Subtitled, Dr. Crapsey Conducting Mission Services at St. James Church" Omaha, Nebraska Newspaper Article, Feb. 22, 1897. In Arthur H. Crapsey Jr. Collection, Rare Books Dept. Rush Rhees Library, Univ. of Rochester, Rochester, New York.

Marsden, George M. *Fundamentalism and American Culture* New York: Oxford University Press, 1980.

May, Henry F. *The Enlightenment in America* New York: Oxford University Press, 1976.

McKelvey, Blake *Rochester on the Genesee* Syracuse: Syracuse Univ. Press, 1973.

—."The YMCA's First Century in Rochester." In *Rochester History* Vol. XVI No. 1 (Jan. 1954).

—. "A History of the Rochester City Club." In *Rochester History* Vol. IX No. 4 (Oct. 1947).

—. "Origins of the Rochester Public Library: Rochester's Literary and Book Clubs." Ruth Rosenberg Naparsteck ed. In *Rochester History* Vol. XLVIII Nos. 1 & 2 (Jan. and Apr., 1986).

Morgan, Lewis Henry *Ancient Society* Tucson: Univ. of Arizona Press, 1985.

Morris, Benjamin Franklin *The Life of Thomas Morris: Pioneer and Long a Legislator from Ohio and U.S. Senator from 1833- 1839.* Cincinnati: Moore, Wilstach, Keys and Overand, 1856.

"Nebraska" Article In Arthur H. Crapsey Jr. Collection, Scrapbooks, Rare Books Dept. Rush Rhees Library, Univ. of Rochester, Rochester, New York.

Newman, John Henry *The Church of the Fathers* London: J. Lane, 1900.

"News and Notes: The Late Dr. Algernon S. Crapsey, The Ethical Societies; Lists of Sunday Morning Addresses." *Standard* 14: 6 (Feb. 1928).

New York Times Column, the proceedings of trail for heresy of A.S. Crapsey (April 28, 1906).

—. Column, Crapsey's speech at Cornell University. (April 30, 1906).

—. Column, "Crapsey Verdict Reached." (May 10, 1906).

—. Column, Crapsey verdict. (May 16, 1906).

—.Column concerning Crapsey appeal. 16: 4 (Sept. 5, 1906).

—. Column, Crapsey appeal. 7: 3 (Nov. 3, 1906).

—. Column, Crapsey's farewell address. 6: 1 (Nov. 29, 1906).

—. Column, Rev. Cox's support of A.S. Crapsey (Aug. 11, 1906).

—. Column, synopsis of the proceedings of the Crapsey appellate court. 6: 4 (Oct. 21, 1906).
—. Column, quotes from Bishop Potter about the Crapsey Case. 4:1 (Nov. 15, 1906).
—. Column, the summary of the findings of the Court of Review. 6: 2 (Nov. 20, 1906).
—. Column, the letter from A.S. Crapsey to Bishop Walker (Nov. 26, 1906).
—. Column, Edward M. Shepard's reply to Bishop Potter. 2: 1 (Nov. 27, 1906).
—. Column, "Judgment of the Court of Review." 2:1 (Nov. 27, 1906).
—. Column, Crapsey's opposition to the Death Penalty. 7:2 (Mar. 4, 1915).
—. Column, the failure of A.S. Crapsey's public lecture series. 13: 3 (Dec. 4, 1916).
—. Column concerning Crapsey Trial 13:3 (Dec. 4, 1916).
—. Column, interview of A.S. Crapsey. 12:1 (May 23, 1924).
—. Column, presentment of Bishop Brown 8: 3 (May 28, 1924).
—. Column, the death of A.S. Crapsey. 19: 1 (Jan. 1, 1928).
—. Editorial opinion concerning Crapsey verdict. (May 17, 1906).
—. Lecture by A.S. Crapsey at the Free Synagogue at Carnegie Hall 3: 1-3 (Dec. 4, 1911).
—. Letter from A.S. Crapsey to A.E. Smith 6:2 (June 27, 1924).
—. Letter to the editor from Bishop Niles of New Hampshire. 11: 3 (Nov. 26, 1906).
—. Letter to the editor from Spencer Trask of Saratoga Springs, New York. (Nov. 26, 1906).
—. Sermon by A.S. Crapsey on John 5: 17. 2: 7 (Nov. 26, 1906).
New York Tribune Column (Nov. 20, 1899).
—. Letter to the editor from Bernard J. McQuaid "Bishop McQuaid Replies" (Dec. 9, 1901).
O'Connor, Sister Mary Edwardine, *Adelaide Crapsey: A Biographical Study* (Master's Thesis Notre Dame, 1931).
"One and Three=Quarters Acres In the Retail District Destroyed." (Newspaper unknown) (Feb. 27, 1904). In Arthur H. Crapsey Jr. Collection, Rare Books Dept. Rush Rhees Library, Univ. of Rochester, Rochester, New York.
Osborn, Mary Elizabeth *The Life of Adelaide Crapsey* Bruce Humphries Inc., 1933.
Outlook "Is Hari-Kari ever the Minister's Duty?" (Sept. 2, 1905).

—. Column concerning Bishop Gore's reprimand of Rev. C.E. Beeby Vol. 76, (Jan.- Apr., 1904).
—. Column, "The Living Church" Vol. 83, (May 5, 1905).
—. Column, Vol. 80 (June 17, 1905).
—. Column, reply by Dr. Edward Abbott to Crapsey's "Honor Among Clergymen" (Sept. 30, 1905).
—. Column, reply by Crapsey to Dr. Edward Abbott (Sept. 30, 1905).
—. Column concerning *Pacific Churchman* editorial (Oct. 15, 1905).
—. Editorial (Sept. 30, 1905).
An Overview of Our Life of Prayer (Pamphlet) Peekskill, New York: published by the Community of Saint Mary, Eastern Province.
Packer, J.I. "The Oxford Evangelicals in Theology" In J.S. Reynolds *The Evangelicals at Oxford* Oxford: Marcham Manor Press, 1975.
Parker, Jane Marsh "Letter to the Editor" *Post Express* Rochester: July 8, 1902.
Parish Record St. Andrew's Church Publication, Lent, 1886.
Philadelphia Press Speech by A.S. Crapsey and arrest at Little Falls, New York. (Oct. 20, 1912).
The Post Express, (Rochester, NY) Column, "Mr. Crapsey to Stay" (May 5, 1899).
—. Column concerning new altar at St. Andrew's Church May 15, 1899.
—. Letter to the editor from Rev. R.R. Converse, Rochester: June 30, 1902.
Potter, Henry C. *Sisterhoods and Deaconesses: At Home and Abroad* New York: E.P. Dutton & Co., 1873.
The Public Ledger Editorial, Philadelphia: March 8, 1899.
Pusey, Edward Bouverie *The Real Presence of the Body and Blood of the Lord Jesus Christ the Doctrine of the English Church With a Vindication of the Reception by the Wicked and of the Adoration of Our Lord Jesus Christ, Truly Present.* Oxford: J.H. Parker, 1857.
Pusey, Edward Bouverie "Letters in Three Parts to John Henry Newman" In *Eirenicon*
Oxford: James Parker Inc., 1870.
Price, William S. Esq. *The Irvine- Talbot Case with Notes on the Presentment of Bishop Talbot* Philadelphia: John McFetridge & Sons, 1902.
Quarles, Benjamin *Frederick Douglass* New York: Athenium, 1969.
Review of A.S. Crapsey's *Religion and Politics* in *London Quarterly Review* London: Charles Kelley, Vol. CV Fourth Series Vol. III Jan.-April, 1906.

Review of A.S. Crapsey's *The Rebirth of Religion* In *New York Times* 746: 2 (Nov. 23, 1907).

Review of A.S. Crapsey's *Ways of the Gods* by "J.C.R." In *Medical World of Philadelphia* (April, 1912)

Review of A.S. Crapsey's *Rise of the Working Class* by W.E. Weyl in *American Economic Review* 5:1/ 2 (1915).

Review of A.S. Crapsey's *Ways of the Gods* in *London Quarterly Review* The Epworth Press, Vol. 185 5th Series, (Jan./ April, 1921).

Review of A.S. Crapsey's *The Last of the Heretics* In *New York Times* III 10: 1 (July 13, 1924).

Review, "The Library: Within It and Beyond It" In Scrapbooks, in the Arthur H. Crapsey Jr. Collection, Rare Books Dept. Rush Rhees Library, Univ. of Rochester, Rochester, New York.

Review of A.S. Crapsey's *Rise of the Working Class* in Milwaukee, Journal. In Arthur H. Crapsey Jr. Collection. Rare Books Dept. Rush Rhees Library, Univ. of Rochester, Rochester, New York.

Reynolds, John Stewart *The Evangelicals at Oxford* Oxford: Marcham Manor Press, 1975.

Richardson, Alan and Bowden, John eds. *The Westminster Dictionary of Christian Theology* Philadelphia: The Westminster Press, 1983.

Ritchie, Arthur ed. *Catholic Champion* (St. Ignatius Guild) New York, 1900.

Rochester Democrat & Chronicle Newspaper "Adelaide T. Crapsey Obituary Notice" Rochester, New York, Jan. 9, 1950.

—. Column concerning the Talbot Case (Jan 7, 1905).

—. Column concerning Dr. Lyman Abbott (Jan. 9, 1905).

—. Column concerning Rev. Nelson Millard D.D. (Feb. 21, 1905).

—. Column, speech by Rev. MacLaurin D.D. to Dewey Class in Rochester, New York (Feb. 24, 1905).

—. Column, the marriage of Bishop William David Walker (Feb. 28, 1905).

—. Column concerning Bishop Walker's confirmation of youth in Rochester, New York (Apr. 4, 1905).

—. "Annual Council of the Diocese Opened at Corning" (May 17, 1905).

—. Column, Crapsey's refusal to leave the church. (May 17, 1905).

—. Column, nomination of the Ecclesiastical Court by the Diocesan Council (May 17, 1905).

—. Column, Rev. Murray Bartlett's views on the Crapsey Case. (May 18, 1905).

—. Column, the refusal of Rev. Andrew Graham to present Crapsey (May 19, 1905).

—.Column, synopsis of Crapsey article in *Outlook* magazine of September 2, 1905 (Sept. 4, 1905).
—. Column, the proceedings of the Committee of Investigation Diocese of Western New York (Sept. 17, 1905).
—. Column, Rev. Edward Malcolm Duff's quote about the Committee of Investigation. (Sept. 28, 1905).
—. Column, the Sixth Annual New York State Conference of Religion (Nov. 10, 1905).
—. Column, the Sixth Annual New York State Conference of Religion (Nov. 13, 1905).
—. "Head of Hobart is a Humanist." (Nov. 25, 1905).
—. "A God Man is Born on Every Human Birthday." W.C. Gannett (Dec. 24, 1905).
—. Column "Denial of Incarnation is to Deny the Gospels." By Rev. Andrew Graham. (Dec. 24, 1905).
—. Column, the consecration of Christ Church by Bishop Walker (Dec. 30, 1905).
—. Column, Rev. Alexander hiring by Rev. Converse. (Jan. 19, 1906).
—. Column, Rev. Murray Bartlett's views on the Crapsey Case. (Jan. 31, 1906).
—. Column concerning the Crapsey Case (Feb. 18, 1906).
—. Column concerning the Crapsey Case (Feb. 25, 1906).
—. Column concerning the Crapsey Case. (Feb. 27, 1906).
—. Column concerning the Crapsey Case. (Mar. 2, 1906).
—. Column, the presentment of A.S. Crapsey (March 4, 1906).
—. Column concerning the MacQueary Case (March 4, 1906).
—. Column, the presentment of A.S. Crapsey (March 9, 1906).
—. Column, the makeup of the Ecclesiastical Court. (April 8, 1906).
—. Column, the members of the Ecclesiastical Court (April 18, 1906).
—. Column, opening day proceedings of the heresy trial. (April 18, 1906).
—. Column, Crapsey's supporters arriving at the Powers Hotel Rochester, New York. (Apr. 25, 1906).
—. Column, legal arguments before the Ecclesiastical Court. (Apr. 26, 1906).
—. Column, quoting Rev. Converse concerning the Crapsey Case (Apr. 26, 1906).
—. Column, legal arguments before the Ecclesiastical Court. (Apr. 27, 1906).
—. Column, legal arguments before the Ecclesiastical Court. (Apr. 28, 1906).

—. Column, hiring of J.B. Thomas as rector of St. Andrew's Church (Apr. 20, 1907).
—. "General Pershing's Thanksgiving Address to the American Expeditionary Forces." (Dec. 1, 1918).
—. Column "In Memory of Mrs. Sibley." (no date). In Arthur H. Crapsey Jr. Collection, Rare Books Dept. Rush Rhees Library, Univ. of Rochester, Rochester, New York.
—. Editorial by Rev. John S. Littell in "Current Topics Discussed by Correspondents of the Democrat and Chronicle" (Feb. 27, 1905).
—. Editorial concerning Church Reform (Mar. 2, 1905).
—. Editorial by Rev. Murray Bartlett "Is Opposed to Heresy Trials." (May 15, 1905).
—. Editorial, "From Heresy Trials, Good Lord Deliver Us." (May 16, 1905).
—. Editorial "Will be no Heresy Trial." (Nov. 17, 1905).
—. Editorial concerning hope for an end to the Crapsey Case. (Nov. 18, 1905).
—. Editorial, "Rolli's Immortals Nominated" (June 11, 1934).
—. Editorial, Bill Beeney "The Hometowner" (Apr. 22, 1960).
—. Lecture by A.S. Crapsey (Dec. 5, 1904).
—. Lecture by A.S. Crapsey (Dec. 12, 1904).
—. Lecture by A.S. Crapsey (Dec.19, 1904).
—. Lecture by A.S. Crapsey (Dec. 25, 1904).
—. Lecture by A.S. Crapsey (Jan. 1, 1905).
—. Lecture by A.S. Crapsey (Jan. 2, 1905).
—. Lecture by A.S. Crapsey (Jan. 9, 1905).
—. Lecture by Rabbi Max Landsberg (Jan. 9, 1905).
—. Lecture by A.S. Crapsey (Jan. 16, 1905).
—. Lecture by A.S. Crapsey (Jan. 23, 1905).
—. Lecture by A.S. Crapsey (Jan. 30, 1905).
—. Lecture by A.S. Crapsey (Feb. 6, 1905).
—. Lecture by A.S. Crapsey (Feb. 13, 1905).
—. Lecture by A.S. Crapsey (Feb. 20, 1905).
—. Lecture by A.S. Crapsey (Feb. 27, 1905).
—. Lectures by Rev. Andrew Graham, Rev. Murray Bartlett, and Rev. Edward Parrott at Church Club (Mar. 4, 1905).
—. Lecture "The Future of Christianity" by Rev. Herbert Symonds on the (Apr. 13, 1905).
—. Lecture by Professor George M. Forbes at Park Ave. Baptist Church, Rochester, New York (Oct. 16, 1905).
—. Lecture by A.S. Crapsey (Dec. 4, 1905).

—. Letter to the Editor from D.B. Lyon, (Nov. 5, 1901).
—. Letter to the Editor from C.S. Moscrip "Dr. Crapsey and Missions." (Nov. 8, 1901).
—. Letter to the editor from A.S. Crapsey (Dec. 12, 1905).
—. Letter to the editor from Rev. John S. Littell. (Dec. 13, 1905).
—. Letter to the editor from C.B. Stoddard (Dec. 23, 1905).
—. Letter to the editor by Louis C. Washburn (Jan 11, 1906).
—. Letter from Bishop Brown to George Foster Peabody (Jan. 11, 1906).
—. Letter to the editor from Rev. William H. Goss (April 18, 1906).
—. "Open Letter from A.S. Crapsey to Rev. Charles H. Brent, Should Not Create a Philippine Bishopric" (Oct. 11, 1901).
—. Open Letter from Archdeacon Louis Washburn D.D. to A.S. Crapsey (Oct. 21, 1901).
—. Open Letter from Archdeacon Louis Washburn D.D. to A.S. Crapsey (Oct. 23, 1901).
—. "Open Letter from A.S. Crapsey to Archdeacon Washburn" (Oct. 23, 1901).
—. Letter from Rev. Andrew J. Graham "For a Bishopric in the Philippines" Christ Church, Rochester, New York (Oct. 26. 1901).
—. Sermon by Rev. S. Frazer Langford (Feb. 27, 1905).
—. Sermons by A.S. Crapsey "God a Presence" and "God a Power." (Mar. 6, 1905).
—. Sermon by A.S. Crapsey "God a Presence." (Mar. 9, 1905).
—. Sermon by Dr. Walton S. Batershall "The Church Today." (May 8, 1905).
—. Sermon by E.M. Martin of St. Thomas Episcopal (Oct. 23, 1905).
—. Sermon by A.S. Crapsey (Jan. 29, 1906).
Rochester Herald Column concerning intentional slight by clergy against A.S. Crapsey. (Sat. Dec 30, 1905).
—. Column concerning Adelaide T. Crapsey Clothing Factory (April 8, 1919).
Rochester Times Union Article concerning the death of A.S. Crapsey. (Dec. 31, 1927).
"Santa Claus at Lyceum Circus." In Arthur H. Crapsey Jr. Collection, Rare Books Dept. Rush Rhees Library, Univ. of Rochester, Rochester, New York.
Sharpe, Dores Robinson *Walter Rauschenbusch* New York: Macmillan Co., 1942.
Shepard, Edward M. *Argument of Edward M. Shepard as Council for Rev. Algernon Sidney Crapsey Before the Court of Review of the Protestant Episcopal Church Upon His Appeal from the Judgement of the Court*

of the Diocese of Western New York, October 19, 1906. (Report in Andover Theological Seminary, 1907).

Shriver, George H. ed. *American Religious Heretics* New York: Abingdon Press, 1966.

Spengler, Paul A. *A Brief History of St. Mathias' Episcopal Church, East Aurora, New York from 1869- 1994 Part I, 1869- 1996.* East Aurora, St. Mathias' Parish, 1994.

Smith, Henry Bradford and McKelvey, Blake ed. "Rochester's Turbulent Transit History" In *Rochester History* Vol. 30, No. 3. July 30, 1968.

Smith, Susan "Adelaide Crapsey: Materials for a Biographical and Textual Study" In *University of Rochester Library Bulletin 25* Nos. 1& 2. 1969- 1970: 5.

St. Andrew's Record (Rochester: St. Andrew's Church Publication, 1889-1896).

"Story of a Cape" Article in Arthur H. Crapsey Jr. Collection, Rare Books Dept., Rush Rhees Library, University of Rochester, Rochester, New York.

Suter, John Wallace *Life and Letters of William Reed Huntington: A Champion of Unity* (New York and London, 1925).

"There in Interest of Advent Mission but Speaks on Race Problem" In Scrapbooks, Arthur H. Crapsey Jr. Collection, Rare Books Dept. Rush Rhees Library Univ. of Rochester, Rochester, New York.

"Twenty Years Ago Today" In Arthur H. Crapsey Jr. Collection. Rare Books Dept. Rush Rhees Library, Univ. of Rochester, Rochester, New York.

Unidentified article concerning accident of Adelaide Trowbridge Crapsey with streetcar. (No date) Arthur H. Crapsey Jr. Collection, Rare Books Dept. Rush Rhees Library, Univ. of Rochester, Rochester, New York.

Unidentified article concerning A.S. Crapsey's eightieth birthday party. In Arthur H. Crapsey Jr. Collection, Rare Books Dept. Rush Rhees Library, Univ. of Rochester, Rochester, New York.

Unidentified article concerning A.S. Crapsey's death. In Arthur H. Crapsey Jr. Collection, Rare Books Dept. Rush Rhees Library, Univ. of Rochester, Rochester, New York.

Unidentified article by Mr. Sanford of *Harper's Weekly* in Scrapbooks, Arthur H. Crapsey Jr. Collection, Rare Books Dept. Rush Rhees Library, Univ. of Rochester, Rochester, New York.

Unidentified article Statement of A.S. Crapsey's Beliefs written before his death. In Arthur H. Crapsey Jr. Collection, Rare Books Dept. Rush Rhees Library, Univ. of Rochester, Rochester, New York.

Venable, William Henry *A Centennial History of Christ Church, Cincinnati 1817- 1917* Cincinnati: Stewart & Kidd Co., 1918.

Weber, Max *The Protestant Ethic and the Spirit of Capitalism* translated by Talcott Parsons (New York: Scribner, 1958).

Webster's Encyclopedic Dictionary New York: Publisher's Guild Inc., 1941.

Works Projects Administration *Inventory of the Church Archives of New York State Exclusive of New York City Protestant Episcopal Church (Diocese of Rochester)* Albany, New York: The Historical Records Survey Division of Community Service Programs, June, 1941.

Wright, Robert ed. "Essays on the Centenary of the Chicago-Lambeth Quadrilateral 1886-88 – 1986-88, The Quadrilateral at One Hundred." In *Anglican Theological Review,* Evanston, Illinois, (Supplementary Series No. 10, Forward Movement Publications, 1988).

INDEX